The True Church and the Poor

THE TRUE CHURCH
and
THE POOR

Jon Sobrino

SCM PRESS LTD

Translated by Matthew J. O'Connell from the Spanish
Resurrección de la verdadera Iglesia:
Los pobres, lugar teológico de la eclesiología
copyright © 1981 by Editorial Sal Terrae, Guevara 20, Santander, Spain

English translation copyright © 1984 by Orbis Books, Maryknoll, NY
(Chapter 5 was translated by Dr Fernando Segovia)

Except where otherwise indicated, Bible quotations are
from the Revised Standard Version (JB = Jerusalem Bible;
NAB = New American Bible)

Sobrino, Jon
 The true Church and the poor.
 1. Catholic Church   2. Church and the poor
 ——El Salvador
 I. Title   II. Resureccion de la verdadera
 Inglesia. *English*
 362.5'8'097284   BX2347.8.P6

 ISBN 0-334-02379-3

334 02379 3

First published in Great Britain 1985
by SCM Press Ltd
26–30 Tottenham Road, London N1 4BZ

Typeset in the United States of America
and printed in Great Britain by
Richard Clay (The Chaucer Press) Ltd
Bungay, Suffolk

To all the men and women of El Salvador
who have given their lives
for the kingdom of God

Contents

vii

viii CONTENTS

Abbreviations

AA	Apostolicam actuositatem (Decree on the Apostolate of Lay People, Vatican II)
AG	Ad gentes (Decree on the Church's Missionary Activity, Vatican II)
CEHILA	Comisión de Estudios de Historia de la Iglesia Latinoamericana
CELAM	Conferencia Episcopal Latinoamericana (Latin American Bishops Conference)
DH	Dignitatis humanae (Declaration on Religious Liberty, Vatican II)
DS	H. Denzinger and A. Schönmetzer, eds., *Enchiridion Symbolorum,* 32d ed., Freiburg im B., 1963
DV	Dei verbum (Dogmatic Constitution on Divine Revelation, Vatican II)
ECA	*Estudios Centro Americanos*
EN	Evangelii nuntiandi (Apostolic Exhortation on Evangelization in the Modern World, Pope Paul VI)
EvKomm	*Evangelische Kommentare*
LG	Lumen gentium (Dogmatic Constitution on the Church, Vatican II)
LTK	*Lexikon für Theologie und Kirche,* 3d ed.
MM	Mater et Magistra (Christianity and Social Progress, Pope John XXIII)
ZEE	*Zeitschrift für evangelische Ethik*

Introduction

The realities and problems I deal with in these pages are, beyond all else, Christian realities and Christian problems. Faith in God, the building of the kingdom of God, the practice of justice, the option for the poor, the holiness of the new being—these are the very substance of Christianity and could well be treated in a theology or a theological anthropology. These things are basic for the Church if it is to be truly the Church of Jesus. Moreover, they make it possible to discuss in a satisfactory way the specifically ecclesial problems presented in this book: unity and division within the ecclesial body, for example; the definition of evangelization as the mission of the Church; the new and important phenomenon of persecution of the Church; and the constitution of the true Church as a Church of the poor.

I am not offering an ecclesiology, that is, a systematic reflection on all that the Church is and ought to be. My intention is rather to shed light on some basic problems faced by a Church that desires to be faithful to its Christian nature and to recover the essence of Christianity in a creative way at this time in history. The book is thus not so much an ecclesiology as it is a theological reflection on the very basis of the Church. On this basis an ecclesiology may then be developed.

THEOLOGICAL METHOD

Let me add a few words on the theological method that lies behind these thoughts and considerations. The first chapter describes the method employed in Latin American theology. I would like to state briefly here how I have used this method in my reflections on the Church.

In my view, theological thinking about the Church must take as its *objective* starting point the present reality of the Church insofar as it is Christian, that is, insofar as it is a present manifestation of God. In other words, the object on which I reflect is the Church itself; my starting point is the reality of the Church and not a doctrine about the Church. Doctrine is of course necessary and important. But in itself, apart from the concrete reality of the Church and apart from the present manifestation of God in the Church, it cannot take any real historical shape. It can be true, but it will remain ineffective and irrelevant. We must then take with utter seriousness the often repeated statement about reading "the signs of the times," and we must be willing to give these signs concrete names. We must give a name to the presence of God, here and now, in the Church; without this presence the Church would cease to be an object of theo-logy.

On the subjective side, reflection must take as its starting point the ecclesial faith as it is practiced or, in other words, the concrete response given to the God who continually manifests himself. While we must make a technical distinction between the revelation of God in the past and the manifestation of God in the present, it is clear that faith here and now can only be a response to the manifestation of God here and now. Theology must therefore be reflection on faith as currently practiced, on the response given here and now to the manifestation of God.

It is vitally important to determine how God is manifesting himself here and now and what form the response of faith is taking. In my opinion, God's manifestation, at least in Latin America, is his scandalous and partisan love for the poor and his intention that these poor should receive life and thus inaugurate his kingdom. Correspondingly, the proper way of being conformed to God is to be concerned actively with the justice of the kingdom of God and with making the poor the basis of this concern. This is the great "sign of the times," a sign which is a fact. Reflection on the Church starts with this fact and attempts to explain it and consolidate it. With this starting point the reflection will then try to integrate everything that tradition has rightly developed concerning the Church. I am not advocating reductionism. However, without this starting point our thinking will not have a real object but only an intention. It will be empty from both historical and theological standpoints.

It may be objected that this approach runs the risk of approving as a source of theological understanding whatever happens in the Church and passing over established doctrine. In other words, this approach seems to do without a set of established and authoritative norms. To this objection I reply with two arguments: one is a priori; the other, a posteriori.

Arguing a priori, if pneumatology has any role to play in the real life of the Church, if we accept that the Spirit of God continually acts in history and in the Church, then we should not be surprised by the idea that we are to search continually for the manifestation of God in our times. Nor should it surprise us that the manifestation will take on new forms during new times. To deny this would be to deny the action of God's Spirit; it would be to deny the "greater" being of God, of which the New Testament and tradition tell us. It would be to deny the first and most orthodox of all truths about God: the trinitarian being. To be frightened of new forms in theology is to be frightened of God. This fright, however, is not the fear and trembling with which we must work out our salvation; rather it is a dismay at the thought of God's word passing judgment on the Church and on the Church's self-understanding and accomplishments.

The history of the Church is part of the being of the Church and must therefore play a part in theological reflection on the Church. This insight has already been assimilated, to a greater or lesser extent, in christology. The history of Jesus concerns the total Christ, the Christ of faith. This is why the historical Jesus is of strict theological importance to ecclesiology. The history of the Church is intrinsic to reflection on the nature of the Church. The essence of the Church does not exist unless it takes historical form. This means that if the historical dimension is neglected ecclesiological thinking will not only be idealistic and triumphalistic on the one hand, and run a serious risk of irrelevance on the other, but it will also not even be theological. A Church that lacks a history cannot be the object of a Christian ecclesiology. Consequently, whatever happens in the Church—predictably or unpredictably—can and must a priori be a source of theological understanding.

Arguing a posteriori, what has been happening in the Church is not just any novel happening. There is no question simply of reflecting on what is new just because it is new. Fidelity to the signs of the times has produced in the Church a mission of evangelization that is directed to and centered on the poor. It has led to cruel and systematic persecution; it has engendered hope against hope, courage in persecution, and faith in God, the Father of Jesus, as the ultimate unshakable rock. In short, the novelty has brought a recovery by the Church of the memory of Jesus; it has made the Church like Jesus.

If this is so, then the novelty must have its source not in just any spirit but in the Spirit of Jesus. For this reason the Church in question is true or at least truer than other historical forms that have been taken by the Church. This is the ultimate justification (impossible to analyze) for taking the reality of the Church as the starting point for reflection on the Church. In this Church God is continually manifesting himself, not only doctrinally, not only on the basis of his word in the past, but here and now through the word that is now being spoken.

THEOLOGICAL CHARACTER OF THESE REFLECTIONS

Let me say a few words, finally, on the theological character of these reflections, a character they share with much of the theology being done today in Latin America. These reflections were set down on paper between 1977 and 1980 in El Salvador. These were years during which Bishop Romero and Fathers Rutilio Grande and Octavio Ortiz lived and died, as did Christian peasant leaders like Polín and catechists like Jesús, whom Bishop Romero used to call "the man of the gospel." All these and many, many others were martyrs. These pages have thus been written in the midst of an unprecedentedly intense ecclesial life and in the midst of a great cloud of witnesses to the faith (Heb. 12:1).

Doing theology in this situation requires that the theology not only follow a specific method but that it also have a specific character. Theology in this situation becomes *responsible.* Theologians do not arbitrarily decide to study this or that theme; the theme is forced upon them by reality. Theology becomes responsible, then, in that it responds to the real world. Theology becomes *practical* because its motivating concern is not pure thought nor even pure truth but rather the building of the kingdom of God and of a Church that will be at the service of this kingdom. Theology becomes *evangelical* in the original sense of that word: it is done with pleasure in the Good News and with joy that there is salvation for the poor. Finally, theology becomes a response of *gratitude* because its starting point is the primordial Christian experience that "something has been given to us." What has been given to us is the mystery of God present in Jesus and in a Church that is poor and is of the poor.

In view of all these remarks the reader will understand that the dedication of this book is not a routine one, and that any light shed by these pages is due to those to whom the book is dedicated.

1

Theological Understanding in European and Latin American Theology

The comparison between European theology and Latin American theology presented in this chapter is not so much in terms of content or method of analysis as it is in terms of the meaning and function of theological understanding and of the consequences which a particular conception of it entails. Before I begin, several preliminary remarks are in order.

1. "Latin American theology" and "European theology" are obviously general terms that can serve only as formal descriptions of two distinct ways of conceiving and attaining theological understanding. In fact, any comparison and contrast between the two cannot be made solely on the basis of geography or language. We must probe deeper than that. What exactly are these two distinct types of theological understanding and what do their operations mean? With these reservations, I describe European theology as the theology that developed in Central Europe; it can be characterized generally as progressive. By Latin American theology I understand the theology of liberation with its various subtypes.

2. When we speak of theological understanding we are dealing with a broad subject that has many ramifications and implications. Theological understanding can be analyzed from the standpoints of the classical theological disciplines: exegesis, biblical theology,

7

the histories of dogma, theology, and the Church, and moral, pastoral, and systematic theology. Each of these disciplines by its nature calls for a particular concrete form of theological understanding and a plurality of methods. It is also possible to analyze the various concrete approaches that theological understanding employs: linguistic analysis, the inductive, deductive, and dialectical methods, hermeneutical horizons, relation to other types of understanding such as philosophy or the social sciences.

In comparing Latin American theology and European theology it is most important to get at the root of that theological understanding which subsequently finds expression in a variety of methods, analyses, and hermeneutics. I shall try to clarify this root of theological understanding from two points of view: (1) if we presuppose that the theological understanding in question is *Christian* and not simply a case of understanding generally, we must ask how Christian *reality* influences theological *understanding* in each of the two theologies; (2) we must also ask what is the ultimate concern that moves us to understand things theologically.

3. Regarding the first of these two points of view, the problem of theological understanding can be formally approached from two distinct vantage points: first, as a human activity, both personal and social in nature, and therefore subject to the laws governing all understanding; and, second, as it is determined, or at least conditioned, not only in regard to its content (this is self-evident) but also in regard to its reality as understanding, by the subject matter which it develops.

The presupposition is that theological understanding, precisely insofar as it is theological, acknowledges and accepts what has been given it: the thing we call revelation, which needs to be made concrete. In other words, this approach makes sense only insofar as we accept the idea of free gift. This approach takes us into the hermeneutical circle, since Christian reality is given precisely as a reality that must be brought to fulfillment. This circular pattern has its history; it is the history of theology itself. But what is of interest to us here is how this Christian reality that is being constantly brought to fulfillment influences the concrete functioning of theological understanding in Latin American theology and European theology in different ways.

Three points that have an impact on theological understanding mark it as Christian. These points can best be made clear from a consideration of the history of Jesus. The first point is the liberating character of the history of Jesus. This point raises the epistemological problem of the liberating character of theological understanding, the problem of the interests that motivate theological understanding. The second point is the dialectic between the present and the future of God's reign as proclaimed by Jesus. It raises the epistemological problem of the relation between theory and practice. The difference between religion and Christian faith is the third point. In theological terms, this is the dialectic of cross and resurrection. It raises the problem of the epistemological break within theological understanding.

4. The second question (see 2 above) to be asked when comparing the two theologies is an important question: What interest motivates theological understanding? Why do theology? This implies another question: For whom and from whose standpoint is the theological understanding done? These questions presuppose that theological understanding as a form of understanding, although possessing a certain autonomy, always takes place in the context of some social reality. Understanding is never neutral either in practice or in intention, but always has, implicitly or explicitly, a practical and ethical character.

From the standpoint of its relation to reality we can ask whether theological understanding is concerned with a concept in the mind or with an existing reality; whether it answers to an intentional demand of the subject or a real demand of the situation; whether its existence serves as a protective screen for that which it denounces at the level of its content (for example, a world of oppression) or whether its existence is due to the experience of oppression.

I think, therefore, that, in comparing different theological understandings, a detailed investigation of the methods of theological analysis is less important than an investigation of the practical and ethical option represented by the understanding. It is equally important to discover the element of practical and ethical option that exists in the concept of understanding. For this reason, in making comparisons between various theologies, a key question is this: What interests motivate—really, and not just in intention—the various forms of theological understanding?

THE "LIBERATING" CHARACTER
OF THEOLOGICAL UNDERSTANDING

Whenever theology has reflected on reality from a Christian standpoint, that is, whenever it has attained to genuine theological understanding, it has envisaged reality according to a bipolar scheme. The presupposition is that reality is not what it ought to be because a negative element exists that can be expressed concretely as meaninglessness, sin, and death. Between this negative element and the truth promised through faith no complementarity or dialectical relationship exists, only contradiction. Christian existence and Christian theology have always endeavored to bring salvation to this divided reality. This salvation is "redemption" or "liberation," terms that have a variety of implications.

The notion of liberation is essential to Christian faith and theology. The question for us here is how this "liberation" has influenced the conception and operation of theological understanding. Very simply, theological understanding in the various theologies liberates from something and for something. What makes liberation necessary and what is its goal?

A complete answer to these questions would require a study of the entire history of theology. But in order to compare European theology with Latin American theology, a brief analysis of the influence of the Enlightenment on the liberating character of theological understanding will suffice. In coming to grips with the Enlightenment, theology became conscious that the role of theological understanding could be liberating or alienating. The manner in which questions were framed by the Enlightenment still influences both theologies, at least to the extent that the critical movement proper to the Enlightenment has made itself felt in Europe and in Latin America.

The Enlightenment represented a challenge to theological understanding, if not an outright rejection of it. Through its response to the challenge of the Enlightenment, that is, through its effort to render an account of the faith over against the Enlightenment, modern theology developed. It is important to distinguish two phases of the Enlightenment. They can be represented by two people: Kant and Marx.

For Kant, "Enlightenment is man's leaving his self-caused immaturity."[1] This immaturity is expressed when people feel no need to think for themselves but are content to accept in an uncritical way what others (philosopher, priest, physician) think for them. As Kant sees it, people must be liberated from the comfortable attitude of infantilism. The watchword of the Enlightenment is: "Have the courage to use your intelligence!"[2] Consequently, even though Kant's ultimate aim was political liberation, the liberation of the first phase of the Enlightenment was the liberation of reason from all authority. The first phase expressed the longing for reality. It was antitheological in that it claimed to free human beings from every form of dogmatism, including that of Scripture, and to liberate the human conscience from all externally imposed religious precepts.

The second phase of the Enlightenment did not see liberation as the independence of reason from which would automatically come the total liberation of the human person. Rather it looked to liberation from the wretched conditions of the real world. Such a liberation requires not only a new way of thinking, that is, independent thinking, but also a new way of acting. The liberation put forward here, then, is not simply a liberation of the mind, but a liberation from the misery of the real world. This calls for and leads to a new way of conceiving of the role of reason. This second phase of the Enlightenment was also antitheological, proposing that religion by its very existence is both an opium of the people and an expression of the wretchedness of reality.

Modern theology has developed within the boundaries set by the challenge of the Enlightenment. In the process it tried to incorporate the critical, liberating movement into theological understanding. Two ways of doing theology can be distinguished according as the challenge to be met and absorbed is that of the first or the second phase of the Enlightenment, that is, according as the motivating interest in doing theology has been the concern for rationality or the concern for transformation.

Broadly speaking, modern European theology has been oriented to the first phase of the Enlightenment. It has understood the liberating function of theological understanding to consist primarily in liberation from all dogmatic arbitrariness, all authoritarianism. Related to this interest is another: the interest in demonstrating the *truth* of revelation at the bar of natural reason and historical reason, or, to put it negatively, in liberating the faith from any element of myth or historical error. Finally, and most recently, the hermeneutical problem has arisen. This is the problem of showing, not the truth, but the meaning of the faith in a situation in which this meaning has been obscured. When the faith is threatened either in its truth or in its meaning, theological understanding is seen as the answer to the threat. Recovery comes by means of understanding the lost truth or meaning. The justification of the faith occurs through the harmony of the faith with some universal truth, with historical truth, or with itself.

These approaches are all responses to the challenge of the first Enlightenment; they have all emerged chiefly within Protestant theology. Here are but a few classical examples. Schleiermacher sought to show the harmony of the faith with the universal truths of the religious consciousness. The study of the history of religions sought to show the harmony of the truth of Christianity with the truth found in other religions. Harnack sought to show the harmony between faith and culture. Bultmann, reacting against liberal thought, claimed that faith is an intelligible yes or no.[3] Barth sought to show the intelligibility of the faith by letting it be precisely faith, that is, by justifying it on its own terms.[4]

Among contemporary Protestant theologians, the clearest expression of this way of conceiving of theological understanding is to be found in Wolfhart Pannenberg. He is a patent example of how the first Enlightenment dictated theological concerns. Pannenberg expressly stated that the greatest need of today's theology is depositivization, since "any authoritarian understanding of revelation is in principle liable to be suspected of clothing human thoughts and institutions in the radiance of the divine majesty."[5] The function of theological understanding is essentially explicative. "Statements about divine reality or divine action lend themselves to having their implications examined in the light of our understanding of finite reality."[6] Theology must by its nature be "true philosophy," but philosophy in its explanatory role; it looks for "a more inclusive understanding of reality."[7] The justification of the truth of theology is "the extent to which the whole of reality can be understood more deeply and more convincingly through Jesus than without him."[8] Theological understanding must free itself from all historical error: "In no case is theology, for example, in a position of being able to say what was actually the case regarding contents which remain opaque to the historian."[9] "The object of faith as such cannot remain untouched by the results of historical-critical research."[10] Hermeneutics, to which Pannenberg has recently turned, has as its central problem the "understanding of meaning."[11] To know an event is to make it intelligible in the light of history as a whole; this is made possible by an anticipation of the end of history as it has taken place in the resurrection of Christ.

The first Enlightenment is in control here; the second is absent. In his books Pannenberg rarely cites Marx, and when he does, the theological problem he raises is subsumed under one of Feuerbach's, namely, the question of the extent to which God may be a human projection.[12] The possible alienating role of theological understanding or, in positive terms, its possible role in the transformation of reality is not given any consideration. Pannenberg develops theological concepts that deal with meaning (God as absolute future; the resurrection as the anticipation of the end of history; hope as expansion of the radical openness of the human person), but he does not analyze their social impact or their significance for the transformation of the real world.

Catholic theology displays basically the same pattern of thought, but it appeared later than it did in Protestant theology, due to the theoretical and, above all, the practical conditions created by the notion of the Magisterium. To give but one significant example: Whatever its merits or its omissions may be, the work of Karl Rahner, beginning with his *Hearers of the Word* and his groundbreaking articles on the Incarnation, grace, and the Trinity, has been a response to the first Enlightenment. As he himself has repeatedly said, his aim has been to save today's Christians from the painful experience of finding theology to be myth. Rahner's concern has been supremely pastoral and liberating (though limited to the educated Europeans of his era) as he has sought to develop a Christian rationality in theology and to show that the Christian mystery, while remaining mystery, is supremely reasonable, although, of course, not reducible to reason.

Generally, then, European theological movements have been conditioned by the first Enlightenment and represent an effort to respond to it. The movement of depositivization (abandoning a theology based on Denzinger), the new historical-critical work in exegesis, the interpretation of dogma, the development of the various hermeneutics—all these have been an effort to liberate theology from authoritarianism, historical error, myth, and from the obscuring of the meaning of the faith. These movements see themselves as movements of liberation, and many well-educated Christians have in fact found them to be a source of real liberation for their own faith. Theological understanding is liberating in a peculiar manner. Its function is first to *explain* the truth of the faith. When the meaning of the faith is under attack, then its function is to somehow restore that meaning. This restoration of meaning is liberating because the crisis in the real world is experienced as a crisis of meaning; the real threat that the real world represents for faith is subsumed under the crisis of meaning and then exorcized by means of a new interpretation.

Without minimizing the liberating value of European theology, I must nonetheless ask two questions: (1) does the liberating character of theological understanding thus interpreted do justice to Christian liberation; that is, can the full reality of liberation consist in the liberation of faith through the bestowal of new meaning, even though such a liberation can coexist in principle with a non-liberated *real world;* and (2) does the liberating function of theology thus conceived not only fail to develop its own full liberative potential but also prevent the attainment of this potential by presupposing that understanding liberates insofar as it explains and gives meaning to the real world. If the answer to the first question is No and the answer to the second is Yes, then theological understanding thus conceived would not only not be completely liberating, but would in fact really be an ideology. It would be an attempt to hide the real wretchedness of the world behind a partial liberation, thus shifting the solution of the real problem (liberation from the wretched conditions of the real world) to the level of ideas (liberation of the meaning of the faith).

If I ask now how "liberation" as the content of theology has influenced theological understanding in Latin American theology, I immediately observe certain major differences from European theology. Bear in mind, however, that when Latin American theology began to emerge in the sixties, it inherited European theology's views on the relation between theological understanding, truth, and meaning, and came up against the resulting problems, at least at the level of thought.

The basic difference between the two theologies lies in this: Latin

American theology is trying to respond to a new kind of problem—not the problem of the meaning of the faith, but the problem of the meaning of the real situation in Latin America. Within this situation the problem of the meaning of the faith also arises. We must not scoff at the intuition expressed in the title under which all that is new in Latin American theology is summed up. This theology understands itself as a theology, first and foremost, of *liberation,* not a theology of the word or the person or history. The focus of theological interest is precisely the desire for liberation. Theology here becomes conscious that it is a theo-*logy,* an intellectual discourse in the service of a real liberation.

Confronted with the movement of the Enlightenment toward liberation, then, Latin American theology spontaneously takes up the challenge represented by the second phase of the Enlightenment. In this theology, the liberating function of theological understanding does not consist in explaining or giving meaning to an existing reality or to the faith as threatened by a particular situation, but in transforming a reality so that it may take on meaning and the lost or threatened meaning of the faith may thereby also be recovered.[13] In this general sense, the influence of Marx on the conception of theological understanding is evident. His *Thesis XI on Feuerbach* is the paradigm for the liberative aspect of theological understanding. To transform does not mean to look for an intelligible form whereby reality may be ordered for the mind; it means to give a new form to a now wretched reality. Theological understanding is thus inseparable from the practical and the ethical and cannot be reduced to the giving of explanations. (This last is a function of theology that has been somewhat neglected in the reaction against the European notion of the autonomy of understanding.)

The aim of theological understanding in Latin American theology is "to confront reality" in the most realistic and unideological way possible. Given this perspective, I will point out some basic differences between the two theologies.

Approach to Reality

In general, European theology approaches reality through the mediations of thought, such as theology, philosophy, and culture. Access to reality comes through dialogue (critical rejection or critical acceptance) with a particular type of *thinking.* For example,

European theological thinking has advanced through *intra-theological* confrontations (Barth in reaction to liberal theological thought, Bultmann in reaction to Barth, Rahner in reaction to decadent Scholasticism, or through critical dialogue with one or another type of philosophical thinking (Bultmann and Rahner with existentialism, Rahner with transcendental philosophy, Teilhard de Chardin with evolutionism, Pannenberg with Hegelianism, Moltmann with Bloch and more recently with the Marxism of the Frankfurt School), or with a particular cultural movement (Robinson with secularism, Moltmann with consumer culture). Behind these theological, philosophical, or cultural movements there is of course a real situation, and European theology has been aware of this. But the tendency has been to approach the real situation chiefly through thought about it.

By contrast, Latin American theology tries to approach reality as it is, even when it cannot draw any clear distinction between the reality as it is and the reality as interpreted theologically, philosophically, or culturally. If, for example, a particular reality is said to be sinful, the reality has already been interpreted with the aid of a thought model that determines why and in what sense it is so. The perspective here is different from that of European theology, in which analysis is an examination of the *interpretation* of the reality as sinful, or a comparison between this interpretation and the biblical analysis of sin, for example. In Latin American theology, the object is first to see that the sin is there and then to ask how to get rid of it. The theological concern is not to explain as accurately as possible what the essence of sin is, or what meaning a sinful world has, or what meaning human existence has in such a world. The concern is to change the sinful situation. In this sense, with certain clarifications and reservations, I think it accurate to say that European theology tends to approach or confront reality primarily as an object of *thought,* whereas Latin American theology tends to confront it as it is, even though in doing this it cannot prescind from interpretative models.

Crises of Meaning and of Reality

European theology comes to grips with the crisis of meaning, that is, with the repercussions *in the subject* of the lack of existential meaning. This lack of meaning can obscure the intelligibility of reality as a whole: nature, history, and the subject itself. Latin American theology is more interested in the crisis within reality and less in the repercussions of this crisis on the subject who may be ideologically affected by it. Latin American theology therefore speaks of the wretched state of the real world, of captivity, of structural sin. It is not so much concerned that the hunger of the masses seems senseless to the contemporary world; its concern is the hunger. Consequently, there is no question here of looking for an interpretative model that will somehow give meaning to Christian faith in a world of hunger (the solutions offered, for example, by the old theodicy, by hope of a just world in the hereafter, by the "eschatological proviso," which says that it is impossible for God's kingdom to become a reality in the present world, and by dialectical schemata of meaning rather than of action, according to which negation is necessary for synthesis). The aim is rather to confront the reality of hunger and not the threat that widespread hunger may represent to the meaningfulness of the subject's faith.

Of course, the theological description of "widespread hunger" as "sin" presupposes an interpretative model. The characteristic thing about Latin American theology, however, is not the creation or development of explanatory models but the call for the transformation of the sinful condition. The interpretative models become relevant to the extent that they arise out of the experienced reality and aim at eliminating the wretched state of the real world.

In European theology it is possible to seek a reconciliation of "hunger" and "meaningful faith" in a single reflection (whence the boom in theological existentialism after World War II), that is, in a single theological understanding. Latin American theology demands that this reconciliation be effected in reality and claims that if it is not, no reconciliation at the level of thought makes any sense.

This description of alternatives—the crisis of meaning in the subject or the crisis in reality itself—does not, of course, solve the difficult problem of the autonomy of understanding as giver of meaning. However, for the purpose of comparing two ways of conceiving of theological understanding, it is enough to show the divergent perspectives from which the crisis is grasped. On the one hand, the emphasis is on the subject, who finds the meaning of faith threatened by the crisis in the real world. On the other hand, the emphasis is on the crisis in the real world. The first perspective leads to an effort to reconcile faith with the meaningless reality within the subject. The second believes a reconciliation to be possible only if an attempt is made to solve the objective crisis.

Attitude of Latin American Theology toward European Theology

Given all this, we can understand a phenomenon that continually astonishes Europeans, namely, the lack of Latin American interest in European theology. Europeans are surprised that "Latin American theologians . . . criticize even more radically the various 'progressive' theologies of the western world."[14] This lack of interest does not mean that Latin American theologians are ignorant of European theology; in fact they frequently cite European theologians. It does not signify any scorn of European theology in principle nor any feeling of superiority toward it. In the search for its own identity Latin American theology would understandably accentuate its own characteristics over "against" European theology. But it does not disdain the achievements of European theology and the theological ideas that have been developed in Europe (political theology, theology of hope, theology of the historical Jesus). The roots of the lack of interest go deeper. The real cause is the lack of agreement on the concern that should guide theological understanding. Latin American theologians believe that as long as European theology looks upon itself, even unconsciously (and this only aggravates the situation), as a theology emanating from the geopolitical center of the world, it cannot grasp the wretched state of the real world and therefore it "share[s] the defect of unconsciously playing the game of western capitalist society."[15] European theology is trying (admittedly in goodwill) to reconcile the wretched state of the real world at the level of theological thought, but it is not trying to liberate the real world from its wretched state.

Uses of Philosophy and the Social Sciences

These differing perspectives explain the differing uses made of philosophy and the social sciences in theological understanding.[16] If the problem of theology is to give meaning, then there will be a spontaneous appeal to philosophy. In this case philosophy is understood in the traditional manner as the model for universal understanding; it can therefore serve as an agent or mediator in the search for an expression of meaning. If, however, the concern is the liberation of the real world from its wretched state, theology will turn spontaneously to the social sciences. For they analyze the concrete misery of the real world, the mechanisms that create it, and consider possible models of liberation from it. The fact that these models are always incomplete and that they are subject to the eschatological proviso is not an obstacle to their use. It would be an obstacle if the aim of theology were to look for an all-embracing meaning at the level of thought. But if the aim of theology is more operational than intellectual, then the social sciences are a suitable mediation for theological understanding.

All this does not mean that Latin American theology ignores the problem of sense and meaning, although it has not reflected very deeply on the subject. It does look for meaning, but in a different form, as we shall see. For the moment it is enough to say that Latin American theology does not look for this total meaning in the situation as given or, to put it differently, does not accept reconciliation with the situation as given. It finds the meaning in historical change, in the real world and not in thought. The mediation of meaning is therefore sought, not in the interpretation that the theologizing subject gives of the real world, but in the interpretation that the real world gives of itself insofar as it is a real world to be transformed by, among other things, theological understanding.

Role of Theological Understanding

Finally, Latin American theology is more conscious than European theology is of its own status as understanding. The task of explaining and giving meaning is good and necessary "in itself," and it is a task incumbent upon theology. But in Latin American theology this explicatory aspect of understanding is seen within the framework of understanding in its totality. Latin American theology asks itself: What usually happens when theological understanding is limited to its role as explicator and source of meaning? What happens very often is that this kind of understanding leaves reality untouched, justified and justifiable. Latin American theology is conscious of the fact that theological understanding, even though autonomous as a form of understanding, is nonetheless never neutral either practically or ethically. If the concern that motivates theology is basically to offer explanations, then by the mere fact of doing theology in *this* way the status quo of the real world remains, and is thereby justified, at least indirectly.

What we are faced with here is the problem of the ideologization of theology. Latin American theology is more sensitive to this problem than European theology is.[17] Latin American theology asks not only what the theologian's intention is in doing theology but also what real use he or she makes of that theology and what the real conclusions are that society draws from it. In dealing with theological pluralism as a theological problem, for example, Latin American theology does not simply inquire into the intrinsic possibility of pluralism in light of the various theologies in the Old and New Testaments, or in light of the different cultural contexts that are responsible for particular theologies. It also inquires into the politico-ecclesiastical interests that come into play in attacking or defending a subject as seemingly theoretical as "theological pluralism." In Latin America, for example, the defense of pluralism may be a subtle way of smothering the theology of liberation. Attention to this real effect, and not simply reflection on the essence of pluralism, is part of a theological understanding of the reality we call theological pluralism.

In summary, European theology is generally interested in explaining the truth of the faith and in clarifying its meaning when it is obscured. The concern that has stirred this theology to its major achievements has been pastoral, although relevant only to a cultural elite. The questions to which it has sought answers are these: How is it possible to believe today? What meaning can faith have today when its meaning seems to have been lost? The task has been to recover the meaning of faith.

Latin American theology is interested in liberating the real world from its wretched state, since it is this objective situation that has obscured the meaning of the faith. Its task is not primarily to restore meaning to the faith in the presence of the wretched conditions of the real world. It is to transform this real world and at the same time recover the meaning of the faith. The task, therefore, is not to understand the faith differently, but to allow a new faith to spring from a new practice.[18]

THE RELATION BETWEEN THEORY AND PRACTICE IN THEOLOGICAL UNDERSTANDING

If we inquire into the way in which theology is actually done, we observe that in European theology the starting point is the presupposition that there is a deposit of truths that must be transmitted, explained, interpreted, and made meaningful. This task does not require a dissociation from concrete reality, but it does involve a responsibility to what is already given as knowledge. European thinking has a long tradition behind it, and the manner of doing theology has been greatly influenced by the history of theology. Thus, European theology has often turned out to be theory or a history of theory, even if in recent years the theory has included reflection on the relation of theory to practice.

Latin American theology, as theological understanding, starts with different presuppositions. Its novelty does not arise from its short history. This theology has acquired its self-understanding, not from theological tradition, but from experiential practice of liberation, however inchoate.[19] In other words, theological contact with reality came first, and only then reflection on the theological implications, that is, on making love and justice a reality among the oppressed. The stimulus to thought and theory came not from a tradition of theological theory but from the faith lived in a process of liberation amid conflict.

Proof of this claim lies in the fact that Latin American theologians view their profession in a way different from European theologians. Many of those who developed the theology of liberation began as counselors to action-oriented groups or were priests immersed in the pastoral life. Even "professional" theologians have interests that are not strictly theological—sociology, for example, or politics. They are often involved in institutions—universities, social action centers, communications media, peasant movements—whose principal goal is not theological research in the narrow sense but contact with reality for the purpose of transforming it. These differing conceptions of the theological profession will serve as the basis for some reflections on the relation between theory and practice in the two theologies.

Orthodoxy and Orthopractice

Orthodoxy as a mode of understanding based on an authority wholly external to the subject has long been discredited in Europe. This is due to the very structure of biblical faith. Today, orthodoxy's need for orthopractice is generally accepted. However, two conditions make this need less urgent: (1) the substitution of an orthodoxy of meaning or method for the orthodoxy of affirmation; and (2) the different standpoints from which the relation between orthodoxy and orthopractice is described—the standpoint of thought or the standpoint of action.

Its best representatives associate European theology with a specific kind of existence and experience of reality. It has never been a matter of pure thought. But orthopractice means more than that. It is not simply a matter of thought based on experience; it is a matter of thought based on a particular kind of experience. It is based, not only on a practice that is influenced by the wretched state of the world (Europe experienced this wretchedness after the World War), but also on the transformation of this wretched state. For this misery is destructive both of the meaning of reality for the subject and of social meaning and unity among human beings. In European theology, even when orthodoxy has been abandoned and reflection on reality has been undertaken, little progress has been made toward orthopractice as understood in Latin American theology.

Theological Method

This leads to a reformulation of theological method. Before methods there is method. Method (in the singular) is simply the process of understanding considered critically and functionally.[20] The transcendental method of Rahner, for example, is identical with his transcendental theology. It is significant that only in volume 8 of his *Theological Investigations* (published in German in 1967) is there any reflection on his transcendental method, even though he had been doing transcendental theology for thirty years.

This suggests the priority of method as a way of understanding over method that explains or justifies this way.

The same phenomenon occurs in Latin American theology. The method of the theology of liberation is simply the road this theology has travelled. But here there is a difference from European theology. "Method" as road travelled is not found in critical reflection on the road travelled to reach understanding, but in the travelling itself. I will explain this statement with an example.

In European theology the "following of Jesus" is a subject usually relegated to spiritual theology; it has had hardly any influence on christology. When it has had an influence, it has taken the form of showing the unique consciousness of Jesus, which finds expression in his call for an unconditional following of himself. The "following" of Jesus as an epistemological source for the "understanding" of Jesus has almost always been neglected and is absent from contemporary systematic theology.[21] Latin American theology, however, understands theological method as a real journeying. To continue with the example of christology: It is the real following of Jesus that enables one to understand the reality of Jesus, even if this understanding must then be explicated by using a plurality of methods, analyses, and hermeneutics. In its deepest meaning method is understood as content.

Abstract Orthodoxy to Concrete Orthodoxy

European theology is aware of the impossibility of an abstract orthodoxy, that is, the impossibility of directly thinking such concepts as God, Christ, sin, kingdom of God, and liberation. Method then becomes the passage from an abstract orthodoxy to a concrete orthodoxy. But this passage can be understood in two fundamentally different ways. Even European theology says that knowledge is inseparable from the road travelled by the knower.[22] For example, an understanding of what the "divinity" of Christ means in the Chalcedonian formula requires one to know the historical development of an *idea* that began in the New Testament and that led to Chalcedon via the Apologists and the Fathers. In this way, naïve, abstract orthodoxy is transcended, and the way to understanding is incorporated into understanding itself.

In Latin America, however, the way to understanding is conceived of differently. The passage from an abstract to a concrete orthodoxy is effected not by means of the history of ideas but by means of practice. The confession of the "divinity" of Christ is not reached through an understanding of the history of ideas such as person, personal union, and divine nature. The truth stated generally by Chalcedon is clarified through concrete praxis. In this case, method in its basic form is identical with the road, the practice of the faith and with what that practice yields.

The issue here is the very idea of theological method. From the theological standpoint, the key is in the history of Jesus: he is the "truth" insofar as he is the "way." Stripped of pietistic overtones, this means that the method of theology is to travel, not to think about, the way of Jesus. Methods (in the plural) will endeavor to explain the real way of Jesus (historical exegesis), the concrete ways that must be travelled today in a geographical and historical setting different from that of Jesus (hermeneutics), the true and false ways followed in the history of Christian life (history of the Church), the way in the contemporary world (social sciences), the all-inclusive and transcendent meaning that is experienced in travelling this way (systematic theology), and the danger, inherent in faith, of turning the way into an ideology (critical theology).

In the concrete development of these themes there will undoubtedly be differing emphases according to differing social, economic, cultural, and political focuses. But the aim of the theology of liberation has been to recover the original meaning of method as the real way travelled by faith. The first question to be asked is whether any and every way is Christian. As long as the kingdom of God is not completely realized, not every occasion, not every practice, not every way can lead to theological understanding. This question takes us deep into the problem of theological understanding precisely as theological. Which way, if travelled, if followed, makes *Christian* theological understanding possible? This is the question, in theological terms, that arises in the course of the passage from the present to the future reign of God.[23]

INTEGRATION OF THE EPISTEMOLOGICAL BREAK INTO THEOLOGICAL UNDERSTANDING

The way leading from the present world to the final reign of God can be conceived of along either of two lines: a way of progressive development and fulfillment of the present or a way of contradiction and transformation of the present. The names of various theologies indicate which way was chosen: the theology of development and the theology of liberation, the theology of the creative Logos and the theology of the redemptive Logos. The two lines bring into play what is most fundamental in any given theological concept and, therefore, what theological understanding should be.

The basic problem here is the problem of the epistemological break within theological understanding. Scripture shows that there can be no theological understanding without this epistemological break. But in Scripture the break takes two different forms: (1) insofar as theological understanding asserts the transcendence of God as futurity, theological understanding must be *distinct* from natural understanding; (2) insofar as it asserts the transcendence of a crucified God, it must be *contrary* to natural understanding. All this is symbolized by the call of Jesus for *metanoia*, a change of heart. The question is how does the epistemological break influence understanding in European theology and in Latin American theology.

In traditional Catholic theology, the classical concept of analogy has always required a moment, a break in the process of understanding. We must negate our knowledge insofar as it is finite if we are to move on to knowledge of the divine. This kind of break meant *going beyond* natural knowledge, but not *going against* it. Theologians focused so intently on certain classical passages of Scripture (Wis. 13–15; Acts 17:22–31; and especially Rom. 1: 20–21) that they did not notice Paul's assertion of the historical failure of all natural theology, that is, of every theological understanding that had not passed through a break. Paul interprets the break as a scandal and a form of madness.

Protestant theology has been very conscious of this type of break, especially in those who rejected the liberal theology symbolized by Harnack. In liberal theology Jesus represents in its sublimest form the good that is to be found in human beings. He thus becomes, in his own historical context, the supreme embodiment of the virtues of the middle-class citizen of the late nineteenth century in whom life and culture, throne and altar, existence and virtue are all in harmony. At this point and against such a background, the discovery by Albert Schweitzer and Johannes Weiss of the eschatological dimension of the person of Jesus and his preach-

ing of the kingdom was of great importance. The introduction of
the eschatological into theology meant the introduction, not only
of the element of *kairos* and the future, but also of another essential
element: *krisis* (crisis, judgment).

This means that the person of Jesus, along with the God who
reveals himself in Jesus and the kingdom that Jesus preaches, is not
accessible to purely natural existence. Theological understanding
must take on the element of crisis if it is to function properly.
Without crisis theological understanding will be only liberal. It will
attempt to harmonize theology with the essential constitution of
the human person or with the truth of historical events, but it will
fail to grasp what is specific to Christian understanding: the conversion needed in order to function. Without crisis, theological understanding will try to develop generic, universal explanatory
frameworks within which it will claim to justify the truth of faith. It
will not suspect that the first thing faith does is challenge universal
frames of interpretation.

How has the epistemological break influenced European theologians? I shall select a few important examples. For Barth the very
essence of theological understanding is to be found in its contradiction of the functioning of natural understanding; theology contradicts religion and unmasks the real interest at work in religious
understanding, which is the justification of the human person in
the sight of God. The epistemological break is inherent in theological understanding.[24]

Bultmann affirms the break when he says that the first point of
contact between God and humanity is the point at which God rejects humanity. The crisis is introduced into understanding when
human beings can accept that they are sinners, they are judged.
Then they are able to understand the word God addresses to them
as the good news of forgiveness.[25]

Bonhoeffer repeated to some extent the views of Barth. He took
a further important step when he pointed out that the break takes
place in objective reality, in the history of the world's suffering. It
follows from this that to know God is to be united with God in the
suffering of the world.[26] Moltmann explored this insight in some
detail during his second period. He held that God is the criticism of
humankind and that therefore all theological discourse must make
this criticism part of itself. The justification of faith cannot be

achieved in continuity with any universal cosmological, anthropological, or historical system, since faith contradicts all of these.[27]

The theology of Pannenberg hardly ever deals with the epistemological break. Pannenberg indeed emphasizes the futurity of God as opposed to a God of origins, but he puts this god in continuity with the god whom the religions conceive of as power. Trust, the fundamental attitude toward God, is here based on and is in continuity with the openness of the human being.[28]

The epistemological break in the theology of liberation is similar to that in European theologies. The difference is that the break is a matter of experience more than of reflective thought. I shall first indicate some specific points of theological epistemology and then consider what impact the epistemological break has on these points in Latin American theology.

Analogical and Dialectical Understanding

Analogical knowledge presupposes that like is known by like (Plato) and, at the practical level, that like gets along with like (Aristotle). A theology based on analogy has not incorporated the epistemological break.

These principles are singularly important in Latin American theology. In a continent where beauty, love, reconciliation, and justice are in short supply and the plight of the masses is catastrophic, theological discourse is much more dialectical than analogical, more practical than analytical. Wretched conditions and a situation of sin and oppression prove paradoxically to be the locus of encounter with God. But God must then be thought of, not as analogous with the God of thought, but as the contradiction of the wretched conditions of real life. The theological is not conceived of as being in continuity with or as the culmination of reality.

It follows that the concrete mediations of theological understanding are those realities that point by contrariety to the wholly other—other not because it is beyond present reality but because it contradicts present reality. This is why the theology of liberation focuses on such themes as the Exodus, structural sin, captivity, and conflict. The very name *theology of "liberation"* points in this direction. It is a theology, not of "freedom" (Pannenberg for example, tries to reconcile the finite freedom of humankind with the infinite freedom of God), but of "liberation," and liberation is only to be grasped dialectically, that is, in opposition to the experience of oppression. In thus opposing analogy and dialectic I am criticizing Greek philosophy, not for its deficiencies in regard to the future, that is, its inability to think what does not yet exist, but for its failure to criticize what already exists.

Wonder and Suffering

Greek thought presupposes that wonder is what motivates all knowing. It presupposes that the positive structure of reality stimulates the human person to know; knowledge brings joy, and joy provides an ultimate criterion for the truth of the movement of understanding.

In Latin America, the suffering of the present, not wonder, plays the active role in the process of understanding. Moreover, this suffering provides the authentic analogy for understanding God: the recognition that the present history of the world is the ongoing history of the suffering of God. At the crowning moments of divine revelation there has always been suffering: the cry of the oppressed in Egypt; the cry of Jesus on the cross (according to Mark); the birth-pangs experienced by the whole of creation as it awaits liberation. Latin American theology gives a privileged place to the cries of the oppressed. They are a stimulus to theological thinking. This does not mean that Latin American theology fails to deal with the positive themes of theology (the love of God, hope, reconciliation, the reign of God). It does, however, mean that it adopts a perspective of its own in dealing with them. It does not approach these great positive themes directly and in isolation. They are always accompanied or even brought into play by some great suffering.

I believe that in the epistemological break to which suffering leads, the practical and ethical orientation of understanding comes into view. Human beings suffer in every part of the world. The suffering on which the theology of liberation focuses is the widespread suffering of others. Berdyaev once insightfully remarked: "If I go hungry it is a physical evil; if others go hungry it is a moral evil." In the face of moral evil there is only one proper response: get rid of it. It is impossible to perceive moral evil in another without experiencing the need to overcome it.

The situation of widespread moral evil that exists in Latin America is a source of suffering for the theologian. This means that Latin American theology is not primarily motivated by wonder, which any system of thought (including theological systems) calls for and arouses. In fact, Latin American theology is regarded not so much as an explanatory schema in which the data of revelation and the data of history are integrated in a consistent way as it is a pattern of response to widespread suffering. The reflection that suffering stimulates is not essentially an effort to explain the nature of suffering or to investigate its compatibility with the data of revelation; it is an effort to eliminate the suffering. An analysis of the causes of the widespread suffering is not excluded; indeed it is demanded. This shows once again the importance of the social sciences. However, the perspective is different: the issue is not the truth or formal beauty of these analyses but the elimination of the suffering.

Natural Theology and Theodicy

Natural theology and theodicy are two traditional and distinct types of theological discourse. In the first, the God-question begins with what is positive in the world. In the second, the starting point is what is negative in the world. The passage from the first to the second supposes a break. What I am interested in here, however, is the meaning of theodicy.

In European thinking theodicy has had a long history and has been represented by great theologians. In Latin America the God-question is basically, though perhaps not explicitly, the same as the question faced in theodicy: How is the existence of God to be reconciled with the real wretchedness and evil in the world? In the Latin American context the question has special nuances. First, it has a historical dimension. Natural catastrophes are a challenge to the existence of God but so are historical catastrophes that result from the free action of human beings. The question also has a political dimension, since it is the structural pattern of oppression rather than the free will of an individual that oppresses human beings. Second, the mediation used in theodicy is anthropodicy: How is the human person to be justified in a world of injustice? Finally, the resolution of the epistemological break in theodicy is not reached by "thinking" about God so as to reconcile God and evil at the level of ideas, but by accepting the task of constructing a world that is in harmony with God.

This approach has its theoretical, if not reflective, phase in which the reality of the Christian God is related to suffering. (Biblical passages that show God related to the suffering of human beings and that meditate on suffering as a mode of God's existence play a special role here.) The question asked in theodicy is essentially practical, because insofar as faith in the God of Jesus leads to a real improvement in the world's wretched state, to that extent God is justified, even if we never succeed in *theoretically* reconciling God and evil.

The "problem of God" is not tackled as extensively and directly in Latin American theology as it is in European theology. The reason for this is not that God has ceased to be a problem or a question (in the double sense of "questions about God" and "the God who questions"), but rather that the theme is approached indirectly. The epistemological break in theodicy does not consist fundamentally in explaining, at the level of thought, the true nature of God, but in experiencing the reality of God in the effort to build his kingdom.[29] The reality of God is proved in the effort to reconcile him with the real world. And although from a theoretical standpoint this kind of reconciliation is more unpretentious than reconciliation at the level of thought, it is the more profound for being a reconciliation in reality.

The epistemological break is not achieved simply by contrasting natural theology and theodicy as different types of theological understanding; it is achieved in the very conception of theodicy, since the basic scandal is not that evil exists despite the fact that God exists, but simply that evil exists. Theodicy is not a theoretical problem that has been constructed by introducing God into the picture of a total understanding of reality; it is a problem that exists independently of any theoretical construction. Consequently the basic question is how the human being is to be justified. This practical task indirectly shows what it means to justify God. It shows the meaning of what the Bible says about God whose sole justification is that he enters history in order to justify, that is, to re-create humankind. The knowledge of God then becomes connatural; that is, anyone who seriously endeavors to do justice to human beings is in continuity with God, even though the problem of theodicy, when formulated in purely theoretical terms, remains without a theoretical solution.

The "Death of God" and the "Death of the Oppressed"

For the past 150 years and especially since the rise of the theology of the death of God, theological understanding in Europe has been influenced by the notion of the "death of God." Independently of how this death has been understood—whether as a linguistic phenomenon, in atheistic or in Christian terms—the very notion of "the death of God" has meant a break within theological understanding. There is no greater break than death and no more definitive way of expressing it theologically than to say that God has died.

In Europe the "death of God" has influenced theological understanding at the level of meaning. In a theistic culture the "death of God" is the most radical expression of the crisis of meaning, whether the "death" be understood as an experience of abandonment (Sartre), as a Good Friday of the speculative mind (Hegel), as a feeling of being orphaned (Neitzsche), or in positive and Christian terms as an ethical exigency accompanying humanity's coming of age (Bonhoeffer).

Among Christians the "death of God" has contributed to a reinterpretation of faith in the specific area of belief. The crucified God is the dividing line between an authentically Christian theology and just any religion, philosophy, or ideology. The crucified God is the most radical expression of God's appropriation of history, not in an idealistic way but in a real way. In this sense Moltmann's book *The Crucified God* marks the most important phase in the incorporation of the epistemological break into European theological understanding. The first thing the cross questions is the interest that spurs a human being (and a theologian) to understanding. The cross unmasks any interest in theological understanding that consciously or unconsciously seeks to find in the divine a justification for present reality and its wretchedness. On the cross, God is the criticism of humankind (and of the theologian). Moltmann has tried to show how the death of God, in the Christian sense of this phrase, produces the epistemological break needed to christianize all the "Christian realities": the God of love, the resurrection of the crucified Jesus, faith against disbelief, hope against hope, love against alienation. All these are shown to be truly Christian and not simply extrapolations of the longings of the natural human being by means of the break within theological understanding.

In Latin America, the "death of God" as ultimate horizon is having an influence on theology, but in a nonreflective way and through a mediation that in its concrete form is different from the European. To begin with, the "death of God" is viewed through the death of the human being.[30] That death is real and widespread. If the death of God is the expression of a crisis of meaning, human death is the expression of a crisis in reality. It is not an experience of being orphaned or of a world that has come of age or of a Good Friday of the speculative mind, but a real experience of the death of the poor, the oppressed, the Indian, the peasant. In Latin America, death does not mean simply the disappearance of that which had supposedly given meaning to things (in this case, God), but the triumph of injustice and sin. The theologically correct statement that sin caused the death of the Son is brought home to people in Latin America through the experience of sin continuing to cause the death of sons and daughters. For this reason the epistemological break is formulated not so much on the basis of the death of God as on that of the death of the oppressed.

In European theology, precisely because the death of God provides the horizon for theological thinking, there has been an effort to reinterpret the transcendence of God. This effort did not use either the language of cosmology (beyond or above), the language of time (in the beginning or in the future), or the language of anthropology (in the depths of the person or as an ethical demand from without). Instead, it used the categories of suffering and power: "Only a suffering God can save us" (Bonhoeffer). In Latin America there is not a great deal of reflection on the new categories that are required by the epistemological break for formulating the concept of God. In a nonreflective way, however, theological language is being influenced by the death of human beings. The new categories appearing in theological language are historical: suffering, power, conflict, liberation. Any talk about God that goes beyond these is spontaneously seen as false, idealistic, and alienating.

In Latin America, theology has been less concerned with the language used in speaking of God than with the concrete mediation of God. The mediation of the absolutely Other takes the form of those who are really "other": the oppressed. In the oppressed the Other is discovered dialectically and through a sharing of suffering. But the break required in order to grasp the Other comes through the real break occasioned by the oppressed. The oppressed challenge us with regard to our own identity. The break therefore takes place not at the level of self-understanding or feeling but at the level of reality. Conversion comes, as in the gospel, through those who are historically "other" in relation to us: the oppressed. Through them we discover what is characteristic of the God of Jesus: his readiness to make himself other, to immerse himself in history, and thus to make real and credible his ultimate word—his message of love—to human beings. Moreover, as concrete mediation of God, the other does not simply occasion a break in our identity; it is by its very existence a call to action, a call for liberation. The other is there in order to be liberated, to be re-created, so that a genuine communion not only in suffering but in joy and love may become possible.

The epistemological break expressed in the phrase "death of God" has been fruitful in Latin American theology, and not simply as a philosophical, biblical, or theological analysis of the meaning of the expression. It has meant for many a genuine break in their lives and indirectly a break at the level of theological understanding. As a result, they have come to realize what is Christian in the "death of God," that is, a crucified God.

The Fundamental Aporia of Understanding

All serious understanding advances because of the presence of an *aporia*, that is, of two seemingly irreconcilable poles. An *aporia* is needed if understanding is to grow, to be serious and not dilettantish. We think seriously to the extent that reality gives us matter for thought. The formulation of the *aporia* will show whether or not there has been an epistemological break.

The *aporia* in theological understanding can be formulated according to ancient Greek theology as the *aporia* of the one and the many, or in Christian terms as the *aporia* of creator and creature, transcendence and immanence. Christian theological understanding has always been faced with some form of this *aporia* and has made it the basis of thought. Classical formulations are seen in the trinitarian and christological definitions and the debates on the relation between freedom and grace, faith and works. In his early articles on christology, for example, Rahner devoted his best energies to reconciling human autonomy with dependence on God. Pannenberg tacked the *aporia* of human freedom and divine creativity and concluded that we must deny the presence of God and conceive of creation in terms of the future. What is common to the approach to and solution of the *aporia* is the development of a new concept of God or humankind or history, thus making possible the conceptual reconciliation of the two poles. The author in question then tries to show that his solution does justice to the thinking found in Scripture.

In Latin American theology the preferred form of the theological *aporia* is the reconciliation of the gratuitousness of the kingdom with its construction by human beings. In principle, this is a modern formulation of the *aporia* of freedom and grace. But concretely the old *aporia* takes on a new meaning. The phrase "to build the kingdom" is not an abstraction that is to be contrasted with the theoretical gratuitousness of the kingdom, but rather expresses a task to be done. Since the task is a concrete historical one, it is always carried out in a world of wretchedness and suffering. It is in the execution of the task that the full force of the *aporia* is felt: Since the kingdom is not built in an ideal form nor simply in human souls, but in a history marked by real wretchedness, the task necessarily involves conflict. In the process, that which is most positive in the real world—the love that effectively does justice—seems impotent in the face of what is most negative in the real world—sin and injustice. Sin is powerful: that is how the *aporia* is now to be formulated.

The *aporia* of the triumph of sin over love cannot be resolved conceptually, but only in life. Theological understanding, insofar as it is a way, develops within the horizon of an *aporia* that is not simply thought about but is experienced and lived. The aim of theological understanding, therefore, is not to resolve the *aporia* intellectually but to find a way of living with the impossible.

The epistemological break occurs in the very conception of what an *aporia* is and how it is to be approached. *Aporia* means literally "without a way through." It is encountered at the point at which there really seems to be no way through, namely, at the point of the powerlessness of love against injustice. When the *aporia* is thus stated, theological understanding is referred to practice, the place of "no passage," and not to more or less subtle speculations by which the *aporia* is to be resolved at the level of thought or which lead to an escapist adoration of mystery. To understand theologically when confronted with an *aporia* is, then, to open a way.

A concrete consequence of this conception of the influence of an *aporia* on theological understanding and on the break involved in such understanding is an appreciation of the eschatological proviso that is different in Europe from that in Latin America. European theology tends to relativize every possible intrahistorical future insofar as it is not yet the kingdom of God. Latin American theology emphasizes that the present state of the world does not embody the reign of God but is a genuine *aporia* and that there is an urgent need to change the situation, realizing that neither will any future state of the world represent the definitive kingdom of God. Latin American theology opts for concrete social and political solutions[31] precisely because it is not trying to resolve the *aporia* at the level of thought, though some ideal resolution might be achieved. Latin American theology tries rather to resolve the *aporia* in the real order, though solutions at this level are always partial. With this outlook, the epistemological break occurs when people accept the fact that, although the faith is not an all-embracing ideology, which can provide complete solutions to the *aporia* in the real order of things, it is nonetheless a "source of functional ideologies,"[32] which, though always subject to revision, are the only way of resolving the *aporia*. This approach derives its validity from the felt pressures of the Latin American reality; this reponse is the present-day equivalent of the concern of Saint Paul: "The love of Christ impels us."[33]

I will summarize the major points of this chapter.

1. When I speak of "European" and "Latin American" theologies I am nominally defining two different ways of conceiving the theological task. Such a definition does not subsume everything theological that is being done in Europe and Latin America. Nonetheless I have attempted to capture in this distinction the essence of theological activity in Central Europe and in the theology of liberation, remaining aware that within "European theology" and the

"theology of liberation" there are divergent theological families.

2. In contrasting these two ways of doing theology (in the strict sense of this last term) I have not attempted to pass a value judgement on them but simply to make a comparison. I think, however, that there is in principle greater harmony between theological understanding and theological content in Latin American theology, at least in intention. I do not want to evaluate European theology in anachronistic terms nor to ignore its accomplishments, which, when judged historically, have been largely positive. For example, European theology made possible the theology of Vatican II. Its exegetical research, its break from dogmatism and abstract orthodoxy, its pastoral concern to give meaning to a faith that seems meaningless or mythical—these have been real gains.

My criticism is directed more to European theology's lack of self-criticism in its accomplishments and, above all, to the historical anachronism of which it is guilty when it supposes that a theological understanding that proved liberating in a particular historical situation must continue to be liberating. Such an outlook implies that theology is profoundly ahistorical. To this historical anachronism must be added a geographical anachronism. European theology was not conscious that it was theologizing from the vantage point of the geopolitical center of the world. It failed to see that the world is not identical with this center and cannot be understood from the standpoint of the center. It failed to realize that the world is instead a whole in which center and periphery are in tension and that from the properly Christian standpoint it is the periphery (the poor) or at least the repercussions at the periphery that are the privileged source of theological understanding.[34]

This is not to say that the theology of liberation should not in its turn be evaluated and criticized. But I pass over this point here.

3. In comparing the two ways of doing theology, I have dwelt not on the concrete methods each uses but rather on what I think are the reasons for the different ways of working toward theological understanding. I have reduced these causes to three, on the basis of the exigences inherent in the content of Christian theology: the liberating aspect of theological understanding, the relation between theory and practice, and the epistemological break.

We have seen that one fundamental difference between the two types of theological understanding is a different motivating interest. This difference may be summed up, with some inevitable simplification, as follows. Ever since the Enlightenment, European theology has been faced with the historical fact that the faith and its meaning have been obscured by various factors: the rise of the democratic-liberal outlook, which attacks all forms of dogmatism; discoveries affecting the truth of biblical passages; the collapse of Western cultures that were based on, among other things, an acculturated Christian faith. The task of theological understanding has therefore been seen as that of restoring the meaning of the faith. In this sense European theology has been both liberating and pastoral, although its effects have been limited to an intellectual elite. The motive for doing theology has been the threatened reality of the believer as believer.

The fundamental problem faced in Latin American theology has not been the restoration of meaning to a threatened faith but the restoration of meaning to a reality that is not merely threatened but is actually in a wretched state. To carry out the liberating function of theology has meant to assist in the transformation of a sinful reality. The enemy of theology has been less the atheist than the inhuman.

4. European theology has claimed in principle that the explanation of the faith and its sources would lead to real liberation. In general, it has endeavored to explain reality in terms of the sources of faith. The relation of Latin American theology to the sources of faith has been different. Theologians in Latin America begin by accepting the Christian faith; the concretizing of this faith runs parallel to real life and is in a dialectical relationship with it. Enlightening the double darkness of obscured faith and the world's wretched conditions is a single process. The sources of revelation are therefore seen less as sources of a knowledge that precedes an analysis of reality and a transformative practice than as sources that shed light on reality because they are themselves illumined by a practice that deals with reality. The relation between sources of revelation and confrontation with reality is established not so much in reflection on the ideas in which revelation and a conceptualized present reality find expression as in a coordination of situations.

Thus, for example, when we draw close to the poor, new light is shed for us on the words of Jesus about the final judgment, and in this life-giving light we understand the words of revelation as words that should in turn illumine reality for us. Clarification of revelation goes hand in hand with practice; the important thing in this conjunction is not to solve the theoretical question of the logical priority between revelation given and Christian life understood as a revelation to be accomplished (the hermeneutical circle), but rather to be aware of being caught up in a process that includes in a dialectical relationship both the sources of revelation and real Christian existence.

5. The basic difference between the two ways of doing theology is to be seen in the degree to which each overcomes dualisms. European theology has made a good deal of progress in this area by unmasking the so-called dichotomies of spirit and body, person and society, private faith and public faith, transcendence and history. But this victory over dualism has been won at the level of thought; in other words, it is within understanding as such that theological understanding has overcome the dualism.

Latin American theology has attempted to overcome the most radical dualism in theology; that of the believing subject and history, of theory and practice—not, however in the sphere of thought but in the real world. It has aimed to recover the meaning of those profound biblical experiences of what it means to understand theologically: namely, that to understand the truth is to do the truth; that to understand Jesus is to follow Jesus; that to understand sin is to take sin upon oneself; that to understand the world's wretchedness is to liberate the world from its wretchedness; that to understand God is to journey to God along the paths of justice.

2

The Promotion of Justice as an Essential Requirement of the Gospel Message

The formal purpose of ecumenism is to pose the question of the unity of Christians and the Christian Churches in such a way as to lead to a good theoretical and practical solution.[1] The union of Christians and the Christian Churches will come about if we take as our starting point a historical practice based on the following of Jesus and if there is a real, effective commitment to the needs and longings of the vast majority of the human race, namely, the poor and the oppressed.

The extent to which the promotion of justice has already proved to be a bond among Christians is an argument in favor of my approach. Historically, it has also divided Christians. The division, however, is not along confessional lines; it comes from divergent conceptions of what the Church is meant to be. The greatest division in the human race today is the division created by injustice.[2]

I shall try to show that this approach is not only effective but also that the gospel shows it to be the right approach in ecumenism. If ecumenism is not to be treated along purely regional lines and not to be reduced to efforts at partial unity (though these are not to be scorned), then we must look for the essential basis on which unity is possible.

This basis exists when there is substantial unity among Christians in their response to the gospel message. The core of this response can be expressed in the traditional triad of faith, hope, and love. Taking this as my point of departure, I want to make two points: (1) the practice of justice as a form of charity or love is part of a total response to the gospel message; and (2) this practice of justice is an essential constituent in the role of faith and hope in this response. In other words, I want to show that the promotion of justice is both formally and materially essential to conformity to the essential gospel message.

THE PRACTICE OF JUSTICE AS ESSENTIAL TO THE RESPONSE TO THE GOSPEL MESSAGE

Determination of the Complete Essence of the Gospel Message

In order to show that the practice of justice is materially essential to conformity to the gospel, it is necessary to determine in a comprehensive way, even if very briefly, what the essence of the gospel is. This essence must be something theo-logical in the strict sense, since even if the reality of God as such is not specific to and distinctive of the gospel message, it would be difficult not to name this ultimate and absolute reality and still come up with something that is truly comprehensive and not partial, truly essential and not provisory. This divine reality must be the one that Jesus proclaimed and that accounts for his own life.

This comprehensive theological reality is what the gospel calls the "reign of God" or "kingdom of God." In the summaries given in Mark and Matthew this reality is given logical and chronological priority and is presented as all-inclusive: "The time is fulfilled, and the kingdom of God is at hand; repent, and believe in the gospel" (Mk. 1:15; cf. Mt. 4:17). In the parallel message that Luke reports at the beginning of Jesus' ministry it is clear that the primary addressees of the good news of the kingdom (Lk. 4:43) are the poor (Lk. 4:18).

The reign or kingdom of God is the concrete content of the *euanggelion,* or good news. The reign of God is the inclusive totality presented by the gospel; within this the basic realities of which the gospel speaks have their place: the God of the kingdom; Christ who proclaims it; its utopian content; its addressees; the practice that human beings must adopt if they are to conform to this reign. The problem of conformity to the gospel thus becomes, in effect, the problem of a true and adequate response to the reign or kingdom of God.

Before proceeding, I must clarify the formal structure of the relation of Christ to the kingdom of God. It might be claimed that the ideal of a reign of God has nothing specifically Christian about it, whereas the person of Christ is indeed specifically Christian, and we should therefore look to this person and not to the reign of God for the all-inclusive element in the gospel message.

A distinction must be made here between a christological reduction and a christological concentration or focusing of the gospel message. I make this distinction not out of any desire for subtleties but because of its theoretical and practical implications.

By a "christological reduction"[3] I mean a presentation of the gospel in which the very appearance of Jesus of Nazareth on the scene is the ultimate thing that God can intend for history. Or, to put it in dogmatic terms, that the incarnation of the Word represents the accomplishment of God's final will. There is no doubt, of course, that this event is fundamental and essential to God's will and that it is a specifying mark of Christianity. At the same time, however, we cannot hastily claim that it represents the final fulfillment of God's will. Christ is obviously related in a special way to this ultimate will at the level both of the revelation and accomplishment of it and of the demands made by God on human beings. But God cannot without further ado be identified as the absolute ultimate. If God were so identified, there would be no meaning, even in christology, to the constitutive relationship of Christ with the Father as ultimate mystery and with the kingdom of the Father as fulfillment of the will of this ultimate mystery.

Nor may we hastily claim that while Christ is not the absolutely ultimate, he is nonetheless the ultimate mediation of God. Here again we must proceed cautiously and by clear steps. On the one hand, it is clear that as Word and Son Christ is the mediator, and the final one, of the Father. According to dogma of the incarnation, in no other person can there be such a union of the divine and the human. But this does not mean that a single person can adequately mediate the mystery of God, God's will for history, and the fulfillment of this will in history. Christ is the mediator of the

Father's word in history, and he is the mediator who shows how to carry out the Father's will, but he does not himself exhaust the totality of mediation of the will of God.

I see, then, a danger in a christological reduction of the gospel message. On the other hand, I want to emphasize the concentration of the message in Christ. In Jesus the will of God is definitively manifested and brought to fulfillment on various levels. The fact that the kingdom of God exists is known to us from the more or less developed ideas of Jesus about it and especially from his attitude and activity in the service of this kingdom. We know how the kingdom is to be proclaimed and brought to fulfillment from his words, his attitudes, his acceptance of the destiny that this proclamation and fulfillment brought upon him. His predilection for the poor tells us for whom the kingdom is meant and in what way it is meant for them. We know what the reign of God demands from the demands made of Jesus himself and from the demands that he in turn makes of his followers.[4]

If I call for a christological concentration of the reign of God but warn against a christological reduction of it, it is because of the theoretical and practical dangers such a reduction brings. On the theoretical level, a christological reduction would ultimately render meaningless the mediation of the Spirit in the accomplishment of the mystery of God and would thus subtly explode the trinitarian reality of God. We must not forget that while Christ is mediator of the Father, it is the Spirit who sets history in motion and is the Lord and giver of life. He it is who renews the face of the earth in order that the renewed earth may mediate the mystery of God. It is important to observe that when the New Testament speaks of the fullness of Christ, it is speaking not of a fullness of Christ the individual but of a fullness that includes others, and that only in this co-fullness, and not apart from it, can we call Christ the adequate mediation of God. This is why Christ is presented to us as head of the human race and as firstborn, that is, in his relation to the rest of the race. It is the renewed human race that becomes the mediation of the mystery of God, although this mediation would be impossible apart from the concrete spirit that Christ inspires and unless human beings conformed themselves to him.

The practical difficulties that a christological reduction brings with it are clearer. When the person of Christ is turned into an unqualified absolute, it is often said that he *is* the kingdom of God and that the encounter with the Thou of Christ is the ultimate reference point of faith. Such a view leads, with historical if not logical necessity, to locating the response to the gospel message more in the line of faith and personal contact with Christ than in the line of the accomplishment of God's kingdom. The demands of Christian practice would certainly be regarded as important, but they would be regarded as secondary to and deducible from the first and fundamental response, namely, faith in Christ and contact with him. This would lead in turn to a one-sided relation with Christ and a devaluation of the kingdom of God.

If we begin with the kingdom of God as the all-inclusive reality, we then see better the meaning of Christ's mediation and the relation between this and the mediation of the Spirit, as well as what is entailed in a response to the essential gospel message.

The Practice of Love as Accomplishment of the Reign of God

If the coming of the reign of God is the most essential and inclusive element in the gospel, then the decisive question should be: How are we to conform to this reign of God? How are we to put ourselves in harmony with it? Conformity to an all-inclusive reality will involve all levels of human existence. If the inclusive reality is the reign of God as proclaimed and inaugurated by Jesus, harmony with it will require a right relation to the reign, to God, and to Christ. It follows that conformity with this inclusive reality must be effected at various levels of practice and meaning, of hope and of transformation of the real world, of the acceptance and attainment of the destiny thus assigned. It also follows that from the outset the triad of faith, hope, and love will be the privileged expression of the total response to the essence of the gospel.

It makes little sense, therefore, to materially divide the triad; it is important that hope does not eliminate the need for love and that love has for its object not only God but also the building of the kingdom of God. Conformity to the reign of God involves not only hope that the kingdom *is coming* but also a practice whereby it actually *becomes a reality*.

The New Testament contains no systematic reflection on this problem, but its reality remains. Whatever the nature of the hope of the coming of the kingdom, it is clear that the New Testament repeatedly calls for the practical dimension, for a doing, an accomplishing. At the level of systematic reflection, all this can be summed up as the accomplishment or bringing into existence of the kingdom. It is secondary here whether this practice is required *because* the kingdom is coming or *in order that* it may come. The important thing is that God's will is *that* the kingdom should come, *that* human beings should act in a particular way, and *that* their action should have an objective content in conformity with the reign of God.

I cannot here discuss in detail what the kingdom of God is,[5] the various ideas about it in Scripture, the diverse expectations regarding the manner of its coming. The important thing from a systematic viewpoint is that the kingdom of God is a reality in which the human world is in harmony with the will and being of God himself. It becomes a world in which human unity and the divine inheritance of all God's children are coextensive.

This short description highlights the indispensable place of the historical and interhuman dimension of the reign of God, and the objective and nonarbitrary coextension of the reign of God with the ethical requirements of love for human beings. Objective conformity with the reign of God would be impossible without a practice that makes the utopian content of the kingdom a reality. Conformity to the coming reign of God consists in a practice that promotes its content, and is the practice of love.

Let me recall briefly here the practical dimension of love as it appears in christology, anthropology, and theology.

The person of Jesus is presented in the gospels chiefly in terms of his mission. He is sent to carry out a mission or, in other words, for the sake of a practice. Whatever may have been the personal consciousness of Jesus and whatever view be taken of his messiahship, it is clear that, as the episodes of his baptism, temptation, and early ministry make clear, his person has no meaning apart from his practice.

The content of this practice is described in various ways: to minister the word, to dispense forgiveness, to work miracles and exorcisms, to have fellowship with the weak, to defend the poor. In systematic terms his practice must be described as salvational. It was for the benefit of others so that they might be transformed.

The practice of Jesus is for others; it is meant to change them and to change their world and its relationships.

Whatever expectations Jesus himself may have had with regard to the coming of the kingdom, they did not paralyze him when it came to practice. It is impossible to determine how in his own mind Jesus unified his hope of the kingdom with his practice of love, but the important thing is to observe that both were objectively real. However imminent Jesus may have thought the coming of the kingdom was,[6] he put its content—love for others—into practice throughout his life and openly denounced the refusal to love.

What is said of Jesus must also be said of his hearers. It might theoretically have been possible for the practice of Jesus to have required of others not a historical practice but a simple doctrinal acceptance of a truth or of a hope in the coming of the kingdom. But this was not the form his practice took. Jesus' statements about the need for conversion and following, his preaching of the commandment of love, are enough to show that an objective conformity to the coming kingdom could not take the form of pure faith or pure hope. Now that the kingdom is coming, change is required. The closer this kingdom is and the more its coming is God's doing, the more must human beings conform to it by a radical change in their way of life.

In its basic structure the change consists in no longer egotistically making oneself the focus of one's attention but instead opening oneself to others in a saving, re-creative activity. It consists in being for others, in a life that is a life-for . . . , in being men and women for others. In short, it consists in the practice of love. Without such a practice there is no entering into the kingdom. Without a saving orientation toward the other there is no conformity to the reign of God.

Underlying these brief reflections is a theological conception of Christian existence and a radical conception of God. For if the practice of love is essential to conformity to the kingdom of God, this must be due to the nature of the God of the kingdom. The proclamation of the approaching reign of God must elicit a response at two levels. First, one must respond in hope that the kingdom is indeed coming, accepting that the immanence of the reign of God unveil the real meaning of human existence, and maintaining at the same time the otherness of the mystery of the

God who is approaching but who is not yet here. Hope is a necessary element in a response to the reality of God seen formally as
mystery, that is, as the ever greater God who is not at our disposal.

The response must also take the form of a practice by which the
human person is assimilated into the reality of God as God and as
understood in Christian revelation. The various descriptions of the
reality of God in the Scriptures have something in common: God is
described as creator, giver of life; as liberator of the oppressed in
Egypt; as *mishpat*, or justice actually operative; as merciful father
or loving mother; and finally as love. These descriptions, each with
its own nuance, point to what is fundamental about the God of
Christian revelation: he is not a self-centered being but one who
goes out of himself to love, re-create, save, and humanize human
beings.

It is for this radical theo-logical reason, and not simply a reason
inferred from the faith, that I say conformity to the reign of God
comes through the practice of love. In this way and only in this way
can human beings do the will of God and thereby come to be like
him. For God's will is not something external to his being; it is the
expression to the world of what he is. In all this I am really reintro-
ducing the classical theme of the divinization of the human person,
but in a form adapted to the present. The ultimate possibility open
to human beings is that they should live the very life of God or, in
other words, do within history that which finds expression in the
essential reality of God, namely, love in a way that re-creates,
saves, and gives life.

To be conformed to the kingdom of God is to be conformed to
the God of the kingdom. An argument based on the mystery of
God would be subject to many difficulties except that it has been
given historical form by Jesus. This ultimate theological appeal is
in the gospel. There we find such bold statements as these: "You,
therefore, must be perfect, as your heavenly Father is perfect" (Mt.
5:48); "Be merciful, even as your Father is merciful" (Lk. 6:36).
Paul even dares to say: "Therefore be imitators of God, as beloved
children. And walk in love . . ." (Eph. 5:1). And John puts clearly
what I have been trying to express in systematic terms: "God is
love. . . . If God so loved us, we also ought to love one another" (1
Jn. 4:8,11).

It is tautological, of course, to say that the practice of love is the fulfillment of God's reign, since without love among human beings God does not reign, and to the extent that this love is practiced, God's reign does come into being. It is another thing to analyze the relation between love of God and love of human beings⁷ and to show in the light of the doctrine of grace how this love becomes possible. The important point here is that the practice of love—and not just of faith and hope—is a primary element in conforming to the kingdom of God; we must not play down this practice by treating it as an ethical rather than a theo-logical matter or by making the practice of love simply a demand flowing from a faith and a hope that exist formally and independent of this practice.

The Practice of Justice as the Historical Form of Love

From what I have said it is clear that if justice is a form of love then the practice of justice is automatically an essential requirement of the gospel message. I believe that this is in fact the case. But we need to clarify the meaning of justice and its relation to love.

By love I understand the proper relationship that exists among human beings when certain relations are established between them. Concretely, love makes the "other" or "others" the addressees of our activity in order that they may exist more fully, may have life and have it in increasing abundance, and that thus we may all be united. Since the relationships among human beings vary according to the different states in which they live, the type of love will differ according as the relationships are those of the family, or marriage, or friendship.

By justice I mean the kind of love that seeks effectively to humanize, to give life in abundance to the poor and oppressed majorities of the human race. Justice is thus a concrete form of love in which account is taken of the quantitative fact that its recipients form majorities and of the qualitative fact that they are poor and oppressed.

For the purposes of this study these general descriptions of love and justice will be enough. I must however dispel two possible misunderstandings, lest it be thought that the basis for the requirement of justice is purely verbal, obtained by including justice in the definition of love.

The first misunderstanding would be to assume that we already know what the generic concept of love is independently of its specific applications. It would be to assume that an understanding of the essence of love is best gotten from matrimonial love, familial love, or the love of friendship. It would then be up to justice to prove that it is a historical form of love, whereas the other forms of love are quite clearly exactly that: forms of love.

The second misunderstanding would be to think that justice is a secondary form of love, either because its existence is required only when charity is absent or because its practice is usually accompanied by conflict, whereas the unitive character of love leaves the element of conflict in the shadow.

I think that justice is a primordial and irreducible form of love because it is called for both by the historical reality of the human race and by the social dimension of the human person. To ignore these basic realities and to reduce love to its other forms would be to indulge in idealism and to disregard the gospel. It would be a similar betrayal of reality to reduce love to justice.

My concern here is to show that the form of love we call justice was practiced by Jesus and that when put into practice this form of love is the best way of embodying important Christian values.

If we do not assume that we already know how Jesus practiced love and if, instead, we attend closely to the gospel narrative, two characteristics of the practice of Jesus emerge clearly (I am speaking of passages other than those occasional ones describing his friendships): his tender mercy [8] toward sinners and his identification with the poor for the purpose of giving them life. These two characteristics are not really separate, but I shall focus on the second and analyze it briefly.

The fact that the kingdom of God provides the purview for Jesus' ministry points to a historical situation in which justice is done to the poor majority. Jesus directs his ministry to the multitudes; the emphasis on sheer numbers alerts us to something fundamental about the service he renders. He loves "the many." Soteriology has been very much aware of this point, but it needs to be reevaluated if we are to understand the historical form that Jesus' love took. Jesus also has compassion on the multitudes. The statement "I have compassion on the crowd" (Mt. 15:32; cf. Mk. 6:34) expresses a basic fact that the gospel narratives use to organize the story of the life and ministry of Jesus according to a logical pattern.

To this quantitative fact must be added the qualitative one: "He has anointed me to preach the good news to the poor" (Lk. 4:18). The "other" to which Jesus directs his practice of love is a collectivity that is well defined in sociological terms: the world of the poor.[9] It is to these impoverished multitudes that Jesus directs his ministry; he serves them and seeks to restore their life precisely because their life has been diminished, and this at the most elementary level. The crippled, the blind, and the paralyzed are symbols of those who have no life or who have it in a lesser degree.

To this collective "other," made up for the most part of the poor, Jesus comes as savior and re-creator. We see this expressed in a positive way in those symbolic scenes in which Jesus makes his own the interests of these others: the poor, the sick, the lepers, the sinners, the tax collectors, the Samaritans. This solidarity of Jesus with the poor finds implicit but no less clear expression in his dealings with the social groups that cause the poverty of the multitudes. An analysis of the disputes in which Jesus is involved and the curses he utters shows that he is defending the poor and not simply solving problems of religious casuistry or denouncing forms of hypocrisy. We can see from his denunciations what it is he is defending.

In the final analysis Jesus is defending life and the right of the poor to life, a right denied them by other groups. Here are but a few examples: The anathemas that Jesus utters are directed not only at the hypocrisy of the leaders but at the oppression in which they engage. The Pharisees are blind guides with no concern for justice; the scribes impose intolerable burdens; they have taken away the key of knowledge and left the people in ignorance (Lk. 11:37–54). Jesus shows up false traditions not only in order to defend God's will in its authentic and orthodox form but also to prevent widows from having their houses devoured (Mk. 12:38– 40) and elderly parents from being deprived of support (Mk. 7:11–12). He engages in controversies about the sabbath not simply in order to defend general anthropological truths about human beings and their dominion over the world, but also in order to defend the right of the hungry to eat (Mk. 2:23–28).[10]

The fate of Jesus can be explained historically only in light of his solidarity with the poor masses and his energetic defense of them and attacks on their oppressors. He certainly does meet death because of his fidelity to the Father's will, but historically his death is the result of a specific love that leads to a specific practice. From the historical standpoint Jesus was put to death by unjust authorities who saw him as a threat.

This brief description of the practice of Jesus does not mean that his entire life is reducible to practice, nor that his mission of evangelizing the poor is reducible to their salvation and liberation. It does not mean that Jesus thought of justice as the only form of love. It does not mean that he idealized the poor and the oppressed with whom his practice was concerned. Neither does it imply that he developed a body of social thought regarding models for a new society and the means of bringing this society into existence.

Nonetheless, the fact remains that Jesus practiced the form of love we call justice; that the gospel narratives give a good picture of this practice; and that such narratives make up a substantial part of the gospels. Whatever Jesus' explicit idea of the kingdom of God was and whatever its apocalyptic or prophetic nuances may have been, one thing remains certain: the service to the kingdom of God that he proclaims is to an important degree one of efficacious love for the poor and oppressed majorities.

This type of love has some historical characteristics that distinguish it from love in general. The possession of these characteristics generates—or can generate—a series of values that I believe to be essential to the gospel and to revelation generally. Justice as a form of love is therefore validated not only by the fact that Jesus practiced it but also by its internal features, which make it consonant with the message as a whole.

I shall list some of these characteristics. They are to be discovered not simply by a conceptual analysis of justice but by observation of the actual practice of justice.

1. Justice takes seriously the primordial fact of the *created world* in its given form; that is to say, it takes seriously the existence of the oppressed majorities. The existence of these majorities is not a fact that can be lightly passed over in speaking of the essence of the Christian message. Otherwise we would have to look for God's will in the signs of the times or by means of subtle efforts to discern it. Justice begins with a judgment, a small but decisive judgment, on the present state of the created world.

2. This initial honesty in dealing with reality leads to the discovery of *sin*. Injustice and the oppression of the majorities reveal to us that which is the most radical denial of God's will and of his very

person: the destruction of the created order and the death of human beings. Offense against God and its correlative, subjective guilt, find objective expression in the death inflicted on human beings, either slowly through oppressive structures or quickly through the techniques used by oppressors. The tradition is fully justified, therefore, in speaking of "mortal" sin, provided the "death" in question be understood as the death not only of the sinner but of the victim as well.

3. When faced with the negation of the life of the majorities, or with the threat to this life, justice tries to re-create human beings and give them *life*. Justice extends to all levels of their existence and seeks to give life in abundance. But justice does not plan too hastily on the fullness of life; it tries first to see to it that life at the most elementary levels is ensured. It endeavors to make God's creation begin to be precisely that. Christianity provides the real possibility of affirming the sublimity of God and, correlatively, the sublimity of the human person. Justice tries to keep these affirmations from being only ideals and to see to it that they start off with the unpretentious reminder of the God of creation and his will that human beings should have life.[11]

4. Justice, operating within history, urges the adoption of a *partisan and subjective perspective* in the practice of love and in the development of Christian existence. This perspective is from below, from the standpoint of wretchedness and oppression, from the underside of history. By taking this approach, one effectively adopts the evangelical perspective, which avoids succumbing to an idealist and alienating universalist attitude by taking as its point of reference the weak, the poor, and the oppressed.

5. Justice fosters objective solidarity with the oppressed and thus an *objective kenosis* or self-emptying. The self-deflation and self-humbling that faith requires takes the concrete form of solidarity with the poor and the adoption of their situation, cause, and fate.[12]

6. The practice of the justice that tries to renew the poor majorities often leads to a personal *conversion*, and a radical conversion at that. Solidarity with the poor may be for the sake of serving them, but it often turns into a service rendered by the poor to those who are trying to secure justice for them. Because of the complex reality of their poverty, and by reason of the fact that their existence acts as a call to break with life as hitherto lived or, to put it in

Christian terms, by reason of the fact that they are the sacraments of the Lord and the suffering face he turns to the world, the poor evangelize those whose initial intention was to serve them. The otherness of the poor gives rise to effective and even affective impulses and conceptual categories that will enable those who serve them to become different, to act differently, and to look on themselves differently; in other words, to be converted, and converted once and for all.

7. By its structure as a historical reality justice highlights one characteristic of love, namely, *service*. In other forms of love, service may be accompanied by personal gratification. In the practice of justice, too, gratification may be present, at least in the form of a profound sense of one's own possession of life. But by reason of those to whom the love and justice are directed and of the kind of relationship that is established with them, personal gratification does not emerge as an immediate affective component. This makes the service aspect of love stand out more clearly; it highlights the fact that love gives rather than receives.

8. Justice recovers the biblical idea of the *neighbor* as being not just someone in close proximity to me but someone I *make* my neighbor. Justice is the movement by which we go out, unconditionally and with a sense of urgency, to the poor and oppressed in order to make of them our neighbors. The situation of the majorities, which is like that of the wounded man by the wayside in the gospel parable, shows clearly what it means to a neighbor. It also shows the fundamental wickedness of passing by, of not actively being a neighbor.

9. Usually, and more clearly than in other forms of love, justice brings *persecution* on those who practice it. Genuine love, of course, implies a readiness to suffer, and this suffering may be very great. Justice, however, brings with it the kind of suffering to which we give the name *persecution*. Sin in its historical reality shows its might and power against those who practice justice. "Taking up one's cross" becomes an unavoidable necessity and turns the life of one who promotes justice into a journey very like that of Jesus: a journey that ends in some kind of historical cross and death.[13]

When I assert that the practice of justice is a basic demand of the gospel, I mean that Jesus practiced this kind of love and that it is therefore essential to the following of Jesus. But I also mean that as a specific kind of love, it generates a series of basic evangelical values. The acknowledgement of God's creation as precisely that, the unmasking of sin as basically the practice of murder, union with the poor in order to give them life, the adoption of a partisan subjective outlook, the achievement of an objective conversion and kenosis, the practice of being a neighbor, the setting aside of self in order to serve, the readiness to suffer persecution—all these to a greater or lesser degree accompany the practice of justice and demonstrate its authenticity from the standpoint of the gospel.

The practice of justice is therefore a basic material demand of the gospel. Without it the gospel would be substantially mutilated. I turn now to the more radical question of whether without this practice the gospel would exist at all.[14]

THE PRACTICE OF JUSTICE AS AN ESSENTIAL COMPONENT OF "FAITH"

I have said enough to show that the practice of justice is an essential material element in the gospel message. It is the form of love that is indispensable if the reign of God is to become a historical reality or if there is to be within history a reflection of the transhistorical utopian reality of that reign. Ecumenism, however, sees the problem of unity as one of unity in faith. I must therefore discuss the importance of the promotion of justice for the existence of faith.

The Formal Relation between Faith and Justice

Faith and justice are not two homogeneous human activities that can exist side by side, each exercised independently of the other.[15] Faith and justice correspond rather to two essential aspects of the human person: the aspect of meaning (meaning of the subject and meaning for the subject) and the aspect of historical practice as the subject acts upon the real world. The two must from the outset be considered together as different but reciprocally related parts of a whole if there is to be a total Christian response.

There is no question, therefore, of assigning absolute priority either to faith or to justice. From the Christian viewpoint priority belongs logically to the decision and action whereby God manifests himself to history and saves it. The response to this initiative is neither faith alone nor justice alone, but Christian existence in its entirety.

Within this unified response faith exerts an influence on the concrete accomplishment of justice. In this essay I shall focus my attention on the influence that justice exercises on faith. I shall not concentrate on a purely conceptual analysis. This would show that when the concepts of faith and justice are understood as they are in Scripture and in dogma each calls for the other. I shall concentrate rather on the real influence that justice exerts on faith in the historical process whereby faith becomes a reality. From a purely conceptual viewpoint, which sees the two as separate entities, it is possible to disagree on whether chronological priority belongs primarily to the element of faith (a general acceptance of the mystery of God that has come among us in Christ), or to the element of justice (a general readiness for the effective practice of love in dealing with the poor majorities).

My concern here is with the process of faith. I am convinced that the practice of justice is necessary for this process. I think that the personal and historical appropriation of "faith," that is, the general content of faith, the mystery of God, requires time. More than that, it requires a particular kind of time in which specific practices can occur. This is required if there is to be what we call "the experience of God." I think, too, that the historical characteristics of the practice of justice are helpful and even in some way necessary if there is to be a process that makes possible the Christian experience of God and enables us to conceive of access to God as being itself a process.

It may be objected that while faith and love are interrelated in the many concrete ways in which love finds expression, it is not necessary that justice should be the particular form of love required for the existence of faith. In response to this objection I call attention both to the content of the mystery of God (the proper object of faith) and to the present historical situation. The first point is one that I shall develop in greater detail. It will be enough here to state that the God who is the object of our faith is a universal God and a creator, and that a practice of love that does not at least try to match this universality reduced God to a regional God. Further, an essential part of God's historical manifestation is his demonstration of partiality to the poor and the oppressed. A love that did not take this aspect of the reality of God into consideration could hardly serve as the channel for an experience of this God.

As for my second point, the historical situation of the human race generally and in Latin America leads to a keen awareness of the fundamental sin that divides human beings and of the unavoidable demand that we overcome this sin and work for a more just world. There can hardly be an experience of God that does not have as an essential component an honest acknowledgment of this state of affairs and a readiness to engage in the kind of practice that will remedy it.

The practice of justice does not exclude other forms of authentic love from shaping the role of faith in Christian existence. I am saying only that the practice of justice is necessary if there is to be a faith that is in keeping both with its own content, which is the mystery of God, and with the present situation of the human race.

Concretization of Faith on the Basis of the Practice of Justice

I want to show now, briefly, how the practice of justice renders the meaning of faith concrete; how it makes the mystery of God manifest in historical reality; and how in the course of history it brings to light important aspects of this mystery that are hardly to be seen in other modes of the practice of love.

The practice of justice makes concrete the point at which we have access to the mystery of God and to God precisely as mystery. We can say, in abstract terms, that God is always greater, precisely because he is a mystery. This ever greater being of God may be apprehended by widening our vision of his limitless being with the help of philosophical reflections on the finitude of creation or with the help of esthetic, intellectual, or sapiential experiences that give rise to wonder *(admirar)* and thus to a looking-toward *(mirar-hacia)* and a looking-beyond the limited objects of our experience.

In the practice of justice the transcendence of God manifests itself in a different and more radical way. The mystery of the ever greater God seems to be mediated through the "more" attached to the obligation to humanize and re-create human beings. No objective limit can be placed on the unconditional "Yes" that God speaks with regard to the humanization of the person and the obligation to do justice, although the absence of limitation can become a reality only in the process of moving beyond the boundaries of a specific humanization already achieved. The process of doing ever greater justice to human beings and the experience of the fact that there are no a priori limits to this "more" and that the person who practices justice cannot establish such limits—this process and this experience are the mediation for an experience of the ever greater being of God. The most radical experience of God's ever greater being comes through the sense of being impelled by the drive to "more" humanization and through the refusal to temper in any way the demand for an ever greater humanization.

By reason of its own historical characteristics justice seeks to humanize directly those who are "littlest" and most deprived of life. This partiality toward the poor and solidarity with them supposes a process of personal impoverishment and a growing connaturality with the being of God as he appears in the Scriptures: one who is partial to the oppressed, one made little and hidden in the little ones. Access to the ever greater and transcendent God comes through contact with the God who is "lesser," hidden in the little ones, crucified on the cross of Jesus and on the countless crosses of the oppressed of our day. The practice of justice with its two sides—effectiveness for salvation and solidarity with the little ones—is suited for mediating a profound experience of the mystery of God as this is attested in Christianity. Christianity emphasizes the ever greater being of God, but—and this is often not brought out in speaking of the experience of God—it also emphasizes the "lesser" place in which access to God is achieved.[16]

The practice of justice uses the rhetoric of opposed alternatives to show how we are to grasp the mystery of God and to test, indirectly but effectively, whether we are really having a faith-experience of God. The gospel often presents the positive reality with which it is concerned by denying its alternative. It is said there that from the theo-logical standpoint "no one can serve two masters: God and money"; from a christo-logical standpoint whoever is not with Jesus is against him; from an anthropo-logical standpoint whoever loses their life gains it. Christian existence is presented at a radical level and a principle is given for judging whether the positive reality has been attained.

The same pattern holds with regard to the Christian experience of God. The practice of justice is a suitable place to pose the alternative to the experience of God. The alternative to doing justice is doing injustice; more harshly put, the alternative to giving life to human beings is to kill them. Here we discover the real alternative to faith in God. The alternative, strictly speaking, is not atheism but idolatry. In the name of the true God we give life to other human beings; in the name of false gods we give death to them.

Idolatry is not simply a lack of faith in the true God, nor simply an intellectual error or an incorrect formulation of the human being's experience of the transcendent. It consists rather in adoring a divinity who requires victims.

By reason of its inherent purpose (which is to bestow life on the people) and our historical context (which makes the struggle against injustice inescapable), the practice of justice is a suitable way to grasp the mystery of God through the giving of life and through resistance to the giving of death. A supposed faith in God that would allow injustice, for whatever reason, or would allow peaceful coexistence with injustice, would not really be faith at all. One who does not struggle against death and against the idols that kill does not have true faith in the God of life. Faith in God means rejection of murderous idols, and this not simply in intention but in practice.

The experience of the mystery of God consists in knowing not only that we are dependent on him but also that he makes demands of us. Even a purely philosophical reflection shows that God has the power to make demands and to make them unconditionally. If a created being, even one accepted as being good, could place limits on the demands God can make, God would cease to be God, and the experience of being subject to God's demands would turn into a matter of human rational calculation.

The practice of justice concretizes, radicalizes, and clarifies the demands made by God as well as the urgent need to respond to these demands. Justice makes it clear that God's formal right to be acknowledged as God is not arbitrary. The oppression of human beings by other human beings must be condemned by every theodicy; conversely, the struggle against this oppression is required by the very nature of that which is at stake: the life of human beings. A God of life does not call for justice as simply one of the many possible demands he might make, but as *the* demand without which his own reality would be empty and his will for the world and history would be meaningless.

Those who do not comprehend the demand (which cannot be completely analyzed) of giving life to the masses will likewise not comprehend, even though they may confess it, the demanding reality of God (which cannot be completely analyzed either). Those who do not feel that the dying masses represent a demand made on them, and a radical demand at that, will try in vain to find in the moral fact of demands made on them a mediation of the experience of the mystery of God. The love of Christ will not urge us on if the situation of the majority of human beings is not seen as urgent. The converse is also true: when we grasp the urgency of doing justice we grasp what is ultimate in the mystery of God that urges us.

God's demands on us become concrete in the practice of justice. Justice demands everything of the subject, everything without exception. In its concrete historical form the practice of justice demands not only that we give of our abilities and talents but also that we give of our life and even give that life itself; it demands a readiness to die in the interests of giving life.

An unqualified readiness for death is a mediation of the experience of God. With his usual acumen Karl Rahner has repeatedly emphasized the fact that in accepting death a person "deeply affirms in his history not abstract ideas and norms but present or future reality as the ground of his existence."[17] If this is true of all death and therefore of natural death (which is never purely natural) as a fate imposed on human beings, then it will be all the more true of explicit readiness to die for the sake of justice. Those who are disposed to give their own life in order that others may have life are in a radical way experiencing the God of life. They may not be able to express adequately the relationship between the mystery of life and the giving of their own life; nonetheless, as in every good negative theology, they affirm what cannot be affirmed in any other way. In their very inability to affirm it in any other way they are affirming the mystery of God. Those who are ready to abide by the paradox that the unconditional promotion of life may demand the surrender of their own life are confessing *in actu* the sovereign demand of life. For a Christian, such a confession is an affirmation of the mystery of God.

There is an element of darkness in the experience of the mystery of God. From an examination of our culture with, for example, the secularization that originated in the Enlightenment, from ordinary observation of history and of our own lives with their absurdities, their failures, and their disillusioned hopes, it is clear that God hides himself and that his silence often makes a greater impact on us than his word does.

The experience of God must include the experience of darkness and therefore be dialectical. If people talk nowadays of "faith in unbelief"[18] or of being *simul fidelis et infidelis* (at once believer and unbeliever),[19] they are but voicing the primal human experience of the mystery of God, the experience that Scripture expresses as "hoping against hope" (cf. Rom. 4:18) and "victory over the world" (cf. 1 Jn. 5:4), or more graphically, in the cross of Jesus, as the dialectical movement of surrendering one's spirit to the Father (Lk. 23:46) while experiencing abandonment by him (Mk. 15:34; Mt. 27:46).

If I stress the experience of God as one that takes place "against" and "despite" the temptation to unbelief, I do not do so in order to dwell masochistically on the difficulties of faith and the temptations against it, nor in order to develop a subtle theodicy that will eliminate what is obscure and absurd in faith by integrating both dimensions of faith from the outset. My concern is rather to emphasize the fact that the experience of God must be accompanied by the experience of negativity and that paradoxically faith is deepened and tempted in the same experience. Faith presents the mysterious God as a God of life; for that very reason the mystery of God may be obscured for us.

Because its primary thrust is to give life, both the affirmation of God and the temptation to deny him are most keenly felt in the practice of justice. Justice looks for effectiveness on the historical scene; it seeks to re-create God's damaged creation. Yet the results are often negative. The just suffer; those who do justice are persecuted; those who try to give life are deprived of life; the poor are told that the reign of God is at hand, but it seems forever distant. These are common experiences; they are also experiences that terrify, not primarily because they leave human beings so insecure, but because they show God powerless in the face of injustice. The fact that "the executioner can triumph over the victim"[20] is an expression of the impotence of God and the scandal of faith in God.

The practice of justice brings us close to the mystery of the God of life; it also exposes us to temptation against this mystery. This practice makes it impossible for us to gloss over the dark side of faith or to trivialize the scandalous statements that Scripture makes about God. The cross is the wisdom of God: these words are a profound expression of faith, but they should not be used by one who has not also been tempted to see them as foolish and scandalous.

The practice of justice makes it clear that we must probe the scandalous side of faith and abide in it without too hastily manipulating it out of existence. We must abide with God in his suffering; we must abide on the underside of history as the place for the obscure experience of God.

It is in the practice of justice that we must sustain our faith in God and believe (with a faith that is maintained and not simply possessed) in the mystery of God. Faith is not faith unless it is maintained as faith amid temptations against it. Faith is less an isolated act than a process that increases (or lessens) the radical conviction that at the heart of everything love and life exist as a reality that is foundational and greater than any other.

Persistence in faith is not the work of naïveté. The practice of justice involves a structure through which faith *can* be sustained and *must* be sustained as an ongoing dynamic process.

Faith *can* be sustained if in the practice of justice sufficient signs are found to support hope. If the poor have the gospel preached to them, if they become aware of who they really are, if they struggle in their own behalf and attain to a greater humanization, if the miracle of kenosis and solidarity takes place, if fear and resignation are conquered—then life is being given to those most deprived of it. These are the signs that are a basis for hope.

It is true, of course, that part of Christian life is an initial general hope (just as there is an initial general faith) that is logically necessary if there is to be an initial impulse to the practice of justice. That hope continues to exist as long as the practice does not cease. The relation between hope and practice is therefore dialectical. But the practice of justice feeds hope through the signs of humanization; this hope, then, differs from concepts of hope that are born of resignation and of a relativization of historical reality. These are viewed as an ultimate refuge in which the subject can find meaning in a meaningless world. Hope persists against hope, but when all is said and done, it is hope. Moreover, this hope, which is maintained at the practical level through the struggle for justice and which never fully realizes its utopian content but constantly looks for "concrete implementations" of justice, is the real way of sustaining faith. The continuation of the struggle for the reign of God is the practical embodiment of continued faith in the mystery of God.

The practice of justice understood in Christian terms has a structure of its own by reason of which faith *must* be an ongoing process. On the one hand, the mystery of the God of life requires that we struggle for life and against wretchedness and poverty. On the other hand, this struggle must entail our own impoverishment. These two dimensions cannot be adequately synthesized in static isolation. They are gradually synthesized in the experienced process of the practice of justice. The tension between the struggle against poverty, on the one hand, and one's own impoverishment, on the other, is the historical mediation of the tension between the mystery of God as giver of life, lord of creation, and the God who gives himself up to the wretchedness of his creation. If the practice of justice is carried on in this light, faith can never be a possession of God but only a search for him. The fact that effectiveness and impoverishment cannot be fully brought into synthesis at the historical level means that the experience of God can likewise not occur once and for all at the historical level but must be a process.

Persistence in this process brings with it the most complete experience of the gratuitousness of faith. I am not denying that a first, general grace gives us new ears for hearing that God has loved us first, that he has drawn near to us in love, and that he will approach us in a definitive way at the end of time. But the practice of justice concretizes this general grace and prevents it from turning into the cheap grace of those who think they have God at their disposal. The culmination of grace is experienced in the gift of new hands with which to build a new creation. The fact that faith in the mystery of God is itself a grace does not become fully or adequately clear in the first act of faith, but only when faith is sustained at the historical level throughout the process of joining God in the shaping of history.

Faith is certainly an act elicited by a subject, but if it is to be a reality, the subjective act as such is not enough. Nor is Christian perseverance in faith accomplished simply by an intention of the will to preserve faith subjectively. If through faith as a subjective act we accept God along with the meaning that such an acceptance imposes on our life, then this faith can exist only in conjunction with something historical and objective. This historical, objective reality is (though not exclusively) the practice of justice as the historical way of proclaiming the reign of God and making this reign real. This practice provides the "material" for making our subjective and transcendent faith in God real and concrete. Because God is ever greater and is defined as love, because he makes absolute demands, because his reality must be apprehended through alternatives and in a dialectical and processual way—for these reasons the believer's subjective decision that that is what God indeed is, or even that he presents himself as such in Scripture, is not enough. Also required is historical material that allows and requires that the mystery of God be presented in this way and in no other. On the basis of this historical material we can see that according to revelation God is this kind of God and no other and that human beings must conform themselves to him in this way and no other. The practice of justice allows and demands that the meaning of faith take a concrete Christian form and that in this historical practice, and even despite it, God can be called "Abba," the God who draws near to us, the God who is love.

The practice of justice as the historical form of love is essential if we are to respond to the gospel message in its entirety. It is also necessary for the existence, in the concrete, of faith formally as faith and as part of our total response. I have not developed another aspect of this relationship, namely, the importance, for the practice of justice, of an explicit cultivation of faith, the importance of rendering explicit the meaning of the faith and of cultivating an openness to the word of faith. Naturally, this aspect can and should be developed too. My only desire here has been to emphasize the fundamental role of practice in constructing the content of faith's meaning; to emphasize, in other words, the role of the "new hands" of practice in forming the "new ears" by which we hear and accept what is offered to us as a grace.

Practice of Justice, Faith, and Ecumenism

The approach I have taken is basic to ecumenism, although it obviously does not do away with regional differences within the various confessions. It is basic for determining the foundation of ecumenism insofar as the latter seeks unity in faith. When Paul says that there is "one Lord, one faith . . . one God and Father" (Eph. 4:4–5), or when Vatican II speaks of "an order or 'hierarchy' of truths"[21] in Christian teaching and implies that ecumenical union would be comparatively easy to achieve in regard to fundamental truths, they are not proposing a solution to the ecumenical problem but rather posing the problem in its most basic form. If the various confessions presuppose that they already know well enough who God is, who Christ is, and what the reign of God is, then ecumenism would take the form of an effort to go all the way by achieving agreement on secondary doctrines or joining in liturgical services. The call to a common practice of justice would then be a pragmatic way of achieving unity at least in this practice, solely at the ethical or social level.

What I have been trying to say goes beyond such an interpretation of ecumenism. The practice of justice is the carrying out of something basic in the gospel. Consequently, union in this practice is union at a fundamental level. But the practice of justice is also the way of making concrete and real the basic affirmations of faith; therefore it also offers the possibility of an authentic union at the level of faith.

The Thirty-second General Congregation of the Society of Jesus said this in its own fashion, not in the context of ecumenism but of the very being of the Church: "The way to faith and the way to justice are inseparable ways."[22] The fact that we are on the way *to* faith and not in definitive possession of it shows the possibility and necessity of a common way on which we will be constantly in search of what is basic in the faith. The fact that the way of faith and the way of justice are inseparable shows clearly what the historical way is that leads to unity in the true faith.

3

The Service of Faith and
the Promotion of Justice

My purpose here is to reflect on the concrete mission of the Society of Jesus. I shall organize my thoughts on this complex matter under three headings: (1) the development of the theme in the Thirty-second General Congregation, especially in its second and fourth decrees[1]; (2) a theological reflection on the relation between the service of faith and the promotion of justice; and (3) the relevance of this mission to religious life.

FAITH AND JUSTICE ACCORDING TO THE
THIRTY-SECOND GENERAL CONGREGATION

The Thirty-second General Congregation opted for Jesuit participation in the crucial struggle of our age: the service of faith and the promotion of justice. The Society's dedication to the defense and spread of the faith accounts, of course, for its very origin, and the task continues to be a necessary one (2:11). However, for the Society to take as its basic choice the service of faith and the promotion of justice was unique, both in its formulation and in its historical practice. Rather than simply repeat the fact that this basic choice has been made, I shall call attention to certain points that are both important and new.

A Dialectical Approach

The General Congregation takes a *dialectical* approach to the basic mission. The issue is not simply the service of faith and the promotion of justice but the pursuit of these goals in a world ruled by unbelief and injustice. The unbelief and injustice affect the Jesuit not only as a missionary, that is, in his dealings with others, but simply as a Christian, that is, in his own living of the Christian reality.

As far as faith is concerned, we are told that we must examine our efforts to enter into real contact with unbelievers (4:52). It is not a question, therefore, of serving the faith in a context which is a *tabula rasa* or in which the prevailing attitude is determined by natural religion, but of serving the faith by overcoming the scandal of unbelief. In their mission, then, Jesuits must keep clearly before them the fact that the faith that they are trying to serve is not something evident, something already possessed socially and culturally, but rather a faith that must win its way. They must be very aware of all that is scandalous and disruptive in the Christian faith and in its presentation.

Furthermore, the dialectical process of serving the faith in the presence of unbelief does not apply only to the *ad extra* mission of the Jesuit. There is at least the implication that for the Jesuit faith nowadays must be a victory won; it must *come into being* in the presence of unbelief. For this reason, any isolation, any lack of "real contact with unbelief" (4:35), is not praised but criticized, since isolation means that we do not allow ourselves to be challenged, in evangelical (though paradoxical) fashion, by unbelief. Jesuits are to be ready to bear witness to the gospel "in the painful situations in which our faith and our hope are tested by unbelief" (4:35).

The same dialectical approach can be seen at work in dealing with the promotion of justice. There is no question simply of promoting something good on the basis of the possibilities and inertia of historical existence. The issue is rather to promote it *in opposition to* the real character of historical existence. Justice is promoted by struggling against injustice. The mission of the Society is to be pursued in a world in which "many grave injustices [are] prevalent" (2:6), a world divided by injustice brought about not only by individuals but also by structures (4:6), a world in which "what is at stake. . . is the very meaning of [humankind: its] future and [its] destiny" (4:21). In other words, the mission is carried out in a world of injustice; even more, it must be carried out *against* a world of injustice, because "it is now within human power to make the world more just—but we do not want to" (2:27)

The opposition of the world to the promotion of justice exists even within the Society in the inertia of the individual Jesuit who tends to ignore injustice (4:35) or to think of the promotion of justice in idealistic terms. For this reason the fourth decree adds that "any effort to promote justice will cost us something" (4:46), and it urges us "to cope with the hardships and risks [we] may encounter in God's service" (4:67).

From this it can be seen that the formulation of the basic choice of mission, even when put in positive terms, must be understood dialectically: in the light of what is rejected, in the presence of this rejection, and accepting the consequences of this rejection. This first observation is important because it "de-ideologizes" our understanding of the mission, locates the mission on the hard ground of reality, and provides it with a first criterion for self-criticism, namely, whether the mission is being carried on *in* the world of unbelief and injustice and *in opposition to* that world.

This dialectical understanding of the mission makes it possible to escape from certain impasses that are created by purely theoretical approaches to what it means in positive terms to serve the faith and promote justice. Faith and justice are in these decrees symbolic or limit notions. (Note how important it is that justice is once again given its status as a key concept of Christianity.) By their nature, therefore, they are utopian notions that can never be completely made real within history. The General Congregation shows its awareness of this when it speaks of "the way to faith and the way to justice" (2:8). It does not often happen that the *positive* statement of the fundamental choice gives rise to purely theoretical discussions of the precise content of faith and justice. It is a priori impossible to make a fully precise determination, and this causes an impasse. The dialectical approach offers something concrete against which we must certainly struggle today. Although the positive side of the choice must be expressed in utopian terms, the negative moment in the dialectic is clear. For this reason the dialectical approach is important and necessary in order to develop the *process* that the choice entails, and to develop it precisely as a process that includes both the rejection of unbelief and injustice and a journeying toward faith and justice.

The Reciprocal Relationship of Faith and Justice

The General Congregation presents the basic choice as having two interrelated aspects. It is difficult to determine from the texts themselves the *precise* relationship between the service of faith and the promotion of justice, but the important point is that the connection exists. If the texts do not enable us to determine exactly how the two fit together, they do allow and require us to conceive of the two as *inseparable*.

The relation between them can be seen in certain *formulations*, in the *theological basis* given for the connection, and in the *historical description* of their mutual connection at the present time.

The texts state that faith requires a struggle for justice (2:2); that justice is inseparable from faith because "faith makes its power felt through love" (2:8); that the promotion of justice is unconditionally required by the service of faith (4:2); that "the promotion of justice is . . . an integral part of evangelization" (4:30). At the level of formulations, therefore, the relation between faith and justice is described in such a way that (1) either faith is a whole of which justice is an integral part (that is, a part without which faith cannot be entire); or (2) faith by its nature gives rise to and requires the promotion of justice. In this analysis, then, the two aspects of the one mission are connected by historical necessity, with logical priority belonging to faith. In this context the term *integral part* should not be taken in the technical sense given to it in the various schools of philosophy; it is to be understood rather in the historical sense that faith cannot be served today unless justice is promoted. No consideration need be given, therefore, to such an essentialist question as whether faith in itself or in some other hypothetical situation (for example, in a world in which there were no sin) would require the promotion of justice.

In addition to the texts in which the connection between faith and justice is brought out, there are others which emphasize their indivisibility and inseparability (4:28, 51) as well as their reciprocal historical connections, both positive and negative. On the positive side, for example, the transformation of social structures is intimately bound up with the work of evangelization (4:40). On the negative side, one of the major obstacles to belief in God today is the prevalence of injustice (2:7), and, correlatively, certain false images of God "prop up and give an air of legitimacy to unjust social structures" (4:26a).

In summary, the General Congregation sees faith and justice as interconnected; the connection is historically necessary; on the positive side the relation is asserted in terms of the priority of faith, which requires justice as an integral part, and, on the negative side, the two are inseparable. Whatever be the ways in which the relationship could be stated more precisely and plumbed more fully, it is important that the General Congregation should have blessed two key concepts of Christianity: faith and justice. This action is a new thing in history, for, while not forgetting other formulations that are of basic importance in Christianity (for example, faith, hope, and charity or love of God and love of neighbor), the Congregation consciously chooses *justice* as a key concept for our time and one without which the Christian life can be neither understood nor lived.

Theological Basis

We must pay attention to the theological reasons given in the texts for connecting faith and justice in the manner described. The texts of a General Congregation are not theological texts in the academic sense, but they do explicitly or implicitly contain one or more theologies. In this theological grounding of the texts or theological accompaniment to them we can distinguish the fundamental and, in a sense, traditional, principles a well as the concrete, nuanced ways in which these principles are applied.

Justice is elevated to the status of a theological category by relating it to the basic gospel category of love. Thus it is said that God is love (2:7) and (in another traditional phrase) that he is "Father" (4:28), that the human being is, correlatively "the image of God" (4:29). From this last, traditional statement the Congregation passes to the ideal of the new being, the human being free of egoism, in whom "the justice of the Gospel shines out" (4:18), the person "converted" to God and neighbor (4:28). The Congregation also recalls the unity of the commandment of love for God and for neighbor (4:18, 28, 31).

The novelty consists in the fact that the Congregation connects love with justice (2:7; 4:27, 28); that it preaches an integral liberation (4:18); that it reformulates eschatology in terms of a "new earth" (4:30), although of course it also says that this eschatology will attain its full development only in an absolute future (4:30); and that a longing for the future must still be cultivated (4:33). Finally, the novelty is also seen in the often cited text regarding the dimension of futurity that is part of both faith and justice (2:8).

These theological reflections accompany, but do not provide the grounds for what is said about faith and justice. They sum up the most fundamental insights of contemporary ecclesial consciousness regarding the dynamics of the faith "which is made operative in love of others" (4:28).

Let me sum up: the Congregation says that the basic mission the Society chooses is the service of faith and the promotion of justice. It makes *justice* a key concept for contemporary Christian life. Both faith and justice are viewed dialectically in terms of unbelief and injustice. The two are interconnected and inseparable. Logical priority belongs to the content of the Christian faith, which is made operative in love and—in our age—in justice.

THEOLOGICAL REFLECTION ON THE RELATION BETWEEN FAITH AND JUSTICE

The theme of the relationship between faith and justice is an important one. Here I can only sum up what I have elsewhere treated in greater depth. Before explaining the positive connection between faith and justice it will be profitable to recall how difficult it is to grasp their mutual relationship at the theoretical level (above and beyond the practical difficulties of living the relationship).

Difficulties in Understanding the Connection

The first difficulty in understanding the relation between faith and justice arises from considering the two as homogeneous. Christian life has traditionally been thought of as based on three virtues: faith, hope and charity. Engendering these three in the hearts and lives of others has been the goal of the Christian mission. What is open to question in this approach is the subsumption of these three areas of Christian existence under the generic concept of virtue. The basic problem is not the assignment of the name *virtue* to all three, but rather the subsumption of the three under a generic concept. This subsumption results in the theoretical difficulty that, though the necessity of all three is accepted, they are presented as simply juxtaposed. The number "three" is canonized whereas it might in fact have been augmented or diminished.

The same problem surfaces when we speak of faith *and* justice as if these were two valuable but homogeneous realities, so that the Society should devote itself to the service of faith *and* to the promotion of justice. When the two are treated as homogeneous contents of the Society's mission, the question arises of the importance of the *and*, along with the difficulty of understanding this connection. I wish only to call attention to the desirability of not presenting Christian existence as a matter of "faith, hope, and charity" or of "service to the faith and promotion of justice," these virtues or actions being regarded as simply juxtaposed, even though all three (or two) are necessary. The Christian reality should rather be approached as an organic, structured whole in which faith and justice are not only necessary components but are organically complementary and not simply added to one another.

The second difficulty is a step beyond the first. Even if the necessity and complementarity of the two components are admitted, it is possible to start with an analysis of them as diverse components. In other words, one might begin by trying to understand in principle what faith and justice are as independent entities, and only then try to bring them together to form a whole. I regard this manner of conceiving the complementarity as inadequate (1) theoretically, because of the trinitarian character of the Christian God and his revelation and of the Christian life that springs therefrom; (2) historically, because of the difficulty that any approach starting from diversity creates for theology and Christian practice (humanity and divinity of Christ, nature and grace, ethics and dogma, history and transcendence); and (3) practically, because of the not necessarily Christian religiosity that springs from an isolationist approach to faith and because of the absolutization of the sociopolitical order that springs from an isolationist approach to justice.

The third difficulty takes the form of starting with faith and justice as complementary (even if the two be unified as well), but analyzing them solely in terms of the origin and present state of Christian existence. Such an approach forgets that both the origin and the present state are at the service of the immediate and remote historical future. It loses sight of the processual character that faith and justice have because of their complementarity and unity of origin. The unification of faith and justice is processual; the reality of the historical process determines in each historical period the way in which faith and justice are to be unified; and this process is at the service of the construction, and not simply the acceptance, of a unifying reality.

These three difficulties have to do with the *manner* of conceiving of the relation between faith and justice. Those that follow have to do with the content of faith and justice. Although great progress has been made in conceiving of faith as more than formulas, there are still traces to be found of a less-than-Christian type of ortho- doxy. This can be seen in the superficial way in which the unity of love for God and love for neighbor is treated, and in the lack of theological reflection on what love of God can mean if it is not mediated in any concrete way through the world. We hear not in- frequently of actions being classified according as they reflect love of God or love of neighbor, with the former assumed to be good and the latter regarded with suspicion.

Another difficulty has to do with the idea of gratuitousness. It is clear that the element of gratuitousness is essential to Christian faith. Without it faith would not exist. Not infrequently, however, gratuitousness is thought of in terms of the origin of faith; that is, in terms of God's action in freely revealing himself and manifesting his love. This is obviously an essential aspect of the gratuitousness of faith, but gratuitousness cannot be reduced to a passive accept- ance of the gift of faith, while all practice is considered to be the work of the human recipient. In practice too, and in the practice of justice, there is gratuitousness, even a high degree of it. Gratuitous- ness is not to be found only in the gift of new eyes for seeing and new ears for hearing but also in the gift of new hands for doing. There is no basis for setting the promotion of justice (which is praxis) and gratuitousness in opposition to each other. I mention this because it can be a difficulty for many people who feel that the area of faith is the area of gratuitousness, whereas the area of justice is clearly an area of human activity.

Still another difficulty arises from the fact that the Congregation approaches the relation between faith and justice primarily, though not exclusively, in terms of mission. In other words, the effort is made to see how the service of faith and the promotion of justice are interconnected as apostolic works. The problem of the interconnection approached in this way may be difficult to solve. Some light is thrown on the problem if the duality in external mission is thought of in connection with the Jesuit's own growth as a Christian. The interconnection of faith and justice is a necessity if Christians are to succeed within themselves in possessing both faith and justice, in being both believers and people of justice. In other words, it is not possible to approach the problem of faith and justice as a mission as if it were to be taken for granted that Christians are already, within themselves, both believing and just.

Finally, important practical difficulties exist. The integration of the promotion of justice into the Christian mission supposes a change of outlook and behavior, a resituating of ourselves in relation to society. It supposes that we are launching something historically new; it supposes that we have the humility to be learners. It supposes, too, that we are willing to run the present or foreseeable risks that the promotion of justice brings with it: conflict within the church and the religious order; conflict with the powers of this world; and persecution in its various forms.

Such are the real difficulties affecting the relationship between faith and justice at this time. I have listed them so that what I say subsequently will not be interpreted solely as a search for a connection between the *concept* of faith and the *concept* of justice. The two concepts and their connection must be given a historical dimension in terms of the real world with which Christians deal and of the real world of Christians where a relatively modern tradition has kept the connection between faith and justice from being an obvious one and still makes the Society's new choice of mission suspect in the eyes of some.

Principles of a Solution

I shall now suggest some principles to use in resolving the problem of the relationship between faith and justice.

In our search for a single unifying reality, we find throughout the Old Testament and especially in the life and teaching of Jesus the concept of "the kindgom or reign of God." Without analyzing the countless nuances of "the kingdom," we can say that, as long as history lasts, the kingdom is a reality in which people live as brothers and sisters to one another and as children of God. In principle, this reality is not limited to any one area of life (familial, social, religious, cultural, economic, political), but must be present in all areas. God's plan for the world is that this kingdom should become a reality.

This kingdom is, furthermore, the kingdom *of God*; that is, it must be shaped according to values that are God's values and must be promoted in accordance with God's values. This, then, is the first and fundamental unity of the Christian faith: that the kingdom should come into existence.

In this kingdom of God history and transcendence are unified. The kingdom must be a historical entity, and it is through and not apart from this historical entity, as well as through and not apart from human beings, that the way is prepared for the eschatological fulfillment, which, as fulfillment, is no longer human work but God's. The vertical and horizontal dimensions of Christian existence are also brought into unity in the kingdom. Unified too are two aspects of the human person—seeker of meaning and maker of meaning. In Christian terms, human beings as seekers of meaning find it by allowing God to communicate with them; as makers of meaning they create it by building the kingdom of God.

The problem of the relationship between faith and justice must be approached from the starting point of this unity that both unifies and is itself unified. In the interaction of building the kingdom and building it in accordance with God, faith and justice are brought into unity in the course of history. Faith and justice are not two homogeneous things; structurally they represent diverse participations in unity. Justice is the way in which the kingdom is built and becomes a reality. Faith is the way in which the kingdom exists in accordance with God, as well as the way in which meaning is found in the process of building, because the meaning comes from God.

In order to understand this unifying unity we will consider how the gratuitousness of faith and the requirement of ethical practice are connected. The connection emerges in the new commandment. In its Johannine version the logical process involved is this: God has loved us first; God has taken the initiative in relation to the world; human beings respond to this love by conforming to its movement and loving the brethren. Here we have an original approach to the relationship between faith and justice. The dynamism in the process of faith does not come to rest simply by turning to God. In fact, this turning, which is pleasing to the God who loved first, takes place only by way of love for the brethren. This love, located in the world, is a result of God's logically prior love for human beings, but also makes possible a faith-response to God. Faith is not simply a response to the love shown by God; it is also a conformity to this love.

The synoptic writers follow a pattern comparable to John's when they refer to the unity of the twofold commandment of love. However, in the early stages of the development of the synoptic passages in question the Johannine scheme is more clearly evident; that is, the commandment is to love one's neighbor. The existence of faith requires this turning to human beings who will mediate our turning to God.

In the New Testament, then, love is clearly not simply a consequence and requirement of God's prior love for human beings. It is also a constitutive factor in making the response of faith possible. This fact shows that there is no opposition between gratuitousness and activity. Gratuitousness does not consist only in referring to God as the origin of the salvific process (though it includes this), but also in responding by an activity like God's. The most complete expression of gratuitousness is the "new hands" for doing. The gratuitous, after all, is not simply the unmerited; it also includes the coming into existence of what seems impossible and even scandalous. "Impossibility" and "scandal" certainly describe the *hearing* of the word of a God-with-us, a God who became one of us and died on a cross and rose from the dead. These words also describe the *doing* of the scandalous thing, the doing of the word that has been heard and even the giving of one's life for others. There is a greater degree of gratuitousness in living like God and giving one's life like God than in knowing that we are loved by God, although this knowing is logically the first step. Love is therefore also essential in order to come into possession of a truly gratuitous faith.

Another approach to the relationship between faith ahd justice is to think of the kingdom (our "unifying unity") as processual, as something already inchoatively present, not as something that will have its full form only at the end. The process is first of all *objective*, in terms of the mission of building the kingdom. This process is evangelization in the fullest sense of the term. To evangelize is to make present a Good News that is becoming a Good Reality. The Apostolic Exhortation *Evangelii nuntiandi* speaks of various ways, all necessary and interconnected, of making this Good News present: the proclamation of the word, the witness of one's own life, and effective action to bring about change. It is through the interaction of these three that the kingdom of God is built. Proclamation is concerned with keeping the source and future of the faith alive, transformative action with concrete embodiments of the reign of God. The two develop dialectically: without the proclamation of the source of the faith there is no direction that can shed light on the process, and without practice there is no process. Faith makes possible Christian judgments on the world as it is and as it ought to be; practice brings to light what is virtually present in the source of faith but does not achieve actuality except through practice. The demand for justice pertains to the virtuality of the Christian truth, only in the effort to practice it has the demand become a real virtuality.

The process can also be studied as something *subjective*, in terms of the Christian subjects who carry it out. This point is important, since my meaning is not simply that Christians are first to realize they have faith and are just and then dedicate themselves to the mission of building the kingdom. No, here again a significant dialectic is at work. One becomes a Christian by constructing the Christian reality. The becoming and the construction must be seen as a process.

Every Christian has in a sense an "initial" faith and engages in an "initial" practice of love. The important thing, however, is not to define this "initial" faith and practice but to determine how the process from an "initial" faith and practice to a final and definitive faith and practice develops. A reciprocal relation between faith and justice exists in this development. Initial faith must give rise to practice; the word of God must be obeyed and put into practice. Once this is done, Christians must respond to the faith as they hear it with the faith they have developed through practice. The initial practice must likewise lead to a further commitment of faith. To *continue* the practice of love in a world of sin and in the presence of sin: this is the way in which a Christian's faith is developed. The activity of love in a world of injustice must be matched by faith against unbelief and hope against hope; such are the correct Christian formulations of faith, hope and charity.

Justice as the Concrete Embodiment of Love

I have been considering faith and the practice of love without explicit reference to justice. What I have said will dispel a naïve conception of the primacy of faith and therefore an inadequate relationship between Christian faith and Christian practice.

If we start with the kingdom of God as the unifying reality, it is clear that the kingdom must make its presence known in human relationships: marriage, family, friendships, ethnic groups, nations. Each of these spheres of reality has its own structure, its own sinfulness, and its own potentialities, all of which must be judged in terms of the reign of God. In each of these human groups, love must be present as the generic form of Christian relationships.

Today, however, people speak more explicitly of justice as a form of Christian love. There are various reasons for viewing justice as a necessary and historically privileged embodiment of Christian love.

1. The reign of God embraces the *totality* of human relationships. In other words, the reign of God includes the social relationships represented by the groups mentioned above, but it goes further. The element of totality is essential to Christianity, since God is not the God solely of individuals or the couple or the family, but the God of all history. To be conformed to this God requires that we think of Christian love in terms of the totality of things. This is what is implied by the ideal of justice.

2. Love in the form of justice has meant historically doing justice to the vast majority of the human race, namely, the poor. It is concerned with re-creating the masses who have throughout history been oppressed and yet at the same time have been given a privileged status by God. Historially, therefore, the concretization of love as "justice" is a necessary and effective way of giving flesh to the great Christian truth that God is partial to the poor majority.

3. Justice reminds us that persons are not pure spirits who relate to each other without a material medium. This is true of every human group. In marriage, fof example, the relationship comes into being through the medium of the body and marital love and therefore has certain characteristics and problems peculiar to it. We must keep in mind in speaking of justice that human beings generally relate through things and, more particularly, through possession of things. In marriage, bodily mediation tends by its nature to unite (which is not to deny that it can also separate). The possession of things has tended throughout history to separate human beings and to entail a formal rejection of the reign of God. To give love the concrete form of justice is to recall the unitive function of material things, even though historically these have separated human beings from each other.

4. Justice concerns itself not only with separation but also with the relationship that arises among human beings as they divide into ruler and ruled, oppressor and oppressed. This type of relationship is formally sin, indeed sin par excellence, since it means the usurpation by a human being of that which is the prerogative of God alone. The consequence of this sin—unlike sins that are found in other types of human groupings—is very clearly death. Injustice kills human beings, albeit slowly and through structures. Injustice reveals the full extent of the evil that is sin, for it repeats in the children of God what was done to the son of God who was slain by injustice.

5. Injustice does not strictly speaking determine the various spheres of human relations, but it does to a large extent condition the whole life of human beings: personal, familial, and associational. Precisely because justice and injustice are terms that cut across the totality of human relations, their impact is felt on the forms these relations take in other types of groupings. For this reason, even though Christian love must find expression in these other

areas of relationships among human beings, we may not abandon
the promotion of justice if we really want to practice Christian love
in these other areas.

6. The process whereby a Christian becomes a Christian through
the practice of love takes typical forms when this practice is in the
concrete form of justice. Every expression of love contains new
possibilities that are not simply interchangeable with those of justice. But the reverse is also true. Love that takes the form of justice
extends the horizon of shared interests and of solidarity with other
human beings. Love becomes more universal, though it may
thereby lose something in intensity. The consequences of doing justice are also very special. Love here—as in no other area—leads to
persecution, risk, the surrender of life, and all this, in many instances, without the gratification which accompanies the sacrifices
called for in other structures (for example, marriage or the family).
In the doing of justice we see manifested with special intensity the
Christian paradox of the powerlessness of love. The doing of justice is in a peculiar way the place where Christian activity obeys the
law of opposition: faith against unbelief, hope against hope, love
against injustice.

7. Finally, the embodiment of love in the form of justice is a
historical necessity, both because the situation of the human race
demands it and because the history of the Church, which has always defended the necessity of putting love into practice, has not
shown itself the best embodiment of love as justice. The Church is
indebted to the human race when it comes to the practice of social
justice, whereas the human race is indebted to the Church in regard
to many other ways of promoting love. Awareness of this debt is
the reason for the holy restlessness that now impels the Church as it
seeks to make clear that Christian love must also take the form of
justice.

This movement toward justice is returning the Church to its
biblical roots. The Church is becoming aware again of what has
over the centuries been expressed in Exodus, the psalms, the
prophets, and the gospels. This conscious return to the source with
the present as point of departure, this illumination of the present
from the rediscovered source is a clear sign and the ultimate justification of the fact that the term *justice* is a key concept for the Christian conscience of our day. We cannot, of course, predict on the

basis of the present moment, and, more concretely, on the basis of the Latin American present, that no other term will ever be able to express the needed concrete form of Christian love. But in our time and for our time the term *justice* has all the aspects which I have pointed out. It is strictly necessary to the proclamation of the *God* of the kingdom and to the building of the *kingdom* of God. In this light some words cited earlier from the General Congregation assume profound importance: "Thus the way to faith and the way to justice are inseparable ways. It is up this undivided road, this steep road, that the pilgrim Church must travel and toil" (2:8).

REPERCUSSIONS ON RELIGIOUS LIFE

What impact will the approach taken to the society's mission in the Thirty-second General Congregation (along with the subsequent theological grounding offered for this approach) have on religious life in the Society and on religious life generally? The theme I have been discussing has implications far beyond its immediate importance for religious life, but it must also influence the latter. Does the choice of this mission as the crucial struggle for our time represent only a more adequate specification of the general mission or does this new definition of the content of the Society's mission implicitly sketch a new theory of religious life as well? In my opinion, the latter is occurring. Indeed it is to be expected a priori, inasmuch as changes in fundamental content always affect structures as well. The following points spell out these changes.

The specification of mission as the service of faith and the promotion of justice sends religious life back to the substance of Christianity, a substance in relation to which everything else, however important and necessary it may be, is secondary. This focusing of religious life on the basics of Christianity is all the more important in that it is based not on ideas but on what objectively needs to be done. The step taken clearly points to the ultimate theoretical standard by which alone religious life can be Christian. It is not a question of one particular mission among many possible ones. Mission apart from Christian life is impossible today.

The elevation of justice to the level of a fundamental theological concept is not self-evident, assuming that it is done in an honest and radical way. For it supposes a historical change, a historical break of sufficient compass that the consciousness of change at the level of mission will lead to readiness for change in the structures of religious life. Readiness for change is very important in religious life, which until recently has tended to regard its structures as canonized and immutable. The assertion that the mission of a religious order is to promote justice marks a historical revolution, which can be put into practice only if there is a readiness to refashion everything in religious life that impedes such a revolution.

When the *content* of mission is determined as the general congregation has determined it, support is given to the idea that mission takes logical priority over the structures of religious life. It is one thing to pay lip service to the priority of mission and quite another to propose a content for mission that will make this priority evident to anyone with an evangelical outlook. The service rendered by the General Congregation to the apostolic and missionary conception of religious life does not consist solely in having issued formal statements about the apostolate of a community. The General Congregation also defined an apostolate that gives clear expression to the Christian eccentrism necessary for Christian life.

By proposing the promotion of justice as the horizon of religious life the General Congregation helps to overcome the isolation or introversion often found in religious life, especially that form of it that has made the life of the religious house an end in itself. More concretely, since the promotion of justice is a mission that has the totality of social relations among human beings for its object, religious life cannot be satisfied with being limited to good but partial works. It will likewise be better able to avoid the dangers of paternalism and of a false professionalism based on a misunderstanding of its charism. The means of promoting justice are concrete and to this extent limited, but at least the purview within which religious life operates can no longer be caritative aid or education or whatever else a given religious order may legitimately have chosen as its apostolate. The promotion of justice, by this very universality, calls upon the religious group to go forth not only to other groups that are known and within reach but to the human race in its entirety.

In view of all this, the concept of vocation becomes more concrete. The idea that persons enter religious life because they have felt a "call" from God represents an important truth that cannot be set aside. It is common for persons receiving such a call to speak of their "response" to it, and this too is a very important notion. But it is necessary to move on from the idea of "responding" to God to that of "corresponding" or conforming to him. Trivial though the point may seem, I must repeat that the correct response to a vocation is not simply a subjective readiness to do anything and everything later on, but rather the kind of response that leads to conformity. This is important in practice, because the reason for remaining in religious life should not be simply the formal one of continuing the response once given to God but rather one's conformity to the reality of God. The point is not to maintain the initial response (even though, hypothetically, the real mission of the order is not in conformity with what is assumed to be the will of God), but rather to grow in likeness to God. The choice set forth by the General Congregation offers a clear criterion by which to judge whether persons have grown in their vocation and whether their response to God is leading them to conformity with God.

This choice of mission is an effective help in dealing with something that gets forgotten in religious life: one's own sins and sinfulness. In addition to their natural sinfulness religious have a Christian sinfulness. An effective way of discovering this is for them to judge themselves in the light of faith and justice. It may be that they will then pass from routine confessions to an honest repentance at having failed in something basic, something that religious life had kept hidden from them.

The choice made by the General Congregation also helps guide religious toward a Christian understanding of the relationship between contemplation and action in religious life. Contemplation is necessary in any Christian life; it may be even more necessary in religious life because of the demands this life makes. But it cannot be assumed that contemplation is the essential element in Christian life or that any particular kind of contemplation is the best. The choice made by the General Congregation implies that the absolutely final and definitive value is conformity to God in the practice of love and, concretely, of justice. Prayer must accompany the entire process so that we may hear God's word regarding a world of injustice, discern the means of promoting justice, ask forgiveness of the Father for our own sins of injustice, and be humbly grateful for the spread of justice on earth.

The General Congregation's choice throws new light on the ascetical side of religious life. Asceticism is necessary by reason of the demands that the structures of religious life make. In its most radical form (though the others are not to be neglected) the asceticism of religious means that a world of injustice will cause them real suffering and even bring them to death. Every type of asceticism must prepare the person for the basic asceticism: not drawing back from the promotion of justice even when this brings suffering, danger, and persecution. The asceticism that is freely accepted in religious life must be placed in the service of the asceticism that is imposed by the world of injustice.

The Congregation's formulation of the Jesuit mission unites two characteristic aspects of religious life: personal perfection or sanctification, and service of others. The choice made by the Congregation asserts that in bringing others to faith and justice we make ourselves believers and people of justice. This is why the content of the mission is so important. There is no question, therefore, of doing just anything, however good, in order that religious, having purified their intention, may grow in faith and justice. Rather, a mission is set before us, and its content is such that its accomplishment will directly bring growth in personal holiness. There are therefore not two ways of sanctification: the characteristic means offered by religious life, which are logically independent of a particular mission, *and* the exercise of a mission. Those who help others to be believers and people of justice are doing the best thing they could possibly do for themselves as well.

I am not saying that spiritual practices are not necessary and efficacious. I am saying only that they will not be necessary and efficacious if they are peripheral to the content of the mission or if their content is heterogeneous to that of the mission. Making other people children of God is the Christian way of making oneself a child of God. Building the kingdom of God is the Christian way of entering this kingdom. To promote faith and justice is to advance oneself as a Christian. We do not reach sanctity by intending it but by following the objective way that leads to it.

Finally, this conception of mission locates religious life in its natural, though often forgotten, place. As the General Congregation says, "If we have the patience and the humility and the courage to walk with the poor, we will learn from what they have to teach us what we can do for them'' (2:50). The Congregation is here saying (though it does not emphasize the point elsewhere in its documents) that before we can serve the faith of others and promote justice among them, we must first let them serve us by their faith and their practice of justice. It also clearly states who these ''others'' are: the poor. This assertion is a very important one for religious life, because the latter is often thought of as a place for serving others but not as a place where one is served by others. This outlook is the source of subtle, or even crass, arrogance on the part of religious. Conversely, true Christian humility in religious life depends on the starting point of the mission: in going out to arouse faith the religious receives faith from the poor. In this way religious life will really become an integral part of the church, not only at the juridical level nor even at the ministerial level, but at the deeper level of ''carrying and being carried.''

4

The Church of the Poor:
Resurrection of the True Church

Given the present Latin American situation a reflection on the resurrection of a Church of the poor is a reflection on a new, historically describable fact, on a new way of being the Church. I will not reflect on the Church of the poor in itself but rather on this Church precisely as representing a resurrection of the true Church. The term *resurrection* means that the Church of the poor breaks away from traditional ways of being Church. In this Church of the poor the Church attains a greater fullness and authenticity.

The application of the metaphor of "resurrection" to the Church may scandalize or seem extreme, as though implying that the Church had been dead and were now beginning to live again in the Church of the poor. That is not what I mean by speaking of the Church as experiencing a "resurrection" in the Church of the poor. If I use the term (as I do) in a way that is more than purely metaphorical, then I am acknowledging that in the Church of the poor there is, first, a newness in substance and a historical break from other ways of being the Church and, second, that in this new situation the Church is returning to life—a life seriously threatened with destruction and irrelevance and even with betraying its own reason for existence if it does not become a Church of the poor.

The Church is always threatened with conforming to the pattern of this sinful world. Recognized or not, these processes of conforming to the world were at work in the great ages of the Church

84

and are repeated throughout its history. The Church, considered structurally and not in the concrete actions of its individual members, tends to suffer declines in its internal life and thus to become incapable of giving life to the world.

But it also happens periodically that the risen Lord appears to the Church and restores it to life again. The experience of the resurrection of the crucified Jesus was not limited to the first generation of disciples, but is one that the Church has at privileged moments in its history. Like Paul, the Church is flung headlong out of its past and is given the grace of having its blindness healed, its sight recovered. It is filled with the Holy Spirit (cf. Acts 9:1-19).

A denial of these possibilities would be profoundly antichristian. To deny the possibility of a sinful degeneration on the part of the Church and of the Church's becoming irrelevant would be not only to blind oneself to the evidence but also to deny what Vatican II said about the sinfulness of the Church. To deny that Christ can continue to appear to his Church and renew the miraculous creativity that accompanied the first appearances of the risen Lord would be to deny that Christ is still risen and that his Spirit still breathes where it will by communicating a knowledge of the truth and creating new life.

The Church of the poor denies neither of these two possibilities. With the same surprise, the same simple joy, and, we trust, the same sense of responsibility that characterized the first disciples, it confesses that Christ crucified has appeared to it as risen. The grace given to the first Christians has been given once again on our continent. A new form of being the Church is coming into existence, just as long ago a new way of being a religious community appeared on the scene. The Lord continues to reveal himself and to show himself where he said he was, and the Church has been given the grace to see him. Those who have been witnesses to these appearances, both then and now, could not but create a new form of being the Church. Gustavo Gutiérrez described this new experience of Christ:

In recent years it has seemed more and more clear to many Christians that, if the church wishes to be faithful to the God of Jesus Christ, it must become aware of itself from underneath, from among the poor of this world, the exploited classes, despised ethnic groups, and marginalized cultures. It must descend into the hell of this world, into communion with the misery, injustice, struggles, and hopes of the wretched of the earth—for "of such is the kingdom of heaven." At bottom it is a matter of living, as church, what the majority of its own members live every day. To be born, to be reborn, as church, from below, from among them, today means to die, in a concrete history of oppression and complicity with oppression.

In this ecclesiological approach, which takes up one of the central themes of the Bible, Christ is seen as the Poor One, identified with the oppressed and plundered of the world.[1]

My purpose in this chapter is to analyze theologically the meaning of "the Church of the poor" and to show not only that it is truly a Church but also that historically it contains the roots of the true Church and that it therefore represents a resurrection of the true Church.

THE THEOLOGICAL ROOTS OF THE CHURCH OF THE POOR

Lest "Church of the poor" be taken as a metaphor or remain simply a description, some analysis is needed in order to find its theological roots and connect it with Christ. This analysis will counter the often-repeated, self-serving accusation that "Church of the poor," "Church of the people," and similar expressions describe the Church solely from a sociological viewpoint.

General Correlation between the Resurrection of Christ and the Rise of the Church According to the New Testament

I will analyze first of all the Church that makes its appearance in the New Testament from a theological standpoint in order to see whether and in what way it can be called a "Church of the poor." I will also analyze the relationship that must exist between the Church and Christ if the Church is to retain its authentic character.

The Church comes into existence *after* the resurrection of Christ. But this "after" is not simply a matter of fact, as though after

Christ's resurrection the Church could have come into existence or could just as well have not. No, the existence of the Church is an integral part of the resurrection of Christ. The "after" describes in temporal terms something that is essential to the very resurrection of Christ. As Rahner says: "Faith in the resurrection [of Jesus] is an internal element in that resurrection and not simply a becoming aware of an event that of its nature could just as well have gone unperceived."[2]

The resurrection of Christ is therefore essentially impossible without the correlative rise of another reality. The resurrection of Christ is impossible unless it in turn launches history. The resurrection of Christ, the supreme symbol of victory over death and over the wretchedness of history, is impossible—provided we understand it in a Christian way and not just as an extraordinary wonder—unless it in its turn launches a movement aimed at overcoming death and the wretchedness of history. The Church is thus an integral and essential part of the very fact of Christ's resurrection. When Christ makes himself known, a historical movement arises. The Church that comes into existence is not simply the depository of the truth *about* the resurrection of Christ but is itself the very expression, at the historical level, of the newness that has come in Christ. "Without new life, without the ability to love and the courage of hope in the lordship of Christ, faith in the resurrection would decay into belief in particular facts, without any consequences."[3]

Clearly, then, there is a correlation between the resurrection of Christ and the rise of the Church as far as the *fact* of the coming into existence of these two new realities is concerned. But the correlation extends to *content* as well. The deepest reality of the Church is correlative with the content of the Christ who rises from the dead. At this point a basic problem arises that will have serious consequences for the Church's self-understanding and mission.

The Church can organize its entire existence around the plenitude already brought into being in the resurrection of Christ. The Church will then be able to render an account of what it knows, hopes, and does (a Kantian phrase for a total response) in terms of the resurrection of Christ. If the Church is asked what it *knows* about the end of history, it will answer by saying that "this Jesus God raised up" (Acts 2:32) and that God "gives life to the dead and calls into existence the things that do not exist" (Rom. 4:17). If the Church is asked what we may *hope* for, it will answer by saying that "Christ has been raised from the dead [as] the first fruits of those who have fallen asleep" (1 Cor. 15:20). If the Church is asked what we must *do*, it will answer by saying that Christ must be "preached as raised from the dead" (1 Cor. 15:12). If the Church is asked *how we are saved*, it will answer that Christ was raised for our justification" (Rom. 4:25).[4]

A Church that arises *solely* on this basis and that looks upon Christ *solely* as the risen Lord will be a Church of glory, that is, a Church that has a sufficient knowledge of the last things and an abundant knowledge of the penultimate things that form the framework of history. It will be a Church that looks forward to the last day with confidence, but with resignation as well; a Church that claims to save and justify human beings by informing them of truths, sublime as these may be; and, finally, a Church that considers itself a depository—a limited one, but a depository nonetheless—of God's absolute power.

The risen Christ can present himself to the Church with the wounds of his crucifixion (cf. Jn. 20:24–27), as the Christ whom God raised from the dead not by an arbitrary act (as if he might just as well not have raised him) but out of fidelity to the Son who was faithful even to the cross. If the one who appears to the Church is this crucified Jesus, this Christ who has now reached fulfillment because he was completely faithful within history, then the Church will respond differently to the basic questions about itself and its mission. The difference in responses does not imply a contradiction; it only requires that the previous responses be given a Christian concreteness.

Thus, if the Church is asked what it knows about the last things, it will answer that God gave his Son (cf. Rom. 4:25), that the power and wisdom of God are "a stumbling block to Jews and folly to Gentiles" (cf. 1 Cor. 1:23–25), and that God is not yet all in all (cf. 1 Cor. 15:20). If it is asked what it may hope for, it will answer that it hopes for liberation, but as one who like Abraham hopes against hope (cf. Rom. 4:18). If it is asked what it must do, it will answer that it must "have the mind of Christ Jesus by taking the status of a slave, humbling itself, and becoming obedient unto death, death on a cross" (cf. Phil. 2:5–8). If it is asked how we are saved, it will answer by saying that "Christ died for us" (Rom. 5:8).

These comprehensive theological formulas show that the Church which arises from the resurrection does not forget that the risen Lord is the crucified Jesus. The fullness that belongs to it in the resurrection of Christ and in its own coming into existence comes because it overcomes a scandal, namely, the abandonment of Jesus on the cross by God and his historical abandonment by his disciples.

The risen Lord who brings a community into existence is not just any human being nor any Christ but the crucified Jesus of Nazareth. Consequently the Church does not achieve existence simply in relation to a universal symbol in which knowledge, action, and hope are unified, but around the consummation of a life that has been brought to fulfillment and yet, being historical, was limited and particular. The first ecclesial nucleus that comes into existence possesses not only the "end product," namely, the Christ, but also—to continue the image—the very process leading to the end product in its entirety or, in other words, a resurrection that has come through the cross. This cross is not something that occupies only a moment in time; it is the ending of the historical life of Jesus. With relative rapidity, therefore, the Church absorbed into its faith and theology the various statements (in theologized form) regarding those things in the life of Jesus that led to the cross and resurrection. This is not the place to review the traits of the historical Jesus, but I must at least recall his ministry to the poor, his solidarity with them, his compassion on the multitudes, his attacks on the mighty, and his condemnation and execution by them.

I may state as a *theological* thesis that according to the New Testament the Church certainly *arises* because of the resurrection, but also that *that which* arises is in conformity with a symbol of fulfillment and with a concrete life of solidarity with the poor and of service to them. It is unimportant whether or not this Church calls itself "Church of the poor." The important thing *from a theological standpoint* is that conformity to the risen Christ is not possible solely on the basis of generic kinds of knowing, doing, and hoping, but on the basis of the concrete kinds of knowing, doing, and hoping that the risen Lord who has been crucified demands. In our day the formula "Church of the poor," when properly understood, expresses this conformity better than any other formula.

I shall not show here that this theological thesis is also *historical*.[5] The proof would require historical investigation and not simply theological reflection. Neither is it possible to ignore certain historical evidence regarding the kind of concrete Church that came into being with the resurrection of the crucified Jesus at its focus. "There is no evidence that the [first] community in Jerusalem included people with power or strong social influence."[6] Writing to the Corinthians Paul says: "For consider your call, brethren; not many of you were wise according to worldly standards, not many were powerful, not many were of noble birth; but God chose what is foolish in the world to shame the wise, God chose what is weak in the world to shame the strong, God chose what is low and despised in the world, even things that are not, to bring to nothing things that are" (1 Cor. 1:26–28).

These assertions are general but important. Most of the first members of the Church were ordinary people, the majority of them poor or even slaves. Soon the basic needs of Christians became clear, along with the perennial problem of the rich and the poor, the oppressor and the oppressed. Persecutions and threats made their appearance, and even accusations of promoting liberation movements. When the Church made its decision (a profoundly theological one) to go forth to the pagans, it decided by that act to turn to a world in which the majority were poor and downtrodden. A nascent Church of this type, which was impelled by historical necessities as well, did not think of itself in terms of power or as a great institution. There was an understandable movement toward institutionalization, and in the long run the Church would come to terms with power and would even assume power in later centuries.

If the early Church was as a historical fact not elitist and did not base its mission and proselytizing on power, and if despite this its membership (mostly ordinary people) grew, the reason was the correspondence between the hopes of the people and the message of Jesus. Whatever may have been the concrete way in which this hope presented itself to the people, if the people turned to the Church it was because they needed hope and saw the nascent Church as embodying this hope for them. The poor, slaves, sinners, outcasts saw something in this risen Jesus that was in profound harmony with their state of wretchedness.

The Manifestation of Christ's New Face and the Church of the Poor

I cannot go back into the history of the Church and show whether the Church has, theologically and historically, been faithful to a risen Lord who was crucified, or whether it developed its organization in an unbalanced way and based its mission on generic symbols of fulfillment that leave aside the wounds of the crucified Lord or that at least do not make these the deepest ground of its existence as Church.[7]

In recent years Christ has appeared again in Latin America. He has granted many Christians the grace of "seeing" him in the poor, and these visionaries have become, along with the visionaries of the New Testament, "witnesses" who are ready for a new mission that will shape a new Church or a new form of existence as Church. It is this new reality that I want to describe. Before giving a positive description of the Church of the poor I want to say what it is not by showing the inadequacy (not the falseness) of certain ecclesiological proposals.

First, the Church of the poor may not without qualification be identified with Vatican II's description of the Church as the people of God. This description was a major advance, and an extremely important one. It served to counterbalance the excessive weight given to an ecclesiology of the "mystical" body by giving the body a historical existence and dimension. It served also to counterbalance the hierarchical conception of the Church by giving the worldwide base of the Church priority over the apex of the pyramid. It served to eliminate a monopolistic view of the faith by locating it first and foremost in "the whole body of the faithful."[8]

From this new vantage point of the people of God certain aspects of the Church came to be emphasized once more: the election and gathering of the Church by God, the historical dimension of its pilgrimage as well as of the temptations and hopes the Church experiences as a people on a journey, the basic equality of all Christians, the humanity of the Church, which accepts every human being as a human being, and the restoration to the local Churches of their proper place. The Council even hinted at a partiality for the Church of the poor.[9]

But the new approach did not go deeply enough into these new descriptions of the Church. Moreover, because of the latent hostility to an elitist ecclesiology (an ecclesiology centered on the hierarchy, the priesthood, and religious life) the emphasis was placed on "all" who make up the people of God. This represented a step in the direction of what may be called a theological democratization of the Church, in the positive sense of this term. But even when the specific characteristics that apply to it as a whole are described, the term *people of God* remained universal in a vague sort of way. The thinking of Vatican II was extremely important in that it approached the idea and reality of a Church of the poor, but this idea and reality were only virtually present in the Council.

Second, "Church of the poor" does not mean only a Church that is concerned for the poor. It certainly does not mean a Church that assists the poor and ignores the poverty. "The Church is not sanctified by poverty when it becomes a 'Church for the poor' and when it especially praises 'alms for the poor.' "[10] Neither is it important that the Church should be a Church for the poor in ways that transcend a purely helping approach to the poor. It is clear, of course, that a "Church of the poor" is an urgent necessity and that many Churches have not gotten even this far. But in principle a Church *for* the poor is not yet a Church *of* the poor. The Church of the poor "is not a Church that stands apart from the world of the poor and offers its generous aid."[11]

A Church *for* the poor represents an ethical and therefore necessary approach, but it is not necessarily an ecclesiological approach. It supposes that the Church is constituted in logical independence of the poor, and then goes on to ask what this Church must do for the poor. A Church *of* the poor, however, poses a strictly ecclesiological problem; it concerns the very being of the Church. This is so even apart from the consideration that historically a Church that is simply for the poor without being of the poor could not succeed in the long run even in being for the poor.

Third, "Church of the poor" does not refer to a part of the Church within the wider ecclesial reality, a part coexisting with the other parts and having the same rights as they. It is not to be denied that there are sociologically distinct groups within the Church and that they are even hostile to one another (this is why sociologists sometimes describe the Church of the poor as the Church of a class). But the Church of the poor is not established by giving a privileged position to a part of the Church, while the other parts remain unaffected, not by waging a "class struggle" in the strict sense within the Church, although such a struggle may in fact really exist.

A Church of the poor, then, requires that we move beyond a merely universalist approach to the people of God, beyond a purely ethical approach by which the Church is for the poor, and beyond a segment approach in which the poor are seen as part of the whole and as coexisting with other, non-poor groups.

Let me turn now to what can be said positively about the Church of the poor. The response is relatively simple at the theological level: The Spirit of Jesus is in the poor and, with them as his point of departure, he re-creates the entire Church. If this truth is understood in all its depth and in an authentically trinitarian perspective, it means that the history of God advances indefectibly by way of the poor; that the Spirit of Jesus takes historical flesh in the poor; and that the poor show the direction of history that is in accord with God's plan. "The union of God with human beings as we see this in Jesus Christ is historically a union with human beings of a God who basically pours himself out into the world of the poor."[12]

For this profound reason I maintain that the Church of the poor is not a Church for the poor but a Church that must be formed on the basis of the poor and that must find in them the principle of its structure, organization, and mission. For the same reason I maintain that this Church does not conceive of the poor as "part" of itself, even a privileged part, but thinks of them rather as the "center" of the whole.

This means that the poor are the authentic *theological source* for understanding Christian truth and practice and therefore the constitution of the Church. The poor are those who confront the Church both with its basic theological problem and with the direction in which the solution to the problem is to be found. For the poor pose the problem of *seeking* God without presupposing that the Church possesses him once and for all. At the same time they offer the Church the place for *finding* him. Christian truth becomes a concrete universal when seen in terms of the poor. In the poor it acquires the potential that theology will develop for an understanding of history as a whole. In the poor we find the primordial conformity with the truth in its evangelical sources. With the poor as its starting point Christian practice recovers its concreteness, direction, and meaning; the poor have the final say about what is ultimate in Christianity—namely, love—about what love really is, about its necessary historical mediations, about its different expressions. The Christian understanding of sin becomes concrete when seen from the vantage point of the poor, for they suffer it, as no one else does, in their own flesh. They make it clear that sin brings death, and they show what kind of death it brings and what kind of hierarchy reigns in death.

When the poor are at the center of the Church, they give direction and meaning to everything that legitimately (by the standard of Christian tradition) and necessarily (by the standard of the structure of any association of human beings) constitutes the concrete Church: its preaching and activity, its administration, its cultural, dogmatic, theological, and other structures. The poor in no sense cause a "reduction" of ecclesial reality but rather are a source of "concretization" for everything ecclesial.[13]

The establishment of the Church of the poor presupposes a willingness to focus specifically on those who at a given historical moment make up the poor and to overcome the frequent temptation to deal with them in such general terms that in fact they vanish from view.

For my purposes here it is enough to keep in mind that "the identity of these poor in the real situation of the Third World is not a problem whose solution requires scriptural exegesis or sociological analysis of historical theory. . . . No self-serving equivocations are admissible in face of the self-evident fact: the real situation of the majority of the human race."[14] One indisputable merit of the Puebla Conference (Mexico) was to have displayed in a concrete way the faces of these poor: peasants, workers, slum dwellers, the persecuted, the tortured. Today, as in the days of Isaiah and Jesus, these poor are those to whom the Good News is primarily addressed. By their material and historical situation they are in the best position to understand what the Good News is about. And it is these same poor, I say, who are the inspirational and organizational center of the Church. I shall not here expatiate on the fact that by reason of their material condition they are apt subjects for "spiritual poverty" and therefore able to realize the human ideal set down in the Scriptures. The important thing to remember is that a Church that arises in solidarity with the poor protests against their material poverty as being an expression of the world's sin, engages in a struggle against this poverty as a form of liberation, and allows itself to be affected by this poverty and its consequences as an expression of its own kenosis. Such a Church is indeed a Church of the poor.

There is no question here of idealizing, much less sacralizing, the poor. The point is rather to recover an ancient idea that has been often repeated in Catholic theology: certain structures play a privileged role in the coming into existence of Chrsitian reality. Just as structures such as magisterium and sacrament have been accepted as privileged channels of truth and grace (although this does not mean that there is no truth and grace apart from them, or even that the existence of the channels proves the reality of truth and grace), and conditions have therefore been set down for the exercise of the magisterium and the administration of the sacraments, so too it can be said that the Church of the poor is a structural channel for the coming into being of the true Church. Paraphrasing the terminology of sacramental theology, I might say that the Spirit is present in the poor *ex opere operato*, though this in no way means simply that with the poor as members the Church will come to exist as the authentic Church. What it does mean is that the Spirit manifests itself in the poor and that they are therefore structural channels for finding the truth of the Church and the direction and content of its mission.

The Church of the poor is not automatically the agent of truth and grace because the poor are in it; rather the poor in the Church are the structural source that assures the Church of being really the agent of truth and justice. In the final analysis, I am speaking of what Jesus refers to in Matthew 25 as the place where the Lord is to be found.

We must not idealize the Church of the poor in an a priori way or revive the false mechanistic concept of the sacramental *ex opere operato*. Neither may we ignore, on the basis of statements about history, the fact that the poor have given rise to a new form of Church that is distinct from the previous form and more in accord with the Church's beginnings as seen in the gospel. What is needed, then, is empirical proof that the Church of the poor provides a structural channel for the establishment of the true Church.

An Epistemology for Recognizing the Church of the Poor as a Resurrection of the Church

To the extent that the Church of the poor is coming into existence, a new mode of being the Church is also coming into existence, and it is this that allows us to speak of a "resurrection" of the Church. At the same time the epistemological problem inherent in the language of "resurrection" also makes its presence felt.[15] We shall see that this problem is not a purely academic one.

In the resurrection of Christ, the Spirit manifests itself as the power of God that is able to restore Christ to definitive life. But the Spirit also manifests itself in order to enable the disciples to grasp the objective resurrection of Christ. The newness of Christ's resurrection is matched by something new in the disciples. This new thing is so far-reaching, even scandalous, that it can only be the work of the Spirit.

With the necessary reservations the same can be said of the Church of the poor. To recognize a Church of the poor as the Church in its true form is simultaneously to recognize that the Spirit is in this Church and to be rendered by the Spirit capable of this recognition. By this I mean that only from within this Church is it possible to grasp this Church as true. Strictly speaking, it is not possible to argue to the existence of such a Church by using previously established criteria, just as it was not possible to argue to the resurrection of Christ by an appeal solely to the Old Testament. The parallelism here is, of course, not perfect. It may be objected, in fact, that the Church of the poor can be known to be the true Church because it reflects best the normative Church of the period when the faith began. I think this is indeed so. But the ability to view the origin of the faith in precisely this way is itself given only from within the Church of the poor.

The basic epistemological process consists then in recognizing that the Spirit is present in the Church of the poor—a recognition that is in its turn to be had only within this Church. Moreover, the recognition of the Spirit's presence in this Church reflects the same work of grace as the recognition that the Spirit was in Jesus. Contrary to contemporary opinions, the first Christians did believe that the Spirit had given a definitive life to Christ. In our day, again despite—or at least in contradistinction to—a great deal of contemporary opinion, many believers recognize the Spirit in the Church of the poor.

It is perhaps not possible to say much more a priori about the resurrection of the Church as a grace and fruit of the Spirit. A posteriori, however, it can be shown why many Christians recognize this Church as the true Church. Every resurrection presupposes an objective and describable newness, break, and change. Starting with this describable newness, we can argue in favor of the Church of the poor as compared with other forms of Churchly existence. That is what I shall do in the second part of this chapter. But before the newness can be grasped as something good and as more Christian than that which preceded it, there is need of a subjective change, which goes by the Christian name of conversion. Without one's subjective conversion one cannot grasp the objective goodness of this new reality. This is why I said that discussion of the epistemological process required for recognizing the Church of the poor is not a purely academic matter. If the Church of the poor has been recognized as such, it is because many Christians have undergone a conversion. The important thing is that the historical reality of the Church of the poor is a structural channel for conversion.

The poor keep alive the question of God, of his kingdom, of Christ, of love, justice, and sin. Their very presence prevents the manipulation of these realities by the Church. The poor challenge previous interests at work in the understanding of these realities and thus make possible the passage from a natural understanding of them to a Christian understanding. The poor keep alive the ethical demands of Christianity and the need to give these a concrete embodiment. It is therefore no accident that the Church should undergo a resurrection when it comes upon the true locus of its own conversion, and that the poor should provide the epistemological standpoint from which it is possible to understand the resurrection taking place in the Church.

By reason of their own concrete reality, the poor are the locus of radical change in the ultimate principles on which the Church has been organized. When Vatican II tried to replace a hierarchical ecclesiology with an ecclesiology of the people of God, it was aiming at a change in the concept of authority. But indirectly it was also aiming at more radical change in the concept of power. It was basically an effort to put an end to the idea of power as a mediation of

God. As long as the Church's center consciously or unconsciously thinks of itself *in terms of* power—whether administrative, dogmatic, or theological—and acts on the basis of this thinking, the Church will not change much (as the Churches of the First World clearly show, despite their liberalization since the Council), even if it avoids certain crass aberrations.

The Church of the poor does not involve a transfer of power from the hierarchy to the poor as a sociological group without the idea of power undergoing change in the process. The process entails a radical change in the notion of power as a mediation of God. The "Church of the poor" concept proposes, first and foremost, that the entire Church should migrate to the periphery and share the powerlessness of the poor, at the feet of a crucified God, so that it might there cultivate Christian hope and develop effective (and, in this sense, powerful) activity. Here, at this level, the most necessary radical change in the Church takes place. To the extent that it does, it is possible to speak of a resurrection of the Church. Such a change means a thoroughgoing conversion; apart from this there will be no understanding of what is central to the Church of the poor. Consequently, those who believe in the resurrection of a crucified man will be called "heretics from the synagogue" (as the Jews called them long ago) or "atheists" (as the pagans called them long ago) by those who have not undergone such a conversion.

THE CHURCH OF THE POOR AS THE TRUE CHURCH

Is the Church of the poor a *true* Church and, more than that, *the* true Church? My question is not meant in the traditional technical sense; that is, I am not trying to distinguish true Churches from heretical or schismatic Churches. I am asking whether in this Church of the poor there exists what might be called the basic substance of ecclesiality, namely, faith, hope, love, the presence of Christ, mission; whether this substance exists in greater fullness here than in other forms of Churchly existence; and whether this basic ecclesial substance is better assured here by the historical structure of this Church precisely as "Church of the poor."

The problem of discerning the true Church is an old one. Long-standing too is the Church's interest in the development of criteria showing where this truth and fullness is to be found. Over and above the radical subjective conviction of possessing the true faith, this concern has provided verifiable historical criteria. However transcendent and therefore not fully verifiable the ultimate truth of the Church may be, there must be something visible and historical that shows where the truth of the Church is to be found and what it is that makes the Church the true Church. Since the Church is a sign of salvation it must be possible to make the transcendent truth of its faith historically credible and, to this extent, visible. Because of its need both to identify itself among other Churches and to make itself credible to the world the Church has developed historical criteria for proving its truth.

As early as the Council of Constantinople in 381 the Church formulated the four historical marks that identify it as true: "We believe . . . in one, holy, catholic and apostolic Church."[16] Vatican I formally repeated the substance of this, not in order to make the Church credible but rather to enable the Church with these characteristics to make the faith credible.[17] At the theoretical level there is room for debate as to whether these traditional four marks are the most adequate, the best suited, or the only ones for proving the truth of the Church. For my purpose here they suffice, since when they include "holiness" they point to what I have called the substance of the Church; when they include "apostolicity" they name both the normative origin and the essence of the Church's mission; and when they include "unity" and "catholicity" they point to an important principle of internal structure and of relationship between the various local Churches. These marks thus indicate important concepts for proving the truth of the Church.

My concern here is to show whether and how these four marks are to be seen in the Church of the poor; whether in this Church's historical reality the substance of the Church is more fully manifested; and whether this "more" is due to the fact that this Church is "of the poor." I wish to show as well (and this is controverted) that the Church of the poor need not fear being measured by theological criteria. More than that, I want to show that in such a Church the traditional marks can recover their force as probative criteria. I say "recover" because, as Hans Küng observed shortly after Vatican II, "the individual signs may be hidden in a church. They may exist in such a way that they are no longer seen to be convincing from outside, perhaps not even from inside, because they have lost their illuminating power."[18]

In traditional Catholic theology these marks have been presented as a piece of apologetics in defense of the Catholic Church. They have contributed little or nothing to making this "catholic" Church a truly Christian Church. In analyzing the marks of the Church I shall describe briefly the treatment given to them in progressive Catholic and Protestant theology in an effort to make them real and capable of building up the truth of the Church.[19] I shall present the marks of the Church of the poor as a way of advancing further along those same lines.

My intention is to judge the Church of the poor on the basis of the traditional marks of the Church. This Church should in turn lend theological and historical truth to the generic marks. With his usual perspicacity, although in a different context, Moltmann has aptly formulated the basic problem involved in proving the Church true: "Where is the true Church? In the fellowship manifested in word and sacrament, or in the latent brotherhood of the Judge hidden in the poor?"[20] There is no question here of an either/or, but rather of seeing that word and sacrament (I say nothing of other ecclesial and disciplinary structures) will set us off on the wrong path to the true Church unless the poor of Matthew 25 are brought in as proofs of Christ's presence in the Church. Without the tension that Matthew 25 introduces into ecclesiology, any criterion of truth, even though generically valid, will remain abstract and open to manipulation. Moltmann asks whether the two things—the presence of Christ in the word and the presence of Christ in the poor—coincide; he answers that coincidence is very rare.

It is essential to the Church of the poor that Matthew 25 be brought into ecclesiology. Once this is done it will be possible to specify other kinds of presence of Christ and to specify in a properly Christian way the oneness, holiness, catholicity, and apostolicity of the Church. If the Church of the poor is a true Church the four marks must be verified in it. In the framework of this Church the four marks will tend to verify the Church, that is, make it true.

The Unity of the Church of the Poor

The true Church is one because its origin is one; in Paul's terms, because there is one God, one Lord, one baptism, one Spirit. That

Church in which this unity is best preserved will be true. However, many confessionally divergent Churches exist today, each with different concrete forms of Churchly existence.

In this context Hans Küng (in *The Church*) emphasizes the point that the ultimate unifying principle is Christ, who "has not only reconciled God and man" but "has also removed all opposition between man and man" (271). Küng then says that the standard of union cannot be "the Church . . . nor . . . the individual Churches, otherwise we will merely perpetuate the division which exists. The only standard is the Gospel of Jesus Christ" (291). On the other hand, this unity which God wants must be effected among a plurality of Churches. "The unity of the Church presupposes a multiplicity of Churches; the various Churches do not need to deny their origins or their specific situations; their language, their history, their customs and traditions, their way of life and thought, their personal structure will differ fundamentally, and no one has the right to take this from them" (274).

The intention that governs Küng's approach to the unity of the Church is clear. It is a unity that must respect plurality and must be based on the gospel of Jesus. Only if these principles are followed will we reach true unity within the Church and among the Churches. But this approach, which is correct in itself and serves to unmask the sacralization of false unities in the name of the gospel as ultimate standard, does not tell us how and by what means the gospel is concretely able to unify the Church.

Moltmann overcomes these objections (in *The Church in the Power of the Spirit*) by looking for the source of Church unity in the Church's mission. The Church "is not 'one' for itself; it is one for the peace of divided mankind in the coming kingdom of God" (345). Christ, the ultimate source of unity, does not unify directly by himself but through his historical mediations. Intraecclesial unity is impossible unless the Church is "a fellowship of believers with the poor, a fellowship of the hopeful with the sick, and a fellowship of the loving with the oppressed" (ibid.). According to this logic unity is sought not simply in a Christ who renders relative the concrete forms of Churchly existence but in the underside of history, which makes demands on the entire Church and on all the Churches alike. This logic applies also to the internal unity of the Church: "The hierarchical build-up of large-scale Church units and of administrations over a large area becomes abstract if it loses its contact with the 'grass-roots' '' (344).

Moltmann points to a historical reality that has sufficient power to unify the Church both *ad extra* and *ad intra*. This reality is not simply Christ but is something here "below" in the human race and in the Church.

What Moltmann suggests on the basis of intuition and as a desideratum is, I believe, becoming a reality in the Church of the poor. The phrase "Church of the poor" does not describe a correct principle of unity but rather the concrete way in which the principle unifies. It radically rejects pluralism where the faith is clear and evident. There can be no pluralism in the ultimate understanding of God, Christ, the kingdom, grace, and sin. This is so not only because Scripture rejects such pluralism nor because no one would in principle dare to engage in a "pluralistic" manipulation of these ultimate realities of the faith, but because from the standpoint of the poor there is nothing equivocal about the mission of the Church and the discernment of God's will for the world.

However trivial this point may seem, it is in fact supremely important. The eschatological proviso, necessary though it be, cannot be introduced to justify pluralisms at these levels. The formal solution to the problem of unity can be seen with clarity in this Church. There is indeed only one Lord: Jesus Christ, the historical, crucified Jesus, the Servant of Yahweh, who is now risen. There is indeed only one God, who wants human beings to live, who hears the cry of the oppressed, who dies with them in history and keeps ever alive the birth groanings of the new creation. There is indeed only one Spirit, who is the renewer of history and the giver of life, and who speaks through the prophets of olden times and of our own day.

Here, then, is the source of unity in the Church of the poor. But this basic unity of faith comes to fruition only when the poor have truly entered the Church as active not passive subjects with their wretched lives and their own faith and hope. This basic unity is achieved when the Church truly decides to understand its total faith as a faith-process in which Christians "bear one another's burdens." Unity in faith does not come solely from the apex of the Church nor does it derive solely from the imposed formulas of faith. Neither does it come from faith as a lived reality in those who are successful on the stage of history. When the Church makes the decision and accepts the risk of listening to the voice of the poor, heeding their faith and hope, and accepting the fact that it must learn from their practice, then there will come to pass the miracle that neither administrative rules nor sermons nor theologies can accomplish. The core of the faith will be understood as an irrenouncible core that cannot suffer death by qualifications or pluralisms. This core of the faith simply demands acceptance.

These reflections might logically be made on the basis of an analysis of Scripture. I am brought to them by reality. In the Church of the poor there exists a unity hitherto unrecognized that calls for a specific kind of pluralism and makes new and effective use of the traditional means of achieving intraecclesial unity.

In the Church of the poor the age-old barriers between hierarchy and faithful, priests and workers, peasants and intellectuals have been broken down. They have been broken down not by a process of formal democratization in which all are made equal, but by the rise of solidarity in the form of "bearing one another's burdens," being "one" ecclesial body, and thus making the Church "one." In this solidarity there is a sharing of the word: no longer the word solely of bishop or priest or theologian but the word of the poor as this finds expression in the liturgy, in prayer, in the interpretation of Scripture by the poor, and in the theological thinking of the poor. There is a sharing of the yearning for liberation and of the various struggles that lead to liberation. There is a sharing of hopes and successes. Above all—and this is the ultimate proof of the unity of the Church of the poor—there is a sharing of what formerly had been the tragic destiny of the poor alone: persecution and martyrdom. This solidarity and sharing is by its nature dialectical: some support others, some learn from others. The times when this dialectic has become operative are the times when the Church has decided to listen to the voice of the poor and to allow the poor to make their voice and their faith heard within the Church.

In the Church of the poor the kind of pluralism that is manipulated at the basic levels of faith is rejected, but a pluralistic participation in the Church as a whole is acceptable and even necessary. This means the acceptance of the hierarchy as providing leadership, expression, and a platform of action for the Church as a whole. It means acceptance of the priestly ministry and religious life, which, because of their special circumstances, bring special understanding and the possibility of great dedication. It also means acceptance of new ecclesial ministries (for example, lay ministers of the word) and new forms of ecclesial organization (for example, the basic ecclesial communities).

These various ways of participating in the one Church of the poor represent the kind of pluralism that is acceptable and necessary. All cannot and should not be doing the same task, but all must build this one Church. It is not simply that all are allowed to participate according to their various charisms; more than that, all are required to set about developing their own charisms. The pluralism of the Church of the poor is the pluralism required for the building of Christ's body in history. Pluralism is thus seen not as a matter of "rights" (to use the language of a particular culture, civilization, or ideology) but as a matter of the "obligation" to build the kingdom of God from below.[21]

The Church of the poor does not disdain the typical ecclesial means of achieving internal unity; on the contrary, it makes them possible. To give but two examples: the use made of the sacraments and the word of God, and the service rendered to unity by the hierarchy.

It has always been said, and with good reason, that the Church calls people together through word and sacraments. Usually, however, such convocations are "regional," that is, they involve different social castes; or else they are universal in an abstract way, as in the traditional celebration of eucharistic congresses. You rarely find the "rich" celebrating a liturgy and spontaneously inviting the poor. The converse does, however, occur. A liturgical celebration held because of something that has happened in the Church of the poor—a martyrdom, a peasant celebration—has the power to draw other Christians who in social terms are not poor. The root cause of the difference in ability to bring people together is that among the poor word and sacraments have power to evoke the source of the faith and challenge people to a true mission. The same is not true of the liturgies of the rich.[22]

The Church of the poor acknowledges, accepts, and requires that the bishop be the unifying head of the diocese and exercise the ministry of unity. This ministry becomes truly unifying only when the bishop hears the voice of the people. They in turn recognize their own voice in that of the bishop and see in him the good shepherd who is ready to give his life for his flock. The unifying role of the bishop therefore presupposes a still more fundamental ministry: that of defending the people. When this condition (demanded in the abstract by the theology of the episcopate and called for in concrete ways in the Church of the poor) is fulfilled, then the bishop is able to unify his diocese because he has become an expression of the reality of this diocese. Then, too, the concrete means that the bishop directs to be used at the pastoral, administrative, liturgical, and other levels as ways of unifying the life and mission of the diocese are not imposed by a purely formal act of authority but become expressions of a much deeper unity.[23]

Thus far I have spoken of the ability of the Church of the poor to create its own unity. It also has the ability to create disunity and division. This disunity does not take the form of schism or heresy as a way of separating from an already constituted Church, nor of division between hierarchy and faithful. When this kind of Church comes into existence, its difference from and opposition to other forms of Churchly existence becomes clear. The poor have the ability to get at what is fundamental and thus unifying in the faith, but they also have the power to divide. It becomes clear through them that Christ is "a sign that [shall be] spoken against" (Lk. 2:34), that the word of God is "sharper than any two-edged sword" (Heb. 4:12), and that the sacraments bring disunity (cf. 1 Cor. 11:17–22; Jas. 2:1–4). The poor are also a way of rejecting Christ (cf. Mt. 25:34–40) and in this way they cause division. When their words are silenced, twisted, or suppressed, there is disunity.

They render a worthwhile service to the Church by setting it on the right path as far as the true meaning of unity and disunity is concerned. They remind the Church that immediate unity is not an end in itself but is in the service of mission. They remind the Church, that unity is eschatological and will be brought to fulfillment in history through conflict and not directly by internal ecclesial methods.[24]

The Holiness of the Church of the Poor

The mark of holiness was chronologically the first attributed to the Church; it is also the mark that logically belongs to the Church.

If the Church is a sign of salvation, a historical sacrament of God's love, it would be a contradiction for it not to be holy. The problem has been to define just what constitutes this holiness and to avoid ecclesial triumphalism. This triumphalism would ignore the opposite of holiness, the sin of the Church, despite the fact that since earliest times it has been admitted that the Church is both holy and sinful or, in the language of the church Fathers, "chaste and a prostitute."

Hans Küng has repeatedly and emphatically called attention to the sinful element in the Church, unmasking the subterfuges by which traditional theology has striven to evade it (322–24).[25] "The Church is a *sinful Church*" (320). "Men in the Church are not, any more than men in the world, holy of themselves. They cannot make the Church holy; on the contrary, they are themselves the *communio peccatorum*, totally in need of justification and sanctification" (327). The one who makes the Church holy is God, "and that is why we do not simply believe *in* the holy Church, but believe in God who makes the Church holy" (325). The formal model of holiness is found in God himself: "Holy things are those which God has set apart" (324), just as his own holiness consists in being separated from what is profane. Concretely the Church attains to holiness under challenge by "the message of Jesus Christ" (337), when it "fulfills the will of God, following in the footsteps of Christ with its eye on the coming of the kingdom" (340).

Moltmann[26] too insists that the Church is sinful (353–55), that it needs conversion (355), and that "the Church is holy . . . not in itself but in Christ" (353). But when Moltmann concretizes, even in formal terms, the reason for the Church's holiness, he moves beyond the abstractions of Küng: "The church is holy because God shows himself to be holy in the grace of the crucified Christ acting on it" (354). It then becomes possible to express the Church's own holiness in concrete terms: "The signs of the sanctification of the church and its members are in a particular way the signs of its suffering, its persecution because of its resistance, and its poverty in the ground of its hope" (355). The Church's holiness must therefore be a "holiness in poverty" (352). "The fellowship of the poor and suffering Christ is the secret of the 'holy church' and the 'communion of saints' " (357).

The Church of the poor believes itself to be both holy and sinful.[27] But it is in terms of the poor that the Church specifies what holiness and sin are, reformulates the essence of holiness and sin, shows how to develop holiness and conquer sin, and develops a clear theological concept of holiness and sin.

For the Church of the poor holiness is ultimately identified with God. God's holiness does not consist simply in his being separated from the profane, in his inaccessibility and mystery; it is to be seen rather in the way in which God separates what belongs to grace and what belongs to sin when he *draws near* to the historical scene. What is really different about God as compared with the profane is not his apartness but the unconditional character of his Yes and No to the world to which he draws near. By this unconditionality he separates himself from the conditionality of human beings; anyone who shares in this unconditionality will be holy. Sanctity therefore consists in continuing God's Yes to the world of love and grace and his No to the world of sin.

The Church of the poor first gives concrete names to love and sin. It is in terms of the poor that it makes clear the supremacy of love at the heart of the holiness preached by the Church. The poor unmask the undialectical love that is not a practice of love in opposition to the world; they unmask the false universalism and pacifism of a Christian love that finds expression in universal declaration of love but does not take into account the concrete situation of opposed and conflicting social groups.

The poor remind the Church that to love does not mean simply to react with good will to reality as given; it means rather to recreate, to make new the situation of human beings by taking into account the concrete causes of the dehumanization by which reality becomes inhuman. It means making new those who have been dehumanized as passive objects of oppression by restoring their dignity and hope and placing them in humane living conditions. It means making new those who have been dehumanized by being active agents of oppression by requiring of them the conversion that will restore to them their lost dignity.

The poor insist on giving concrete names to the practice of love. The concrete situation of the poor renders intolerable mere declarations of principle regarding Christian love. Throughout history love for the poor has taken the form of a love that helps and promotes. Now it must take the form of a structural love, that is, a love that becomes justice and renews the structure of society.

The poor give love its urgency. Love is not just a commandment; it is not even the greatest of the commandments simply because Christ said so. If love were only a commandment it would retain an element of arbitrariness. Love is rather a conformity to the demands of reality, a conformity that is marked by urgency. The poor are the historical mediation of Paul's cry: "The love of Christ impels us" (2 Cor 5:14 NAB). This urgency explains the two characteristic traits of Christian love: its effectiveness and its gratuitousness. Because the purpose is to save those who have no salvation, a loving intention is not enough nor are the means history shows to be limited and inadequate. The need is for an effective love that makes use of the practical and ideological means that will make justice a reality. And because the situation of the poor is desperate, love must be gratuitous, that is, more ready to give than to receive; it must not count the cost even if this be the surrender of life itself.

The poor give a concrete name to sin. By their very presence and with dreadful simplicity they remind the Church that sin is what kills human beings. They know the kind of death sin causes and what the methods of killing are. They know what it means to confront sin and what the consequences of the confrontation are.

Against this background it is easy to see what the sin and holiness of the Church are. The basic sin of the Church is to participate in the sin of the world and to make this sin possible and effective. In this sense the Church is sinful: it has connived with the sin of the world; not infrequently it has even justified this sin. Karl Rahner's profound reflections on how the Church is sinful and how this sinfulness is not simply a matter of there being sinners in the Church are eminently validated by the participation of the Church in the sin of the world.

What constitutes the essential holiness of the Church is also clear. The first component of this holiness is the Church's liberating and re-creative mission, its promotion of justice and integral liberation.

In its activity the Church becomes holy or sinful. The Church of the poor offers the Christian model of action that befits God's closeness to the world and his judgment on it. This model is none other than that provided by the Servant of Yahweh. The holiness of the church of the poor is the holiness of the Servant, who begins by seeking justice and right for the nations. In so doing he takes upon himself the sin of the world thereby taking it away and replacing it with justice.

By serving as the Servant did, the Church acquires Christian holiness. It restores love as the form of holiness, and this according to the two basic aspects of love: the effectiveness of love as liberating and the gratuitousness of love in the form of martyrdom. Simple though it may sound, the Church of the poor is the church that restores the fundamental gospel truth: no one has greater love than those who give their life for the brethren. All love and holiness is to be understood by analogy with this supreme giving.

The Church of the poor sees holiness as a matter of saving the world as the Servant did and as Jesus did, not by an exercise of power but from below: through poverty and solidarity with the poor, their cause and destiny, their persecution and martyrdom. The Church thus recovers the deepest dimension of the holiness of Jesus, namely, his kenosis or self-emptying. If the Church of the poor succeeds in doing this—and to see that it does we need only recall the thousands of Latin American Christians who have been threatened, persecuted, slandered, imprisoned, tortured and murdered—it is because the poor compel it to do so. The holiness of the Church and the kenotic dimension of this holiness are not in the intention of stooping in to save the world, but in the objective, structural exigency that the poor represent. To opt for the poor is automatically to opt for the form of holiness proper to the Servant. The two choices authenticate each other.

I believe that the Church of the poor is living the "holiness in poverty" of which Moltmann speaks. In the real order and not simply in the conceptual interrelation between "holiness" and "poverty," poverty and impoverishment are the structural channels of holiness, and holiness cannot come into existence except through these channels. At the same time, Küng's abstract statement about the holiness of God being his separation from the profane is also being verified. The ineffable transcendence of God is manifested in the crucified God. Those who abide faithfully at the feet of this crucified God are really separated from the profane world; they are truly holy.

The Church of the poor therefore says in a definitive way that the church does not know a priori what holiness is or what specific means exist for the sanctification of the Church. It only knows that if it remains faithful to the suffering of the world and tries to transform this suffering into resurrection, then it does all it can and must do and it is in conformity with the deepest reality of God. This is *the* means of holiness, in light of which all other traditional means of holiness find their importance: sacraments, asceticism, virtues. However the reverse is not so.

The fact that the holiness of the Church proves it is true does not mean that a Church yields fruits of holiness comparable to those produced by other Churches or forms of Churchly existence. The fact that the true Church is holy means rather that only by being holy does the Church exist. If this holiness is lacking, the Church is not only not true, it is not a Church at all. Holiness serves to distinguish not so much between true Churches and false Churches as between various degrees of realization of the Church. The Church is "more" true according as it is "more" holy, whatever be its doctrinal structures and confession. I believe therefore that the Church of the poor is truer because in it the holiness of the Servant of Yahweh is found more fully and more perfectly.

The holy Church, then, is the Church that takes shape in history after the manner of Jesus, in a particular situation and among a certain group of people whom it tries to save. The Church follows the way of Jesus: a way of solidarity and brotherhood, a way of controversy and conflict with power. Above all the Church lives the paschal mystery of Jesus. The Church dies when the poor within it and the poor who are in solidarity with it are killed by those in power; it dies when it is ignored and attacked. The Church constantly experiences resurrection because death does not do away with hope, and danger does not paralyze the practice of love. The Church of the poor is today a martyr Church that is repeating the life and "passage" of Jesus.

The Catholicity of the Church of the Poor

The term *catholic* hardly appears in the New Testament. It came to mean *universal* (without polemical overtones). In the third century, *catholic* took on a distinctive, polemical connotation: they are "catholic" who are united to the universal Church and not sepa-

rated from it by heresy. With the spread of the Church throughout the world its catholicity took on a positive sense: the essence
of the one Church was concretized in the local Churches. At the
same time the problem of the relation of the local Churches to the
universal Church arose. Consequently, catholicity as a mark of
the true Church came to mean that local Churches stood in a correct relation to the universal Church, that the local Church
was properly integrated into the Catholic universal Church. It
meant the correct location of the Church within the plurality
of Christian Churches and within the universal human community.

Hans Küng emphasizes that catholicity does not exclude but
rather calls for the establishment of different local Churches.
Sociocultural plurality is a sign of catholicity (*The Church*, 304).
He stresses the point that these local Churches are true Churches
"inasmuch as they are the manifestation, the representation, the
realization of the one *entire,* all-embracing, universal Church, of
the Church as a whole. While the individual local Church is *an*
entire Church, it is not *the* entire Church" (300).

For Moltmann the catholicity of the Church means universality,
but with two important qualifications. The first is that the Church
as catholic is related to the whole of the "world" (*The Church in
the Power of the Spirit*, 348). The second, which is extremely important for us here, is that the universality implied in catholicity is
not achieved except through partisanship (350–51).

> But because not all are "people" in the same way, as far as their
> means, rights and freedom to live are concerned, the fellowship
> in which all are to see the glory of God "together" is created
> through the choosing of the humble and through judgment on
> the violent. This form of partisanship does not destroy Christian
> universalism, nor does it deny God's love for all [human beings];
> it is the historical form of universal love in a world in which
> people oppress and hate each other. . . . Universality and parti-
> sanship are not opposites when they are historically intertwined
> in this way. The church is related to the whole and is catholic
> insofar as, in the fragmentation of the whole, it primarily seeks
> and restores to favor the lost, the rejected and the oppressed
> (351–52).

I cite this lengthy passage from Moltmann because it explains what is happening in the Church of the poor. Through this partisanship toward the poor the Church in Latin America is discovering simultaneously its "local" character and its "universal" dimension, both of which were veiled in the abstract universalism that was preached in the past.

At the level of the "local" Church the poor have made possible the discovery of the originality and specificity of the Latin American Church. In theory this discovery might have been made in some other way: through the culture-bound ideas that differentiate the Latin American Church from other Churches, or through heresies and schisms. The cultural dimension would not have been capable *by itself* of shaping the Latin American Church unless it were grafted on to a much more comprehensive reality, the whole world of poverty, and there have been no heresies or schisms.

There is a good deal of evidence to prove that the Church in Latin America is becoming an authentic "local" Church and not simply an appendage or prolongation of the Churches of the parent countries. This development is a result of the Church's option for the poor.

The Latin American Church is regaining its historical identity and consciousness by recognizing itself not in some event of the past, but rather in those deeds and personalities of the past (significant here are Bartolomé de las Casas and the role of the bishop as "Protector of the Indians") which made the Church of that time a Church of the poor. This selectivity of historical consciousness shows that the present-day Church has a self-awareness that causes it to reread the history of the Church from the standpoint of the poor. The very fact that it has this self-awareness and exercises this kind of historical selectivity is itself the doing of the poor. The poor concretely embody the principle that gives rise to the self-awareness of the Latin American Church as a local Church.[28]

This Church is developing its own type of theology, the theology of liberation, and doing so with unparalleled originality and power. We must keep our eyes on what is essential. This theology is indeed proclaiming liberation and remembering captivity; it is rediscovering what is best in the religious soul of the people and is seeking new forms; its concern is to be for the poor and to share their lot. What is central in this theology, what gives it its reason for existence is the breakthrough of the poor in the Church. The poor are not theologians, but they are the ultimate source of any originality the theology of liberation may have.[29]

For the first time in many centuries the Latin American Church is exercising a teaching office. Many and diverse are the episcopal voices being heard on the continent. If the bishops are no longer content to repeat the universal magisterium or to make superficial applications of some of its conclusions without concretizing the Church's teaching in a creative way, the reason is that they have heard the voices of the poor, have tried to find solutions to their problems, and have gone to their defense. The poor are the ones responsible for the originality of so many of the pastoral letters now being written in Latin America. The Medellín Conference—the most important symbol of the new magisterium—was possible not simply because of Vatican II. Vatican II was indeed a condition for Medellín, but the real efficient cause of that Conference is to be found in the poor. "It is the viewpoint of the poor that gives Medellín its character and originality, whatever may have been its inevitable lacunae and shortcomings."[30]

The new historical consciousness, the new theology, and the new magisterium are expressions of something basic: the Latin American people themselves have become conscious of being the Church, without on that account ceasing to be Latin American but, on the contrary, becoming more fully and deeply Latin American. For the first time in many centuries, being Latin American and being the Church have become one and the same thing. For the first time it is possible to be a Christian in Latin America without borrowing one's ecclesiality from other Churches. For the first time a truly *local* Church exists in Latin America. The reason is the breakthrough of the poor in the Church.

Through its consciousness of being a local Church, the Church understands what universality and catholicity mean. Once again this understanding comes about because of the poor. The grasp of catholicity and universality is apparent in a negative way in that the Latin American Church does not seek to translate its consciousness of being a local Church into any kind of schism or heresy in relation to the other Churches.[31] It is apparent in a positive way in that the Latin American Church's rediscovery of itself as the Church of the poor makes it see itself as part of a larger Church that is living in the same kind of poverty and captivity and feels the same longing for liberation, though the longing may take different forms in other latitudes and seek different solutions. As a Church of the poor the Latin American Church feels part of the Third World Church in Asia, Africa, and Third World enclaves within affluent worlds. This perspective of a universal Church of the poor is the starting point for the Latin American Church's understanding of catholicity.

Thus the Church in Latin America is recovering the "catholic" meaning of the words at the beginning of Vatican II's *Constitution on the Church:* "By her relationship with Christ, the Church is a kind of sacrament or sign of intimate union with God, and of *the unity of all mankind.*" [32] But the Church of the poor endeavors to give concrete and historical form to the meaning of "all mankind." "Mankind" is made up of those sharing the same human essence. This fact, though true, is abstract. For the majority of humankind to be human is to be poor. At the historical level, then, the Church of the poor is more a sacrament of the unity of the human race than other forms of Churchly existence are.

At a basic level it is possible to understand and make real the *oikumene* that is the universal Church if we take poverty and not abstract humanness as our starting point. The Church of the poor offers a twofold model for the building up of catholicity: (1) the understanding of catholicity from the periphery, that is, from the Third World; and (2) the understanding of catholicity as a process whereby various local Churches bear one another's burdens.

From a theological point of view, as well as from a historical point of view, the thing that can unify and is now unifying the local Churches of the entire world is the resolute service of the poor. This service must be offered, of course, in the sociological, cultural, economic, and political conditions peculiar to the Churches in the various parts of the world, but when this service is given there is catholicity. I need only mention the close relations that spring up between countries of the Third World and countries of the First World when together they defend the rights of the poor, denounce repression, and collaborate ideologically in efforts at liberation.

In this context Churches of the Third World are bringing their faith and life to the Churches of the First World for the first time in many centuries. Third World Churches are gladly accepting many

First World Churches as a source of inspiration and not as something imposed on them. A catholicity based on the poor takes the form of mutual help, mutual inspiration, mutual enrichment. This new approach is undermining the traditional concept of catholicity as the epiphany and manifestation in divergent forms of the "one" Church in its various parts. It marks a recovery of the Pauline intuition of catholicity as built up through the sharing by the Churches of one another's burdens.[33]

The paradox is that the Church of the poor in Latin America has discovered at one and the same time its local character and its universal character. It has discovered that catholicity is not simply universalism nor the concrete application of universal principles but rather mutual responsibility within the Church. It is the mutual bearing of burdens within the Church and the active cooperation of each as it gives what it has to offer to the building of the universal Church. The Church in Latin America is beginning to understand which things have been authentic in the influence of other, foreign Churches on it and which have represented an antichristian imposition. It is also beginning to understand what it can and should contribute to the faith of the other Churches, not by way of imposition but by way of urgent pressure on them to become aware of the poor and take action on their behalf. In this way the Latin American Church is coming to understand its localness, its catholicity, and the interrelation of the two.

What I have been saying of catholicity within the "Catholic" Church applies as well to relations with the Protestant Churches[34] and with groups of people representing other religions and ideologies. The partisanship I spoke of earlier leads to Christian solidarity across Church lines, to authentic human solidarity. Wherever the poor make their presence felt "locally" and the decision is made to side with them, Christian and human groups recover their own identity and open themselves to the fact of universal poverty and the need for universal liberation.

Ecclesial catholicity, like everything authentically Christian, adopts a partisan point of view in conformity with a God who is greater but who is also lesser; a God who is for all but whose Spirit is in the poor; a God who wants to reach all, directly but through his privileged ones, the poor; a God who wants to raise up all through his hidden presence in the cross and death of the oppressed.

Paul is right to emphasize the fact that we have but one God, one Lord, and one Spirit (Eph. 4:4–6). This unity must govern the universal Church and find varied expression in the local Churches. The Church of the poor shows us what this unity must accomplish, where it must be embodied, and what choices must be made if it is to become a reality. This same passage from Paul contains the resolution of the difficulties. The Christ who ascended above the heavens in order that he might fill all things, the Christ who gave a variety of charisms so that we might all attain to the "unity" of faith (Eph. 4:10–13), is identical with the Christ who had previously "descended into the lower parts of the earth" (Eph. 4:9). This is catholicity from below, a catholicity that takes sides, a catholicity based on the poor.[35]

The Apostolicity of the Church of the Poor

To say that the true Church is "apostolic" is to say two different but related things. The first is that the Church must go back to the apostles, that is, back to the origin of the faith, "origin" here having a chronological sense. The second is that the present-day Church must retain its apostolic structure, that is, it must be sent, it must be missionary.

Hans Küng has correctly posed the problem of the Church's apostolicity. "The Church is founded on this apostolic witness and ministry, which is older than the Church itself" (*The Church,* 353). Three important points are contained in this statement. The first is that the apostles are logically prior to the Church; they are its foundation. "An apostle is a messenger of another. . . . The apostle is not simply the messenger of a community, but has been appointed by Christ" (351). Apostolicity therefore points to something prior to the established Church both chronologically (in the beginning) and logically (even today).

The second point is that the testimony of the first apostles is "the original, fundamental testimony of Jesus Christ, valid for all time; being unique, it cannot be replaced or made void by any later testimony" (355). The apostolicity of the Church is, therefore, simply the way in which the Church is connected with its real source, Jesus of Nazareth, through those who were his privileged witnesses at the beginning.

The third point is that apostolicity continues to be an essential dimension of the Church. "The apostles are dead; there are no new apostles. But the *apostolic mission* remains" (355). "The apostolic Church least of all can be an end in itself. Everything the Church does must be directed towards fulfilling its apostolic mission to the outside world; it must minister to the world and to mankind. To be a Church and to have a mission are not two separate things" (358).

Moltmann offers basically the same view of apostolicity, although he formulates the present meaning of apostolicity in forceful terms. "What we must learn is not that the church 'has' a mission, but the very reverse: that the mission of Christ creates its own church. Mission does not come from the church; it is from mission and in the light of mission that the church has to be understood" (*The Church in the Power of the Spirit*, 10). Because of the existence of this Christian mission, Moltmann stresses a basic characteristic of the Church as apostolic: "The apostolate in the world is never undisputed. . . . Participation in the apostolic mission of Christ therefore leads inescapably into *tribulation, contradiction and suffering*" (361).

The Church of the poor highlights the apostolicity of the Church, both in the first sense of making clearer the origin of the faith (I shall not dwell on this point here) and in the second sense, affirming that the Church has its existence through the apostolate. The apostolate is logically prior to the Church as an institution and to any of the Church's structures. Even if these structures precede the apostolate in time, only the apostolate concretizes them in a Christian way and supplies the reason for their existence. In saying this I am only repeating the profound insight of the *Apostolic Exhortation on Evangelization in the Modern World (Evangelii nuntiandi):* "The task of evangelization is to be regarded as the Church's specific grace and calling and the activity most expressive of her real nature. The Church exists in order to evangelize" (no. 14). Moreover, the Church living within the community—praying, listening to the word, practicing brotherly and sisterly love, sharing bread—"cannot attain its full meaning and vitality unless it issues in witness, stirs wonder and leads to conversion, and finds expression in the preaching and proclamation of the gospel" (15).[36]

I believe that the Church of the poor is an authentically missionary Church dedicated to evangelization. Mission is much more important now than in the past; it has changed the very being of the Church. The Church is carrying out its mission at the levels called for in *Evangelii nuntiandi*, as we shall see. But the important point here is that all this has happened because the Church has become the Church of the poor and not because it has arbitrarily decided to dedicate itself "more fully" to mission. Once again, the poor have brought about a spectacular change whereby the Church has become truly "apostolic."

What Gustavo Gutiérrez said about the historical origin of the theology of liberation is also true for the Church of the poor. "From the beginning, the theology of liberation posited that the first act is involvement in the liberation process, and that theology comes afterward, as a second act."[37] Further, it became clear that "the poor appeared within this theology as the key to an understanding of the meaning of liberation and of the meaning of the revelation of a liberating God. . . . It is not enough to say that praxis is the first act. One must take into consideration the historical subject of this praxis—those who until now have been the absent ones of history."[38]

It is no accident that the Church should become missionary and apostolic and should give priority to the apostolate over itself as an institution. This has come about to the extent that the poor have demanded and carried it out. Let us examine briefly the way in which the characteristics of evangelization as described in *Evangelii nuntiandi* have been realized and concretized by the poor.[39]

The first element in the Church's mission is the proclamation of the Good News, the proclamation of God's coming kingdom, which we know is not identical with the Church. This last statement is generally accepted and is to be found in every updated manual of theology. Nonetheless this basic truth is generally not operative. It is not enough simply to remind ourselves that Church and kingdom of God are not equivalent. Nor is it enough to appeal to the words of Scripture. If this truth is to become operative we must find out where it can be clearly seen.

It is the poor, the oppressed majorities, who make the non-equivalence clear. As long as these majorities exist in the world, the kingdom of God has obviously not come, and no Church can be presumptuous enough to identify itself with the kingdom. Moreover, as long as the poor have not regained their dignity, even in the

Church, then no Church will ever be a sacrament of the kingdom of God, much less the reality of the kingdom.

The first contribution of the poor to the mission of the Church is to show at the historical level the difference between the historical reality and the proclamation of the Good News, to give a first description, even if a negative one, of the Good News itself, and to require in an objective way that the Church ground itself in this proclamation. The poor make it clear that the Church must be at the service of the proclamation of the Good News.

Because the proclamation of the kingdom has been forced upon the Church by the poor, the mission of the Church includes another aspect which *Evangelii nuntiandi* describes as "the preaching of the mystery of iniquity" (28). This means that in the presence of the poor the proclamation of the Good News must be accompanied by a denunciation. The proclamation is issued in a world of sin. In a neutral world the only need would be to proclaim the existence of a better hope. Consequently the mission of the Church is to proclaim not only beatitudes but also curses; its mission is not only to proclaim the Good News but to unmask what passes itself off as good news but is in fact a set of sinful structures.

In addition to proclaiming a hope, the Church must stress the fact as the first apostles did that "you have put the just man to death" (cf. Acts 2:23). Death points not simply to the absence of the Good News but to its negation and destruction, which is what in fact happens.

The testimony given by the apostle's own life, which is an integral part of the Church's mission, does not consist in an abstract holiness but in a holiness arising from mission. "The proclamation of this liberating love in a society scarred by injustice and the exploitation of one social class by another will transform this 'emergent history' into something challenging and conflictual."[40] The apostolate will therefore be accompanied, as Moltmann says, by conflict and persecution. This will happen over and over because the mission is a mission to the poor. "The poor" and "persecution" go together in history. For this reason the basic testimony of a Church of the poor will consist in remaining with the poor despite persecution. The basic testimony of the apostle's life takes the form of courage in persecution, a readiness to surrender life itself. History will thus repeat what tradition tells us about the first apostles:

not only were they witnesses to Jesus; they were also martyrs to their apostolate.

The mission of the Church of the poor consists in bringing to pass what is proclaimed, in making the Good News become a Good Reality. This important advance in the idea of evangelization is due to an understanding of the privileged addressees of the Church's mission. Joachim Jeremias says that although the proclamation of the kingdom is fundamental for Jesus it does not describe the most basic characteristic of mission. This essential characteristic is that "the reign of God belongs to the poor alone."[41]

But when the "poor" are understood after the manner of Isaiah and the synoptic gospels, they determine the concrete content of this *eu-aggelion*. Evangelization includes both the proclamation of the Good News and the concrete application of the message proclaimed. "This news will be *good* only to the extent that the liberation of the oppressed becomes a reality."[42] Consequently, "material liberation from every form of oppression that is the result of injustice belongs to the biblical message as an essential religious value."[43] The Church's mission consists in making liberation a reality, precisely because the message is addressed to the poor.[44]

Finally—and this I regard as basic—the poor bring to the accomplishment of mission something analogous to, though not identical with, what the first apostles brought. The apostles are logically prior to the establishment of the Church because they are the witnesses sent forth by Christ. They are the evangelizers par excellence. The first apostolate cannot be repeated in a historical sense. This does not answer the question as to who in our day (albeit in a way different from that of the first apostles) enjoys a logical priority in regard to the ongoing establishment of the Church.

A first, and true, answer to the question is that the bishops, who as a body are the successors of the apostles, have the ministry of constantly creating the Church anew. This formally true answer does not specify the sense in which they are sent today by Christ. The bishops are the successors of the apostles in the sense that they are a sacramental expression of an entire Church, which, as an entire Church, is also in our day a witness to Christ and sent by him.

This witnessing and sending occur when the entire Church becomes a Church of the poor. If the poor are the privileged recipients of the Good News, then there is a transcendental correlation be-

tween the Good News and the poor. It is therefore useless to look
for the content of this Good News without reference to the poor.
Whenever the Church has taken the poor seriously it has become
apostolic. The poor set the process of evangelization in motion.
When the Church directs itself to them in its mission, paradoxically
they in turn evangelize the Church and establish it. In this profound
and more than poetic sense we must understand the often heard
statement: "The poor evangelize the Church." In an analogous
sense, they continue the role of pillars of the Church that the first
apostles had before them. They are not witnesses to but a sacrament of Christ who through them continues to send (in the form of
a demand) the entire Church on its mission of proclaiming the
kingdom and making it real.

"Evangelization will be genuinely liberating only when it is the
poor themselves who become the bearers of the message, the actual
agents of evangelization," says Gustavo Gutiérrez.[45] For the sake
of greater conceptual accuracy perhaps we ought to say that the
Church will be truly apostolic and will carry out its mission in a
Christian way when the poor turn the Church into a Church of the
poor. The entire Church will then be the successor of the apostles,
while allowing for functional differences within itself. It will be a
Church in the measure in which it constantly becomes so through
its mission. And it is the poor who will give this mission a Christian
direction.

The Church of the Poor as the True Church

This brief analysis of the marks of the true Church has been
made with the positive and polemical aim of showing that the
Church of the poor is really a Church and that the characteristic
marks of the Church are best realized in it. But in showing this we
have advanced very little in posing the basic problem of the
Church.

Applying terminology that is customary in christology we may
say that the Church of faith and the Church of history are not
identical. The Church can be described "in the light of faith" as
"people of God," body "of Christ" and temple "of the Spirit."
But this same Church must be described "in the light of history,"
that is, in terms of historical accomplishments and values that best

point to the content of what is said in the light of faith.

The marks of the Church are expressions of the historical truth about the Church and thus indirectly of its correspondence to the Church of faith. These historical marks are verified in the Church of the poor. This Church has also made these marks concrete[46] and hierarchical[47] in such a way that they can be criteria of the true Church of history.

The concretization does not consist in applying these marks first and foremost to the structures and mechanisms of the Church, for these, though necessary, do not manifest the substance of the Church.[48] Uniformity in the formulation of the faith, the institutional mechanisms for maintaining unity, the sacraments as vehicles of holiness—all these, though important in themselves, represent a second, deeper stage that surfaces only when we bring in "Christ," "God," and the "Spirit." I have endeavored by my analysis to relate the marks of the Church to that basic ecclesiality, to the level at which Christ, God, and the Spirit are actively engaged. It is for this reason, and not simply as a matter of interest, that I made brief mention of Küng and Moltmann, who have attempted, each in his own way, to rescue the marks of the Church from the triviality to which the usual theology has condemned them.

The Church of the poor introduces the poor as the ultimate mediation of the transcendental reality of the Church, the Church of faith; thereby it concretizes this ultimate reality in a Christian way. It also concretizes the historical marks of the Church in a Christian way. The four marks are criteria of verification, and in this sense a posteriori criteria, of a particular Church. At a deeper level these four marks are ways in which the Church is continually established. In this sense they are a priori criteria for the establishment of the true Church.

This is the sequence: the poor constitute the true Church, and then, once the Church is established, the four marks, concretized in terms of the poor, verify it. Establishment and verification are basically one and the same thing. We have not then *proved* anything in a sense that would require the existence of universal criteria already valid in themselves and independent of the concrete reality of the various forms of Churchly existence. What I have tried to *show* is that the Church of the poor is most like the Church that is a continuation of Jesus.[49] No one, therefore, is obliged to accept my argument unless he or she has already accepted the idea that the Church of the poor is in our day the historical form of the Church of Jesus. However, as I said earlier in reflecting on the epistemology of the Church of the poor, I regard such an acceptance as possible only to one who is already within this Church.

I have presented here a Church that is structured by a desire to live today in accordance with the gift of God that is present in the crucified Jesus and the crucified human beings of history; a Church set apart from other forms of Church that are based, consciously or unconsciously, on an assimilation of this world and its powers. At this ultimate level I have endeavored to explain the Church of the poor, and thus show the structural difference between the *two* fundamental historical forms seen today in the light of the ultimate criterion just mentioned.

> The real and fundamental problem is not to be seen in a contrast between a Church structured with a historical body of its own and an unstructured, spiritual Church. It is between a Church which, as a social and political power, connives with other social and political powers and this same Church which, as the people of God who are unified by the Spirit and have become a historical body, is directly at the service of God's reign: a Church that follows Jesus.
>
> In this Church that follows Jesus there are bishops, perhaps episcopal conferences, and even a general conference of bishops such as met at Medellín. There are religious congregations, parishes, pastoral letters, and so on. This Church has always been alive and has contributed and is now contributing to the liberation of the oppressed.
>
> But there is the other aspect of the Church: the worldly, secular Church that conforms to the powers and dynamism of a world of sin. This Church lives on side by side with the people of God. When the institutional Church is rejected, it is this worldly Church that is being rejected, and rightly so.[50]

When we say that the Church of the poor is the true Church we are not speaking of "another" Church alongside the Catholic Church or the various Protestant Churches. Nor are we saying that where this Church of the poor exists it exists in a pure form, uncontaminated by sin and error, nor that it is coextensive with the Church of faith. What we are saying is that the Church of the poor is in its structure the true way of being a Church in Jesus; that it provides the structural means of approximating ever more closely to the Church of faith; and that it is more perfectly the historical sacrament of liberation.[51]

If all this is the case and if it is happening in Latin America, it is because Christ has willed to show himself not in any place whatsoever, nor even in the structure, good in principle, which he established, but in the poor. We must describe this new phenomenon of the Church of the poor as representing on the one hand a conversion of the historical Church and on the other its resurrection.

5

The Experience of God in the Church of the Poor

In this chapter I wish to honor the theological work of Karl Rahner. I have chosen a theme that has been present in his work from the very beginning: the theme of God. As Rahner himself declared, Christianity basically proposes only one thing: ". . . that the great Mystery remains eternally a mystery."[1] If some have claimed, often by way of criticism, that Rahner's theological work is anthropological in character, it is no less true that his anthropology is also deeply theo-logical: "Whether he is consciously aware of it or not, whether he is open to this truth or suppresses it, man's whole spiritual and intellectual existence is orientated towards a holy mystery which is the basis of his being. . . . It is our most fundamental, most natural condition, but for that very reason it is also the most hidden and least regarded reality. . . . We call this God."[2]

Rahner has always insisted that this radically theo-logical point of departure is the only one that can do justice to any type of reflection on the ultimate nature of Christian faith. Consequently, he has cautioned against beginning the theological task with too hasty a christological and *a fortiori* ecclesiological reduction.[3] Yet, at the same time, he has claimed that the experience of God as absolute mystery is always a historical experience, that is, it can be experienced only through an experience of that which is categorically historical. Thus, the experience of the mystery of God, of the whence and whither of transcendence, can take place only within specific historical experiences.[4]

In this chapter I wish to describe the experience of God from the perspective of a specific historical reality which I shall call "the Church of the poor." That is, I wish to describe how the mystery of God is experienced as mystery in this relatively concrete and historically specific channel, a channel that can be clearly differentiated from other such channels. In so doing I believe that the Church of Latin America and Latin American theology can contribute directly to the task of theological reflection on the mystery of God. It is precisely this type of reflection that many superficial critiques and evaluations would argue is missing from Latin American theology, given the latter's supposed preference for the historical efficacy of liberation rather than for the mysterious or numinous element of the faith.[5]

Before proceeding to elaborate the theme in question, I wish to make certain preliminary observations that will be of help in understanding the meaning and direction of this study:

1. When I speak of "the experience of God" or of "the Church of the poor," I do not pretend to shed light directly on these concepts or on this mutual congruence. Nor is it my intention to demonstrate thereby the reasonableness of faith or, in the words of Rahner, "to give people confidence . . . that they can believe with intellectual honesty."[6] My goal is simply to show that such an experience of God does exist—and this in itself may prove to be a valuable pastoral aid.

2. I take it for granted that the transcendental experience of God is made concrete in specific historical channels. Thus, although theoretically one could give a generic description of the universal experience of the mystery of God, such an experience, given its concrete character, will always be conditioned by and made possible only within specific historical channels. More specifically, I wish to affirm that it makes quite a bit of difference whether one believes in God within an ecclesial configuration or outside of one, or even within one particular historical configuration of the Church, such as the Church of the poor, or another such configuration. Moreover, the difference arises not only because of the different doctrines of God that are formulated in the various ecclesial channels, but also because of the concrete historical nature of the channels themselves.

3. I also take it for granted that one can experience God within the Church of the poor and that one can do so as mystery, that is, as an experience that goes beyond the concrete channel itself. I also believe that in this concrete channel of the Church of the poor one can recover certain fundamental Christian doctrines of the experience of God that, from a historical point of view, have not been as palpably present in other ecclesial channels.

4. When I speak of "the experience of God" in "the Church of the poor," I wish to emphasize the fact that individual believers cannot exclude, even in their own transcendental experience of God, their dependence on other human beings, on their own specific historical situation, and on the experiences of God that these others have. It is not the same to believe in God as an individual as it is to believe in God as a member of a community. Indeed one could even argue whether the former option is a possibility at all, given the social nature—itself transcendental—of human beings. Be that as it may, however, I do wish to emphasize here the latter option: the importance of the ecclesial reality as a social and communitarian reality for the experience of God.

5. I take it for granted as well that the faith of the individual believer is colored not only by the ecclesial reality as a communitarian reality but also by the concrete characteristics of that same reality. More specifically, I take it for granted that a real and historical configuration of the Church as the Church "of the poor" will influence directly the life of the individual believer. Further, such a configuration will affect not only the most obvious levels of that individual's life, for example, those of liturgy and ethical praxis, but also the theo-logical level of the experience of God.

6. In what follows, I will describe the experience of God in the Church of the poor, first of all, from a descriptive and expository point of view rather than from a directly polemical or apologetic one. I am, therefore, quite aware that this study represents a description of ecclesial life within a specific time and situation, namely, that of various churches in Latin America today. Strictly speaking, this description does not pretend to be universal in character. Yet if the description should yield more accurately, from a historical point of view, that which is essential to the experience of God according to revelation, then the description becomes to a certain extent normative as well as indirectly polemical or apologetic. Further, one would also have to affirm that one could find today

within the Church of the poor a "better"—though by no means unique—channel for the experience of God.

If it is correct to say that both the transcendental nature of the experience of God and the eschatological reservation prevent one from singling out a unique and exclusive locus for the experience of God, it is also true that they do not demand that all possible historical loci for such an experience be considered to have the same validity. If one takes all of revelation into account, such a minimalist position demands and justifies a search for the "most adequate" locus for the experience of God. That which comes at the end does not relativize all that precedes; rather, it demands a proper subordination or hierarchy.

7. Whatever is said here concerning the experience of God in the Church of the poor does not presuppose or give way to triumphalism or mechanicalism. I speak of the Church of the poor as a structural channel for the experience of God. As such, I do not claim that all individuals within that Church share the same profound experience of God, nor is it my claim that Christian faith within that Church is beyond all dangers, as if completely protected by life insurance and no longer borne in fragile vessels made of clay. I do wish to affirm the structural importance of the Church of the poor for the individual believer's experience of God. I have deliberately chosen to reflect on that structure because I believe that therein one does find an experience of God of such substance that is not only important, but also, in its character as channel, normative.

8. Finally, I wish to affirm that whatever is to be considered normative in the Church of the poor is ultimately, but not exclusively, to be attributed to a very specific understanding of Jesus Christ and of christology. The fundamental goal of this christology is to reevaluate the historical Jesus, specifically his status as Son of God, that is, as the one who is historically related to the Father and dependent on his own historical situation.[7] Briefly stated, the fundamental goal is to reevaluate Jesus' *own* faith: to let Jesus become not only the primary content of our faith, but also a structural model for that faith, that is, to let him emerge "as extraordinary believer,"[8] the one who first lived the fullness of faith (Heb. 12:2).

The second goal of this christology presupposes that the radical historicity of Jesus demands that his own subjective experience of the Father be mediated through his concrete, historical life, through the actions and goals of that life. Therefore, it seeks to single out the more important and, from a historical point of view, the more firmly established aspects of Jesus' experience of the Father. Among these one would have to include his fundamental and foundational relationship to the kingdom of God as the mediator of that kingdom; his ministry toward the poor as the primary recipients of his message; his historical solidarity with the socially oppressed of his time; his total immersion in the historical conflicts occasioned by his mission; the persecution and death that he accepted as part of his own destiny and as logical and historical consequences of his own mission.

The third goal of this christology is to accept the fact that it is possible and necessary for the experience of God to relive these fundamental historical structures of Jesus' life. The possibility of reliving these structures is quite evident in Latin America, even though new mediations are always necessary. The need to relive these structures follows ultimately from one's own acceptance of Jesus' call to follow him. Furthermore, the intrinsic reasonableness of this call, given its character as call, cannot be analyzed or debated. Indeed if the call is not accepted as an essential part of one's own experience of God, then any further reference to Jesus as the historical revelation of the Son of God would have to be seriously questioned.

The Church of the poor claims no monopoly on the experience of God or on the understanding of Jesus, but it does believe that it can relive more adequately Jesus' original experience of God within its own channel.

THE IMPORTANCE OF THE ECCLESIAL CHANNEL OF "THE POOR" FOR THE EXPERIENCE OF GOD

When I speak here of "the Church of the poor," I refer to its primary historical constitution or to what one could call its first ecclesial substance. In what follows I select from that historically primary ecclesial reality only three elements that can shed light on the importance that a determined ecclesial reality has for the experience of God. These are: the communitarian nature of the experience of faith; the variety and complementarity of historical experiences within that communality; the importance of the active presence of the poor in the Church.

Historical Communality of Ecclesial Faith

From its very inception, the Church was to embody a double dimension of immanence and transcendence, of historical channel and experience of faith. This double dimension appears in pro-grammatic fashion in its first self-definitions: the Church as "the people of God," "the body of Christ," "the temple of the Spirit." That which one calls faith in God has been found to entail from the very beginning a double relationship. The first relationship is with its own direct object, namely, God, while the second is with the historical locus in which that object appears as an object of faith in correlation with that locus, that is to say, with whatever it is that is meant both historically and materially by such terms as "people," "body," and "temple."

If the importance of the locus in which the experience of God takes place is taken seriously, then, for example, whatever it is that is meant by the term "people" will have important consequences, not only at the level of administrative organization, liturgy, and ecclesial praxis, but also at a more profound theo-logical level. Further, these consequences flow not only—as is obvious—from the teachings *concerning* God that the members of this "people" receive from the revelation, the tradition, and the magisterium of the Church, but also from the very fact that being a "people" will influence directly the act of faith *in* God.

If that is the case, then the individual who has an experience of God should not be seen merely as an individual subject, but rather as an individual subject *in* the Church, *in* the people of God. Like-wise, that individual's experience of God will be dependent on and influenced by not only the object of his faith, but also the histori-cally concrete ecclesial reality in which it takes place.[9] Given the familiar ring of this terminology, this distinction may appear prima facie to be trivial, but it is extremely important. It is clear—as every form of existentialism and personalism has emphasized—that only the individual person and not a corporate structure can have an experience of God. Yet, at the same time, if the faith of that indi-vidual is to be ecclesially Christian, then it must of necessity be shared with others and open to the faith of these others in the Pauline sense of "bearing and being borne." One could even de-bate, given the transcendental character of the communality of the individual subject, whether at the philosophical level an experience of God can take place that is not essentially related to or dependent on the experience of God that others have. Be that as it may, at the ecclesial level the faith of the individual subject cannot properly be called faith unless it is both a witnessed faith (a faith that is shared with and actively oriented toward others) and a faith that needs witness (a faith that is influenced by and dependent on the faith of others). A properly ecclesial faith is, therefore, a faith that is experienced before "a great cloud of witnesses" (Heb. 12:1) and needs "the mutual encouragement of each other's faith" (Rom. 1: 12).

Consequently, at a very generic and formal level, the individual subject's experience of God must of necessity be open to the faith of others, and an important part of that experience of God is the individual's own awareness of the fact that he or she is dependent on and influenced by others in the experience of the mystery of God. In this profound sense faith is ecclesial by nature, and the adjective "ecclesial" is not to be understood from a doctrinal point of view—that is, as a presentation of teachings and doctrines concerning God—but rather as making explicit the essential communality of the individual subject, even at the level of the experience of God. In this way, one may speak radically of the Church as "the people" of God.

Variety and Complementarity of the Historical Experience of Faith

It should be clear from the preceding presentation that a simple multiplication of the individual subjects of a faith does not of itself establish the ecclesial nature of that faith. That is not the proper way to understand how this reality of being a "people" influences or determines the faith of the individual. It should be clear by now that the ecclesial character of the experience of faith refers to the different and complementary configurations signified by the term "people." From the very beginning the Church accepted a historical configuration of that term. In so doing it also accepted the different historical situations of its members as well as the different historical mediations of the experience of God.

Paul's declaration to the effect that "there is neither Jew nor Greek, free nor slave, male nor female" (Gal. 3:28) should not be seen as contradicting this fundamental point. If a particular theological reading of this study could conclude that therein the importance of the concrete historical situation for the experience of faith is relativized, a different theological reading of the same study—and specifically one that would pay close attention to the polemical undertones of that text—could very easily reach the opposite conclusion: even a Greek, or a slave, or a woman can be a mediation of faith. From its very beginnings it must be said that the Church never sought to abolish historical differences—indeed these cannot be abolished!—but rather to accept and incorporate them into its own self-definition as a "people."

Thus the Church accepted a diversity of cultures and of social configurations regardless of their minority or majority status. It accepted the diversity of abilities and of "charisma," of talents and contributions from different individuals and groups of individuals necessary for the constitution of a social body. It accepted the diversity of functions essential to any social organization. It accepted the historical deprivation and misery of many—indeed, of the majority—of its members as well as the spontaneous and related desire for redemption and liberation. Finally, it accepted the heartfelt urgency on the part of other members to dedicate themselves to that task of liberation.

It does not really matter to what extent the Church consciously accepted such a diversity into its own historical configuration or what theological reflections flowered from such an acceptance; what does matter is that the acceptance took place. The fact that one finds in the Church any members in different historical situations presupposes ipso facto that they have different historical experiences and that these experiences cannot be relativized by any subsequent theologizing, but must be shown to be mediations of faith. This means that the Church automatically accepts diversity and complementarity in the experience of God, an experience which, insofar as it is transcendental in nature, can be formally described as being universal to all human beings, but, insofar as it is concrete, depends on concrete historical configurations.

This diversity of experiences should give way to complementarity both for historical reasons, such as the social nature of a human being, and theological reasons, such as the mutual encouragement of faith. The historical situations and experiences of others as well as the way in which God is experienced within them will be extremely important for one's own experience of faith. For example, the experience of God that takes place in the midst of historical deprivation and is lived in situations of real and permanent misery will be quite different from the experience that urges others into the service of God. However, the deprivation of the former will turn the urgency to serve of the latter into a determined mediation of the experience of God. Similarly, the altruistic service of the latter will influence and modify the experience of God of the former, that is, of all who live in total misery. Yet another example: The experience of God that takes place among Church officials in positions of power, be they of an intellectual, administrative, or pastoral nature, will be quite different from the experience of the dispossessed. However, the faith of the latter can influence the service and the faith of the former, and this service in turn can influence the faith of the historically dispossessed.

This diversity of historical situations among the different members of the Church prevents the experience of the individual subject, even at the level of the experience of God, from ever becoming a purely individual experience. If one takes seriously the unlimited breadth of the mystery of God then this fact of diversity will not only be accepted, it will be positively received and valued. This multiplicity of experience constitutes in effect the only way to correspond asymptotically to the mystery of God. Because of this mystery, which of necessity belongs to God, the proper experience of God can take place only when there is an openness to the different historical experiences of others. It is in this sense that I refer to the importance of the diversity and complementarity of the different experiences and situations within the Church and to their importance for the individual's experience of God.

The Importance of the Poor in the Church for the Experience of God

The only reason that I have taken time out to recall something that is already well known is to prepare the way for a fundamental assertion: a specific Church will offer a specific historical channel for the experience of God by vigorously adopting the historical primary fact of the poor and by allowing that historically primary fact to become the center of its own ecclesial self-definition and mission. Such an emphasis on the importance of a historical fact, insofar as it is historical and free of any theoretical reflection, for the totality of the Church is nothing new either in principle or in fact. The Church has been historically organized, for example, on the basis of such facts as hierarchy or celibacy. As a result these facts of hierarchical power or celibate life have become historically primary facts on the basis of which both the totality of the Church and the hierarchical ordering of its values have been understood historically. For example, if one accepted the hierarchy of the Church as its primary ecclesial fact, then one would propose the use of authority and the demand for obedience as historical mediations for the experience of God. Similarly if one accepted the celibate way of life as the primary fact, then one would propose freedom for service and the aloneness of the person before the mystery of God as proper historical mediations.

What I wish to affirm above all is the importance of the adoption of what one could vaguely call "the world of the poor" as the primary and central fact within the Church, so that the Church itself may be called "the Church of the poor." In what follows I will begin a description of this Church by giving examples of what may not yet be properly called "the Church of the poor," even though one may find in these descriptions scattered elements of the proper definition.

First, the Church of the poor goes beyond what the Second Vatican Council understood and proposed by the term *the people of God*, even though the Council may have in effect prepared the way for the emergence of the Church of the poor by abandoning a very effective hierarchical conception of the Church, namely, a Church that was conceived and organized from the very top of a pyramidal structure of ecclesial power. The new description of the Church as "the people of God" helped to restore a fundamental historical and corporate reality to the Church, but that was the extent of the change. The Council, depspite its profound consideration of charisma, did not go beyond a theological democratization of the Church. It failed to find in that new description of the Church a center with sufficient historical strength to reorganize all Christian and ecclesial realities.[10]

Second, the Church of the poor goes beyond the image of a

Church that shows concern for the poor, even though such concern is desirable in itself and represents a fundamental dimension of the Church of the poor. Strictly speaking, however, such an interest in the poor remains an ethical, not an ecclesial, concern for the poor. A Church *for* the poor is not necessarily a Church *of* or *from* the poor. In such a Church, the poor would not yet constitute a historical principle for the configuration of the Church, even though they may very well be the principle recipients of the mission of that Church.

Third, the Church of the poor goes beyond the collectivity of all the poor and the oppressed, whether in the Church or outside of it, even if they are fully aware of their oppression and self-interests and thus constitute a very specific class within the Church. In principle, the Church of the poor does not emerge from a negation of other ecclesial elements in a social conflict, even though such a conflict may in effect exist.

The Church of the poor thus goes beyond these three descriptions—the Church as the universalistic, theologically democratic people of God; a Church with an ethical concern for the poor; a regional or class Church—even though elements from these descriptions may be found in the historical process of the Church of the poor and important channels for the experience of God may exist within them, for example, the experience of democracy and solidarity, the experience of conflict, and, to be sure, the ethical experience of service.

At this point, I should like to turn to a positive description of the Church of the poor.[11] The Church of the poor is a Church the social and historical basis of which is to be found among the poor. As such, it is a Church that has as its basis the majority of human beings, who both individually and collectively constitute the real poor not only because of their natural condition of poverty, but also because of their historical condition of impoverishment by others. It is these poor, therefore, that are said to constitute the very basis of the Church. Such a description shows how different the Latin American understanding of the phenomenon of "base communities" is from that of the developed nations. The developed nations take the essential characteristics of these communities to be the small number of their members and, by comparison with the institutional Church, judge them to have a greater degree of freedom and initiative for the Spirit of God.

The poverty that characterizes the poor of this Church can be concretely distinguished from the spiritual poverty that constitutes a basic openness to the spirit of God and from the metaphysical poverty that is correlative to and inherent in the limited condition of every human being. The final document of the Third Conference of Latin American Bishops (Puebla, Mexico) gives a vivid description of the poor from the point of view of this first social level:[12]

—the faces of young children, struck down by poverty before they are born, their chance for self-development blocked by irreparable mental and physical deficiencies; and of the vagrant children in our cities who are so often exploited, products of poverty and the moral disorganization of the family;

—the faces of young people, who are disoriented because they cannot find their place in society, and who are frustrated, particularly in marginal rural and urban areas, by the lack of opportunity to obtain training and work;

—the faces of the indigenous peoples, and frequently of the Afro-Americans as well; living marginalized lives in inhuman situations, they can be considered the poorest of the poor;

—the faces of the peasants; as a social group, they live in exile almost everywhere on our continent, deprived of land, caught in a situation of internal and external dependence, and subjected to systems of commercialization that exploit them;

—the faces of laborers, who frequently are ill-paid and who have difficulty in organizing themselves and defending their rights;

—the faces of the underemployed and the unemployed, who are dismissed because of the harsh exigencies of economic crises, and often because of development models that subject workers and their families to cold economic calculations;

—the faces of marginalized and overcrowded urban dwellers, whose lack of material goods is matched by the ostentatious display of wealth by other segments of society;

—the faces of old people, who are growing more numerous every day, and who are frequently marginalized in a progress-oriented society that totally disregards people not engaged in production.[13]

The poor described above deserve preferential attention on the part of the Church in their own concrete historical situation and regardless of ". . . the moral or personal situation in which they find themselves."[14]

The poor within this Church become the hermeneutical principle for a primary concrete expression of important Christian concepts and realities.[15] Thus, for example, the notion of objective sin may be interpreted from this perspective as anything that brings death upon human beings and the children of God; the concept of Good News as that which is addressed to the poor as its privileged recipients[16] and thus forms a transcendental relationship with them; the first objective of the ethical praxis of the Church as the liberation of the poor through the establishment of justice and the decision to achieve this objective in active solidarity with them; the concept of a theology of history as one that is presented from the point of view of the poor, "from the underside of history."[17]

The Church of the poor, however, goes beyond an acceptance of the poor as the social basis of the Church or as the primary recipients of its mission. A true Church of the poor must look at poverty from the perspective of the beatitudes. They propose in effect a salvific kenosis, which in order to be salvific must be a kenosis. "Become poor as long as there is poverty in the world; identify yourselves with the poor."[18] The spiritual basis of the Church of the poor must include a voluntary acceptance of poverty, the adoption of an attitude of effective solidarity with the poor, and an acceptance of the persecution that results from the just nature of this solidarity. The Church of the poor represents, therefore, an attempt to find the ecclesial and Christian *spirit* of poverty, that is to say, to spiritualize poverty and misery and not simply to endure them as cruel facts of human existence. It must be emphasized, however, that this proposed spiritualization cannot be achieved by a mere desire to become poor. In order to be truly a sacrament of salvation, if salvation is understood as a real kenosis,[19] the Church must accept real poverty, must become poor itself in an act of solidarity with the poor, and must actively defend the causes of the poor. Poverty, powerlessness, and persecution constitute the real and material conditions for a Church in keeping with the will of God to arise and for the possibility of an experience of God within such an ecclesial channel to take place. If we take seriously the promise of the kingdom of God to the poor and the persecuted, then we must affirm that there is something inherent in poverty and persecution that directs human beings to the kingdom of God. As a result, the Church of the poor can provide a historical channel for an authentic experience of God, and it is the nature of this experience that I wish to pursue in the following section.

THE EXPERIENCE OF GOD IN THE CHURCH OF THE POOR

The mystery of God has been historically conveyed in many different ways by many different experiences, even though these experiences may be considered to be formally similar insofar as they are channels for that mystery. The sapiential, apocalyptic, prophetic, and existential tradition of both the Old and New Testaments testifies to this diversity. The absolute nature of the mystery of God does not prevent specific historical experiences from pointing to or conveying that mystery. Rahner, for example, emphasized the importance of three types of experiences for what he calls a searching christology: an appeal to absolute love for the neighbor; an appeal to readiness for death; an appeal to hope in the future.[20]

From the perspective of the Church of the poor, the unconditional rejection of scandalous poverty and the unconditional acceptance of salvific and liberating impoverishment may be said to constitute the fundamental appeals. While it is true that any of the above-mentioned experiences can be a channel for the mystery of God if and when such an experience is taken to its ultimate expression, it is also true, given the historical situation of all human beings, that the choice of one or the other of these experiences in coming to know the mystery of God is extremely important. Rahner emphatically declared that ". . . it is equally obvious that the present-day situation of man, in which he has to achieve the total fullness of his own selfhood . . . also in a very essential sense imposes its own distinctive stamp upon this experience. . . ."[21] What does remain theoretically open to question—although I am of the opinion that the point is beyond discussion—is whether the present situation of the Latin American believer, a situation that in its concrete historicity is quite different from that of the European believer, is essentially determined by the massive, oppressive, scandalous, and challenging fact of the absolute poverty of the masses.

This situation of the Latin American believer and the primary experience obtained therein give rise to different expressions of the experience of God. Such expressions may be found in other ecclesial channels, which cannot be historically described as the Church of the poor, but it is only within the Church of the poor that these expressions allow their own contents to become much "more evident." At first glance, this process of allowing the contents to become "more evident" would appear to be a rather small contribution to the task of theoretical reflection on and logical analysis of the experience of God, particularly since the contents, once conceptualized, can be subsumed under other ecclesial realities. However, I argue that the process is extremely important because the evidence for the concept becomes thereby more operatively transparent as it becomes "more" evident. What is more evident can be easily subsumed under what is evident and, as a result, can be presumed to be known, but one can also argue that in becoming "more" evident the contents become absolutely evident.

I should like to emphasize this point because what follows is not new, or at least not radically new, in terms of its purely conceptual formality. To speak of life, love, conversion, or hope appears to be nothing more than a routine repetition of what is frequently discussed in theology. Yet in making concrete the formality of the concepts, the concepts themselves acquire new "evidence," since the reality that lies behind the concepts does not exist as universal "genera," of which the "species" are but an application, but rather as concrete and specific realizations.

The Experience of the God Whose Kingdom Is Near

Rahner declared that "there is really only one question, whether this God wanted to be merely the eternally distant one, or whether beyond that he wanted to be the innermost center of our existence in free grace and in self-communication."[22] Christianity assumes this question by claiming that God has shattered his symmetry of distance and nearness and in his free grace has drawn near.

The Church of the poor makes concrete this fundamental experience of God as nearness in grace by affirming, in biblical language, that the kingdom is near and the Good News is being preached to the poor. Thus, the introduction of the poor as the hermeneutical principle in the primary experience of God makes concrete all generic truths concerning the God of the kingdom. Several important points concerning the experience of the mystery of God follow from this position.

First, the transcendental relationship between the God of the Good News and all human beings is mediated by the more concrete correlation between the Good News and the poor. The poor are accepted as constituting the primary recipients of the Good News and, therefore, as having an inherent capacity to understand it "better" than anyone else. The obediential capacity of the human being to become a hearer of the word is thereby made concrete as the obediential capacity of the poor and the impoverished to hear that word as the Good News and thus as a word of grace. It follows logically that only to the extent that we adopt the perspective of and show solidarity with the poor will we have the capacity to hear the Good News as it was preached in history.

This historical disposition of the poor presupposes their historical capacity to hear the Good News in its formal character as "grace," that is, as something totally unexpected and freely given, and as "content," that is, as life itself. In this regard the response of Jesus to the disciples of the Baptist is well known: "The blind receive their sight and the lame walk, lepers are cleansed and the deaf hear, and the dead are raised up, and the poor have the good news preached to them" (Mt. 11:5; Lk. 7:22). This text clearly identifies the poor and, at the same time, shows what happens to them when the kingdom of God draws near. What happens is that the poor receive life once again, since from the point of view of both the ancient world and linguistics, these types of persons—the blind, the lame, lepers—are always described in terms of death: "According to the thinking of the time, the situation of such men was no longer worth calling life; in effect, they were dead . . . now those who were as good as dead are raised to life."[23]

Thus, the preaching of the Good News in the Church of the poor becomes the recovery of the original truth concerning God the Creator among those who would appear to have the least claim to be his children. God is a God of life, and, therefore, life itself becomes a primary mediation of the experience of God. All the complexities of life—its abundance, its threat, its demand, its misery—reflect the complexities of the experiences of God. The words of the famous dictum "gloria Dei, vivens homo" should not be looked upon as mere words. Life is the primary mediation of God. Only within the Church of the poor is that insight recovered in the very midst of that life, which is for the most part threatened, stymied, and destroyed. The life that emerges out of such a historical situation is well acquainted with the mystery of God.

Second, although the affirmation that the God of the kingdom "is near" breaks through that fundamental symmetry of distance and nearness, it does not abolish the dialectic of the presence and the hiddenness of God—a dialectic that has been summarized in the well-known expression, "already, but not yet." Indeed the need to preserve that dialectic represents one of the fundamental experiences of the mystery of God as mystery, since the "not yet" of God is perceived as always surpassing his "already." That dialectic may be expressed in several ways. Philosophically it is the presence of the ground of being in all beings and the inadequacy of concrete beings vis-à-vis absolute being. Existentially, it is seeing God as that which is most intimate to a human being and, because it is most intimate, overflowing the human being. Biblically it is the tension that exists between creation and eschatology, between absolute origin and absolute future.

The experience of the dialectic that takes place in the Church of the poor does not discredit the ones mentioned above, but it does concretize them from the perspective of the poor. This experience becomes ultimately an experience of a history that includes both grace and sin, both manifestation and hiddenness on the part of God. The Church of the poor knows that the kingdom of God has not yet come because sin, the very nature of which is to cause death, is still very much present. The Church of the poor knows that as long as there exist innumerable victims of oppression and that as long as countless other human beings are regarded as human refuse, undone by the appetites of the powerful, the kingdom of God cannot be said to have come. However, if the Good News is preached to the masses, if this ultimate dignity as children of God and this status as the privileged before God is effectively proclaimed, if the masses manage miraculously to achieve human solidarity, if they actively regain their dignity and begin to defend their so-called "rights"—a situation that amounts in effect to a reliving of the original creation—then it may be said that the kingdom has come. It is true that the experience of the manifestation and the hiddenness of God, of the "already, but not yet," may be expressed in many ways. However, the description of that experience within the Church of the poor is privileged, because it captures from within and in its most historical essence what it means to let God be God.

Third, it is a typical feature of the Church of the poor, and one that is historically demonstrable, to experience the coming of God in his kingdom not only as destiny (joyful because of its character as grace and yet somber because it occurs in the midst of sin) but also as a task that is demanded by God and that corresponds to God's own mode of approaching. It is an experience that seeks to correspond to that God whose kingdom approaches. Obviously that correspondence is as complex as the mystery of God itself. In recent years, many have pointed to hope as the primary mode of corresponding to that God who is coming. To be sure, hope, as I shall point out later on, is an important element of the experience of God that takes place in the Church of the poor. But a mode even more primary than hope, a mode that will provide the necessary conditions for that hope to be Christian is the practice of love. If hope hopes that the otherness of God will one day become fullness, the practice of love attempts to correspond to that eternal content of the mystery of God. Ultimately, the praxis of love is an attempt to capture the mystery of God from a Johannine perspective: "If God so loved us, we also ought to love one another" (1 Jn. 4:11). That is to say, it is an attempt to grasp at the same time the character of the mystery of God as a free gift and of its content as a task to be carried out.

In the Church of the poor, this basic affirmation concerning the practice of love as the primary element in the experience of the mystery of God is mediated by its own historical situation. Within that situation the practice of love cannot be considered simply as one of the many possible mediations of God or even as the one that is the most privileged; rather, love becomes the mediation that lies at the very center of the experience of God and gives meaning to all other mediations. Such a conception of the practice of love recapitulates both the Pauline teaching of Galatians 5:14 and Romans 13:8–9—"For the whole law is fulfilled in one word, 'You shall

love your neighbor as yourself' ''—and the Johannine message of
1 John 4:16 and 18—"God is love."

The practice of love in that Church is an urgent task. The poor
cannot wait. It is, therefore, not a question of calmly and col-
lectedly accepting the proposition that love is the ground of being
and concluding that the practice of such love befits its character as
ground; on the contrary, it is a question of realizing that love demands of its very nature its urgent actualization. Love consists, to
put it in biblical terms, in becoming a neighbor to someone in need
before that individual becomes a neighbor to oneself.

The neighbor is seen in this Church in his or her concrete historical reality. It is true that, given the social nature of a human being at
every level of life, interpersonal relationships will develop so that
some human beings will become one's neighbor at every level of
life. However, it is also true that there exists the overwhelming historical fact of the impoverished masses who demand that we become their neighbors. Indeed, one could find in this situation the
basis for a solution to the problem of justice. At this time, however,
all I wish to affirm—and that is sufficient in itself—is that the practice of love in the Church of the poor includes of its very nature the
attitude of Jesus that is reflected in the "misereor super turbas" of
Mark 6:34, that is to say, the act of becoming a neighbor not only to
individuals whom the "I" encounters as a "you," but also to collective entities such as the great majority of the human race and of
the Latin American continent. Any practice of love that excludes
from its center the urgent task of becoming a neighbor to these
masses cannot be called a mediation of the experience of God. Such
a conception of love would constitute a docetic view of creation, a
view that would not accept creation as it actually is, but would
restrict itself to those areas of human experience where one could
choose ahead of time to become a neighbor to someone else.

The above discussion does not represent by any means a new
theoretical truth concerning God or the experience of God. Many
have claimed that God is a God of life and of love; many have
claimed that life and love constitute mediations of God and that sin
is the reason for his hiddenness; and many have claimed that a
practice of love which gives life to those without it is a privileged
mediation of the experience of God. I would add that the Church of
the poor provides a structural channel in which these generic affir-

mations may become fully operative and effective truths. The reason for this claim lies in the historical and material constitution of the Church of the poor. Within that Church, the affirmation that life is a mediation of the mystery of God becomes obvious in the midst of institutionalized death; similarly, the affirmation that the praxis of love is a privileged mediation of the experience of God also becomes obvious amid those who have surrendered to apathy, indifference, and injustice. After all, those narratives of the Old and New Testaments that speak of the self-revelation of God and of his offer to become our God and to make us, all of us, his own people, begin with the following words: "I have seen the affliction of my people . . . and have heard their cry . . ." (Ex. 3:7; cf. 6:5). To this exalted truth of the loving nature of the mystery of God the Church of the poor would simply add that such love is historically preceded by the cries of the poor that reach God. Given this position, the Church of the poor will always proclaim that which is eternally true concerning the mystery of God, namely, his loving nature, but it will do so only from the perspective of those who find themselves the most deprived of any love.

The Experience of the Greater God

The nature of God as mystery includes of necessity being beyond all control, being the totally other, being "the greater being." This aspect of God may be experienced in various ways. In this section, I wish to discuss only two elements of this experience of God as the greater being, both of which are common in the Church of the poor: conversion and the permanent process of conversion.

Conversion may be defined as a turning toward the "true" God. Such a definition has two important components: (1) the aspect of "turning," of changing the direction of one's life; and (2) the idea that such a "turning" is directed toward the "true" God. As a turning toward God, conversion implies the notion of change, but it is a change that should be more precisely understood as a rupture. There is no question that a change without rupture can be indicative of an experience of the greater God; however, such a change would not fundamentally alter basic human nature and human experience. A rupture, however, is a change that allows human beings to come face to face with the greater God as the one who is totally other.

Given this definition of conversion, the Church of the poor attempts to find that concrete historical situation which—in unison with the workings of grace—can provide the channel for such a radical change and, indeed, demand it. For the Church of the poor, that concrete situation is to be found historically whenever the radical nature of "the other" becomes most obvious, questioning directly one's own identity and demanding that one become "another." Such a concrete historical situation, it claims, is to be found among the poor.[24] Thus, for this Church, the poor historically constitute otherness, that is, they constitute that which becomes "the other" to the individual and to the Church as such; the poor embody the unconditional "No" of God to the world. They embody that which one must become, that which cannot be ignored by any theodicy; the poor provide a positive direction for the initial stages of the process of conversion. They provide the task of their liberation as the unconditional "Yes" of God to the world, a liberation that cannot be relativized by any eschatological reservation. It is clear, therefore, that the Church of the poor locates and identifies a historical situation where conversion can take place, a situation where "the other" exists and demands that one become "an-other."

Perhaps the most important point—although from the point of view of pure theoretical reflection it would appear to be rather trivial—is that the experience of conversion takes place frequently in the Church of the poor. Just as Rahner has correctly pointed out that it is very difficult for a modern human being, that is, for a human being within the perspective of the developed nations, to experience guilt and, therefore, conversion,[25] conversion does take place in the Church of the poor and it can be conceptualized precisely because it does take place. Further, as far as the phenomenon can be analyzed empirically, that conversion takes place because the very real presence of objective sin in this Church makes it extremely difficult to repress subjective guilt. It is "easier" to be aware of one's own status as a sinner in the midst of sinful poverty, even though one may not be able to define in exact terms the relationship between one's subjective guilt and objective sin. Objective sin makes it easier to differentiate between what is and what ought to be, to grasp the qualitative as well as the quantitative dimension of this difference, and to realize how urgent it is to change from what is to what ought to be.

As a human experience, therefore, conversion involves a "turning," an experience of change and rupture. As a theological experience, however, it also implies a turning toward the "true" God. What I propose here is not fundamentally new; the difference lies in the perspective from which it is presented, namely, the poor as the locus for conversion. From that perspective, to turn toward the "true" God takes on a very specific meaning: it means to turn toward a God who lives and gives life. In Latin America—at least in the way it is generally experienced—conversion does not mean a turning toward God in the face of agnosticism and atheism, but rather a turning toward the true God in the presence of other gods who cause death. The faces of the poor become a positive mediation of the true, but hidden, God, insofar as they are also a mediation of those false gods who choose death as the channel for their revelation.

Thus, conversion as a theological experience is not a turning toward God in the face of atheism, but rather in the face of idolatry. The experience of the Church of the poor is not one in which human beings call upon many gods, some of which are true and some false, or in which they fail to call upon any god at all. It does not involve the question of epistemological disagreement when calling upon the gods or when failing to call upon them. It has to do with an experience of two very real alternatives: a situation where people encounter death, where they are dehumanized and impoverished, in the name of a specific god, be it a religious god or a secular god such as "democracy," "private property," and "national security"; or a situation where, in the name of a different god, life is given to them or, at least, actively sought for them. Idolaters, therefore, are not those who err epistemologically in the process of defining their transcendental experience of God, but those who bring death upon others in the name of some god. Similarly, true believers are not those who have correctly defined their transcendental experience of God, but those who give life to others in the name of this God.[26]

Consequently, the experience of conversion is an experience of God as the greater being primarily because he differs radically from all human beings. When this experience takes place among the poor, it includes the realization that one must turn toward life, because the real alternative is to cause death. Rahner declared:

"God is always greater . . . than culture, than science, than the Church, the Pope, and all forms of institution. . . ."²⁷ The Church of the poor provides an objective basis for such a claim. God is not only greater because what is uncreated is greater than any creature and because what is unlimited is greater than what is limited, but also because all that is created and limited can ultimately be measured by only one criterion: whether it brings about life or death. God is greater because he guarantees life and because no creature can call upon the name of God in order to disregard life, or to discourage it, or, even worse, to destroy it. Herein lies the fundamental experience of conversion, of turning toward a true God.

Conversion is, first of all, a turning toward the God of life; however, this is but the beginning of the process of conversion. If conversion is to be Christian, it must also include a constant search for the concrete will of God. Rahner wrote: "Is it necessary to discover the will of God because it is not possible fully to know what is willed, here and now, by God, simply by way of a Christian use of reason (principles of reason and faith plus analysis of the situation), because a man must take into account on principle and not merely as a hypothetical case not normally met with in practice, that God may make known to him some definite will of his over and above what is shown by the Christian use of reason within the framework of Christian principles applied to the particular situation?"²⁸

Given the possibility that God may reveal his will to a human being, the conclusion is inevitable: we must always be open to the process of coming to know the concrete will of God in varied ways. However, particular attention must be given to the historical channel that makes it possible for the diverse will of God to be revealed in the course of history. This channel includes, first of all, life itself—its transitory character, its different stages, its surprises and disappointments, its changes and failures. I argue—and I do not mean to deny thereby the importance of the channel of human changeability—that the Church of the poor provides a historical channel that demands that life become a theological process in search of the will of God. This channel is made possible by a dialectic inherent in and essential to the Church of the poor. In this Church, one finds two fundamental affirmations that are true only when considered dialectically. The first one includes an unceasing condemnation of oppressive poverty and a determined resolve to eradicate it; the second involves the adoption of a real kenosis, that is, a life of voluntary poverty and an attitude of solidarity with the poor.[29] It would be relatively easy from both a theoretical and a practical point of view to designate only one of these poles as the mediation of the experience of God. A much more difficult task is to claim that both poles represent the correct mediation of that experience. However, precisely because of this structural and therefore permanent difficulty the experience of God has to be characterized as a process and the human task described as a search for the will of God, as an attempt to discern that will. Further, to undergo this process and undertake this task is to relive Jesus' own process in his search for a "messianism" that could adequately describe his own mission.

The lack of knowledge that is inherent in our knowledge of God, the a priori inability to manipulate God that is inherent in the process of letting God be God, and the possession of God that is true possession only when understood as a way of God further characterize this process. As a result, the Church of the poor may be said to undergo the experience of a search for the will of God and thus the experience of the greater God. This experience should not be seen as the result of a decision made by the Church of the poor on the basis of knowledge acquired through theoretical reflection, but rather as a process that is demanded by its own structure, that is, as an attempt to sustain the search for a synthesis that can never be adequately attained. It is this experience that constitutes the historical mediation of letting God be God.

The Experience of the Lesser God

The privileged perspective of the previous reflection should be obvious: this is also a historical characteristic of the Church of the poor. At this point, I believe it would be helpful to treat this perspective thematically, that is, as an element in the experience of God. The proposition that God's nature has to be absolute in character has long been an accepted teaching in both the philosophical and the Christian traditions. If this claim were to be denied, then God could in no way be considered the absolute origin or the absolute future or the absolute Lord of history.

However, this true proposition may give rise to a rather serious error in the understanding or description of the experience of God. God can be said to be present in all things as their ultimate ground and horizon, but he cannot be said to be present equally in all things. This is a traditional Christian doctrine: God is present in me and my neighbor. If God is present in all things, he may be found in all things; however, this proposition in and of itself does not solve the problem of a concrete access to God or that of a hierarchical arrangement within such an access so that he may indeed by found in all things. Consequently, out of this situation emerges the expression, "the lesser God," an expression metaphorically correct, but no less metaphorical than that of "the greater God." This expression means that one cannot approach God in the same way from all experiences, but rather that such an approach must take place from adequate experiences and, more specifically, from those experiences which prima facie would seem to have absolutely nothing to do with God.

Rahner has correctly stated that the claim "whoever searches for God has already found him" represents authentic Christian teaching. However, this teaching must be made concrete through another authentic Christian teaching: "The question is not whether someone is seeking God or not, but whether he is seeking him where God himself said he is."[30] That locus consists of the world of the poor as I have described it above. The search for this concrete locus may be historically difficult—a real difficulty, for example, in the context of the developed nations. However, the difficult nature of this task does not prevent one from emphasizing formally the privileged position of the poor in the experience of God or from claiming that the very attempt to determine who the poor actually are—regardless of the success of such an enterprise—is important for the experience of God.

From the point of view of philosophical reflection, it is clear that God cannot be reached directly from the absolute character of the totality of existence and history. The position that he must be reached only from the perspective of the poor is possible only within Christian faith. The Church of the poor, in recalling what it takes to be the fundamental truths of revelation, "justifies" an access to God that is privileged in nature.

First, the revelation of the mystery of God has been accomplished in terms of a "lessening," a kenosis. Indeed the incarnation of Christ presupposes a double "lessening." The first one consists in the fact that he became human—a teaching that has been held and revered by all of Christian tradition. The second, proclaimed and emphasized by the Church of the poor, consists in the fact that he became weak and showed solidarity with the poor. Although from a logical point of view, this second "lessening" could be regarded as being accidental to the life of Jesus—that is, as if his incarnation could have just as easily taken place in another context and showed a different kind of solidarity—from a historical point of view this is impossible. "I have been sent to preach the Good News to the poor." It is always possible to interpret this text as one more text of the life of Jesus and not to draw any logical conclusions from it. Likewise, it is also possible to interpret "the poor" to mean "all humankind." However, if these words have not totally lost their meaning and if the entire life of Jesus is taken into consideration so that his own partiality can be observed from the point of view of his tragic end, then it is clear that in Jesus' life one may find a partiality and a solidarity that are historically constitutive. Such a partiality, which takes place at the second level of kenosis of the Christ and not at the first, forms part of the "surprise" that the incarnation brings and that corresponds, as Rahner tells us,[31] to a certain lack of knowledge on our part concerning humankind prior to the incarnation. If Christ has something really historical to say concerning what is means to be human and concerning the kinds of relationships with others that are necessary in order to become human, then it is clear that the person becomes a mediation for the experience of God if seen from a very specific perspective: "person" as someone who is poor or who shows solidarity with the poor.

Second, if the proper appellation for Christ is not only that of "man," but also that of "son," then it follows that he himself has an experience of the Father, an experience of God, and that that experience becomes a prototype for our own experience of God. He is the faithful witness who has lived the faith first and in fullness (cf. Heb. 12:2). In his concrete way to the Father, Christ becomes the way for us to the Father. I cannot analyze in detail at this point the way of Jesus, but I do wish to affirm that both his objective way as well as what can be discerned of his subjective experience have been shaped by the perspective of the poor and by his partiality for them. Neither the controversies nor the exposé of oppressive religious traditions nor the prophetic denunciation of the rich, the priests, the intellectuals, and the politicians, nor the threats and persecutions in the course of his life, nor above all his own end can be understood simply as consequences of his defense of "the person"; rather, they should be seen as direct results of his defense of "the poor." It is this partial perspective of his mission—a partiality which may also be observed in his subjective experience, given his messianic temptations, his prayers, his knowledge or lack of knowledge with respect to the coming of the kingdom—that Jesus fundamentally requires of anyone who wishes to follow him. Further, it is this following which in turn constitutes the only way for us to become children in the son and thus to have the experience of the Father. Finally, this following, which may also be described as a taking up of the cross, is also historically privileged, given the reasons why the way to God is a way to the cross.

Finally, the Church of the poor finds its constitutive partiality on the well-known passage of Matthew 25 (vv. 31–46). The passage may be read in two ways: as a simple demand for ethical action in the Church or as having more pronounced consequences for an understanding of the formal nature of the experience of God. In the first reading, the act of reaching out to the neighbor in an attitude of love and service already constitutes a historical gesture in which the transcendental necessity of love for the experience of God is made concrete.

In the second reading, however, this act of reaching out to the neighbor, as presented in Matthew 25, also functions as a mediation of the experience of God. The unity of love of neighbor and love of God constitutes a profound truth; however, this truth will remain simple tautology or be construed as pure idealism unless the generic aspect of the three terms in question—love, neighbor, and God—is shattered and made concrete. I believe that the description of Matthew 25 carries out this historical function of shattering and making concrete. The poor as poor and not simply as human beings serve to shatter the previous interest of the natural human—and "natural" should not be understood here in its technical meaning of opposition to a "supernatural" elevation—and to provide the basis for a response to questions such as, what is love, who is the neighbor, and, more fundamentally, who is God. This natural ego-centric interest of humankind—and "egocentric" should not be understood here in a moral sense but in a structural sense—is shat-tered when love takes place where there is no reason or hope for a fulfilling gratification. When this happens, the natural understand-ing of God may also be shattered in a fulfilling extrapolation of human self-understanding.[32] The claim that God may be found in the poor of Matthew 25 should hardly be called self-evident, and the acceptance of that claim should be even less self-evident. How-ever, if the claim is true, then the contrary affirmation is also true: the experience of God demands in and of itself a certain amount of scandal, but a scandal that can be perceived only from the perspec-tive of the poor.

This constitutive partiality of the experience of God does not invalidate the universality of other experiences where God can be found, and it does single out that experience without which the others could be considered generic experiences of a mystery but not necessarily Christian experiences of God. There is an ultimate theo-logical reason for this assertion: "Become poor as long as there is poverty in the world; identify yourselves with the poor."[33] One must seriously ask whether all Christian teaching should not be mediated by this partiality, whether the locus for raising a question and awaiting a response concerning truth, love, or freedom should not be the privileged world of the poor, and whether ultimately the above mentioned correlation, "gloria Dei, homo vivens," should not be understood in terms of yet another correlation, "gloria Dei, pauper vivens."

If this partiality—this "preferential option for the poor," as the Puebla Document calls it—is rejected or dismissed as being exag-gerated, opportunistic, and manipulative, then the question must be raised as to whether there exists any other locus for the expe-rience of God that can be considered more Christian and more historically possible than that of the Church of the poor. It is im-possible to reject this partiality in favor of a position that empha-sizes the universality of the experience of God: the total character of any experience must always be expressed through a more con-crete element of that experience. Similarly, it is impossible to re-ject it in favor of a position that emphasizes the fundamental equality of all concrete experiences of God: both from the point of view of history and of Christian tradition this would be a mis-understanding of the fact that poverty is a historical product of the dialectic of oppressive wealth. Although one may claim to be at the margin of these two poles of history, such a position can never be actually realized. History presents a very real choice: to understand the absolute mystery of God from the perspective of power or from that of poverty. To reject one partiality is to accept the other. If one does not think and live from below, one will think and live from above. If one does not experience God as a God who empties himself for us, one will experience him as a God of power without dialectic, that is, as power without service, where service is under-stood historically in terms of the cross and of scandal.

The Experience of the Crucified God

As scandalous as such a proclamation may seem, one must af-firm vigorously and without compromise that the experience of God implies in and of itself the notion of scandal. Many of the teachings of the faith point directly to it. That God became flesh, that the son humbled himself even unto death on the cross, that the wisdom of God was manifested in the cross, that the anguished cry of Jesus on the cross was met with silence, and that grace now overflows where sin used to abound: from the point of view of both philosophical and religious reason, these truths are not self-evident but scandalous. Indeed even with the Christian faith, it is difficult to take these truths seriously or to preserve them as a substantial element of the experience of God.

In the Church of the poor, this scandal appears first and fore-most through the scandal of history and points directly to what has traditionally been called the problem of theodicy. The difference is that neither the problem nor the solution are formulated in tradi-tional terms. Thus the primary scandal in this Church is not the need to reconcile the misery of the world with the nature of God, but rather the very existence of this misery in the world.[34] Likewise, the solution is not sought in an understanding of God that would allow for a conceptual reconciliation of the misery of the world with the nature of God. The Church of the poor accepts, con-sciously or unconsciously, the fact of the scandal of history and—this is the fundamental point—uses it as a basis for its own structure. It does not seek to organize itself on the basis of what the world calls power, wisdom, or beauty, but rather on the basis of the poor, the persecuted, and all those crucified by history. It does not blame God for this situation. That attitude, as surprising as this may be, simply does not exist. On the contrary, the Church of the poor looks upon God as its own ally on the basis of a certain intuition into the nature of God and its relatedness to the historical scandal as well as on the basis of a concomitant realization that salvation and liberation have to be secured through this scandal of history and not outside it.

Moltmann has spoken of a "crucified God." We are all aware of the difficulties of that terminology and of the necessary qualifications that have to be made. Nevertheless the fact remains—and this is specially evident in the Church of the poor—that unless one introduces the notion of scandal into one's conception of God, the nature of his salvific redemption will be thoroughly misunderstood. This does not mean that the expression is frequently used in the Church of the poor; it does mean that the reality conveyed by the expression is commonly found in that Church. Indeed one may even speak in that context of a "crucified people" as the primary scandal and as no longer a partial but rather a specifically privileged locus for the experience of God.

At the same time, from the abyss of this scandal hopes rise triumphant, confessing God as the absolute future or, in typical Latin American language, as the liberator, the one who can be trusted. There is hope in the Church of the poor. It is not a naïve kind of hope, since the Church itself is born out of a situation where one would expect only despair or resignation. The Church of the poor knows that the just do not fare well, that the poor who struggle for their dignity are oppressed, and that those who show solidarity with them are persecuted. Indeed, it almost seems as if the oppressor has the final say in and concerning history. In such a situation only one kind of hope can exist: that peculiarly Christian mode of hope that Paul calls hope "against all hope." At the same time, it is precisely in such a situation that one finds a possible structural channel wherein the scandalous aspect of God may be truly grasped. The characteristic darkness of faith—that element of *sacrificium intellectus* that is always a part of faith—is mediated by the black darkness of hope. If in spite of and through such a situation hope arises and endures, then it is clear that a very profound experience of the totality of history and of existence takes place in the Church of the poor. This experience goes beyond a simple hope for a favorable outcome or a naïve trust in optimistic mechanisms and solutions; it is much more profound than that. It is above all an acceptance of the enduring presence of truth, love, and justice in the world. It is, furthermore, an affirmation to the effect that God can be found in the world, specifically in the abysmal misery that exists in that world. Thus the most important task of the Church of the poor is not to attempt to formulate or employ these theological positions explicitly, but to continue to hope. If such hope does endure, then one may conclude that there exists within this Church a mediation of the experience of God, a knowledge that God's silence is not his final say concerning history, and a conviction that the executioner does not ultimately triumph over his victims.

The ability to continue to hope in this way constitutes the Christian utopia. To believe despite everything in the resurrection of Jesus and of all history becomes its generic formulation. This is the privilege, both tragic and joyful, of the Church of the poor: to opt for hope where there should be none. Such hope goes against hope, but it is not groundless. If on the one hand the power of sin again and again clouds our understanding of God as the Creator, as the guarantor of life, and points us toward the crucified God, then on the other hand the generosity of service, the raising of the consciousness of the poor with respect to their dignity as children of God, and their struggles and concrete gains serve to ground and strengthen anew this very vulnerable attitude of hope. Within such a dialectic, hope endures as a process toward the mystery of God. Those who hope do not possess, but are on the way to possession. Those who hope against hope, who keep that absolute mystery alive, are on the way to God, a God whom they will have to regard both as a crucified God and as the absolute future without any possibility of ever synthesizing the two affirmations. In undertaking and continuing in this difficult way of hope, one believes that the road does have an end.

To keep hope alive refers not only to the subjective experience of continuing to hope, but also to the adoption of and perseverance in the Christian praxis of love and justice in a world marked by conflict in which persecution and martyrdom abound. This hope against hope, this mediation of the experience of God, is not grounded on its own power or on the act of waiting or on a belief in a promising future. It arises out of the historical practice of love despite the seemingly impotent character of this love. For this hope the darkness of the future is grounded in the darkness of the present, that is, the persecution that characterizes the lot of the just. But the light of the future is also grounded in the light of the present, that is, the ultimate human experience that those who love have fulfilled the law and that no one has greater love than the one who dies for another. In the end, the Church of the poor will be able to describe this experience only by way of negation, as is the case in all sound theological work. It has no adequate knowledge of the future, of the meaning of fullness, or of the mystery of God. However, it is quite aware of the fact that unless it adopts this attitude of hope—that is, a hope that is active and fruitful, but also against all hope—it will have failed to correspond adequately to this mystery.

CONCLUSION: HISTORICAL EXPERIENCE AND FAITH IN GOD

The acceptance of the claim that specific historical experiences can serve as authentic mediations of the experience of God is an act of faith and indeed the most fundamental act of faith, since it accepts a correspondence between the historical and the theological structures of reality. This faith always presupposes "more"—and this quality of "more" may be interpreted in different ways, for example, as "beyond" or "in the future" or "in the past" or "more profound"—than the historical experience itself conveys. Faith always implies a leap that cannot be adequately analyzed from the purely historical level of the experience.

Thus, faith in the mystery of God does not arise automatically from specific historical experiences, not even from those I have described above. This claim is historically correct: many who have not approached history or its meaning from the perspective of the mystery of God have had experiences fundamentally similar in nature to the ones described above. It is also theologically correct: faith in God has always been regarded as a grace and a gift, categories theology employs to affirm the discontinuity that exists in principle between faith and historical experience.

It is also true that there can be no faith without a historical experience. There are two basic reasons for this: faith does exist, one does come to believe; and the quality of faith does differ, since faith—when it is understood as concrete reality in the believer and not only as a true, generic formulation—will vary according to different historical experiences. Therefore, while it is true that history does not automatically give rise to faith, it is also true that faith cannot exist without the historical experience.

Consequently, in analyzing what I have called the "experiences" of God in the Church of the poor, I have attempted to describe how the Church of the poor, in its concrete historical reality, provides different types of experiences that can be accepted as historical mediations of the experience of the mystery of God. I have tried to do no more than this, but also no less. The fundamental point of this enterprise has been to make all subjective experiences dependent on objective historical reality. In so doing I have tried to avoid a noble but dangerous position: that of a purely conceptual view of the nature of faith. It is true that in the act of desiring to have faith, an individual is adopting a subjective atttiude that corresponds to that element of faith we call availability. However, that desire by itself, independent of all objective conditions of history, may remain nothing but a pure and empty desire, or worse, it may try to interpret, even by basing itself on a reading of the Scriptures, the content of faith, the mystery of God, from the perspective of its own subjectivity, ignoring all objective criteria. By way of contrast, the Church of the poor offers a historically objective channel for the experience of God, a channel through which all generic attitudes and contents of the faith, which as generic realities are certainly to be found in the Scriptures, can be made concrete.

In the Church of the poor, one may also find that element of *sacrificium* essential to faith. It is clear that faith implies a *sacrificium intellectus*: although the Church has always proclaimed the mystery of God as comprehensible, it has also declared it to be incomprehensible. It is impossible to relate to that mystery unless one is willing to abandon reason by an act of reason. In order to have an adequate knowledge of God, one must be willing to give up knowledge, even though one may know the reason for the lack of knowledge. The Church of the poor interprets this *sacrificium* of the intellect in terms of a greater and more complete sacrifice, the *sacrificium vitae*. It is in the context of real life, of history, that we must give up an understanding of the ultimate mystery of life as well as the claim to have the final and absolute say concerning history. It is also in that context that we must be willing to give of our own life and even give up our own life in order to be able to correspond to the mystery of life. The mystery of God will remain hidden without this fundamental sacrifice in and of life. The *sacrificium intellectus* will become a part of that *sacrificium vitae*; the reverse, however, is not necessarily true.

One may also find in the Church of the poor a locus for understanding God, a locus where faith can become an *obsequium rationabile*. The experiences I have mentioned above—the emphasis on and the urgent call for love and justice, the creative nature of history, the hope that endures—make this God in whose name they take place a "comprehensible" God. In these experiences individuals come to an awareness of themselves by unleashing a positive type of history, that is, by immersing themselves in the flow of life and of the creation of life. Viewed in this way, faith does not alienate; on the contrary, it reflects and embodies what is most positive in history and it unleashes true history.

Finally, in the Church of the poor one finds a locus where faith can be experienced as an *obsequium*, that is, in terms of gift and gratitude. The endurance of hope where there should be only despair, of love and justice where a prudent withdrawal would be much more realistic, of the conviction that love grounds all reality: these are all signs that what is impossible has become possible, that we have been given something greater and stronger than our own selves, something that imposes itself upon us and before which all we can do is utter a final word of thanksgiving.

Like any other ecclesial channel, the Church of the poor has limitations and, as such, is subject to a characteristic element of danger with regard to its faith in God. This danger is grounded not only on the natural limitations and sinfulness of its members, but also on its own specific structure. It may appear, first of all, as a weariness in continuing to hope against hope and in striving to preserve the tension between the struggle against scandalous poverty and the commitment to an active life of poverty. It may also appear as an increasing desire to look to the historical process for some hope of a solution, thus limiting the role and reality of the mystery of God.

Despite these dangers, the Church of the poor provides an objective—and indeed the best—locus for a life of faith. It does not in and of itself weaken the mystery of God, as many of its detractors have claimed; rather, it strengthens and widens it. It seeks to recover the tradition of the Church and to enrich it. In attempting to make faith in God more concrete in its own specific way, it provides a verification of that faith: it recovers much more adequately the evangelical roots of belief in Jesus and it unleashes new history according to the Spirit of God. This verification constitutes the ultimate warranty for its own faith as well as for the claims that its historical experiences can serve as mediations of the experience of God and that it is the nature of God that unleashes these specific experiences.

6

The Witness of the Church in Latin America: Between Life and Death

In this chapter I will attempt a theoretical and theological analysis of the witness being given by the Church in Latin America. My aim is more than a simple description of this witness, although a theoretical development of the subject must of course take into account the concrete witness given in recent years by the Churches faithful to Medellín.[1]

I must answer at the outset a fundamental question that arises when one speaks of the witness of the Church. The Church's witness is usually understood as its subjective holiness, which lends credibility and, indirectly, effectiveness to its practice. The direct focus, therefore, is on the subjective life of the Church rather than on its objective practice.

Such an understanding of the Church's witness is inadequate, however, if we are to get at the root of the Church's historical activity and even if we are simply to understand the essential nature of its testimony. The basic thing about the Church's witness is its objective aspect. Witness is witness to something; testimony is given for or against something. This objective "something" both logically and historically requires credibility on the part of the testifying subject. The subjective aspect of witness becomes necessary and acquires meaning because of the objective aspect. The more important the objective content of the testimony, the greater the demand for the subjective credibility of the one giving it.

As far as the Church is concerned, this means that there is a basic question to be asked: To *what* does the Church bear witness in its evangelizing activity? This question gives rise to a second: *How* does the Church give witness?

At the objective level the Church bears witness to life; at the subjective level its testimony and holiness take the form of surrendering its own life. To put these general formulations into historical form: the Church in Latin America is bearing witness to a *just* life and it is surrendering its life in the specific form of *martyrdom*.

This approach to the testimony of the Church is important for three reasons. At the *formal systematic* level it brings the two aspects of testimony into unity; it unifies them, although dialectically, in terms of the objective aspect. The subjective testimony loses its autonomy and even arbitrariness; it can and should be understood only in terms of the content to which witness is given. This is important if the subjective holiness of the Church is not to be understood in idealist and voluntarist terms but as a response to an objective demand of history as mediation of God's will. The content of the Church's holiness will therefore not be simply a seal of credibility on any and every type of ecclesial practice but will be a content that is in objective conformity with the demands of reality.

At the *historical* level this approach brings together the two elements that are the newest and most basic in the practice of the Church: the active participation of the Church in the processes of liberation and the persecution that has come upon the Church on this account. There can be no reflection on the Church's witness if these two basic facts are not taken into account and if they are not made central to its historical testimony.

At the *theological* level, this approach brings together the points that are constitutive of the experience of the faith in Latin America. The content of the *fides quae creditur* is the God of life, who is concretized and to whom the Church is related as God the creator, God the crucified, and God the liberator. It is in conformity with this God that the *fides qua creditur* develops; that is, there is a surrender of the human person to God in faith, this being understood as a following of Jesus, who is called the primordial witness to faith, "the pioneer and perfecter of our faith, who for the joy that was set before him endured the cross, despising the shame" (Heb. 12:2). In what follows I shall offer a theological analysis in explanation of what it means to say that the Church bears witness to life, to the just life, to life in its fullness, and how the Church bears this witness by giving of its own life and even by giving that very life itself.

THE OBJECTIVE TESTIMONY OF THE CHURCH IN BEHALF OF THE JUST LIFE AND IN THE PRESENCE OF DEATH

"Bearing Witness" in the New Testament

The New Testament frequently states that the disciples of Jesus are to bear witness as an activity essential to their faith. There is no Christian faith unless there is something to which public and unconditional testimony is given. The act of bearing witness certainly requires a conformity of life in the believing subject, but it derives its meaning primarily from that with which the testimony is concerned, that is, from something objective.

In various New Testament formulations the objective content to which testimony is to be rendered is expressed in christological terms. Witness is to be given to Jesus Christ, to his entire historical life and especially to his resurrection.[2] In strictly theo-logical language, the witness must be to Jesus Christ as definitive mediator of the Father.

If we look more closely at the content of the testimony according to the New Testament, we see it includes not only the person of Jesus Christ but also the historical mediation in the service of which Jesus acts or which becomes present in him. If we examine the historical Jesus, it is clear that he bears witness not to himself but to the kingdom of God. And if we look closely at the Christian community as it reflects on Jesus, it is clear that the community connects Jesus the mediator with a mediation that becomes present in him but includes more than him. It is possible to bear witness to Jesus only by bearing witness to the mediation of God, which Jesus himself proclaims or expresses.

In the New Testament the testimony of Jesus the mediator is combined with testimony to the mediation of God. "This Jesus

God raised up, and of that we are all witnesses" (Acts 2:32). The testimony does not stop at the christological level but proceeds to the strictly theo-logical level. Testimony is given to God who "raised from the dead Jesus our Lord" (Rom. 4:24) and who is now defined, in systematic terms, as the one who "gives life to the dead and calls into existence the things that do not exist" (Rom. 4:17). Life and resurrection are the mediation of God to which testimony must be given.

In the theology of John, too, testimony to Jesus is connected with testimony to the mediation in the service of which he acted: "I came that they may have life, and have it abundantly" (Jn. 10:10). Against this background Christians understand what it is to which they must testify: We proclaim "the word of life—the life [which] was made manifest, and we saw it, and testify to it" (1 Jn. 1:1-2).

The important points in these brief observations are two. First, whatever be the further exegetical determination of the precise meaning of "kingdom of God," "resurrection" and "life" in the New Testament, testimony to Jesus the mediator is inseparable from testimony to the mediation. Second, the content of the mediation is not a limited area of human existence or a narrowly "religious" sphere, but what we may call life as a whole.

Testimony in Behalf of Life in the Latin American Church

This testimony in behalf of life reveals the deepest roots of the activity of the Church in Latin America. Life in this context is understood as a fullness of life that touches every level of existence. This is why the Church aims at an integral liberation. I shall speak of this fullness of life in the third part of this chapter.

For the moment I wish to concentrate on a basic historical determination of what is meant in Latin America by the life to the service of which the Church has pledged itself. The most fundamental datum in making this determination is the fact that life is threatened and is being taken from the masses, and this at elementary levels, by structural injustice and institutionalized violence. It follows that the testimony of the Church in behalf of life takes very seriously these elementary levels of life and that it promotes a "just" life through a struggle against injustice.

The Church can make this kind of historical determination of what life means because of the breakthrough of the poor[3] on this continent and in the Church, and because of the partisan option for the poor that the Church has made in response to this breakthrough. As a result of this option, the testimony in favor of life can be correctly specified at the historical level and not deteriorate into an abstract and idealist type of testimony. The option for the poor emphasizes the historical fact that when we speak of life we are speaking of the life of the masses, of a life that is being threatened and destroyed. This being the option, the witness given by the Church is not hastily focused on the "fullness" of life, thus causing the elementary levels of life to be effectively ignored and theologically devalued; instead, the Church pays serious heed to these elementary levels of life as the object of its testimony and as the mediation of a spiritual experience of the God of life.

This means that an authentic theology of creation is being restored, even if unwittingly. I do not mean a return to theologies of creation that pay no heed to the sin that objectively cuts across creation and that promote a linear development based on the dynamic "seeds" present in the created world. Such a return would amount to an endorsement of developmentalist socioeconomic theories. The point is rather to see creation as the (logically) first mediation of the being of God. It is to see in creation the first manifestation of the God of life and to see it in places where theology frequently fails to look: in the fact of having life and managing to go on living, in work, in the use of nature and its resources for the service of human beings. The issue, then, is not to fall into the trap of turning too quickly to eschatology but rather to turn soberly to protology. The real problem in Latin America is not that the eschaton has not come but that the realities and values present at the beginning have not achieved their full being.

I thus reject the practical, if not theoretical, view that asserts that the elementary levels of life and the very fact of living are data having to do only with nature and the socioeconomic sphere. They merit study in an anthropology, a sociology, an economics which may serve indirectly as a basis for the understanding and practice of various parts of Christian ethics but are not in themselves data that require integration into a theo-logy in the strict sense. Theo-logy, according to this view, begins at a different level: the level of "true" life, "Christian" life, "eternal" life.

I regard this approach as erroneous and deadly in its consequences. In fact it was denounced at the very start of evangelization in Latin America. Bartolomé de las Casas pointed out the error in his own way. Exercising profound theological insight, he saw the Indians first of all as created beings and described them as poor and oppressed; only then did de las Casas go on to see them as unbelievers. Thus he drew the well-known conclusion: better "a live heathen Indian" than "a dead Christian Indian."[4] He thereby attacked a method of evangelization that made destruction and death the necessary condition for the conversion of the Indians; he attacked the corrupt ethical results of a certain practice of evangelization. More profoundly, he was attacking, at the theo-logical level, an erroneous conception of God. A living infidel is a sacrament of the God of love, while a murdered Indian, even one who had been a Christian, is a sacrament only of idols. It is not possible to bear witness to God while neglecting the elementary levels of life, even if one goes on to add that this God offers a fuller life than mere natural life and that the fullness of this God is mediated through the fullness of Christian life.

This restoration of the elementary levels of life may seem a minimal achievement, but it is fundamental to an understanding of the Church's activity and of the experience of God via this activity. It seems minimal because life is not exhausted by its elementary levels. It is basic, nonetheless, because these levels are the foundation of all life, and unless they are taken into account it is vain to try to bear witness to a God of life. A created order in which life is neglected, threatened, or destroyed is a corrupt creation. It would therefore be vain, illusory, even blasphemous to claim to bear witness to God without a practice geared to restoring creation. Given the basic, primary needs that exist, any experience of God on this continent and any testimony of the Church must *logically* begin with them.

Antilife and Unjust Structures in Latin America

These reflections on testimony in behalf of life at its elementary levels seem radical when we consider the concrete reality of the continent. If that which made itself known in Christ was the word of life (as John says), then that which is manifesting itself in this continent is the antichrist and his word of antilife. On this point the documents of Medellín and Puebla and many pastoral letters are in agreement.

The manifestation of antilife is not something natural; it is not a mere absence of life at elementary levels because creation does not give more fully of itself. On the contrary, it is a historical product of human wills, crystallized in structures that produce injustice. Antilife is not a product of nature; it comes from an antichrist. The absence of life that is being manifested takes the form of injustice, which manifests in turn the essence of sin. What sin is reveals itself in historical form through the death that human beings inflict on one another. Unjust structures bring death near and inflict it daily, and anyone attacking them is killed. God's created world is thus corrupted not only by the de facto absence of life at the elementary levels, but also because this life suffers positive oppression from injustice. Witness borne to the elementary levels of life is thus witness in favor of justice, and such witness includes participation in the conflict and the struggle against injustice. Witness to God the creator necessarily becomes witness to God the liberator.

The connection between the experience of God and witness to a just life becomes even clearer in Latin America because structural injustice is there given explicit or implicit theological sanction. The presently prevailing structures—a capitalism of dependence and national security, whatever their forms—function as real dieties with divine characteristics and their own cult. They are deities because they claim attributes that belong to God alone: ultimacy, definitiveness, and inviolability. They have their own cult because they demand the daily sacrifice of the masses and the violent sacrifice of any who resist them. These deities require victims in order to survive, and so they produce such victims.

The true ruler of the continent, then, is an injustice that is given theo-logical sanction in the name of deities that are gods of death.[5] By contrast with these false deities and their deadly mediations there arises the conviction of what the true God, his authentic mediation, and his authentic cult must be. If sin reveals itself in the death of human beings, then grace reveals itself in the human life that is God's first and basic gift to us. If the doing of injustice shows itself to be worship of false gods, then the practice of justice shows itself to be worship of the true God. If capitalism and national security reveal themselves to be idols, the true God shows himself as the one who gives life and desires liberation.

Because the realities of the situation on the continent make abundantly clear the irreducible alternatives of life and death, grace and sin, justice and injustice, there is no room for a "third way" kind of testimony from the Church in this area. To put the point negatively: there can be no testimony to God that effectively relativizes the life and death of human beings in the name of the eschatological proviso or that relativizes the elementary needs of human beings in the name of the fullness of life. To put it positively: testimony to God is correct only if it includes the practice of justice as an essential.

Let us keep this in mind: the practice of justice has become so necessary historically and so basic theologically for the testimony of the Church because antilife, the widespread oppression of life, takes place at elementary levels where it cannot be hidden. The question is not of some generic need for justice (after all, in any historical situation there will always be some kind of limitation and oppression), but of a need for justice at those elementary levels at which the ethical conscience and the experience of God take their basic shape. The need is not to demand "human rights" in general. This approach generally does not yield much fruit in ecclesial life and practice, nor does it change the self-consciousness of the Church. The need is rather to demand the "rights of the poor." This approach has the ability to convert the Church and to bring new depth to its practice.

The cries of the Latin American people rise up from the elementary level. God hears these cries. Only by hearing these cries and turning them into hope and the practice of liberation will the Church be conformed to the basic reality of God himself and will it bear witness.

The Latin American Church's Response

The two facts I have mentioned—the absence of life at the elementary level and injustice as the cause of the absence—are well known. Both are central to an understanding of the activity of the Church. Only in light of these facts can the new dimension of the Church's activity be understood. As the Church entered into the true reality of this continent the first thing it experienced was the unjust death inflicted on the masses. Seeing this obverse side of life it began an ecclesial and pastoral work directed to the conquest of death and the cultivation of justice.

As far as programmatic formulations are concerned, the Church has asserted a preferential option for the poor. This option has its basis, of course, in Scripture and, more concretely, in the mission of Jesus. But it is not the result of a purely formal fidelity to the texts of the Bible nor of a mechanical, voluntaristic imitation of Jesus. The option has been taken rather because the poor, as individuals with real faces and unsatisfied elementary needs as a collectivity that exists because of injustice (see the Puebla Final Documents 31–39, 63–69), mediate a basic call to conscience. The preferential option for the poor represents something basic that is its own justification. The Puebla Document states this point in sober language: "The poor merit preferential attention, whatever may be the moral or personal situation in which they find themselves. Made in the image and likeness of God (Gn. 1:26–28) to be his children, this image is dimmed and even defiled. That is why God takes on their defense and loves them (Mt. 5:45; Jas. 2:5)" (1142).

This statement shows that the Church's conviction is based on ultimates; therefore it is a profoundly theo-logical statement. It is not in the proper sense a deduction from an already constituted faith in God. Rather it gives voice to a foundational experience of ultimate things and therefore of God. Far from being discretionary or necessary only because of circumstances, the option for the poor is an unconditional affirmation of life and an unconditional rejection of injustice.

Here is the root—in one sense, minimal, but in another the deepest—of the Church's practice. In recent years the Church has carried on an unusual and extensive practice of prophetic denunciation and has accepted the risks that go with such a practice. It has acted as defender of human rights, not of the "civil" rights dear to liberals but of the most elementary rights: the right to live and the other rights necessary if life is to be sustained. It has chosen to speak of the "rights of the poor." It has demanded and promoted, as far as it has the means, the structural changes needed at the social, economic, and political levels. It has fought for trade unions and the organization of the masses of the people as means of breaking the power of the oppressor and bringing into existence a more human and humanizing kind of power. And it has done all this not simply by offering instruction on these problems but by often taking part in the struggle so that this struggle may become a reality.

All this activity cannot be understood simply as a response to specific ethical demands or as an application of an already constituted social teaching. It must be understood rather as the fundamental response to a demand that emerges from reality itself and therefore to the fundamental demand made by God himself. It must be understood as the most basic way of bearing witness to life.

The radical character of this conviction can be seen historically in the new way in which the Church has supported specific projects aimed at unifying the people along socialist lines and has even given its approval to a popular uprising.[6] This is not the place for discussing in detail these complex situations and the precise meaning of the Church's support. The important thing is that neither ideologies, usually regarded with suspicion by the Church, nor the serious nature of the conflicts in question, which may include armed struggles, can set limits to the Church's witness in behalf of a just life. This does not mean either naïveté or a loss of specifically Christian substance. What we have here is rather the conviction that the Church cannot continue to adopt a third party attitude and remain apart from the processes in which the life and death of human beings are literally at stake. It cannot adopt a supposedly more important standpoint from which life and death are relativized as things that in the final analysis are not truly ultimate. However necessary and basic the need to criticize what is limited and dehumanizing in these processes, the Church regards it as even more basic to demand life and a just life. The Church can effectively voice the necessary criticism of these processes or any other kind of process only if it makes its own the option to promote life and to accept the ambiguity and conflicts that such promotion involves. The Church cannot effectively voice such criticism on the basis of some general truth that would supposedly make possible a more insightful judgment about life.

Roots of the New Eccelsial Consciousness

This manner of bearing witness to life manifests a new ecclesial consciousness, which has its origins in the ecclesiology of Vatican II but which is more radical than that ecclesiology because the Church has identified itself with the death and injustice of the continent and with the continent's longing for liberation.

The Second Vatican Council teaches that the Church does not exist for itself but to serve the world; that the Church is to bear witness not to itself but to something distinct from and greater than itself. This teaching has been applied in Latin America. The Church in Latin America is not bearing witness to itself, but neither is it bearing witness to "Jesus" or to "God" without qualification. It is bearing witness to Jesus as the Word of life and to God as the God of the kingdom and of life.

Something profound is at work here, the first results of which we are now seeing. It has power to shape the future of the Church and indirectly of the Latin American continent. In this logical distancing from itself, in the apparent distancing from a Christ who had been absolutized as a person and disjoined from the Word of life and from a God who had been formalistically absolutized as the Ultimate and disjoined from his mediation by the kingdom, the Church is recovering its own deepest identity and at the same time recovering faith in Christ and in the true God.

This recovery is occurring at levels that are elementary but no less theological. The Church is effecting a theological recovery of those traits of Jesus that led him to meet the elementary needs of human beings, as when he had compassion on the multitudes (Mk. 6:34) or asked the disciples to give the people food (Mk. 6:37) or asked the Father for daily bread (Mt. 6:11; Lk. 11:3) or healed the sick. The Church is recovering for itself the logic that guided Jesus in his disputes (Mk. 2:1–3:6), his exposures of falsehood (Mk. 7:1–23), his curses (Lk. 6:24–26; 11:37–52; Mt. 23:13–32): the logic of defending the life of the poor and struggling against injustice. The Church is rediscovering the meals of Jesus as a sign of the fullness of personal, social, and transcendent life, a fullness that is signified precisely through the sign of elementary life. All this does not mean a reduction in the scope of the following of Jesus; it means rather a concentration on that which provides the basis and direction for the following of Jesus.[7]

The Church is also rediscovering and reviving that which gives basis and direction to faith in the mystery of God. Those who imprison the truth in injustice, those who do violence to the truth of things through lies cannot know God, as Paul tells us (Rom. 1:18–22), because their hearts are darkened and they prevent creatures from being sacraments of the creator. Those on the contrary who respect the deepest truth of things and allow reality to manifest itself as it truly is can know God. In being honest about reality in Latin America, in refusing to manipulate the truth about antilife on the continent, and in not closing its ears to the cry for life rising from the entrails of the continent and to the longing for liberation the Church is refusing to manipulate God. It allows him to reveal himself through unmanipulated reality; it allows him to be God. In so doing the Church is able to make the great act of faith in a God of life and justice.[8]

Summary

What I call the objective testimony of the Church can be summed up as follows. The Church bears witness on behalf of life. Given the real conditions of our continent, this life must receive a historical embodiment at elementary economic, social, and political levels. The witness must take historical form in a struggle to master these elementary levels, a struggle against the injustice that operates destructively there. This type of witness, though in itself it does not exhaust the fullness of life, is an integral and fundamental part of the witness the Church must give to the God of life. At the same time it is a condition for the possibility of faith in God. For many groups in the Church there is no retreating from this kind of witness.

THE SUBJECTIVE TESTIMONY OF THE CHURCH IN PERSECUTION AND MARTYRDOM

I turn now to the subjective aspect of the testimony the Church gives through the objective promotion of a just life. This subjective testimony is another name for the holiness of the Church. But what repays analysis here is not holiness in the abstract, as though we already knew what holiness was independent of objective testimony. I am interested rather in the kind of Christian holiness, attitudes, and virtues that are generated in the process described in the first part of this chapter. More concretely, I want to show that when the Church gives the objective witness described, there is generated at the historical level what the New Testament regards as holiness in its supreme form: the giving of one's life for the community as the greatest possible proof of love.

I need not dwell on the fact that the Church, which has given its testimony on behalf of life, has been persecuted and has produced martyrs. Thousands of peasants, workers, catechists, students, and intellectuals have suffered persecution and death. There is something new and eye-catching: hundreds of priests, religious women and men, and bishops have been attacked, slandered, threatened, expelled, tortured, and murdered.[9] I want to undertake a theological analysis of persecution and martyrdom and to show that these two are the most typical and most complete form of holiness for the Church, precisely because the Church therein gives testimony in behalf of the just life.

Theological Reflection on Persecution and Martyrdom

The Second Vatican Council acknowledged the importance of witness as a form of life that opposes faith and spiritual values to the reigning materialism. It also emphasized—and this was something new—that the laity have the duty of giving this kind of witness to the world. The Council did not, however, analyze theologically the importance of persecution and martyrdom. There is a general reference to the Church being persecuted in the pursuit of its mission (LG 8). When the Council becomes specific, it holds up for praise those persecuted in mission countries (AG 42) or in places where there is no religious freedom (AA 17). It also mentions in a general way the supreme value of martyrdom (LG 42) and the history of the martyrs (DH 11).

In Vatican II, then, persecution and martyrdom are not made the object of specific theological reflection, nor is any close historical connection established between them and the testimony of the Church. As far as the present-day situation is concerned, the emphasis is on other forms of this testimony. There is certainly no thought that persecution and martyrdom might become widespread in traditionally Catholic countries such as those of Latin America.

Neither *Evangelii nuntiandi* nor the Medellín Documents put any great stress on persecution and martyrdom. Both repeat the need for subjective testimony in the work of evangelization, and both—especially the Medellín Documents—emphasize the need for poverty and the sharing of destitution. But testimony is still not viewed in terms of persecution and martyrdom.

When I point out this lacuna in such important Church documents, I am not indulging in anachronism but simply trying to show how new persecution and martyrdom are to the Church of Latin America. The presence of this new reality became clear at the Puebla Conference (Mexico). Despite the reserve of the Puebla working document and the effort to suppress this subject during the meeting, the Final Puebla Document mentions a number of times the situation of persecution in which the Church finds itself. Here again reality forced attention upon itself.

More important than the simple mention of the fact of persecution is the inchoative theology of persecution that is found in these texts. First, the texts reflect on the reasons for the present persecution. These reasons are to be found in a practice that originates as a response to "the cry of a suffering people who demand justice" (87) and takes shape in "the Church's prophetic denunciations and its concrete commitments to the poor" (1138; cf. 92). Second, according to the texts, to face "persecution and death" (668) is the culmination of the witness of holiness, which also shows itself in the spirit of sacrifice and abnegation in the face of loneliness, isolation, and incomprehension (668).

According to the Puebla Document, then, persecution is widespread and occasions the perfect form of witness. In addition persecution cannot be understood according to the classical model of the persecution of the early centuries nor according to the model of mission countries with their nonchristian religions or of countries with an official and militantly atheistic ideology. In other words, the theological understanding of this persecution will be different from the theological understanding of traditional forms of persecution. The reason for the persecution here is not at the level of ideological superstructure but at the level of infrastructure. The Church is being persecuted because it defends the life of the poor, denounces the unjust destruction of life, and promotes the historical practice of justice. This is all the clearer inasmuch as those who are persecuting the Church today often verbally profess the Christian faith (cf. 49). Therefore the persecution cannot be understood at the explicitly Christian level but only at a really human level. It must be understood as a response to the objective testimony of the Church on behalf of a just life.

Theology of Persecution

The inchoative theology of persecution sketched at Puebla represents a recovery of a fundamental dimension of New Testament ecclesiology, although this in turn needs a fuller theological development and translation into historical terms. It is clear from the New Testament that persecution came upon the Church at a very early date and that being persecuted was soon declared to be a de jure characteristic of the true Church. In other words, the new Church at an early date experienced persecution from the Jewish and Roman authorities. Soon there was a declaration of principle regarding the Christian necessity of such persecution. In the earliest New Testament document Paul says: "You yourselves know that this is to be our lot. For when we were with you, we told you beforehand that we were to suffer affliction" (1 Thes. 3:3-4). The communities see this necessity as having its theological ground in the lot of Jesus (Jn. 15:18, 20; Mt. 10:24-25) and the prophets (Mt. 5:11-12).

The persecution of Jesus, which from a theological standpoint has to be understood in terms of the Father's will, has a clear historical cause: his activity in opposing, denouncing, cursing, and unmasking the powerful and the rich, the Pharisees, scribes, and rulers. Jesus fought against every kind of oppressive and unjust power, in order to promote and defend a life of justice for the poor. The struggle was not simply a personal conflict between Jesus and other individuals, that is, a conflict between "mediators." It was a struggle between different "mediations." On the one hand, the defense of a just life for the poor; on the other, the defense of a life of injustice exercised by the powerful. This emerges clearly in the death of Jesus. The *pax romana* and the Jewish society symbolized by the temple are unjust sociopolitical formations that oppressed the poor masses. Because Jesus attacked both in the name of the reign of God, he was persecuted and put to death.

The gospel narratives supply abundant evidence of the persecution against Jesus, and they present this persecution as religious.

Beneath the religious level lies the properly human level. If the apparent issue in the persecution of Jesus is his religious orthodoxy, the real issue is the *doxa* or glory of God, which is manifested in a life of justice for the poor.[10]

Practical Consequences for the Church and the Kingdom

These brief reflections are important if we are to have an adequate theological concept of what persecution of the Church means, and this concept in turn is important for its practical consequences. The starting point for understanding what persecution of the Church means is not the Church but what we call the kingdom or reign of God, the *glory* of God as the life of human beings. The Church has a twofold relation to this reign of God. The Church is a servant and an instrument in the coming into existence of the reign of God. The Church, insofar as it brings together many men and women, also tells us whether or not the reign of God has in fact become a reality. The concept of persecution must be developed in terms of this twofold relation of the Church to the reign of God.[11]

The Church is persecuted, in a *formal* way when, in carrying out its express pastoral mission in the service of justice and integral liberation, its bishops, priests, religious men and women, lay ministers of the word, or simple faithful are hindered, threatened, or destroyed on account of this mission and in order to prevent its being carried out. In other words, persecution means that the Church is frustrated as servant of the kingdom and instrument of its building and growth.

In this context, the Church is not persecuted formally as an institution nor as a religious entity. The persecution is not an attack on the institutional aspect of the institution nor is it inspired directly by an *odium fidei* (hatred of the faith). The Church is persecuted insofar as it is a community that effectively defends life and justice; the persecution is inspired by an *odium justitiae* (hatred of justice). In practice it is clear that not every Christian, priest, or bishop is persecuted (a number are praised, given privileges, and manipulated), but only those who have chosen, like Jesus, to bring to the poor the life and justice of the kingdom. It is also clear that behind this *odium justitiae* there does exist, indirectly but really, the true *odium fidei*.

The Church is persecuted in a *material* but real way and with intense fury if not with great frequency when it is looked upon as a "world," that is, as a community of human beings whose real life is threatened or denied. In other words, the Church is persecuted when the people who make it up are oppressed and crushed. When the people are oppressed by structures and, even more, when they are crushed because they struggle for life, then not only are the promoters of the reign of God being persecuted, but the very kingdom of God is being destroyed.

It can be debated whether it is theoretically appropriate to use the term *persecution of the Church* for both situations on grounds of the analogy between them. What cannot be denied, however, is the existence of the second kind of persecution or the fact that this touches the Church in its very essence. By reason of its faith in the God of life, the Church must consider itself the guardian and protector of life. If an attack is made on the life of human beings, then because they are his creatures the attack is also on God and indirectly on the Church, which is founded on faith in this God. Daily persecution of human life and of God's kingdom, even if it is not explicitly a persecution of Christians, is a major attack on the Church, since the reason for the Church's existence is to make God's reign a reality.

This theoretical determination of the theological concept of persecution is important by reason of its practical consequences for the Church. If the Church understands persecution in this way it will act differently than it usually has, and it will act in what is ultimately a more Christian way.

If the two senses of "persecution" are accepted, the Church will gain a better understanding of the origin of material persecution of the people. To the extent that it does, it will raise its voice in protest and as a result will be formally persecuted. If it looks on oppression and repression of the people as persecution of itself, it will be unable to affect ignorance of it because the attack will be on the Church's own being. This is the historical reason why many Churches have been formally persecuted whereas others have been tolerated and even praised. The reason for this difference of treatment is that the one group of Churches has made its own the persecution of the people, and the other has not felt affected, as Churches, by the persecution of the people.

If the two senses of persecution are accepted, then the Church will understand the essence of formal persecution of itself. Such persecution consists not in the loss of privileges or even of certain civil rights but in being frustrated and crushed when it endeavors to defend life. It is even possible to say, as some bishops have said, that persecution of the Church and repression of the people are one and the same thing, even if the formalities differ. If both meanings are accepted the Church will learn through a continuing dialectical process what is involved in persecution. When it experiences in its own flesh the persecution of its leaders and the reason for their persecution, it will understand more fully what is involved in the oppression and repression of the people. Conversely, when it accepts as real persecution what happens to the people, it also understands the meaning of formal persecution of itself.

This real, experiential dialectic is one way, and an important and effective one, in which the Church learns important lessons, since persecution in the twofold sense described concretizes truths which the Church professes in generic terms. For example, the Church learns who the poor really are, not as individuals who ruffle no feathers, but in their collective, challenging reality that incites repression. The Church learns what it means to become part of the world of the poor and to make their cause and lot its own. It learns the ec-centricity that is constitutive of its being; for persecution takes place precisely when the Church goes out of itself, ceases to defend its own rights, and commits itself fully to defending the rights of the people. Persecution and repression help the Church to recover its own true nature, and in this sense (and not in a purely eschatological sense) it can consider itself fortunate and blessed in persecution.

Martyrdom

The persecution here described can generate and in fact does generate a series of Christian attitudes and virtues that are difficult to come by apart from persecution. The most noteworthy of these are impoverishment, solidarity with the poor, courage in suffering, and hope against hope. All these form an important part of the subjective witness of the Church and reach their climax in what has traditionally been regarded as the supreme testimony: martyrdom.

I maintain that martyrdom is the most complete form of holiness, not only for general theological reasons but also for contemporary historical reasons, which make martyrdom a real and not a remote possibility and show clearly that it is the greatest proof of love. Although martyrdom will obviously not be the lot of all Christians, it is theologically and historically the *analogatum princeps* (primary analogue) on the basis of which, and in relation to which, the holiness of the Church and what I have been calling the Church's subjective witness are to be understood.[12]

In theory this has always been the case in the Church. The important thing is to specify in a historically concrete way what martyrdom is and how it should be understood at the present time. The usual definition of martyrdom is "the free and patient acceptance of death for the sake of the faith (including its teaching on morality) either as a whole or in regard to a particular doctrine (which in turn is always seen in relation to the faith as a whole)."[13] This definition captures the basic idea of martyrdom as a bearing witness to Christ (this element of martyrdom is clear in the New Testament) and as a bearing witness with one's own life (martyrdom has been thus understood since the middle of the second century). It implicitly includes another New Testament tradition according to which the giving of one's life for another is the greatest act of love (cf. Jn. 15:13; 1 Jn. 3:16), that is, the supreme form of holiness.

If we are to understand the death of so many present-day Latin American Christians as martyrdom, we must give historical concreteness to some of the ideas contained in the definition just given. Three points need to be stressed.

1. The "confession of faith," which is an inherent element in martyrdom, must be historically specified in the way indicated earlier as a confession of the just life. According to the usual definition, martyrdom is a bearing witness with one's life to a basic moral teaching, namely, the call for a just life, with this teaching seen as related to faith in the God of life.

2. At the present time, it is necessary to give a different historical content to the notion of "patient" (the "patient" acceptance of death). It usually means "not provoked by acts of physical or moral violence," as the working document for Puebla puts it.[14] As I said earlier in speaking of persecution, death normally comes through the struggle in behalf of justice. Objectively, every struggle

generates some kind of violence. Martyrdom in our day cannot be understood without this element of violence, just as Christian life in general cannot be understood without it, although it is of course necessary to determine what kind of violence is just.[15] Martyrdom cannot be understood without bringing in this element of violence, just as the death of Jesus cannot be understood without it, since, at least objectively, Jesus made use of moral violence. It would be ironic if we found ourselves unable for purely terminological reasons to speak of "martyrdom" in contemporary Latin America when in fact so many Christians suffer the same fate as Jesus and when many of them use the same kind of violence that he did.

3. Finally and most importantly we must see death suffered out of love for one's neighbor as taking the historical form of death out of love for an entire people and for the sake of the liberation of this people. As Saint Thomas shows,[16] love is the formal element that gives martyrdom its excellence. This love need not be a love directed exclusively to one or another individual; it may be a love for an entire people.

The reality of martyrdom is today abundantly present in Latin America, where it takes various forms. I shall analyze two of these. There is first the kind of martyrdom that most clearly reproduces the characteristics of the martyrdom of Jesus. There are many Christians—simple faithful, community leaders, priests, religious women and men, and bishops—who have denounced the sin of the world, struggled to promote justice, come in conflict with the powerful, done violence to the mighty in the name of God, and been murdered for their deeds. These Christians have been murdered because of their love for their people and their desire that the poor might have a just life. This is the kind of martyrdom suffered by the priests Héctor Gallegos, Rutilio Grande, Hermógenes López. In the light of what I have said there is no doubt that these men were martyrs; the people celebrate them as such, and some of the hierarchy acknowledge them, though others are skeptical.

There is another way of giving one's life. It has some of the same traits as the first kind of martyrdom but it also has characteristics proper to itself. I am referring to the martyrdom of a people as a people.[17] Given the situation in so many Latin American countries, the sufferings and struggles of the people of Nicaragua, and the state of affairs in El Salvador and Guatemala, it would be scandalous to pass over these deaths and the kind of holiness they reflect, whether or not we call the deaths martyrdoms.

I will describe these martyrdoms in a somewhat sketchy way. It is clear, as I said earlier, that vast majorities surrender their lives daily because of unjust structures, and that there are frequent instances of massacres and genocides being inflicted on the ordinary people. I might speak here of a "material" martyrdom because in many instances the murdered die without knowing why they die or to what they are bearing witness by their deaths. But the basic and overwhelming fact is there: countless individuals among the people die or are slaughtered each day.

In many cases these oppressed majorities accept their situation of wretchedness and martyrdom in a Christian spirit[18] that leads them to an awareness of their own poverty and death and to a practice of liberation. Their personal privation and death express love for others and an efficacious desire for a just life.

This love of the masses usually leads to the social organization of the people, to their political organization, and even to their politico-military organization. In this ongoing struggle many suffer despoliation and the loss of everything, even torture and death, simply for having organized as a people and having demonstrated peacefully. When, as in Nicaragua, the conflict turns into an armed struggle, hundreds and thousands die.

These are the plain facts about phenomena that occur often on this continent. What kind of holiness is manifested therein and, though this is not the most important point, may not this kind of death be described as indirectly a martyrdom and an ecclesial testimony.

As far as the deaths of the people and the deaths of those who organize themselves socially and politically are concerned, it is clear that these persons give their lives with great freedom. They know from historical experience that death is inevitable for an organized people, even more so than in the first type of martyrdom, since the people are usually more defenseless than the leaders of the Church are. Although the giving of their lives is not "patient," neither can we ignore the massacres of defenseless populations or the inequality of the forces taking part in the social struggle. As a result, while the dead in these instances are not completely defenseless victims, they do need the "historical patience" of those engaged in self-defense with disproportionately small means. It is also clear that generally speaking, the deaths suffered by the people are for love of the people and out of a desire that the people might be really free.

These considerations must be extended to include the case of an armed popular insurrection. Two points need to be made here. The first is the ethical legitimacy of the insurrection as judged in the light of the conditions required by moral theology. The bishops of Nicaragua maintained the legitimacy in the concrete situation of that country, and Bishop Romero of El Salvador spoke realistically of the possible legitimacy of an insurrection in his country.

The next point is of great pertinence to my purpose here, namely, the holiness that can be developed by means of an insurrection. An insurrection can by its nature engender dehumanizing and sinful values such as hatred, vengeance, disproportionate violence, and outright terrorism. However, if the passions that logically accompany a struggle are overcome, then the struggle can engender a number of Christian values such as fortitude, generosity, forgiveness, and magnanimity in victory. All this means that it is very possible for even an armed struggle, if it is inevitable and just, to be a means of holiness, and that the life given in such a struggle can be regarded as a testimony of the greatest possible love. Saint Thomas saw no difficulty in regarding the death of a soldier as a martyrdom, since "the good of the community is the highest of human goods" and "any human good can become a reason for martyrdom insofar as it is referred to God."[19]

Whether or not these deaths are suffered with historical necessity by a people that organizes itself can be "theoretically" disputed. God alone can judge when this greatest possible love in fact exists. The considerations I have offered are not an effort to overlook the defects and sins of the Christians in question. I am not trying to idealize these people, nor to say that each individual who fights in behalf of the people possesses *all* the Christian virtues. The point I am making is that we must not ignore the widespread and surprising fact that many Christians freely give their lives in order that the people may live; they give their lives with the kind of generosity that requires human beings to abandon everything and not shrink in the face of persecution, death, and even cruel torture. We cannot overlook the fact that there is here a form of that greatest love of which the gospel speaks, even if in each individual case it is accompanied by faults and weaknesses. The point is that we must not overlook the most important thing, even if there is need to be critical of lesser faults.

If we take into account the two ways just explained of giving one's life for the life of others, the situation of the Latin American Church in regard to martyrdom resembles, in its newness and extent, the situation of the Church during the first three centuries of its history. As far as pure theological theory is concerned, we could go on discussing whether or not we are dealing here with martyrdom in the strict sense. Perhaps we would give evidence of greater conceptual clarity if we were to speak of an "analogue of martyrdom." But none of these considerations can justify our ignoring the widespread reality or our hiding the important fact that the Christian communities and sometimes even the hierarchy regard as martyrs and true Christians those who have given their lives in order that the people might live. Without entering into a theological discussion, the bishops of Nicaragua acknowledged the Christian value of the blood shed in Nicaragua:

> Our people struggled heroically to defend their right to a life of dignity, peace, and justice. This is the deeper meaning of the activity they undertook against a government that violated and crushed human rights both personal and social. . . . We make our own the deeper motives animating their struggle for justice and life.
>
> The blood of those who gave their lives in this prolonged struggle . . . signifies the deployment of new energies in the building of a new Nicaragua. The hopes set on this revolution rest chiefly on the young people of Nicaragua. They have shown a generosity and courage that have astonished the world and they will be the principal builders of the new "civilization of love" which we want to fashion [Puebla 1183].

Marytrdom and Faith in the God of Life

This holiness that takes the form of martyrdom, this subjective testimony given by the Church is connected with the objective testimony of the Church. I do not regard an analysis of this connection to be of purely academic and conceptual interest. I think that a deeper grasp of the relationship between believing in life and giving one's life is the way to a grasp of the essence and practice of the Christian faith.

The witness of martyrdom is *historically* a consequence of the objective witness in behalf of life. Only if we understand witness to God and Jesus as witness in behalf of life can we understand the inevitability of persecution and martyrdom. More concretely, only when testimony is given to the elementary levels of life in a world of injustice can persecution and martyrdom be explained. In other parts of the world there will be other forms of injustice and violation of human rights; when these occur at the elementary levels, the defense of life provokes persecution and martyrdom. The defense of life causes the witness of holiness on the part of the Church to take this radical form not merely in isolated cases but on a broad front.

From the *theological* standpoint the relationship between God as object of faith and our way of reaching him becomes clearer. Although the question might seem a transcendental and a priori one (and to that extent academic), it is not out of place to ask what objective content of the faith can require human beings to give even their lives for it. The formal answer to the question is simple: the will of God. No created thing, not even one's life, can be allowed to be an obstacle to the doing of God's will. But it is not idle to ask what there is in the will of God to prevent such a demand from seeming arbitrary. If the giving of one's life is ultimate for the subject, then we must ask what the ultimate focus of God's will is that makes the giving of one's life "plausible" and "understandable" (I am trying to find words for a case for which language provides none).

In view of what I have said, the "ultimate" with which God's will is concerned is the life of human beings and, concretely, a just life for human beings. This ultimate concern, precisely because it is ultimate, renders plausible the ultimacy called for in the witness of martyrdom. Conversely, death accepted in order that others may have life is a profound experience both of God and of the unqualified ultimacy of life. When one gives one's life for the life of others, one affirms by that very act the God of life.

There is a paradox here: one must give one's own life in order that others may live. The paradox is real because creation and history are permeated by the sin that produces antilife. We do not know whether in a created world in which there were no sin it would be necessary to give one's life for the life of others. But in the created world as we have it, the sin of antilife can only be overcome by allowing one's self in a first stage to be overcome by it. In our experience of God, the experience of sin's effects and then the giving of one's own life is the way of asserting our faith in the God of life.

Perhaps no more than this can be said at the notional level, nor is it possible to look at this level for a rational synthesis that brings into harmony the ultimacy of the God of life and the ultimacy expressed in the giving of one's life. The experience in question here fits in better with a negative theology. In martyrdom as in every death there is a not-knowing, a necessary mediation of the element of not-knowing in order that the mystery of God be maintained. But in this supreme not-knowing there is manifested a profound knowing of the supremacy of life, a knowing to which testimony is given in action but over which there is no conceptual control.

From the *historical* viewpoint this is how the two aspects of faith—the *fides quae creditur* and the *fides qua creditur*—are brought into unity. The content of faith (*fides quae creditur*) is not simply "God," nor does the act of faith (*fides qua creditur*) consist simply in the "giving" of the human person to God. "God" and "giving" reciprocally concretize and explain each other from within and not merely in terms of conceptual formalities, when we are dealing with a God who wills a just life for human beings and with a total self-giving in order that this just life may come into being.

From the viewpoint of *salvation*, the mysterious relation between the giving of one's own life an an abundant life for others comes into play. I call the relation a mysterious one because it is impossible to prove a priori that life springs from martyrdom. Historical observation yields no religious conclusions here, but within the mystery of faith martyrdom is seen as salvific in its effects, that is, as not simply an expression of subjective holiness but as something actually productive of life for human beings. The mystery of the Servant of Yahweh and of the cross of Jesus is repeated.

The testimony of martyrdom is in the service of historical salvation. There is no question of choosing pain as if suffering were something good in itself or of choosing sacrifice as if the first and essential step in approaching God were sacrifice. We are dealing with what we see in the testimony of the Servant of Yahweh whose immediate goal is historical liberation (Is. 42:4) and who by his travail justifies many (Is. 53:11). This mystery of the Servant is experienced with all the greater intensity in Latin America to the extent that it is the entire people that seeks liberation and shares in the travail of the Servant. In christological terms it is the entire people that provides Jesus with a historical body; in it what is lacking in his sufferings may be completed (Col. 1:24).[20] Because persecution and martyrdom are accepted in the spirit of the Servant, they keep alive the hope and struggle for liberation and are therefore salvific, even within history.

The Church's witness of martyrdom draws its vitality from the original option in favor of life, justice, and liberation. It represents the acceptance of the historically inevitable suffering that the option in favor of life entails. Since the suffering is accepted with the same faith that animated the Servant of Yahweh, it becomes effective for salvation. There is no rational explanation. The important thing is to see that this is what is occurring in the Church and that by reason of it the Church is growing as Church. The historical response to the historical conditions in Latin America is making the Church deepen and unify its faith in the God of life, making it give its life after the manner of the Servant. For this reason its practice and its hope do not fail.

THE TESTIMONY TO THE FULLNESS OF LIFE: THE CHRISTIANIZATION OF THE HUMAN

In this consideration of martyrdom I have indicated what the fullness of the Church's essential testimony, or at least the central core of that testimony, is. I wish now to offer some reflections on the objective testimony of the Church in favor of the fullness of life. These considerations are important if we are to be faithful to God, who is not only the creator and liberator but also the consummator who bestows fulfillment. They are also important for understanding what I said about witness to a just life at the elementary level being part of the overall testimony of the Church, and therefore for answering the charge (often motivated by self-interest) that the Church is reducing its activity to the sociopolitical level.

Humanization and Christianization

My basic thesis is that the Church's service to the fullness of life takes the form of a constant humanization of the human at all levels and in all situations. This presupposes that the human is always able to grow and deepen. The positive reason behind the statement is that the Christian faith has the power to humanize in a way specifically its own, which we may call "christianization."

The human that is to be christianized develops at three levels: (1) the historical level, which includes the basic fact that the human being is both material and spiritual, personal and social, partly the product of history and partly the active shaper of history; (2) the transcendent level, which includes the fact that the human being is related to something that is prior to and greater than itself and in which it finds its fulfillment; (3) the symbolic or liturgical level, which includes the fact that human beings give expression to the deeper meaning of history and that, if they are Christians, they do so in terms of and in view of the transcendent.

These three levels are to a certain extent independent and relatively autonomous, in the sense that the levels correspond to different areas of human life. Thus the humanization (at least in its conscious and explicit form) of one level does not automatically follow the humanization of another. The practical consequence of this for the Church's witness to the fullness of life is that the Church must explicitly give witness at each level.

The three are also connected. This assertion is based not simply on a transcendental a priori anthropology but on the Christian understanding of the human person and God. This means concretely that even the proclamation of the fullness of transcendent life is connected with the testimony regarding the fullness of historical life.

The conclusion from this statement is that the Church has an obligation to humanize *all* levels of historical reality and this in *every* historical situation, and that it will thereby also bear witness to the fullness of transcendent life, which it celebrates and anticipates in its liturgy.

The Church and the Humanization of History

In order to understand what is meant positively here, let us first look at the matter from a negative viewpoint, that is, from the standpoint of the Church's temptation not to act in this way. The first manifestation of this temptation would be for the Church—in its explicit testimony to the fullness of life—to focus on the liturgical and transcendent levels as being its proper field and to abandon the historical level. This can happen for theoretical reasons, derived from a bad theology, or for practical reasons, such as the competence possessed by other "humanitarian" ideologies that deal with the historical level, in comparison with which the Church is supposedly incompetent. The error would consist in trying to approach the transcendent plenitude independently of a "less complete" historical plenitude. This would be not only an error but also a temptation because such a course would be an abandonment by the Church of faith in the God of life.

The temptation could also arise if the Church were to agree that it must bear witness to the fullness of life at the historical level but then it would distinguish various historical spheres, some of which (spiritual and moral) could be fulfilled while others (material, economic, and social) could not. Or it would distinguish between certain situations in which the Church can promote the fullness of historical life (peaceful situations, situations in which there is a formal democracy), and others which do not permit it to do this (situations of conflict, situations in which the society is socialist).

The error here does not consist in saying that at certain levels and in certain situations (for example, the level of basic human necessities or in situations of conflict) there is no dynamic exigency to overcome the situations and turn them into "better" ones. It consists rather in abandoning these levels as not proper for the testimony of the Church and in considering any activity of the Church at these levels to be transitory and provisional. It is the temptation so often met in the Church: seeking to bear witness to the fullness of life "in itself" without being willing to pass through the prior levels, each of which needs to be planned and makes historically possible the access to the more fully human levels of life.

Expressed in positive terms the Church's obligation is to christianize the historical level. This means that it must humanize the structures in which human beings live and by which the human beings who create them are shaped in the process.

In Christian language this means that structures must be humanized along the lines of the reign of God so that they may promote the satisfaction of elementary needs, basic equality among human beings, solidarity among them, and sharing of power.

Human beings must likewise be humanized so as to develop toward what the New Testament calls the new person. The new human beings are those who are able to learn, change, and be converted and thus to be honest with themselves; persons whose values are those of the Sermon on the Mount, whose eyes and heart are pure, who show mercy, are devoted to justice and ready to run the risks that this devotion entails, who prefer peace to needless struggle; those who are ready to forgive their enemies, are generous in victory, and always give their adversary another chance. They are, finally, disposed to be thankful for life and to celebrate it; they believe in life and continue to hope.

All this, though formulated in the categories of the gospel, is in itself historical. There is no need to be explicit on the liturgical and transcendent levels. The first task of the Church is to deal with all this when it seeks to bear witness to the fullness of life. Of course in themselves these traits, because historical, are limited and therefore do not embody the fullness of life in an unqualified sense. At the same time, these limited realities contain within themselves an exigency of a "more," an ever closer approximation to the ideal of the reign of God and of the new person. The witness of the Church properly consists in encouraging and fostering this "more" and penetrating ever more deeply into the historical realm in order that the latter may yield ever "more" of itself in the direction indicated.

The fullness of life to which the Church must bear witness must not consist in something borrowed from the liturgical and transcendent levels. Fulfillment is not quantitative. It does not add to the limited historical fulfillment a "plus" of transcendence. This is precisely the temptation we see at work at the beginning of the Church's history in the form of the docetism, gnosticism, and enthusiasm that are condemned in the theologies of John and Paul: the temptation to look for fulfillment and salvation outside history instead of finding it by penetrating more deeply into the historical.

The Church must, in addition, give witness to the fullness of historical life in any and every situation, although the fullness will have to be understood analogously according to different situations. It is therefore not to be claimed or insinuated that certain occasions are not favorable to the Church's witness, either because the situation is one of conflict or because in a situation in which rebuilding is going on the more elementary and urgent levels of life take priority. I mention these two examples because they are topical and because they present a new challenge to the Church's testimony.

Let us take the first example. The Church will have to humanize two important aspects in a situation of conflict: the appearance of new human values and the appearance of serious, even armed conflicts. The Church must encourage the emerging values of the people, for example, conscientization, organization, solidarity, the ethical responsibility imposed by struggles, and generous selfgiving. At the same time, the Church must exercise constructive criticism in order to prevent or minimize the antivalues that arise as negative by-products, such as disunion, excessive claim to a leadership role, the tendency to vengefulness, and the abuse of power.

The Church must try to humanize the conflict when this becomes inevitable and serious. Such humanization extends to an overall ethical judgment on the conflict and a signaling of the side on which basic truth is to be found. In extreme cases it includes a declaration of the legitimacy of an insurrection, a declaration that calls to mind the conditions for a just war. These conditions come down to this: the conflict must produce more life, not less. In addition to passing basic judgment on the conflict, the Church must also try to humanize the conflict. In Latin America we often find verified what Paul VI once said: the very struggle "frequently finds its ultimate motivation on noble impulses of justice and solidarity."[21] It is the Church's role in the process of humanization to see that these "noble impulses" be followed in as rational a way as possible and transformed into effective forces that are as human as possible.

Without going into the complex case histories of various Latin American situations, we can draw a conclusion from these considerations. The Church must bear witness to life even in situations of conflict, including serious conflict. It cannot act as if a given situation were not favorable for its testimony and it ought therefore to wait for a better occasion. The Church as a human, historical reality must, even in conflict, bear witness to hope and do all it can so that life may attain a greater fullness. Here I think there is something new. It may be formulated theoretically: the Church's role is not simply to pass judgment on situations of conflict and possibly to decide which party reason supports. No, the Church's task is to humanize the conflict from within in order that it may engender prolife values and that the solution to the conflict may engender more life. The Church's witness in favor of the fullness of historical truth must accept history as it is; this witness cannot be given from a position apart from the conflict.

When a nation is being rebuilt along anticapitalist, socialist lines (as is the case now in Nicaragua), the Church must accept the situation as it is and from within it give its own testimony to the fullness of historical life. It will have to be conscious of the new situation in which it is living and make this newness the object of profound theo-logical reflection. It is understandable that the newness should lead to a certain confusion and not-knowing within the Church. It is important, however, to distinguish between a fruitful not-knowing and a paralyzing not-knowing. The latter may be due to the fact that the revolution has taken the place within an old humanism, which the Church defended in the past; it may be due to the basic question of how the Church is to conduct its life within a new regime that is oriented to socialist principles; or it may be due to the more immediate fact that the Church is losing its importance as an institution.

There can also be an immensely fruitful not-knowing which, when formulated in theo-logical terms, means taking this question seriously: What is God saying today about the history of Nicaragua? The question gives evidence of a theo-logical not-knowing that is radical, precisely because the question has to do with what is new about a historical event. It is a fruitful not-knowing because it makes the Church exercise discernment on points that are fundamental: the kind of life to which the Church's witness must be given; how its testimony should be given; how it can and must promote the fullness of life in this new situation.

I believe the Church must bear witness to life by supporting those structural changes in the economic, social, and political spheres that favor life at its elementary levels and that reorganize the sharing of power so as to guarantee a better life. The Church must bear witness by promoting the human values that are being engendered but that need careful cultivation: solidarity, generosity, austerity, joy among the people at large, magnanimity in victory, the practice of reconciliation, and what the bishops have called revolutionary creativity. By promoting all these things the Church will bear witness to the fullness of historical life.

Liturgy and Transcendence

This manner of bearing witness to the fullness of historical life is geared to the historical situation but reflects nonetheless the specific nature of the Church, that is, the Christian faith. I give the name *Christianization* to this kind of humanization, because the latter is objectively in conformity with the values of the Christian faith, even if these values may not be explicitly put forward as Christian.

The Church believes that if it is to humanize fully it must also bear witness to the fullness of life at the transcendent and liturgical levels. This is obviously one of the Church's obligations. It offers this witness to others so that they may freely accept it. At the transcendent level the Church offers an explicit cultivation of faith in the eschatological life wherein God will be all in all. It also offers faith in Jesus who is the first fruit of the new creation; the following of Jesus puts us on the road to this new creation.

At the liturgical level the Church offers the celebration of historical life at a depth made possible by its transcendent faith, for it believes that the word of God is constantly revealing the depths of the human and pointing out the direction in which the human can become even more fully so.

The Church believes in the necessity and importance of historical life for its celebration of the liturgy and the formulation of its transcendent faith. Let us not forget that "resurrection," "new heaven," and "new earth" are all described as the fulfillment of historical life. Let us not forget either that only through incarnation and the assumption of the flesh of history can we share in the fullness of the divine.

Conversely, the Church also believes that the explicit cultivation of transcendent faith and the celebration of this in the liturgy, that is, the explicit remembrance of Jesus and the celebration of this dangerous memory, far from separating us from history, are a doctrinal spur to a greater incarnation and a more intense search for historical fulfillment. In its faith the Church finds a powerful incentive to transform history; it also finds therein the basic lines along which history is to be transformed. This is why testimony to the fullness of life at the level of faith is so necessary: both for the sake of fidelity to the Church's own nature and for the sake of the humanizing efficacy present in the Church's explicit message. The Church believes in God and in his Christ; it believes that human beings will attain to a greater humanization with God and his Christ than without them.

The Church must maintain its own specific character when it bears witness to the fullness of life. This means that the Church must unify the historical and transcendent levels and do so in the way proper to itself. Here I must call attention to the "utopian" character of the Church's witness and to the Church's consequent task of proclaiming utopian principles. The Church must maintain the utopian principle that on the one hand God's reign inspires historical accomplishments and on the other it refuses to absolutize these accomplishments; that God's reign inspires effective action in the process of liberation and increasingly humanizes the persons who are active in this process.

I call these principles "utopian" because they cannot be adequately translated into historical reality and are at times difficult to put into historical form at all. This is due to the "transcendent" element in the Church's testimony. I call them "principles" nonetheless, because they can set in motion something of positive value for the historical world. The mission of the Church is to give historical shape to these principles. This is the historical contribution made by the Church's testimony. The witness of the Church in behalf of the fullness of life is meant to help history along the road to God's utopia by effecting a partial realization of this utopia within history.[22]

Conclusion

By way of conclusion I would like to emphasize the serious responsibility the Church has of taking part, in its own specific way, in the new processes that are coming into existence throughout Latin America. The Church's testimony to the fullness of life and its humanization and Christianization of these processes will be possible only if it takes part in them, accepting what is new, ambiguous, and conflictive. A humanization from outside, a humanization that is purely a matter of statements, would be a formal denial of the Christian incarnational plan and would represent a lapse into the most basic of Christian temptations: docetism and gnosticism. This temptation might today take more sophisticated forms, appealing to the transcendence and specific character of the Christian faith as not adequately identifiable with any concrete historical embodiment. But when all is said and done, it is the gnostic and docetic temptation to seek salvation through ideas and not through incarnation, through a supposed truth and not through love that takes concrete historical form.

In the present situation in Latin America the Church has a serious responsibility to bear witness in the way I have explained. For *ethical* reasons, the Church, like any other social body in Latin America, cannot be indifferent to the task of humanizing and bringing justice to the continent. For *ecclesial* and *institutional* reasons humanization is a key factor in the Church's credibility and in the possibility of the Church's being accepted by other, nonecclesial groups that promote humanistic projects. For *theo-logical* reasons it is only through humanization, in the radical way that I have described, that the Church will be able to bear witness to God and even itself believe in God. It would be a tragic mistake for the Church not to take seriously this responsibility for humanization because then, especially in places and processes of liberation, the Church would simply wither and deprive these processes of the potential inherent in its faith.

In many places in Latin America the Church is meeting or attempting to meet this serious obligation. When it does so we see what is most original in its witness. Despite all the limitations, fears, mistakes, and sins that accompany its activity and that of the other, nonecclesial groups with which it joins forces, the Church is coming to realize that its witness can be truly given only where the stakes are life or death, the humanization or dehumanization of the men and women of the continent. It is also coming to realize that its obligation is to bear witness to life and to life in its fullness, even if to this end it must give of its own life and even that life itself. As it thus gives itself, it is in turn given the grace of preserving and growing in its faith in God and in its following of Jesus.

7

Unity and Conflict in the Church

Unity and division, reconciliation and conflict, are human realities that run through the history of the human race and the history of the Church. They point to the presence of different values, different stands on what the Church should and should not be. They are first and foremost historical realities, the existence of which cannot be denied. My purpose in this chapter is to analyze and consider the relation between the conflict and the division in the Church. I emphasize the existence of these two in order to deideologize the theological understanding of unity and to help show what unity should involve and what the Christian conditions of its possibility are.

Conflict in the Church is a fact that has emerged in a new way since Vatican II. We often hear high Vatican officials speaking out in criticism of protest as a widespread fact of life in our day. Rare in Latin America is the country or diocese in which there is no conflict between the hierarchy and Christians at the base and—this is even more striking—among the bishops. Despite all efforts to give an appearance of unity, divisions and conflicts at the national and continental levels are an inescapable fact.

The fact, then, is undeniable. It is of greater interest and importance, however, to see in what way it is new and what its roots and meaning are. This is what I shall try to analyze here, with the focus of my attention being on the structural and ecclesial aspects of conflict. In focusing on the *structure* of the Church, I want to move beyond a merely personal and psychological analysis of the causes of conflicts. Of course personal sin and the will of individuals and groups forcing their ideas on others are a cause of conflicts. *Ubi peccatum, ibi multitudo*: where there is sin, there is disunion. It is more important to discover the concrete forms that this sinfulness (inherent in every individual and social group) takes in the structure of the Church. I shall also focus my attention on the ecclesial aspect of the structure we call the Church. In other words, my concern is not so much with the tendency toward conflict inherent in any institution (a general fact that holds for the Church as well) as with what the fact of being a "Church" brings to the existence of conflict. I shall also be concerned with a statement of what the unity of the Church should be and the way of achieving this unity.

THE FACT OF SOCIAL CONFLICT IN OUR DAY

In the period just prior to Vatican II the Church gave the appearance of internal unity. Major tensions between the various bodies of Christians existed, especially between Catholics and Protestants, but the Catholic Church thought of itself as being by its nature the "one" Church and therefore endeavored to show itself as such on the stage of history. It regarded this unity as one of its constitutive marks. It ideologized this "unity" not simply as an eschatological ideal toward which the ecclesial community must tend but as a historical reality that would also show the Catholic Church to be the true Church of Christ. Not only public conflict with its attacks and disputes, but even simple differences of opinion were regarded as dangerous, as something that should not exist. Disciplinary means were used to secure a single liturgy, a single theology, even a single philosophy, as well as a single ethic. The Catholic Church gave the impression of monolithic unity, although when examined more closely the unity was often nothing more than uniformity.

At the same time the hierarchical structure of the Church as conceived and developed in practice before Vatican II supposed a latent tendency to conflict. The distinction between hierarchy and faithful, superiors and subjects, which was understood in the light of a monarchical ecclesiology with its roots in posttridentine controversial theology, supposed a situation of unstable balance. In theory and in practice all power—doctrinal, executive, and judicial

—was reserved to the hierarchy; the faithful were certainly a part of the Church, but only a passive part.

Whether the hierarchical concept of the Church and the passage from ecclesiology to hierarchology had a strong basis in Scripture and early tradition or not is irrelevant here. The important thing is that the Church was structured as a set of groups—not simply groups that legitimately exercised different functions in the Church, but groups that were sociologically and ecclesiologically distinct and sometimes antagonistic. The situation was one of latent—and at times, real—conflict. An effort was made to suppress conflicts by administrative means; they were condemned at the ideological level in the name of the absolute unity of the Church.

Initial attempts to break out of this situation of uniformity, which had been historically imposed and justified in the name of unity, and to conceive of the Church's unity as a unity in complexity were made in the name of pluralism.[1] The supposition with which the defenders of this new position started was that neither ideologies nor cultures are eternal (as could be shown from philosophy and even from the history of the Church). They are historical and changeable. Pluralism thus becomes a necessity, especially in theology and the liturgy. Some rather timid voices called for pluralism in the priestly life: for example, in the priest-worker movement and in the petition made in the time of Pope Pius XII that priestly ministry should not entail obligatory celibacy.

These attempts met with varying degrees of success. Pluralism was sanctioned by Vatican II or at least by the theology that developed around the Council. The important thing for us here is to observe that pluralism, as a theoretical model for reconciling unity and multiformity, was not essentially conflictive. The model called for a diversity of forms, especially in theology and liturgy, while maintaining the generic unity of which the various theologies and liturgies were applications. Unity was presupposed; problems, if any arose, would appear in the various expressions of the originating unity. Presupposed, therefore, was the peaceful coexistence of various ways of Churchly existence. Pluralism lacked the concept of unity based on mission, that is, based on what the Church existed to do, both proximately and in the future. Above all, the element of partisanship proper to this mission was absent. Turning to the poor and the oppressed, if considered at all, was just one more demand made on the Church; it did not give concrete form to the Church's entire activity. Because this constitutive partisanship was missing, no attention was paid to the fact that the Church and the world were made up of antagonists: the oppressed and their oppressors. Yet this deepest cause of conflict provides the perspective in which the unity of the Church must be considered.

Today, especially in Latin America, the problem appears quite differently. I am not denying that the problem described above did exist in the past. It arose from a particular understanding of the hierarchical Church. However, it is not now the most typical problem nor does it explain either present unity or present conflict. There are two ways in which our present situation differs from that of the past. First (and this is a matter of objective description), the line along which today's Church is divided or united is not that of authority and obedience but that of the understanding and practice of the faith. This is something new. Today we have distinct currents cutting across the hierarchy and the ordinary faithful. It is not possible to speak of a *single* hierarchy, a *single* clergy, or of *the* laity. Each of the various currents brings together and serves as a focus for many bishops, priests, religious, and laypeople; as a result, social status within the ecclesial institution becomes relative. The fact of adherence to an ideological and practical trend serves to divide the currents or trends from each other. The present situation is therefore characterized by an ecclesial unity of a kind unknown in the past; this in turn sparks division between the various currents and, as a result, conflict in the Church.

The problem of unity and division is seen not as an intraecclesial problematic but as the reality of the Third World. It is seen as a reality outside the Church, but one that is the source of the currents uniting and therefore also dividing Christians. Because this source of differentiation is outside the Church, what could once have been a simple division or separation or diversity of mentalities has now been transformed into a conflict. The conflict is inevitable, necessary, even called for in the name of the gospel. It is the price to be paid for authentic union.

Let me be more concrete. The conflict of recent years within the Church might be symbolized by the different stands taken by various groups of Christians toward the Medellín Conference. Medellín is a symbol that both unites and separates. In theory no Christian, no member of the hierarchy, would dare reject Medellín. In practice, however, this is precisely what is being done. Some speak of a "withdrawal from Medellín," others of a "correct interpretation of Medellín." For some Medellín was the beginning of a new stage, the potential of which needed to be developed and given concrete form. According to these individuals Medellín is now dying the death of a thousand qualifications and distinctions. Little is now left of the original substance that even an unsophisticated reading would find in its documents. For others Medellín came as a surprise that they accepted in principle without knowing just what the surprise was and what its historical consequences would be. Once these consequences manifested themselves the withdrawal began: the qualifications, the "correct" interpretations, and, finally, the effort to eliminate the surprise, to return to the familiar ground of traditional Church life and politics, and to avoid confrontations with the powerful and with persecution.

This situation cannot be properly called pluralism. This is not a case, like the one mentioned above, of the base asserting itself against the uniformity imposed by authority. In the new situation hierarchy and base alike are divided. In addition, pluralism supposes a variety of opinions and currents, whereas in Latin America the options are effectively reduced to two.[2] In a situation of pluralism peaceful coexistence of the various ways of thinking is conceivable: but in the present situation where there are two polarized currents—not only of thought but also of practice—peaceful coexistence is not to be found, only opposition between the two currents.

Pluralism was originally a way of regaining freedom in the face of an imposed uniformity; in present-day Latin America, however, it often becomes an alibi for not moving effectively along the lines set down by Medellín. To put it another way, the appeal to pluralism (which even in contemporary Latin America does have meaning within the area of the theology of liberation) often becomes a weapon of ecclesial politics in defense of clearly conservative attitudes and interests.

Recent years have made it abundantly clear that the present ecclesial situation is structurally one of conflict. Many important posts in the CELAM (the Latin American Bishops Conference) and its commissions have been filled by those who adhere to the ideological position of the bishops. Institutes that came into existence on the basis of Medellín have been suppressed or relocated. However, a number of bishops have found platforms for gathering and communicating other than those provided by CELAM or the episcopal conferences. Various movements at the level of basic groups, at least by structure and independent of the intention of individuals within them, work along opposite lines. Many movements are attempting to get back to the interior life proper to the Christian faith, to find a common ground in the liturgy or in the ordering of private and familial life, whereas other groups are directly concerned with making their Christian faith effective on the sociopolitical scene.

A number of groups of priests are at odds both in theory and in practice with the traditional exercise of the priestly ministry. Economic support is given (indirectly through influence with European and North American organizations) to this or that Christian group depending on its type of activity. There is competition at the ideological level with some groups orbiting, so to speak, around the theology of liberation in one or other of its forms, and others fighting against this theology, offering as an alternative a more or less tidied up version of traditional theology or even a watered down, nominal version of liberation theology that is in fact ultimately antiliberationist. There is competition in the organizing of congresses of theology and the pastoral life. The type of theologian invited depends on the organizers. The question of the orthodoxy of certain theologians has even been raised, not because these theologians show any desire to bring back old heresies, but because the question serves as a way of discrediting them. More recently there was the sad, secret manipulation in the preparation for the Third General Conference of the Latin American Bishops at Puebla in 1979. "Scandalous conflict" is the only way to describe the varied and even contradictory reactions of the different bishops to situations affecting the Church, especially the persecution that has led to the martyrdom of priests and catechists.

These observations show clearly that the present situation of the Latin American Church is one of conflict and not of pluralism. If we prescind from details, we must say that the two present trends are antagonistic in their overall direction. Perhaps the most interesting thing about the conflict is that it will apparently not lead to a schism or heresy in the traditional sense of these terms, since the Christians in the vanguard claim that they are remaining in the Church. If this turns out to be the case, then the conflict will be with us for a long time. It is not likely to be resolved by an appeal to the general unity of the Church or to the legitimacy of pluralism or to any doctrine on the charisms, since the two currents do not understand themselves to represent complementary functions in the Church. On the contrary, both claim to embody a comprehensive concept of ecclesial existence and will therefore be antagonistic, at least in practice.

I have taken some time to analyze the conflict and to show that it is not reducible to simple pluralism. I have done so in order to clarify the positive meaning of the unity that is desirable for the Church and to "deideologize" this unity on the basis both of the real facts and of the theology of the Church. I continue this task in the following reflections.

THE NEW ECCLESIOLOGY AND THE POSSIBILITY OF CONFLICT IN THE CHURCH

My purpose in this section is to show how a new ecclesiology has made conflict in the Church both possible and real. I am not claiming that simply by its existence as a theory this ecclesiology has given rise to the conflicts in question. I am saying that a new ecclesiology has done away with the justification for identifying Church unity with uniformity and has brought the Church into real contact with the world, the place of conflict. I can make this point only in a sketchy way, concentrating on the really significant phases in the development.

The Church Is Not the Kingdom

The Church is not the kingdom of God. Later on I shall consider the positive relationship between the Church and the kingdom. At the moment I must emphasize the denial of identity because this is the first step in getting rid of an ecclesiology that is false both in its content and in the method used for justifying the content.

This discovery in ecclesiology, taken for granted today, was made around the turn of the century. It was realized that the message of Jesus was an eschatological message. In analyzing this eschatological or ultimate reality in the service of which Jesus was acting, it was discovered that the properly eschatological reality is not the Church but the kingdom of God. Jesus did not preach or establish (in the conventional sense of the term) any Church; he simply proclaimed a kingdom of God that was at hand. The ultimate, definitive reality in the eyes of Jesus was the kingdom, not the Church.

This is not to say that there was no theological and historical continuity between Jesus and the Church (which came into existence after his resurrection) or that we may not speak of the Church as having been "founded" by Christ. This is not the place for a positive development of this subject. The important thing here is that the ultimate reality is the kingdom and that the Church is not absolute (that quality belongs only to the kingdom) but relational. As in the case of Jesus himself, the nature and plenitude of the Church comes from its relation to the kingdom.

Implied in the message of Jesus about the kingdom of God is the message that the kingdom brings a judgment (*krisis*) inasmuch as the coming of the ultimate criticizes and makes relative any and every created reality. The kingdom of God does not come as a possibility inherent in present existence but only and always as the result of a break. There is nothing created or historical that must not pass through the same break. Jesus could not speak of the break through which the Church must pass, but it is clear from his attitude to structures, even those salvational (according to the Old Testament) and dear to God, that the kingdom of God makes everything relative: the institutions of Israel, the covenant, the Law, the very traditions about God and his kingdom, insofar as these took concrete, particular form. The kindgom of God as a new reality and the God of Jesus as the ever greater God make creation relative and put it in a state of crisis.

All this has two consequences: one has to do with the Church as a whole; the other with the institutional structure of the Church. If the Church as a whole is not identifiable with the kingdom of God, then it is open to criticism; moreover, inasmuch as the kingdom subjects every created reality to judgment, then the Church must be criticized. These statements are general and as such can be accepted without great difficulty by anyone who does not wish to deny the evidence of exegesis. Such statements do not directly and adequately explain the present conflict within the Latin American Church, but acceptance of them is nonetheless basic for understanding the possibility and meaning of such conflict. Of course, few people would claim that the Church is identifiable with the kingdom of God or, in other words, that it is absolute; in practice, however, many often act as if the Church were indeed the kingdom and an absolute—absolute in the pope or the Vatican or an episcopal conference or in a particular avant-garde movement.

The greatest structural temptation for the Church arises out of its relational character. On the one hand, the Church is entrusted with the tradition of the kingdom and the requirement to make the kingdom a reality; on the other hand, it is not itself the kingdom. This combination of factors puts the Church in a situation of "concupiscence," that is, of wanting to be, by identity, that which in fact it can and must only point to and serve, namely, the kingdom of God. In consequence, the possibility of conflict is always present; and when a particular situation clearly shows the difference and distance between Church and kingdom, the conflict breaks out—and cannot but break out—spontaneously. The discovery that the kingdom of God is the ultimate reality has brought an elemental truth to light: the Church, even in its entirety, is not absolute and therefore its structure is open to criticism.

If the Church is not an absolute, then neither are its structures. Each of its structures exercises a function, positive in principle, in regard to the entire ecclesial body. But in the final analysis something else passes judgment on hierarchy and faithful alike. The structure of the Church is not salvific by its own inherent nature. And someone can rise up within the Church to remind it of this truth—someone in the hierarchy or among the faithful. When account is taken within the Church of the difference between the Church and the kingdom of God, then a Christian conflict may arise. There is in principle no institutional mechanism within the Church for stifling this kind of protest, provided the criticism is made not for the sake of self-interest but for the sake of the kingdom.

All this does not tell us how conflict is to be handled, who has the right and duty to incite it, and how it is to be resolved. The point here is that if the Church is something relational and not absolute, then it ceases to be untouchable, it is open to criticism. This truth was recognized from the beginning of the New Testament but was forgotten after Trent; it was rediscovered at the level of theory when the eschatological message of Jesus was analyzed.

The Church Must Follow Jesus

The Church must follow the real historical Jesus. The Church engages in various activities; it has a liturgy, a doctrine, an organization. But the most fundamental and important thing about the Church is that it follows Jesus. If it does not do this, it corrupts its own nature; if it does do it, it will do everything else in a Christian way.

In what sense has the rediscovery of the historical Jesus been one of the causes of conflict? Let me present my answer in three parts. First, Jesus was a relational entity: he did not preach himself or even God; he preached the kingdom of God. He preached the God who is at hand in his kingdom. This means that Jesus is not a self-contained absolute, but stands in relation to the kingdom of God and to the Father who is going to reveal himself through him. In absolute terms, Jesus is the Son; but he is in absolute terms the Son only insofar as he lives from and for the Father.

Second, Jesus is related to the kingdom not only through his preaching but also through his action. He does not simply declare a truth for the purpose of making it known; he places his entire life at the service of the truth so that truth may become a reality. He does not merely preach that the kingdom of God is at hand; he tries to make the kingdom real. The modern Church has followed a doctrinal concept of revelation. Vatican II tried to complement this view by adding that revelation comes through both *words* and *deeds*, but the Council did not pay enough attention to the relation between the words and the deeds of Jesus. The discovery here is that Jesus does not simply preach the coming of the kingdom but also tries to establish it, to make it a reality. His life is dedicated to the practice of the kingdom, as can be seen from his activity in behalf of the oppressed, his miracles, his exorcisms, his criticism of a society that is a negation of the kingdom, his consistency in action until he is put to death. Here there is no opposition between word and deed because the word in the form of prophetic cricitism, or the consciousness-raising word, or the challenging word, or the word as theory of what must come, is also a practice. The real opposition is between two conceptions of the activity of Jesus: teaching about the kingdom, and practice of the kingdom that includes both words and deeds.

Third, Jesus tries to make the kingdom of God a reality within his own concrete history. This history is dominated by sin in its various forms: the selfishness and will to power of individuals and structures that are clearly unjust. Jesus tries to make the kingdom a reality within this structure, not apart from it. His words pass judgment on the structure from within; his moral preaching presents an alternative to this situation; his vision of the future stands over against it; his practice of miracles and liberation is directed against those in power. For this he is persecuted and dies on the cross. He attempted to make the kingdom a reality within his own conflict-ridden history, and therefore the power of sin crushed him.

This rediscovery of the historical Jesus has important consequences for the Church's self-understanding. If the Church sees in its founder not just any Christ but the Christ who is Jesus of Nazareth, then it cannot be grounded solely or primarily on instructions that Jesus may have given regarding the organization and mission of the Church; it must be grounded first and foremost on the life of Jesus.

If this be so, it implies consequences for the Church that will cause conflict, at least in our present historical situation. The first is that the Church cannot and must not preach itself, any more than Jesus preached himself. If the Church consciously or unconsciously puts itself first, conflict becomes likely as soon as someone reminds the Church that this is its first and fundamental sin. The basic conflict will take the form of a tension between the Church's preaching of itself, its boosting of its own institutions, its attempt to make itself more important, and its preaching of the kingdom as something that is distinct from it and may even be opposed to the historical shape the Church has taken.

This conflict is aggravated if the Church, like Jesus, moves on from a purely preaching mission to a practical implementation of the content of what it preaches. As long as the Church considers its mission to be simply one of proclaiming something, even something so sublime as Christ, God, or the kingdom, conflicts within the Church will be relatively minor; they will be reducible to problems of orthodoxy or scholastic discussion about the hermeneutic and the pastoral approach that are best calculated to make the message intelligible. But when the Church passes from "proclaiming" something to "doing" the content of what it proclaims, then serious conflicts begin.

The key question that must be asked of today's Church and that will condition all conflict in the Church is this: Does the Church seek only to proclaim Christ or does it seek also to do what Jesus did and in this way declare him to be the Christ? Obviously these are not mutually exclusive alternatives nor are they even historically exclusive, since there has always been something of each present in the Church. But the emphasis in each case is different and so will be the ensuing conflict. If the inclination is to the first alternative, then the historical situation will have to be known so that the message may be made intelligible; but if the inclination is to the second, then the historical situation will have to be suffered so that the content of what is preached may be made a reality.

We have here in the theoretical and practical concept of the Church's mission the deepest root of present-day division and conflict in the Church. Today both the union and the division of Christians are rooted in different views of mission: mission is seen as a matter of proclaiming or it is seen as a matter of doing. The conflict intensifies if the doing is the kind considered above in the third point about the historical Jesus.

The type of mission that involves itself in the historical situation of Latin America and does not ignore the sin in this situation will rouse opposition, rejection, and persecution on the part of the mighty, whereas a mere preaching of the word will usually be tolerated. If to a particular practice of mission as a bringing into being of the kingdom we add the empirical consequences to which such a practice leads, we will understand the deepest root of conflict in the Church. The real division is between those who want to defend the Church—and its members—against the sin of society, even if this is done in a subtle way by limiting the Church's activity to a generic proclamation of the truth of Christ, and those who want to bring the Church into a sinful society with all the consequences such a move entails. The conflict is therefore not a simple divergence of views on how the Church can carry out its mission while acknowledging pluralism; rather it arises from the theoretical and practical conception of what it means to make the kingdom a reality.

If the Christian mission is to bring the kingdom to pass (a very complex business indeed), then the possibility of conflict acquires a new nuance, since the mission then has to do with the good of third parties and concretely with the good of the poor. I have elsewhere explained in detail what is meant by the Church of the poor, who the poor are, and the kind of partiality for the poor that is required if evangelization is to take place. From the viewpoint of an analysis of conflict the most important point is that the conflict does not reach its point of greatest intensity when it is a question of defending the internal nature of the Church or even (this is more characteristic of First World countries) of defending the rights of the individual Christian when these are threatened by the application of Church discipline. The conflict becomes most intense when it is a matter of defending the rights of a specific group of people, who in our continent happen to be the majority. I mean the rights of the oppressed, who are for the most part Christian and even Catholics.

This reference to the poor, which is justified by essential Christian theology and by the facts of our situation, shows that such a mission is urgent to the point that it cannot be postponed. A consequence of this urgency is a tension between those committed to such a mission and those others in the Church who directly or indirectly, but effectively, hinder it, depreciate it, or rob it of its necessary intensity. Since the poor are part of a dialectical relationship (that is, there are poor because there are rich and there are oppressed because there are oppressors), a mission that is directed to the poor becomes historically a source of antagonism. To pursue such a mission, to be of help, to give preference to the poor is impossible without making the causers of the poverty feel under attack. Even though the Church's mission is to all human beings, its partiality for the poor leads it into a historical conflict that divides the Church into those who side with the poor and those who do not.

This explains the intensity of conflict in the Church. The conflict is not a matter of divergent opinions proposed by dissenting schools nor of the lot of the Christian within the Church. It concerns a mission undertaken in behalf of the poorest and not in behalf of the Church. It concerns a mission to the poorest that has for its aim not simply to tell them that they have a Father in heaven but to help them live here and now with at least the minimum of dignity proper to the children of this Father. It is therefore a mistake to look solely to the subjectivity of individuals for the basic cause and basic solution of the problem of conflict. Of course the character of individuals and groups will determine the outward shape of the conflict, but the root of the conflict is not to be found there. The problem for the Church today is not a problem of psychology, as is often supposed, nor a problem of psychological docility or rebelliousness; it is a problem of mission. The will to power, in the form of self-assertion, will be present in all the groups that are implicated in a conflict, but the conflict will not be resolved simply by rejecting this will to power. It will be resolved by making it clear what the Christian mission must be.

In summary, the deepest source of conflict in the Church lies in divergent conceptions of the Church's mission. As long as this mission remains a matter of mere preaching (this does not of course exclude the addition of certain ethical demands), conflicts in the Church will be minimal, as is clear in those parts of the world or in those Christian groups that are concerned with problems of orthodoxy or hermeneutics or the pastoral approach best suited for making the message intelligible. But if the Church's mission is understood as a doing, an action taken on so that Jesus may be proclaimed as the Christ, then serious conflicts arise, as the Latin American situation proves. The doing in question will be that of Jesus, a doing that will explain Jesus, but in the final analysis it will be a building of the kingdom of God and not a mere giving of information about what the kingdom is or what form it should take. Thus understood, the mission of the Church has power to draw many Christians and to break down the barriers that have separated bishops, priests, and laity. Mission thus understood also divides and is therefore a source of conflict because it means defending not the cause of the Church but an outside cause, that of the poor.

If we specify the Church's mission in the way I have described, all the problems Christians have inside and outside the Church will not disappear, nor will we have explained all the nuances of intraecclesial conflict. There is need therefore of a complementary study of the will to power as manifested by various individuals and groups. But the basic statement stands: the major conflicts in the Church arise when the Church conceives its mission as primarily one of making the kingdom a reality.

Conflict in the World Is Reflected in the Church

When the Church conducts its mission as Jesus did, the conflict in the world enters the Church as well. According to the earliest biblical tradition the world is a world of sin. What contemporary thinking has added to this truth is the vision that the prophets of Israel and later Jesus of Nazareth had of this sin, namely, that the sin in the world causes human beings to be divided and to pursue competing interests; they separate into groups or classes that are at odds with each other. The exercise of the Church's mission in such a world certainly "poses problems to the universality of Christian love and the unity of the Church. But any consideration of this subject must start from two elemental points: the class struggle is a fact, and neutrality in this matter is impossible."[3]

As long as the Church's mission is conceived in doctrinal terms the conflict in the world will not besmirch the Church. "Christians of the left, right, and center will agree that Jesus Christ is true man and true God, that God is one in three persons, that through his death and resurrection Jesus redeemed the human race. . . ."[4] Furthermore, if in its preaching the Church emphasizes the absoluteness of God, then it is possible, as we see in Europe, to keep reminding people of the eschatological proviso, which this Absolute imposes on any and every human accomplishment. Then the conflict in the world will be regarded as regrettable but (in practice) not very important. There will indeed be frequent reminders that the Christian faith brings certain ethical requirements with it, that Christians must make the world a better place, and so on, but the eschatological proviso will remove any forcefulness from this ethical message.

If the Church's mission is to make the kingdom a reality as Jesus did, that is, within history, then Christians must locate themselves within this real history with its inherent conflict.

To try piously to cover over this social division with a fictitious and formalistic unity is to avoid a difficult and conflictual reality and definitively to join the dominant class. It is to falsify the true character of the Christian community under the pretext of a religious attitude which tries to place itself beyond temporal contingencies.[5]

The social division then becomes a division within the Church. There would be no reason why it should if the entire body of the Church took the same side and defended the same interests. But in fact this is not the case; first, because Christians themselves belong to different social classes and, second, because in their work in the world outside the Church they adopt different attitudes.

What makes the division so acute is that action deals with the concrete. Christians must, of course, act with critical judgment; they must accept and experience the tension between a love that in principle extends to all human beings and a love that to be efficacious must opt for certain concrete individuals. Even when all these conditions have been met there is no denying that action means choice and concreteness. It means that the Christian ideology must take concrete form in ideologies which though onesided set us effectively on the way to a concrete liberation; it means choosing concrete ways of acting. In this process of concretization effective and affective identifications with various groups are formed and risks are taken. From this concretization, which is required by Christian mission when it is understood as action, conflict arises in the Church. By way of this action the conflict existing in society is introduced into the Church.

Conflict is a fact in the Latin American Church; the conflict bursts into the open when Christians choose to make the kingdom a reality and when they select in a critical spirit those concrete mediations that seem most effective at this point in history. To understand the nature of the conflict it is important not to analyze it solely in its final stage. If analysis is thus restricted, voices will be raised saying that what is really an ecclesial conflict is being analyzed in sociological terms and that certain Christians are trying to "assign a sociological meaning to 'people of God.' "[6] Such an objection is an attempt to avoid a theological analysis of the conflict; the supposition at work in it is that the unity of the Church is "the very heart of any ecclesiology"[7] and that conflict is therefore undesirable.

It is for this reason that I went beyond a mere description of present conflict when I began my own analysis of the problem. As long as the Church has not assimilated the "discovery" that the kingdom of God is the ultimate reality and brings judgment with it and that the activity of Jesus is an effort to make the kingdom a reality through word and action, conflict will always appear to be something undesirable. Even then the deepest root of division and conflict will not yet have made its appearance although it is present. A particular conception of the Christian faith entails by internal logic a particular concrete option. This is why it is so dangerous to naïvely repeat that "the essential unity of the Church must be clearly seen to be a unity in faith."[8] This statement is formally correct; however it does not resolve the problem but only poses it in a more radical way. If the Christian faith is a faith in an ever greater God and a crucified God, if it means following Jesus amid the conflicts of history in order to make the kingdom a reality, and if this following brings dangers and persecutions and calls for the making of concrete choices between oppressed and oppressor, then the source of division is the faith itself and not the character of the individual. Faith also has the task of creating unity in the Church; it is true that we must strive for this unity; it is certain, too, that the individual in the Church must be ready to sacrifice personal fulfillment for the good of the body of the Church. But none of these truths justifies giving the internal well-being of the body of the Church priority over the mission that the Church must carry out even if this entails internal conflict.

THE REAL NATURE OF THE UNITY OF THE CHURCH

It is often said that unity—in general and of the Church in particular—is a good. Expressed at this level of generality the statement is correct, but it is idealistic. In the New Testament the unity of the Church is seen as something eschatological, something that is not simply given but must be brought about, something to be built in the course of history. Thus we are back once again in the sphere of history.

It may be objected that the unity of the Church is not just another kind of unity but has a theological and supernatural dimension logically prior to efforts made in behalf of unity. This is partly true and partly false. It is true insofar as the principles of the Church's unity are Christian principles, as Paul tells us in a classical passage: "There is one body and one Spirit, just as you were called to the one hope that belongs to your call, one Lord, one faith, one baptism, one God and Father of us all, who is above all and through all and all in all" (Eph. 4:4–6).

Paul is aware that these are only principles of unity and that a statement of them does not suppose the unity to have been already achieved. In fact he says that we must be "eager to maintain the unity of the Spirit in the bond of peace" (v. 3). It seems important therefore to emphasize that while the Church does have certain principles of unity proper to it, we must not presuppose but rather determine whether these principles have in fact brought about unity.

These same principles are often enunciated in what we might call the second stage of Christian reality: the stage of orthodoxy and theology. It is more important to enunciate them in their first and original stage. Thus seen these principles do not seem identifiable with the utopian reality of God's kingdom or with the following of Jesus as dedicated service to the historical construction of this kingdom. The principles of unity then have a content of their own, and it is in the historical realization of this content that real unity is to be found.

The problem of unity in the Church is not correctly posed or solved by focusing on unity as such but rather by focusing on the content of the principles that give rise to unity. With this content as our starting point we must judge both the positive aspects of the Church that promote this content and the intraecclesial conflict insofar as it is, paradoxically, at the service of this content.

In order to show in greater detail how the unity of the Church is built up in a Christian way and what kind of positive role conflict can play in effecting Christian unity, I shall look at two aspects of the Church. Formally considered they are not characteristic of the Church alone but they do play a part in the Church as a historical and theological reality. I am referring to the institutional and the prophetic aspects of the Church.

By *institutional aspect* I mean not only or even primarily the hierarchy but rather the dimension of the Church expressed in the physical existence that is organic and hierarchized in various doctrinal, administrative, and liturgical structures and that exists to give consistency and effectiveness to the Church's mission. At the historical level the institutional side of the Church tends to preserve the self-awareness that the Church has already attained as well as the direction taken by it in its mission. On the positive side the Church's institutional character tends to give a universal and wide-ranging effectiveness; on the less desirable side the Church as institution tends to avoid conflict and distrust the new until its truth has been theologically justified.

By *prophetic aspect* I mean the Church insofar as in allegiance to the utopian horizon of God's reign and of God as an ever greater God it claims to open up the future to seek out new ways and to reaffirm the reality and mission of the Church in changing situations. At the historical level the prophetic aspect usually involves conflict, since it is accompanied by denunciations of the sins of the Church and since it challenges the collective conscience of the Church as this exists at any given moment.

In the course of history the concrete individuals who embody the institutional aspect and the other individuals who embody the prophetic aspect may well be different. In the past the institutional side of the Church has often been represented by the hierarchy, the prophetic side by those who were not members of the hierarchy (priests, religious, theologians, or simple faithful). Today this division is no longer so clear, although it can be said that the hierarchy in general still tends to defend the institution (in the sense described) as something self-evident and to be suspicious of the prophetic.

Let us consider the role that the prophetic element has played and is now playing in the Church. As far as its structure is concerned, this element may take two forms: heresy and intraecclesial prophetism (I shall refer to this simply as "prophetism"). In conceptual terms, heresy can be defined as the denial of an ecclesial truth leading to separation from the body of the Church. Understood in this sense, heresy destroys the unity of the Church. If we look at heresy from a historical standpoint, we find that, paradoxical though it seems, heresy can play an important social role within the Church. This positive role consists in challenging the Church as a concrete reality and pointing to "forgotten truths" of revelation or truths that are ignored at the practical level but are nonetheless fundamental.

Clearly the heretical answer is unacceptable to the Church. Yet when confronted by heresy "the Church learns to know more clearly its own truth by hearing and rejecting contradictions of its own truth and of its growing self-understanding."[9] Heresy is thus one historical way in which the Church grows in understanding of its own reality and mission. When a heresy first makes its appearance, the Church goes on the defensive, issues condemnations, and perhaps tries to justify itself. Even this first attack leads to enlightenment, as the history of the councils shows. However it is with the passage of time that the Church discovers what is of positive value for it in a heresy. The history of the modern ecumenical movement supports this analysis. As a result of the Protestant movement the Catholic Church has recovered important values it had forgotten; it has rediscovered the true place of the Scriptures, moved beyond a one-sidedly intellectual conception of faith. When a heresy has become an ecclesial movement with a long history and broad dimensions, it is clear that the problem of unity can be resolved only by appealing to the "principles" of Christian unity and not simply to the historical structures that supposedly embody this unity. Insofar, then, as heresy has positive content it forces a rethinking of the approach to unity and supplies a content that makes it possible for unity to become fully Christian.

Prophetism is similar, except that the prophet remains within the Church and thus causes conflict within its bosom. The great Christians (in this case, Catholics) who have formed new movements have met their primary opposition within the Church; they have caused conflicts and have been the first to suffer from these. The only difference between these individuals and "heretics" is that the "prophets" have remained within the Church and have given rise there to a contradiction that has brought clarification. A history of prophetism in the Church shows that the ecclesial body does not progress unless there has first been a rejection of something within the Church. Prophetism does not turn into heresy because the Church is able to absorb the step forward. If the Church does not succeed in accepting prophecy it will stiffen into immobility.

The Church has unreservedly acknowledged the necessity of prophecy. Not infrequently the Church canonizes these prophets after their death and misses them when it does not have them. The problem is that hopes are strong about the effects of prophets until they actually arrive on the scene, and official praise is heaped upon them only after their death. During the prophets' own time they are usually looked upon with suspicion and they cause conflict in the Church. The lives of many saints and doctors of the Church support this statement. It is a historical fact of the Church's life, therefore, that there have been prophets, that the ecclesial body needs them, that they cause conflict, and that once the Church absorbs the new thing they have brought (although the Church almost never does this immediately) the life of the Church progresses.

Both prophecy and (in its own way) heresy render a service to Church unity by challenging the "principles" of unity that a given period has made absolute. They supply new content enabling the desired unity to be more truly Christian. They also (if we look at the history of prophetism and heresy as a whole) show that full unity is always in the future and that the history of the Church will be marked by a necessary but always provisional unity until the day when at last God is all in all.

Let us look now at the role of the institution in the Church. Prophecy is, at least initially, often a secondary phenomenon. The Church, however, is in principle a universal body and accepts millions of individuals into its bosom.

Historically and theologically, faith in Christ is not an individual or small-group phenomenon; it is lived by individuals-in-community who form a Church. This fact received early theological formulation in the New Testament. Christians are there described as the people of God, the body of Christ, the true Israel, the temple of the Spirit. Such images speak of an ideal Church insofar as they relate it to God, Christ, and his Spirit. They also make a historical statement: faith is lived in a community and within a body meant to be universal. It follows that some kind of structure is needed as a means of making possible and expressing this universality. Needed too is a declaration of principle regarding the fundamental openness of the Church to the various groups of human beings: educated and uneducated, strong and weak, worldly-wise and simple. Moreover, all these persons will in principle have equal rights and obligations in the Church, and all will help to build the Church by the positive contribution of each person as he or she has been shaped by cultural and social conditions.

This basic fact of history and theology was immediately important in the New Testament, especially with the delay of the parousia. As the Church's awareness that it must live in history grew, the process of institutionalization was accelerated. *Institutionalization* here is a much more comprehensive term than *hierarchization*. The process was rendered ambiguous not only by the tendency to institutionalization (in the sense described) but also by the principles that directed this institutionalization.

The temptation was to structure faith in Christ along the lines of the traditional religions. The danger here lay not in choosing a line, but in the presuppositions held by that line that are not the presuppositions of Christian faith. This temptation has always been attacked by prophetism, whether heretical or intraecclesial.

Institutionalization was however a historical necessity and was in principle at the service of a Christian goal: the effectiveness of the Church's mission. The decision of the first Christians to "go forth to the Gentiles" meant the taking of a stand against an elitist and sectarian Christianity. As a result of this decision the Church grew to a size that could be handled only by institutional means. The institution became increasingly necessary for decision making in the areas of doctrine and ethics, in liturgical life, and in the discipline of the community. A tradition about Jesus had to be formulated that would remain alive, be transmissible down through history, and be maintained in its purity at least in its fundamentals. This first institutionalization of the Church gave body and effectiveness to the initial prophetism, that of Jesus.

In its beginnings, then, the institutionalization of the Church took place in the service of the initial prophetism and was intended to give this historical effectiveness. In principle the institution is also needed today in order to integrate and make viable the prophetism now taking place which cannot be repudiated and which must be made accessible to all. This is what Hugo Assmann means when he says that "the Latin American Church is a Church in captivity and one that keeps captive the gospel and its own dogmas. But this is also the Church which, as an undeniable pole of power, will make it possible to take the next steps in the process of liberation."[10] He accepts the fact that prophecy must be embodied in some institutional form if it is to be influential.

The institutional element in the Church is at the service of unity. One of its explicit functions is to remind us of unity and to keep unity alive especially by means of the hierarchy. The institution at any given period brings unity to the many and various aspects of the Church's reality and mission, whereas prophecy tends to emphasize particular aspects.

The two dimensions, the prophetic and the institutional, must by their structure be a real help to the process whereby unity is established in the Church. This is not to deny that both prophecy and institution by their very structure tend to be sinful and that they provoke conflicts that are neither necessary nor Christian but are rather the product of sin. But it is part of the historical character of the Church that the two dimensions, the two forms of service to unity, should be often in tension and even in opposition and that the two must therefore be brought into historical unity. This will be accomplished not in virtue of some general sociological law but in virtue of the very substance of Christianity.

The Church exists to serve the kingdom of God, the ever greater God; but the kingdom is a utopian reality. The Church as institution will tend to forget the true reality of the kingdom and to equate its present reality with the kingdom of God; it will tend to think that it already knows and possesses the ever greater God. For this reason the sign that the Church is alive is the fact that from within the institutional Church Christians rise up to recall and give concrete form to the elemental truth that the Church is not the kingdom and that the God whom the Church preaches is greater than any of the Church's structures. Ernst Bloch, a Marxist who judges the phenomenon of religion as an outsider, has said that "the best thing about religion is that it makes for heretics," because in his view "where there is religion there is hope."[11] Put in Christian terms this means that the Church is alive when it is able to put its finger on hope and keep it alive. But this is not historically possible without concrete rejections showing that the content of Christian hope cannot be identified with specifically ecclesial content. For this theological reason conflict is a necessity in the Church. It is the way of keeping the Church from becoming rigid and from denying by its existence the very thing it preaches, even if at times it preaches it without conviction, namely, that God is greater and that the kingdom of God is greater than the Church. The institutional Church embodies for the long run what begins as pure prophecy (the type of thing that made its appearance at, for example, Vatican II and Medellín).

Without prophecy the Church would literally disappear. It would become the custodian of an abstract truth to which it could not give concrete form. It would deny the fundamental truth it preaches: that Jesus is the Son who has power to make human beings his brothers and sisters in the changing and conflict-ridden situations of history. It would deny the God of the future who for the sake of utopian plenitude demands that the historical process of liberation continue.

If the Church lacked the institutional dimension it would cease to be a true body and would turn into a minority group of ethically superior individuals. It would exclude the vast majority of human beings who by reason of the social structure of the race cannot be prophets, even though they are capable of traveling the new paths opened up for them by the prophets. It would rob the Church of the positive contribution of so many human beings who may have nothing to offer but their suffering, their ignorance, their wretched poverty. Just how the Church as institution is actively to integrate all human beings into itself is another problem. But it is certain that without the institutional element the Church could not exist at all, especially not as a Church of the people, a Church of the poor.

I have thus far shown in this brief analysis that both prophecy and institution are necessary if the Church is to have an ongoing unity. Paradoxically both are needed because by their very structure they are in tension with one another. This tension is what makes the process of unification both correct and Christian. The tension allows and requires that we speak of the unity of Church not as something already given, which must be maintained, but as something that by its nature must go on being achieved until eschatological unity becomes a reality.

PRACTICAL CONSIDERATIONS AND CRITERIA OF DISCERNMENT

Thus far I have offered some general thoughts on unity and conflict, the relationship between them, and the role played by the institutional and prophetic dimensions of the Church in this relationship. I turn now to a few concrete points that may shed some light on how problems are to be posed and resolved.

The Hierarchy

Let me begin by considering the problems arising from the institutional element in the Church and more specifically from the hierarchy. I pointed out earlier that institution and hierarchy are not identical but that the hierarchy is part of the institution. Although there have been hierarchs who were prophets, generally speaking to hierarchs and lay people alike any talk of the institutional element immediately brings to mind the hierarchy.

The hierarchy exercises a function in the institution. This function takes concrete form in a direct concern for union and in the proclamation of what serves Christian unity. Medellín is a clear instance of the way in which the institution serves unity through concentration on certain contents of faith.

Certain bishops, especially those who have made Medellín their own without weakening its message, have been catalysts for Christians in their dioceses. In this way the institution, even working through the hierarchy, has rendered a service to Christian unity.

Since Medellín, because of the interest in the theology of liberation at the theoretical level and because of the conflicts resulting from a mission based on Medellín and its theology, a number of the bishops are trying to achieve unity on the basis of the command that unity should exist rather than on the basis of Christian contents that bring unity and, still less, by way of the conflicts to which the new prophetic direction gives rise.

We usually find a sizable part of the hierarchy ignorant of theology's (including First World theology) rediscovery of the priority of God's kingdom over the Church. They are even more often ignorant of the contribution that the theology of liberation at its soundest and most Christian has made to the concrete realization of this kingdom of God. We see efforts being made to retain in their abstract scholastic form truths that must be made concrete if they are to be grasped and put into practice.

We also see a fear of the consequences of Medellín. The difficulties and persecution that the Church is experiencing in Latin America have caused many bishops to retreat or to settle for a defense of human rights (highly laudable in itself) without denouncing the violent structure that gives rise to concrete situations of violence.

We see, too, a tendency to appeal to the hierarchy, as formal source of unity, for the resolution of the problems that prophecy necessarily creates. The result has been to throw suspicion on theological and other movements simply because they create problems for certain members of the hierarchy. No effort is made to analyze in depth what is Christian or unchristian in these movements.

In regard then to the hierarchy as one of the concretizations of the institutional element in the Church we can see a double movement toward maintaining Christian unity: by means of the substance of Christianity and by means of the consciousness of the hierarchy. The second movement is no solution nor is it a contribution to the Church, since even the service that the hierarchy gives to unity must be concretely based on the mission of the Church. This is why even the New Testament affords us clean examples of division within the hierarchy when the mission of the Church is at stake.

What is said of bishops can be said with even greater reason of nuncios, since they tend to represent and look for a unity based on them, not in the concrete mission to be carried out. They certainly do not look for a unity to be attained through the conflicts to which this concrete mission gives rise.

Whenever the bishops of Latin America, whether singly or as a body, have been able to harness and combine the best evangelical impulses—a clear option for the poor, a courageous defense of human rights, a denunciation of the roots of injustice—then they have become true pastors leading the people to God and in so doing unifying them. Then there is no longer any dichotomy between what is worldly and what is religious; instead the proclaimed word falls upon favorable soil and grows organically in all its dimensions. Then, finally, pastors unify the people of God not from without but from within, and the people spontaneously acknowledge this.

When the bishops do not harness and combine the best evangelical impulses, the service the hierarchy renders to unity is perceived as something imposed, something coming from outside. At the administrative level the bishops may claim to be unifying the people, but at the pastoral level no true unity is achieved.

Prophecy

Let us look now at the problems arising from the existence of prophecy. Prophetism's positive contribution to unity is to remind the Church that unity is attained only through the application of

Christian truths, truths often forgotten. Prophets are very necessary today if the institutional element in the Church is to adapt to the times. Prophets remind us of the creative and renovating character of Christian faith, which makes it possible to transform the times in accordance with the faith. A further reason why prophecy is important: it reminds us of the sin of the Church as a whole and it counters the tendency of the institutional element to a conservatism that not infrequently degenerates into reactionism.

In our time prophecy is important because it emphasizes a necessary and legitimate secularization or incarnation of the faith. We must continue to remind ourselves that the history of God is the history of human beings and that therefore the Christian faith has to be mediated through secular realities.

But prophetism also runs the risk of dividing, not insofar as it opposes the hierarchy but insofar as it opposes the institutional element as such. From the sociological standpoint prophecy is a secondary phenomenon. As such it provides a necessary leaven for the entire institutional mass, but it may overlook the differences in rhythm between majorities and minorities, and it may leave the majorities in helpless confusion unless it accompanies theoretical and practical progress with an understanding of their needs and capacities. It can fall into a kind of dogmatism, not by making absolute what is unconditional (the crucial struggle for a world of justice that is inspired by love of God, that is, the unconditional struggle for the reign of God), but by disregarding the difference in the mediations suited to minorities and majorities.

The typical conflict to which prophecy gives rise is therefore not a conflict with the hierarchy but a conflict with the much broader thing I call the institutional element. The first of these two conflicts seems to me to be still necessary; the second must be carefully analyzed, lest the poor be in fact left orphans.

Criteria for Discernment

Criteria for discernment in cases of conflict or, in more positive terms, criteria for building unity, are not easily come by. For unity is not simply one of the characteristic notes of a Church that already exists and about which everything is known—what it is, what kind of structure it has, and who determines its unity. At a second stage such an approach might be valid, but at a first stage the problem of the unity of the Church is identical with the problem of creating the one Church. The problematic element lies both in *oneness* and in *Churchness*. I shall now analyze some of the criteria for discernment, which seem at first to be obvious but which are in fact not.

First, authority is not the final or the sole criterion of discernment. This is not to say that authority does not have a function in the Church and in cases of conflict. But it cannot serve as an ultimate criterion. This is true for several reasons. The conflict may be between prophecy and authority. Those in authority can resolve the conflict at the administrative level but not at the objective level, because then they would be both a party to the conflict and the judge who resolves it. The prophet may be challenging the sin affecting the institutional element; therefore, at least on methodological grounds, those in authority should allow themselves to be judged by something higher than themselves, namely, the word of God.

Second, recent history shows that prophets who were initially condemned in one or other manner by the authorities of the Church are later accepted and even praised. This is one of the more curious phenomena that accompanied Vatican II. Almost all the great theologians who made the Council possible had once been suspect; administrative measures had even been taken against them. This shows that in the conflict something objective lay beyond the normal range of judgment by the authorities.

We also see here the danger of "psychologizing" the handling of conflict in the Church. It frequently happens that the authorities analyze the psychology of the prophet and ask her or him to be docile. But this is not where the real problem lies. Many prophets did choose docility and submitted to administrative measures taken against them, but the cause they defended eventually was accepted by its own objective weight. This simple fact of history should make us reflect on the role of authority in cases of conflict. The authorities must intervene and bring their best insights to bear; they may even have to take administrative measures. But they should be very conscious that when the point at issue is new and rejects something in the present life of the Church, their position as authorities does not make them more capable of discernment than others; in fact it often makes them less capable.

Strange though it may sound, neither is the New Testament the sole criterion of discernment. More accurately, the New Testament as a body of teaching is not the ultimate criterion. The simple reason is that the New Testament contains several doctrines of the Church, and these cannot be fully harmonized. The real story in the New Testament is the story of the Church during the first three generations of Christians, of how conflicts occurred and were resolved. What emerges from the New Testament is the fact of conflict and how in each case a resolution was sought that would lead to unity.

The ultimate reason why the New Testament cannot be the sole or final criterion of discernment is to be found in the very structure of the Christian faith, which has its source in Jesus of Nazareth but which is not reducible to an "application" of the teaching of Jesus to subsequent history. This Jesus of the past is truly grasped, and grasped as a norm, insofar as he gives rise to a present history. It is not enough to repeat the abstract truth that the Christian faith is historical, that revelation takes place within history, and that the Church must carry out its mission within history.

History "means the understanding and transformation of historical reality."[12] If conflict in the Church occurs as part of our history and of our effort to make history, then it is not possible to resolve it simply by appealing to the New Testament. This is the basic problem expressed in the "hermeneutical circle." Christian existence "implies a reading of revelation in the light of historical practice and a reading of historical practice in the light of revelation."[13]

In today's situation conflict is due in part to ignorance, sometimes crass ignorance, of what is in the New Testament. This ignorance shows itself in several ways. First, the New Testament is often regarded as a body of doctrine; the fact that it narrates a history is overlooked. This leads, especially among some of the hierarchy, to a method of arguing that relies on isolated passages taken almost always from the Pastoral Letters in which we find the Church already possessed of a rather fully developed organization, and that ignores the tensions that other New Testament writings show to have existed in the Church. Second, the great truths of Christian ecclesiology are usually ignored. It seems that the discovery of the theological concept of the "kingdom of God" has still not been sufficiently assimilated. As a result, individuals continue to use concepts of Church, authority, and institution that have no basis in the New Testament. They act as if the Church were an end in itself; as if those possessing ecclesiastical authority stood above and apart from the Church as people of God; and as if the structures of the ecclesial institution were in themselves a source of salvation.

Many do not know that conflict in the Church made its appearance at the very beginning of New Testament times and that this conflict existed between hierarchy and faithful, among the faithful, and even among the hierarchy. While unity is certainly a desideratum in the New Testament ("that they may be one," Jn. 17:11) and Christians must work for this unity (cf. Eph. 4:1–6), the mere assertion that there is one Lord, one faith, one baptism, one body, one Spirit, one God and Father, is not enough to make this unity a reality. Any ideologization of Christian unity must take this into account. One Lord, one faith, and so on, are the Christian bases that make unity Christian, but they do not of themselves make the unity real. We need only recall the divisions in the Pauline communities; the situation described by the Letter of James when it speaks of liturgical assemblies and relations between rich and poor; the celebration of the Eucharist at Corinth; and the disputes between Peter, Paul, and James.[14]

The removal of this kind of ignorance is not enough by itself to resolve the conflict, nor does it provide conclusive criteria for resolving it, but it is a necessary condition if dialogue is to have a minimum of clarity. If the unity of the Church is regarded as something absolute and if it is justified in an unqualified way by an appeal to the New Testament, then any discussion in cases of conflict is meaningless, since it has been decided in advance where right is to be found. There is need, therefore, of the kind of knowledge of the New Testament that "leads us to exegetical suspicion, that is, to the suspicion that the prevailing interpretation of the Bible has not taken important pieces of data into consideration."[15] Even though the New Testament taken in isolation is not the sole criterion of discernment, yet an up-to-date knowledge of it that will cause us to examine it with new eyes is a necessity if conflict in the Church is to be resolved in a lucid rather than a dogmatic and authoritarian way. The acquisition of such knowledge is incumbent on every Christian but especially on the most conservative sector of the

Church, which gives the impression that there is no need to go to the New Testament for the truth since it is already known and set down in the documents of the Church.

The Hermeneutical Circle

Neither ecclesiastical authority nor the New Testament is the sole and univocal criterion for exercising discernment in cases of conflict if either is regarded as absolutely autonomous and independent of history. It follows from this that the criterion must be historical in character and must originate within concrete history. I have already indicated the objective reason for this: Christianity is not a truth that appeared on the scene two thousand years ago in order then to be applied down through history; Christianity has its basis in the concrete history of Jesus of Nazareth, which in turn gives rise to further history. In the Christian faith God is described as Father (he is ultimately an absolute mystery), as Son (in Jesus we are shown the right way to understanding of this Father), and as Spirit. The Spirit signifies the incorporation of human beings to the history of God and the immersion of God in the history of human beings. The trinitarian God cannot be what he is without continuing to create history and not simply interpret it.

Here we have the reason for the hermeneutical circle, which is located not in the line of "interpretation" (as is usually the case with an existentialist or transcendentalist hermeneutic) but in the line of "action." Jesus gives rise to a history and the history thus launched can be traced back to Jesus. This is how the circle is created. But insofar as the circle unfolds within history, the return to Jesus will always be different if indeed the history to which Jesus gave rise is truly a history. The Christian's participation in history "forces us to interpret the word of God afresh, to change reality accordingly, and then to go back and reinterpret the word of God again, and so on."[16]

We have renounced a clear and univocal criterion of discernment in cases of conflict, but we have located the problem where it really belongs: at the intersection of revelation and history, of the history of salvation and salvation in history, of Christian faith and Christian practice, of meaning and action. This meeting does not take place through a comparison of doctrines but in action. The hermeneutical circle can be seen in the New Testament, although only in principle, since there had not yet been "enough" history to be able to formulate it as we can today. But in principle it is there: "He who does what is true comes to the light" (Jn. 3:21). The truth must be done in love.

The same declaration of principle has been made in more contemporary terms by the Thirty-second General Congregation of the Society of Jesus: "The way to faith and the way to justice are inseparable ways. It is up this undivided road, this steep road, that the pilgrim Church must travel and toil."[17]

Only a posteriori, then, and in the doing of the truth can it be seen where "truth" and "unity" are to be found in cases of conflict. This approach presupposes a pre-knowledge of what the truth is. For this reason, the New Testament is one of the Christian's sources of discernment; but it is only in doing the truth and in passing from generic truth to truth in historical form that we can know in what this truth consists and how it is in harmony with the New Testament. The present concrete situation is therefore the second source of discernment. Put another way, the fact that history brings salvation can be known from the New Testament, but precisely what this salvation is is made known only within salvation in history.

The New Testament and the present situation are in reality a single thing, but reflection turns them into two sources or poles. From the New Testament we learn some general criteria to be applied to conflicts; these criteria are usually stated only implicitly—that the Church exists for the sake of the kingdom of God; that this "for the sake of" involves secular mediations such as the practice of love and justice; that the Church's mission must be carried out in a world of sin and that the Church must therefore carry the burden of this sin and not simply declare it to be evil; that the primary and privileged object of the Church's mission is the poor of Matthew 25; that this mission brings danger and persecution for those in power. In the historical exercise of its mission the Church will gradually recover its Christian essence and approximate the Church of faith; it will make real its faith in Jesus as the Christ and will understand its mission as a journeying of the people of God to the Father.

Viewed in light of the present situation these general criteria become concrete, and the concretion assures us of finding these and

not other criteria in the New Testament. This is what the hermeneutical circle means. The concretion also supposes a rejection of
certain aspects of the Church's mission as concretely exercised;
such a rejection is not because of any a priori intention of condemn-
ing the Church's past. It is because the present situation makes it
clear that the Church cannot continue in its previous self-
understanding nor can it justify that self-understanding by an appeal to the New Testament. The present situation brings to light the
truth about the Church: whether it preaches a God who is a source
of real hope for the majority who are oppressed, instead of too
quickly appealing to the eschatological proviso; whether it looks
for secular mediations that make its preaching effective, instead of
too quickly distinguishing between the natural and the supernatural; whether it names the concrete sin, the capitalist structures that
are shaping our society today; whether it looks explicitly to the
great masses of the oppressed and focuses its mission directly on
them, instead of too quickly calling for a universal love that introduces a one-sidedness into the Christian option; whether the
Church is ready for danger and persecution and is actually experiencing these, instead of retreating into activities that by their nature are socially and politically neutral. In this kind of activity the
Church will grow in understanding of itself as the continuation of
Jesus and will give expression to its faith in him, but from within its
own history. Its faith in Jesus will be based on its living of the faith
of Jesus. Its liturgy will be the expression of God's grace, which
takes possession of it in its living of the folly that the following of
Jesus implies.

The criterion of discernment in conflicts is not to be found in the
truth alone but in the communal doing of the truth. No one, of
course, would be so presumptuous as to claim to be doing the truth
in all its purity. I have provided some general criteria, which explain in the light of the New Testament what it means to do the
truth. A formal criterion is at the basis of everything I have been
saying: whether a conversion is taking place in the Church, "conversion" meaning not simply a change or an adaptation to a new
situation, but a doing of the very opposite of what had been done
previously. This criterion derives from the essence of Christian
faith in a God who is a crucified God, a God who constantly challenges the truth of the status quo in the Church and breaks through

the concern with, and internal clinging to, what is commonly regarded as good.

Can there, then, be unity in the Church? This unity is an eschatological gift that will be given when God is all in all. What is required within history is the search for unity, a search based not on an imposed uniformity or on a faith expressed in general terms but on mission and on acting like Jesus in particular situations. The unity of the Church within history will always be relative, partial, and provisional. As an institution the Church must seek out the means and forms of this unity; insofar as prophecy exists in the Church, the unity achieved must repeatedly be broken, until the institution manages to integrate the prophecy while waiting for another prophetic movement to arise. The unity of the Church comes into existence through the dialectic of union and conflict. The institution reminds us that Christians must be united; prophecy reminds us that their unity must be Christian.

8

Theological Significance
of "Persecution of the Church"
Apropos of the Archdiocese
of San Salvador

"The Church, 'like a stranger in a foreign land, presses forward amid the persecutions of the world and the consolations of God.' " "The fathers of the Council together with the Roman Pontiff, being deeply conscious of their duty to spread everywhere the kingdom of God, affectionately salute all preachers of the Gospel, and making themselves sharers in their sufferings, they especially salute those who suffer persecution for the name of Christ."[1]

These texts, from two documents of the Second Vatican Council, show that the Council knew persecution of the Church was a possibility and even a part of the Church's lot (LG 8). It is to be expected in the Church's missionary work (AG 42). But there is some difficulty in applying these texts to our present situation. They need clarification in the light of this situation.

The difficulty with the first text is that it states the necessity of persecution for the Church in general terms and does not specify details or forms of persecution. The difficulty with the second is that is supposes the classical pattern, that is, persecution in mission countries where the gospel is being preached for the first time and meets with rejection.

The situation in the archdiocese of San Salvador today is different from the situation that the Council presupposes. This is true for two reasons. First, the activity of the archdiocese (following the teaching of the Council and of Medellín) is very different from that of the early sixties when the Council teaching was formulated. Second, the archdiocese is not a mission country in the classical sense of the term, and therefore the persecution now going on cannot be interpreted according to the traditional pattern of persecution. There is, then, a need for a theological reflection on the meaning of *persecution of the Church* as the basis for a theological reading of recent events and of the reaction of the Church in the archdiocese to these events.

CONFUSION ARISING FROM THE PHRASE "PERSECUTION OF THE CHURCH"

Since these reflections are meant to be historically situated, it is important to give a concrete description of today's use of the word *persecution*. It is important, first of all, that the word has become current, appearing as it does both in ecclesiastical language of archbishop, clergy, and religious, and in everyday language. Many Salvadorans take it for granted and use it spontaneously. The simple fact that the word *persecution* has become so important in the vocabulary of society shows that something real is occurring that is different from what went on before. We cannot treat the problem in a nominal way by reducing it to a matter of "terminology." When people speak as they do about the present situation of the Church in the archdiocese, it is clear that the situation is quite different from that of previous years and that to describe it they feel compelled to resort to such words as "attacks," "slanders," and "persecution."

Second, the term *persecution* is relational; that is, it implies that someone is persecuting someone else. In the minds of the people it is the government and the dominant economic groups that are doing the persecuting; it is the Church that is being persecuted.

The events of the past months have led the Church to claim that it is being persecuted—expulsions of foreign priests; the imprisonment and torture or mistreatment of priests, both local and foreign; accusations that priests have been falsifying the faith of the

Church; accusations that the hierarchy has been covering up and defending these deviations by priests; accusations against an entire religious order; the murders of two priests and several laypersons; assaults on the Church's communications media; the obstructing of meetings of catechists and delegates of the word; the imprisonment, torture, and mockery of lay ministers of the word; the profanation of the Most Blessed Sacrament; the prohibition of liturgical gatherings in some places.

Through the archbishop of San Salvador and through its communications media the Church denounced these acts as persecution of the entire Church of El Salvador. The government responded that it was simply applying the law to priests who overstep their religious duties and meddle in the politics of the country. It has likewise stated that other incidents are part of the legitimate struggle against subversive individuals and movements on the part of a state devoted to its laws.

Alongside the government and its official response other forces are at work. Their precise origin is usually shadowy but they certainly represent the economically and politically dominant sectors of the country. These other forces have reiterated the government's reply through a steady flow of publications. They have gone a step further: they have unearthed dark pages of the Church's history. By appealing to these without any regard for historical context, they have tried to strip the Church of all moral authority as far as persecution is concerned. They have even gone so far as to give an interpretation of the facts diametrically opposed to those facts: the state is being persecuted by a Church attempting to satisfy its own ambition for temporal power.

A further source of confusion can be found in some ecclesiastical circles and certainly in reactionary groups where it serves their self-interest. I mean the confusion generated by certain ways of defining "persecution of the Church." The definition has to do both with the facts and with their institutionalization. It is admitted, for example, that profanation of the Blessed Sacrament does constitute persecution, but the repeated instances of the torture and murder of peasants is not considered persecution. As for the institutionalization of persecution, this is present (it is said) if there is an organized, permanent attack on the Church, but the name "persecution" cannot be given to attacks by individuals, whether or not these attacks can be justified in accord with their own criteria and interests.

This confusion does not originate solely or even fundamentally in the varied use of terms, but rather in the ideological attitude toward the Church and its mission and therefore toward the attacks and/or persecution of the Church. It is therefore not possible to understand what "persecution of the Church" is simply by an abstract analysis of terms; also required is an analysis of the various social, political, and economic interests that are consciously or unconsciously being defended. For this reason, before beginning a theological analysis I shall first briefly describe what is usually understood by "persecution of the Church," and thus be in a position to detect the ideologized use of the phrase.

The Model Taken from the History of the Church

According to the model taken from the history of the Church, "persecution" is what went on in the first three centuries of Christianity, what has gone on in societies whose governments have not accepted the Church, and what has gone on in certain mission countries where at times there have been direct attacks on the Church. The external signs of this persecution have been the deaths of ordinary Christians, priests, and bishops, and the juridical order of a society in which the Catholic religion has not been allowed or tolerated and in which Catholic institutions such as seminaries, schools, universities, and parishes have been prohibited or restricted in their activities.

The Model Taken from Socialist States

The model taken from socialist states is basically the same as the previous model, but because of its historical currency it is the more influential. In the socialist states persecution has varied according to country and period (I am passing no judgment at this point on the possible objective causes of persecution). It has included the killing of ordinary Christians, priests, and bishops, the declaration that the Catholic religion is illegal, the hindering in greater or lesser measure of worship, seminaries, freedom of Catholic education, and so on. There is another fundamental point that must be kept in mind. The socialist states that are based on a form of the Marxist ideology are logically atheist in principle, whether or not this finds explicit mention in the constitutions of these states. The atheistic starting point can also be seen at work, depending on cases, in systematic campaigns against religion. This model differs therefore from the model taken from Church history in that it adds the presupposition that is the ultimate theological basis for persecution of the Catholic Church: atheism.

The Model Found in the Ideology of "National Security"

The two models I have just described are not of much help in understanding the present situation in Latin America and, more concretely, in the archdiocese of San Salvador. Those who exercise political and economic power claim that these two models provide us with the official model of what real "persecution of the Church" is and that therefore Cuba is the only Latin American country in which the Church is being persecuted. This kind of persecution, and it alone, must be regarded as the official definition of persecution. It is in the interest of these people to defend such a definition; they want to get this definition into the minds of the citizenry and of high-ranking members of the hierarchy. Then they will be able to continue their "justified" attack on Christians whom they characterize as subversive delinquents and at the same time deny that any persecution exists.

Since this is the model that is now effectively functioning in my country, let me dwell on it briefly. Our starting point must be the presupposition that both the Church and the forms of government in Latin America have changed substantially in recent years, especially as far as their relationship is concerned.

Latin American governments and the economic powers that represent them maintain that these countries are officially or unofficially "Catholic," even when other kinds of "Christian" communities are allowed. It is often in the interest of people in government to put in an appearance at religious events in order to give public, symbolic expression to this "Catholicism." In these countries a great deal of emphasis is placed on strictly religious terms such as "God," "the Almighty," "the Supreme Maker," or on symbols that are religious in origin, such as "fatherland" and "freedom." The important thing is to get into people's minds a sense that there is a religious absolute because this same sense can subsequently be extended to other absolutes such as private property, the state, and so on. If the state is to maintain its unqualified power the people must have a sense of the absolute. For this reason the state values the use of religious symbols of the absolute, which it can manipulate; it also favors and promotes everything to do with religion (many elements of popular religion, certain kinds of Protestant sects, certain Catholic phenomena such as Pentacostalism with its remoteness from history) that will help maintain an uncritical sense of the absolute. Along with all this there may also exist constitutional guarantees of freedom of worship, freedom in principle for Catholic educational institutions, the appointment of chaplains to the armed forces, including a military Ordinary with the rank of colonel or even general.

The purpose of all this is to defend special interests under the cloak of a defense of "Western Christian civilization." The Catholic religion is thus seen as providing religious justification for political institutions, while an appeal to the complete incompatibility of communism and religion makes it possible to defend any and every attack on real or supposed communists as a defense of religion.

Something new has made its appearance in the Church of Latin America. Let me describe its most important elements. Ever since Medellín there has been a movement in which absolute realities and their symbols are expressed with increasing clarity through historical mediations, especially the human person and, more concretely, the oppressed. The absolute that is "God" is translated into another absolute, "the kingdom of God," which includes God but also includes and treats as an absolute the reign of justice.

When Christians begin to work seriously for this reign or kingdom of God, they are persecuted. This is undeniably the case throughout Latin America where countless ordinary Christians, religious, priests, and bishops have been slandered, attacked, mistreated, tortured, banished, and murdered. Documents published by many bishops and episcopal conferences in the last few years have called attention to these facts and have interpreted them as an attack on the *mission* of the Church. They are saying that the deepest reality of the Church, its mission, is now under attack, even though there may be legislation on the books that respects the Church as an *institution*.

These attacks, which are an undeniable fact, must properly be described as persecution. Further on I shall offer the ultimate theological basis for this statement. For the moment it is enough to point out that the cases of individual attacks are too numerous for them to be considered, even at a purely descriptive level, as nothing more than sad and regrettable incidents. The mere number of such attacks takes us to a qualitatively different level: the "attacks" become "persecution." Further, the attacks are institutionalized, not in the form of laws, but in the political and economic structures of each country. As long as a political structure is that of a national security state and the economic structure is capitalistic, the conditions are present for these attacks to continue. Finally, the attacks will continue. I say this on the a priori ground that the conditions giving rise to the attacks are not likely to disappear, and on the a posteriori ground that the attacks have been occurring with growing frequency during the last few years. When such attacks are institutionalized and permanent, it is no longer possible to speak of them simply as regrettable incidents; they represent persecution in the proper sense of the term.

In recent years, then, Latin America has seen a new type of persecution of the Church—one based, on the one hand, on the ideology of national security, and, on the other, on a new conception and practice of the Church that is opposed to that ideology both in theory and in practice. The doctrine of national security, which conceives of the world as divided Manichean-fashion into two opposed systems that are engaged in a continuous and irreconcilable conflict (the two systems being Western civilization and communism), claims that the state is the ultimate source of all rights, "God, Country, Unity," "Tradition, Family, Property," "God, Country, Freedom" are old and new slogans giving expression to the ideological values of a system that manipulates a religion that has nothing left in it of the substance of the Christian faith. The Latin American Church, which has been renewed in accordance with Vatican II and Medellín, is being persecuted because, in its effort to make its faith historically real under the guidance of the Spirit of Jesus Christ, it has no choice but to challenge regimes that are everywhere destroying the historical effort to bring justice to the oppressed masses.

Far from seeing the decline of ideologies, our world is finding that they are assigning ultimate meaning to social, economic, and political projects and interests, even if these projects and interests are depicted as resulting simply from technological calculations. In such a world, the Church's exercise of its right to "pass moral judgments even in matters relating to politics, whenever the fundamental rights of man or the salvation of souls requires it" (GS 76) must inevitably be interpreted as the expression of a competing ideology. Although the Church insists that "the social teaching of the Church is part of the Christian vision of life" (MM 222), and therefore claims that this teaching is an essential part of the Christian message and the Church's own task of evangelization (EN 29,30), when the Church moves into the area of the juridical order and of value judgments concerning the effects of economic systems and political regimes on human and social life and when it proposes evangelical ways of resolving problems, it enters into competition with other authorities that hold jealously to an autonomy they consider to be more absolute than that which the Church allows them.

All that I have said of Latin America in general is true of El Salvador in particular. Recent events have their roots in an earlier time and show that there is indeed persecution of the Church in the archdiocese. This is clear from the number of the attacks, from their institutionalized source, and from their duration through the present and the foreseeable future, unless the Church backs off or finds itself unable to pursue its present policy because of the substantial losses it has suffered.

The important conclusion of this brief analysis of models of persecution of the Church is that our present situation can only be understood in terms of the third model. This does not mean that there have not been persecutions throughout the Church's history or that there is at present no persecution in socialist countries. The point is simply that for *us* neither of the first two models can be of service. This is true if for no other reason than the verifiable fact that it is not the socialists who have launched the attacks (whether or not you call them persecution) on the Church of the archdiocese but political and economic powers that are certainly not socialist. These persecutors are trying to have the second model of persecution accepted because then they can continue to persecute without having to present themselves as persecutors.

CRITERIA FOR DETERMINING THE SIGNIFICANCE OF "PERSECUTION OF THE CHURCH"

Thus far I have described what is meant by "persecution" and have shown that there is a new situation in Latin America in which "persecution" is no longer found in its traditional form. But all this is still descriptive and not normative.

What I am seeking now are some criteria for determining what, from a Christian viewpoint, persecution of the Church really is. Insofar as these criteria are "Christian" only the Church has the right to define what persecution means. Given the present situation it has not only the right but the pastoral obligation to do so, especially since in the campaigns against the Church that are being carried on in the press the aim of many writers is to act as arbiters of what Christianity is, what the Church is, and what is to count as persecution of the Church.

As basic criteria for determining from a Christian standpoint what "persecution of the Church" is I assign first place to the historical significance of the "persecution of Jesus" and second place to the real mission of the Church as the Church sees this in its present self-understanding. Our thinking on both Jesus and the Church has been renewed in the last ten years; the theological concept of "persecution" shares in this historical renewal.

The Persecution of Jesus

If there is any well-attested historical fact about Jesus of Nazareth it is certainly that he was persecuted during his life by the powers of the day and that this persecution was climaxed by his condemnation and death. The subject is a broad one. In order to make it vivid for us, I shall follow closely the gospel of John in which the theme of the persecution of Jesus appears in the beginning and runs throughout.

Even at the beginning, during his first stay in Jerusalem, Jesus distrusted the Jews (2:24). During his second stay in Jerusalem "the Jews persecuted Jesus because he did this [the healing of the paralytic] on the sabbath. . . . The Jews sought all the more to kill him, because he not only broke the sabbath but also called God his

Father, making himself equal with God" (5:16, 18). When the time came to go up to Jerusalem for the feast of Tabernacles, he "went about in Galilee; he would not go about in Judea, because the Jews sought to kill him" (7:1). In the temple he asked them: " 'Why do you seek to kill me?' " (7:19). The people took the attempt for granted and said, " 'Is this not the man whom they seek to kill?' " (7:25). "So they sought to arrest him; but no one laid hands on him, because his hour had not yet come" (7:30). "The Pharisees heard the crowd thus muttering about him, and the chief priests and Pharisees sent officers to arrest him" (7:32).

In a new debate with the Pharisees Jesus bore witness to himself as he taught in the temple, "but no one arrested him, because his hour had not yet come" (8:20). At the end of this discourse "they took up stones to throw at him; but Jesus hid himself, and went out of the temple" (8:59). At the end of his discourse on the feast of the Dedication "the Jews took up stones again to stone him" (10:31); "they tried to arrest him, but he escaped from their hands" (10:39). On his way to Bethany to visit the family of Lazarus his disciples said to him: " 'Rabbi, the Jews were but now seeking to stone you, and are you going there again?' " (11:8). After the raising of Lazarus many Jews believed in him; the Pharisees met with the council and Caiaphas and "from that day on they took counsel how to put him to death. Jesus therefore no longer went about openly among the Jews" (11:53–54). At his final Passover "the chief priests and the Pharisees had given orders that if any one knew where he was, he should let them know, so that they might arrest him" (11:57). Then came the arrest, the religious trial, the civil trial, the condemnation and death of Jesus.

According to John's gospel, therefore, persecution marks the entire life of Jesus. It is not something incidental that occurs at the end of his life; it is typical of his career from the beginning. A similar analysis might be made of the other gospels.

John gives the persecutors the generic name of "the Jews" (this attribution plays a key part in the theology of the fourth gospel). More specifically, they are the Pharisees, the high priest, and finally Pilate. According to the synoptic gospels the persecutors include all who wield power in the religious (Pharisees, priests, high priest) and political (Herod, Pilate) spheres.

The *fact*, then, that Jesus was persecuted is clear and undeniable.

More important, however, is the answer to the question *why* he was persecuted. It will give us the basic criterion for understanding the persecution of the Church. The reason for the persecution of Jesus can be studied at two complementary levels: Jesus was persecuted because of the God he preached (the religious level, where the accusation of blasphemy has its place) and because of the visible, historical consequences to which his proclamation and inauguration of the reign of God and his denunciation of the sin of injustice led (the political level, where the accusation of subversion has its place).

It is an oversimplification inspired by ignorance or self-interest to claim that Jesus died simply because the Father so willed. At the level of abstraction the statement is certainly true. The question that needs to be answered, however, is what this will of the Father was that explains why the life of Jesus was one of persecution and why it ended on the cross. The will of the Father was that Jesus should be faithful to his mission. His mission can be summed up in three words: proclaim, denounce, realize.

Jesus did not *proclaim* just God; he proclaimed the kingdom of God. From the outset the preaching of Jesus was concerned not simply with God but with a human society in harmony with God, a society that will reach its fullness only at the end of time but that must make its presence felt here on earth. In thus proclaiming the kingdom of God Jesus took the side of the poorest. His very preaching therefore had social repercussions even though his message was a religious one. Here the revolution that Jesus brought is to be found: the religious message is neither possible nor real unless it clearly has to do with relationships among human beings. Jesus *denounced* sins against the kingdom. He therefore denounced every form of oppression that was practiced by the economically strong, the intellectuals, the religious leaders, and the political leaders. He did this in his well-known debates with the Pharisees, in the curses he uttered, in his attitude toward Herod, Caiaphas, and Pilate. Finally, Jesus made the kingdom a *reality*; he showed the signs of its presence (miracles, exorcisms, unity with the outcast) and the prophetic signs of its absence (expulsion of the merchants from the temple).

If we understand the mission of Jesus in this way we will also understand that persecution was his inevitable lot. For although he came to preach salvation to all and sought to convert the powerful as well as the weak, yet the nature of God his Father, whom he preached, was such that the execution of his mission gave rise to profound conflicts. In those days as in our own, society would tolerate a preaching about "God" that did not entail a prophetic denunciation of the basic sin of injustice, which prevents human beings from being brothers and sisters and which does not call for any action. But Jesus understood his mission in a different and contrary way; as a result, the powerful, who had no desire to be converted, felt threatened and therefore persecuted Jesus.

The first Christian communities, as made known to us in the New Testament, were very conscious that persecution was to be a fundamental mark of their Christian life. For this reason they kept in mind or reinterpreted certain sayings of Jesus on the persecution his disciples would suffer, and with the help of these they reflected on the persecution they themselves were experiencing.

"Blessed are those who are persecuted for righteousness' sake" (Mt. 5:10); "Blessed are you when men . . . persecute you . . . on my account . . . for so men persecuted the prophets who were before you" (Mt. 5:11-12). To his disciples he says: "When they persecute you in one town, flee to the next, and if they persecute you in this one too, flee still to another" (Mt. 10:23 JB). A lukewarm Christian is one who is not ready for persecution (cf. Mt. 13:21). In the discourse at the Last Supper as recorded by John Jesus says to his disciples: "If the world hates you, know that it has hated me before it hated you. . . . 'A servant is not greater than his master.' If they persecuted me, they will persecute you" (Jn. 15:18, 20).

Many passages in the Acts of the Apostles and in the letters of Paul tell of Christians being persecuted. This passage is representative: "We sent Timothy . . . to establish you in your faith and to exhort you, that no one be moved by these afflictions. You yourselves know that this is to be our lot. For when we were with you, we told you beforehand that we were to suffer affliction" (1 Thes. 3:2-4).

I cannot here discuss the concrete reasons for the persecution of the first Christian communities. In general terms these persecutions were not due solely to the fact that the Christians were preaching a new doctrine, a new Lord, and a new God; they were due also to the visible social consequences of this teaching.

The Conception of the Church Based on Vatican II and Medellín

The Second Vatican Council and the Medellín Conference led to a new conception of the Church: the Church rediscovered its biblical and patristic roots. This new conception of the Church explains the new concept of "persecution of the Church."

Since Vatican II and, in Latin America, even more since Medellín, the Church is sure that in its preaching of the gospel it cannot focus solely on individuals nor can it adopt a purely otherworldly perspective. The Church is convinced that the salvation of souls does not exhaust the Christian task. The task is a broader one: "It is man himself who must be saved; it is mankind that must be renewed" (GS 3). The Church realizes that if it is to be true to its faith in Jesus Christ it "must avoid the dualism which separates temporal tasks from the work of sanctification" (Medellín, *Justice* 5).[2] The Latin American Church in our day is deeply aware of the unity of history and of the connection between the history of salvation and the history of the human race. Because the Church proclaims a salvation that it understands as a total liberation, a redemption of the entire person and the structures in which she or he lives, and because it denounces both personal and structural sin, its mission today affects public life in a profound and constant way.

The basic presuppositions of this conception of the Church, a new conception as far as practice is concerned, can be reduced to the following. First, the Church is the *people* of God; any distinction between hierarchy and faithful is secondary. The Church is also a sacrament, or *sign*, in two ways: it is a sign of the entire human race as it journeys to the Father, and it is a sign of the historical presence of Christ among humankind. In addition, the Church is an *assembly* gathered to hear the word of God which calls it to account and to which it responds in its liturgy. The Church is also a *community* that lives the faith and practices love. Finally, the Church is *partisan*; this is perhaps the greatest novelty in the present-day Church. It "recognizes in those who are poor and who suffer, the image of her poor and suffering founder. She does all in her power to relieve their need and in them she strives to serve Christ" (LG 8). Moreover the Church proclaims that its duty is to cultivate solidarity with the poor in which it will make their problems and struggles its own (cf. Medellín, *Poverty* 10).

If we take this description seriously we will have a glimpse of the meaning and even the historical necessity of "persecution of the Church." When the Council speaks of the Church as a people, it adds that this is a *pilgrim* people. This term is meant to indicate, among other things, the participation of the Church in the real history of human beings, and especially in the difficulties, confusions, and conflicts that are part of this history. The term implies a change at the practical level from a Church of power, which sought and received privileges, to a Church of poverty, whose sole privilege is to share the wretched poverty of human beings and to be their companion in affliction.

When we speak of the Church as a sign we are saying that it signifies "something" to "someone." The thing that it signifies is the saving and liberating will of Christ for all human beings and for human beings in their entirety, that is, integral liberation now and eschatological liberation in the fullness of time. Because the Church is a sign it is by nature a relational entity; it has no meaning in itself except to the extent that it signifies love of God (service of God) to human beings (service to human beings). The conclusion from this is that the Church's reason for existence is not itself but its mission. In this specific sense it can be said that the Church does not create the mission; the mission continually engenders the Church. Obviously, the Church as institution determines and decides what must be done concretely in a given situation, but this action of the Church has meaning only as a response to the continual summons of God that comes to the Church through the signs of the times. The response to this summons constitutes the Church as mission.

Finally, Medellín makes it clear that the privileged recipients of the Church's mission are the poorest and most oppressed. This partisanship within the mission of the Church is called for by the signs of the times, at least in Latin America. The privileged recipients of its action are the peasants, the outcast natives, the shantytowners.

If the Church really acts in this way, we have a Christian criterion of persecution. Persecution of the "Church" does not typically take the form of a direct attack on it as an institution, a stripping away of its historical privileges, a refusal to treat it as a "perfect and autonomous" society. In misguided attacks on the institution there is indeed the element of human persecution, but not of typically Christian persecution. The Christian notion of persecution makes its appearance when the attack is on the Church's mission. In simple terms an authentic persecution of the Church exists when by some means its threefold mission of proclaiming the kingdom, denouncing sin, and making the kingdom a reality is made more difficult or is hindered. The mission of the Church is devastated when the purpose of that mission is made difficult to achieve or is attacked or destroyed. That purpose is the creation of a fraternal society, the creation of the kingdom of God in its inchoative state, that is, a society in which God can be called Father because human beings are truly brothers and sisters. The mission of the Church is undermined when the work and reflection of its communities is made impossible, when they can no longer be assemblies summoned by the word of God for the purpose of responding to this word.

The crucial form of persecution of the Church does not consist therefore in direct attacks against the Church as an institution. When such attacks are unjustified, the Church can and must defend itself in virtue of the right that belongs to any human institution. The most telling form of persecution is to prevent and destroy the Church's mission and the goal of its mission.

We have now determined in Christian terms what it means to persecute the Church. From the brief christological analysis we can conclude that to persecute the Church means to attack and kill those who carry out the Church's mission. From the brief ecclesiological analysis we can conclude that it also means to attack and kill the recipients of this mission, that is, human beings and in particular the poor and the oppressed. On the stage of history these two kinds of persecution fuse and become one. To persecute Jesus today is to persecute his historical body, the mass of human beings who in a privileged way represent him in his suffering and poverty, as he indicated in his cry to Paul: "Saul, Saul, why do you persecute me?" (Acts 9:4).

This Christian definition of "persecution of the Church" will seem novel only to those who have failed to grasp what is new in the ecclesiology of Vatican II and Medellín. The assertion that the Church is persecuted when the people of God, the people who are poor and oppressed, are persecuted will seem a demagogic slogan only to those who still have not realized, or have not tried to realize, that the ultimate reason for the existence of the Church is the service of this people.

Concrete Application to Latin America

As long as the Church in Latin America did not understand and carry out its mission in the way I have been describing (the failure to do so is understandable on historical grounds), the Church was respected, aided, and given privileges; any persecution of it was persecution in the literal sense of an attack on the Church as institution. But now that the Church understands its mission as set down in Medellín, it has been persecuted in the manner I have been describing.

This kind of persecution can be seen in the persecution of Christian leaders, those who are the Church's agents in its mission. Everyone is aware of how many leaders (priests, laypersons, and even bishops) have been murdered, threatened, banished, tortured; of the systematic newspaper campaigns accusing these leaders of subversion; of the bombs set off in the agencies of the Church's mission (libraries, printing houses, and universities); of the bombs set off in the homes of Christian leaders; of the effort to limit the Church's mission to the interior life without allowing it any social repercussions; of the aid, even economic, given to Churches that limit their efforts to the purely spiritual.

The point to be stressed with regard to this list is that these activities can be called "persecution of the Church" not because they trample on civil and human rights but because they attempt to take from the Church the concrete means it needs in order to carry out its *mission*. From the standpoint of human rights it is the same kind of crime to murder a priest because of his commitment as it is to murder him in order to rob him. But from the Church's point of view the two crimes are different in kind. Persecution consists in hindering the Church's mission and not in attacking a churchperson.

Persecution at another level is persecution of those to whom the Church's mission is directed: the people, especially the poorest and most oppressed. This type of persecution is familiar to us. The many massacres of peasants and Indians amount to genocides; malnutrition and unemployment cause slow deaths; complete inequality of opportunity brings inequality and oppression.

Medellín put this whole matter very clearly and described the structural root that leads to this kind of persecution: "There are in existence many studies of the Latin American people. The misery that besets large masses of human beings in all of our countries is described in all of these studies. That misery, as a collective fact, expresses itself as injustice which cries to heaven" (*Justice* 1). This situation of wretched poverty and injustice is not a static one that will be passively undergone; it contains an active dynamism that leads to active disorder: "If 'development is the new name for peace,' Latin American underdevelopment, with its own characteristics in the different countries, is an unjust situation which promotes tensions that conspire against peace" (*Peace* 1). This tragically active dimension of structural injustice unleashes what I have called persecution of the people, the historical body of Christ:

> [The Christian] recognizes that in many instances Latin America finds itself faced with a situation of injustice that can be called institutionalized violence, when, because of a structural deficiency of industry and agriculture, of national and international economy, of cultural and political life, "whole towns lack necessities, live in such dependence as hinders all initiative and responsibility as well as every possibility for cultural promotion and participation in social and political life," thus violating fundamental rights (*Peace* 16).

The thinking of Medellín is clear. Where institutionalized injustice exists institutionalized violence is its direct consequence. The language of violence is the same as the language of persecution; it speaks of the consequences for those who live within these structures. To act unjustly is to do violence to the masses; it is to persecute them, to deprive them of their basic human rights. In the theological sense that I developed earlier, institutionalized violence is nothing else than institutionalized persecution of the people of God and the historical body of Christ. The particular "persecutions," the murders, the slaughtering of Christians, are simply tragic expressions of the basic "persecution" being inflicted on the people of God.

The two kinds of persecution of which I have been speaking—

persecution of Christian leaders and persecution of the recipients of the Church's mission—coincide in the present situation in Latin America. Not just any Christian leader is persecuted, but those precisely who have sided with the people in order that the latter might cease to be persecuted. People are not randomly persecuted, but those groups precisely that have undergone conscientization through the efforts of, among others, Christian leaders. The murder of a priest is therefore not simply an attack on a particular churchman, but an attack on the people, who historically have depended on the priest for direction and organization. The murder of a group of peasants is not simply a direct attack on the fundamental rights of individuals, but an attack on their leaders inasmuch as it destroys their mission or attempts to scare them off. At the risk of generalization I must assert that in Latin America the two types of persecution of the Church are coextensive at this historical moment. The fundamental persecution continues to be the persecution of the people of God: they are denied their basic human rights, and in consequence the reign of God is formally rejected. This persecution then takes for its object all those Christians—leaders, priests, pastoral workers, lay ministers of the word—who have been at the people's side in their conscientization and who, through the word of proclamation and denunciation as well as through concrete works, have helped the people to organize themselves with a view to the reign of God.

PERSECUTION IN THE ARCHDIOCESE OF SAN SALVADOR

The events of the first five months of 1977 made tragically clear what had been going on for a long time. The archbishop did not hesitate to voice the unanimous view of true Christians and to assert that a real persecution of the Church was in progress. He did so despite pressure from rulers, oligarchs, and even some high-ranking members of the ecclesiastical hierarchy who regarded the term "persecution" as too strong.

The empirical evidence for this persecution and for the ways in which the Church reacted at various stages in the process is given elsewhere.[3] My purpose here is to offer a theological evaluation of the Church's reaction to the persecution.

The Church's Understanding of "Persecution"

The Church's decision to assert the existence of persecution has certainly been due to the many attacks on its leaders and institutions. This shows that there are still certain deficiencies in the Church's understanding of persecution. These deficiencies are understandable in the light of the Church's past history and in the light of group psychology, since a group becomes conscious of the meaning of particular events when those affected by these events belong to that group.

In denouncing persecution because those being persecuted are Church leaders, the Church is also, at least indirectly, including the people among the persecuted. Not just any priest has been attacked nor just any bishop nor just any Catholic school nor just any Catholic communications medium, but precisely those that have most distinguished themselves by their partiality for the oppressed. The Church has clearly realized, if only unconsciously, that these Church leaders and institutions are being persecuted because they have sided with the oppressed people. Denunciation of this persecution means a denunciation of the ultimate cause of the persecution: the violence to which the majority of the people are subjected and which is such that anyone who draws close to the people, identifies with them, and gives them concrete help in getting out of the situation of injustice becomes a victim of the same persecution.

This implicit consciousness of the Church has become explicit in various ways, even if the term "persecution" is not always used. To take only what I regard as more significant examples, I shall cite some passages from recent documents in which the persecution of Church leaders is seen in relation to and as part of persecution of the people.

In its Message of March 5, 1977, the Episcopal Conference said:

> Our concern is with the repression of the peasants, the number of individuals killed or spirited away, the increase in the incidence of torture, the anguish of the families affected by these happenings. We call for the cessation of every kind of violence by social groups, paramilitary organizations, security forces, and the army; a guarantee of the safety of all citizens; the restoration to public life of those who have been spirited away; the

cessation of the use of torture; the observance of the strictest legality during the state of siege; an end to the trampling on human rights.

In this context we must regard as attacks on the Church the expulsion of priests and the campaign of slander, and we call for a stop to these abuses and for consultation prior to any planned expulsion of priests.

In his communiqué of March 15, 1977, the archbishop wrote:

The violence abroad in society has shown itself in unjust attacks on organizations that promote the integral development of the peasantry; it showed itself next in the expulsion and torture of priests; it culminated in the triple murder of a priest, Fr. Rutilio Grande, S.J., and two peasants, Manuel Solórzano and a young man, Nelson Rutilio Lemus, all three of them symbols of the sufferings and deaths among the dispossessed and helpless majorities of the Salvadoran people.

In the communiqué issued by the archbishop and clergy on May 5, 1977, we read:

We are concerned about the inequitable distribution of land, the kidnapping of the Chancellor of the Republic, the fear that the address of the President would lead to more tragic consequences, the armed confrontation of May 1, with the liquidation of eight dead civilians and a number of wounded, among them some policemen of the Guardia Nacional. We therefore ask that the situation of those arrested be clarified, that justice be done them, and that human rights be defended.

In this context we must mention the persecution of Christian leaders, members of the Justice and Peace Commission, and the priests who have been expelled; the campaign of slander being conducted in the press and leaflets; the vilification of the Jesuits in particular; the attacks on the printing house of the archdiocese in which a bomb was exploded. We ask therefore that a stop be put to these campaigns and that the rights of priests be respected.

The archdiocesan Bulletin of May 20 (no. 16), after reporting the arrest of three priests of Aguilares, stated:

> In denouncing these new acts of persecution against the Church we also denounce the military action carried out in Aguilares, El Paisnal, and their territories, against the city-dwellers and peasants who are already oppressed by the terrible inequality in land ownership in our country. We want to express our disquiet at the atmosphere of terror and the personal insecurity to which Salvadorans are subjected whose only crime is their despair at the lack of land and work. The lot of these fellow countrymen, poorest of the poor, concerns us as much and even more than the injustice suffered by the priests to whom we referred earlier. In the name of national security and of the safety of property the fundamental right of an entire people to live in dignity and justice is being trampled underfoot.

These documents all show a clear awareness that the persecution against the Church is intelligible only as part of a more basic persecution of the people. The documents express a fundamental awareness of the Church and its mission and depart from traditional ideas. I am not trying here to strike a triumphalist note nor to claim that the Church of the archdiocese has fully assimilated the great truth that the Church is the servant of the people. I said earlier that there are still deficiencies in the Church. I think that the Church's reaction to the persecution of the people of Aguilares under military occupation was not as energetic as it should have been, since according to all indications that was a real massacre of the people of God, the historical body of Christ, in that part of the country.

Neither can it be denied that the Church of the archdiocese has grown in the awareness that it is the servant of the people of God and that the persecution of the Church can only be understood as part of a systematic persecution of this people. There has been a growth in consciousness of the ultimate cause of the persecution: the continuing, institutionalized injustice under which the majority of Salvadorans live. Let the following passage from the bishops' Message (March 5, 1977) stand for many others:

> These serious incidents [listed earlier] are the expression of a much greater and more radical evil. Everyone knows the tragic

social conditions of our country. . . . The situation has been described as one of "collective injustice" and "institutionalized violence." . . . This is the basic sin which we pastors must denounce. We cannot ignore the people nor gamble with them and their hopes. As long as we make no determined and effective effort to resolve the problems of the distribution of wealth and land, political participation, and the organization of the urban and rural population, we are ignoring the people both as citizens and as children of God.

Reaction of the Archdiocese to the Persecution

The sheer number of the events of the first five months of 1977 makes it impossible to follow a chronological order in discussing the Church's reaction. I shall follow instead a logical order and describe the types of reaction to the persecution. The intensity of the reaction varied from instance to instance; the important thing to observe is the basic structure of the reaction. I shall distinguish three forms.

Defense of the civil rights of Church leaders and key laypersons. In the course of the general persecution of the Church ("persecution" understood in the theological sense already explained) the civil rights of many Church leaders have been violated. At this level, which is not the one most typical of persecution of the Church, the Church has tried to respond using the means best suited to particular cases. Thus it has called upon the government to investigate the murders of Fathers Rutilio Grande, S.J., and Alfonso Navarro. It has sought to prevent the expulsion of priests, the mistreatment and torture of priests arrested and detained; it has tried to win the freedom of imprisoned priests and laypersons.

The methods used in the Church's response have been the normal ones: official and unofficial conversations with representatives of the authorities; contacts with embassies; the creation of public opinion; international pressure. It is important to emphasize this type of reaction in order to show that the Church has not conducted itself in a naïve manner. Without ceasing its ethicoprophetic denunciation it has tried to find effective ways of resolving the tragic plight of its priests and of preventing still greater evils. At this level the Church has acted as a "human group," endeavoring to defend its legitimate interests, even if in thus defending ecclesiastical persons and institutions, it is also defending and making possible its own mission.

Participation of the Church in important situations. In the many social conflicts in El Salvador recently the key element in the Church's activity has been its effort, more or less urgent according to cases, to be in solidarity with those who are persecuted. A typical example is the mediation of the archbishop in the conflicts around siezures of land. In these cases the mere fact of trying to mediate when the law did not protect the peasants was itself a denunciation of the legal situation and a support to the landless peasants. Other examples: the services offered by the archbishop on May 1, 1977, after the repression of demonstrators; the effort to mediate in the Borgonovo case; the welcome given to the families of many individuals who had disappeared and the speaking out on their behalf; the effort to reach the beseiged populace of Aguilares.

This general response shows that the Church is concerned that the human rights of the oppressed should not be violated or, in other words, that the people not be persecuted. The Church has defended the human rights of all the citizens of El Salvador, but it has shown a partiality for the most oppressed. This makes clear the Church's understanding of what real "persecution" is; it also shows that the Church's fundamental reaction has been to lend its voice to a voiceless people, even if at times it could not do much more than this.

The humanization of the country. The majority of Salvadorans, be they Christians or simply people of good will, recognized that the Church is today the only social force capable of confronting persecution in a positive way. In several official statements, by means of the *Seminario Orientación* and the archdiocesan YSAX program, the Church has tried to humanize the country as it passes through one of its deepest crises. The Church is the only social force capable of bringing all other social forces together in a bold effort at ethicoprophetical proclamation and denunciation. By denouncing the roots of the national crisis and by showing what the true roots of the nation should be, it has humanized the country.

The characteristics of this effort at humanization seem to me to be the following. At a time when human words have no value and have been degraded to a degree hitherto thought impossible; at a time when words are not vehicles for truth and appear to have no connection with reality; at a time when words are not an expression of the person but a way of defending anonymous interests—at such a time the Church has restored value to human words by being accountable for what it says, proving what it asserts, and signing what it writes.

The Church has restored the proper meaning to the word *sin*. The powerful are anxious to have sin regarded solely as a violation of a law, but the Church forcefully reminds us that sin is "inflicting death on human beings," whether in a quick and violent way or a slow, institutionalized way. It also reminds us of the elemental truth that every human life has the same value, whether it be the life of a high public official or the life of the most disregarded peasant.

The Church has restored the true meaning of *justice* and *law*. It reminds us that behind laws there must be a supreme law of justice without which other laws have no meaning and serve only to defend various interests. It repeatedly tells us that the person does not exist for the law but the law for the person. It reminds us that the supposed neutrality of the law is deceptive since in fact it shows partiality to the powerful; whereas both historically (in view of the origin of human laws) and biblically (in view of God's predilection for the oppressed) the intention of the law should be to show partiality for the oppressed. The powerful do not need this kind of protection.

The Church has restored seriousness to history. Against an anecdotal conception of history that focuses on isolated events, however tragic and lamentable they may be, the Church reminds us that history is not just something that happened; it is what we human beings have made. Therefore, instead of concentrating on and bewailing the sad events now occurring, it points to the ongoing institutional causes of these events. It has repeatedly said—as a voice crying in the wilderness—that as long as present structures are not changed, the sad events the country is experiencing will be repeated.

The Church is restoring a sense of the future. The condemnation of vengeance is not simply an expression of a particular ethical conscience; it is also a condemnation of the attempt to tie human beings to their past. In opposition to that kind of outlook the Church proclaims the future. Its mission is to open up the future to all persons, oppressed and oppressors; the manner of opening the future to them will depend on which they are. The Church reminds us that it is not by giving primacy to the past and to the eternal order of things (supposedly reestablished by the exercise of vengeance) but by moving into a re-creative future that we will be able to escape from the present sociopolitical impasse.

The Church, finally, is restoring hope to the people. Without indulging in triumphalism and recognizing that the Church still has a long way to go, we may say that the Church has given the people a voice and opened a way for them. It has asserted that justice and the struggle for it contain the seed of a deathless hope giving ultimate meaning to our historical life and that we can, on the basis of this meaning, look forward to final fulfillment.

What I have here called "the process of humanizing the country" is the Church's deepest and fullest response to persecution. I am talking here not of fighting for the return of peace or for the privileges of the institutional Church but of fighting, with means that are weak and in principle ineffective, to turn the country into something that resembles the kingdom of God. All this shows that the Church understands the present persecution as persecution directed at the kingdom of God and that therefore, whether or not the result will be of immediate advantage to the institutional Church, its own first reaction to this persecution must be to struggle for the proclamation and realization of the kingdom and for the humanization of the country. It must respond in this way even when its own institutional life is under unjust and bitter attack.

9

Evangelization as Mission of the Church

The purpose of this chapter is to reflect in a systematic way on the Christian meaning of evangelization. The term *evangelization* includes two related but distinct things: content to be communicated and the action of communicating. Evangelization is the communication of good news.

The history of evangelization has clearly applied and specified the sense of this nominal definition. Not every evangelization is Christian. Put negatively: we must not assume that every "good news" that is proclaimed is Christian or even that the good news that has been proclaimed throughout the history of the Church has been fully Christian. Even more important, we must not assume that any and every way of presenting this good news is Christian. That is, we must not assume that the true manner of evangelizing has the same structure as other kinds of proclamations of good news or other kinds of proselytism. Put positively: if evangelization is to be Christian there must be a reciprocal and specifically Christian relationship between the content that is presented and the way of presenting it. Not every manner of spreading the faith does justice to the content of the Christian good news, nor does every understanding of this content call for its communication to others.

I wish to emphasize that in dealing with the subject of evangelization we must determine the Christian meaning of the term in both its aspects. I shall develop and elucidate this general point in the course of this chapter.

The importance of the theme is reflected in its topicality. It looms large in the ordinary life of the Churches, both in a treatment of evangelization as such and in any inquiry regarding the mission of the Church as a whole or of basic communities, religious orders and congregations, and parishes, vicariates, and dioceses.

The theme of evangelization has also been taken up by the Church's official magisterium. The Third Synod of Bishops (Rome, Sept.-Oct. 1974) was devoted to it, as was the Apostolic Exhortation *Evangelii nuntiandi* of Paul VI and the Third General Conference of the Latin American Bishops (1979).

Evangelization is topical because it is being discussed; it is being discussed because it is so relevant. Evangelization is not simply one of many possible subjects that the universal Church and the local Churches may and should discuss; it has become a central subject due to the rediscovery (since Vatican II) of the relational nature of the Church. To rethink evangelization is to rethink the relational nature of the Church and its reason for existence.

There is no question simply of rethinking methods of catechesis or pedagogy or even of rethinking the content of an evangelization whose nature is already essentially clear and fully grasped by the evangelizing Church. We are dealing here with a prior and more elemental problem: What does it mean for the Church to evangelize? This question has to do with both evangelization and the nature of the Church, with both the good news to be communicated and the way of communicating it.

It follows from this that the crises in evangelization are the most radical crises now affecting the Church. *Evangelii nuntiandi* names three of the most fundamental crises. The first is the enveloping atheism that prevails in various parts of the world (55). As a result of it the Church is no longer taken for granted as a social and cultural phenomenon, but is an entity that will be meaningful only if it can offer an encompassing meaning for life and history superior to the meaning, or meaninglessness, offered by atheistic ideologies. The widespread atmosphere of atheism calls into radical question the Church's nature and mission. It can no longer be taken for granted in the work of evangelization that human beings are naturally religious and that the Church can simply come along and offer them the "true" religion. The need is rather to provide a global alternative meaning for life and history, an alternative in which the God of Jesus is beyond conventional atheism and theism. This problem is a serious one; its resolution calls not simply for a new way of evangelizing but for a new way of existing as Church. The need is not for new catechetical methods but for a change in the understanding and practice of existence as Church.

The second crisis is the need for inculturation in evangelization (20). *Evangelii nuntiandi* asserts the inadequacy of an evangelization that does not take account of the diversity of cultures and that tries, consciously or unconsciously, to impose forms of expression of the Christian faith that are alien to the specific character of the various peoples. This crisis, which Vatican II had already singled out, is felt with increasing acuteness and calls for serious reflection on the work of evangelization, in regard both to the language of faith and to the symbolic manifestations of faith in liturgy and sacraments. But this crisis is also radical for the Church itself in at least two ways. First, it challenges the uniformity that has been imposed on the Church by the European conception of "Christendom." It is one way of challenging the model of Church unity that works outward from the center of Christendom and ignores the Churches on the periphery of the circle or even treats them as subjects. This challenge, most obvious in the disciplinary arrangements the center has imposed on the periphery, is only an expression of something deeper. What is ultimately at stake is the true radicalness of the universality of Christ as seen here in the self-expression of various peoples. If the Jewish Jesus of the first century cannot be expressed and confessed as the Christ through the medium of different cultures, then he is not truly the Christ. The ultimate question that the crisis of inculturation raises for the Church is: In what Christ does it believe?

The third crisis has to do with the very idea of evangelization. It is the crisis that occurs when evangelization is conceived of as simply a proclamation of sublime realities without any accompanying effort to make this content concrete. We are dealing here not with alternatives but with the problem of combining the two aspects of evangelization. The crisis makes its appearance when the preaching of the redemption brought by Christ is not accompanied by a practice of effective liberation or, to put it another way, when preaching about God is not accompanied by the building of God's kingdom. The problem is a serious one and *Evangelii nuntiandi* devotes several paragraphs to it (29–38). This crisis affects not only evangelization but the very idea of what the Church is. The failure to accompany proclamation with an effective practice of liberation is not simply one of the possible faults that the Church, like any human institution, can commit; it is a failure that denies the Church itself. The ultimate issue is whether the Church is an institution of the gnostic type, that is, one whose function is to transmit saving knowledge, or whether it is a people who continue the saving action of Jesus. The ancient gnosticism that rejected the flesh, the human history of Christ, is not a danger now. However, it may be replaced by an ecclesial gnosticism if the Church settles for communicating a noetic content without setting history in motion, if it settles for confessing Christ (including his earthly history) without continuing the history of this Christ.

The crises of evangelization named in *Evangelii nuntiandi* are fundamental; they are also profound crises of the Church. They cannot be resolved, therefore, unless we explain what the Church is. This is why the subject of evangelization is so relevant and so much discussed: because it raises, explicitly or implicitly, the question of the ultimate reality of the Church.

The method I shall adopt is that of systematic reflection. If my aim is to determine the Christian significance of evangelization and the relation between evangelization and Church, then I must relate each of these realities to its most basic principles. This means, in the concrete, connecting evangelization with the ultimate content of Christian reality: with God, the kingdom of God, Christ, sin, love, justice. These realities determine whether and how the manner and content of evangelization are in fact Christian. In this way I shall try to determine the fundamental structure of evangelization without dwelling too much on its necessary concrete mediations. The criticisms made, explicitly or by allusion, of other models of evangelization will be based not only on the ideologies associated with them (which can be discovered especially on the basis of the social sciences) but also on their Christian inadequacy (which it is the unavoidable task of theology to establish).

Since I wish to begin by listing fundamental Christian principles of evangelization I shall take as my point of departure the theological principles set forth in *Evangelii nuntiandi* especially in its first three chapters (6–39). I shall offer a theological development of these principles and then go on to examine other themes connected with evangelization that are relevant to our situation but are either not discussed in *Evangelii nuntiandi* or are not discussed in sufficient detail to regard them as set forth for the universal Church.[1]

The Christian definition of evangelization must take into account the concrete history of Latin America as part of the Third World. Even the various realities I named above become concrete only in the perspective of concrete history. In addition to *Evangelii nuntiandi*, therefore, we must keep in mind other letters of the pontifical magisterium of Pope Paul VI, which by reason of their social themes were directed explicitly to the Third World; above all, we must keep before us what was said at Medellín. We will have to remember that evangelization takes place in a world of sin (cf. Medellín, *Justice* 1–2) but a world in which nonetheless there is widespread desire for liberation (cf. Medellín, *Introduction* 4); that the poor and the oppressed, who constitute the vast majority in Latin America, "place before the Latin American Church a challenge and a mission that [it] cannot sidestep" (*Poverty* 7). Medellín gives us a hermeneutical principle from which there is no turning back when it says that "we wish the Latin American Church to be the evangelizer of the poor and one with them" (*Poverty* 8).

These are the themes I consider most important in dealing with evangelization: the Church's establishment through evangelization; the ways of evangelizing; the content, transcendent and historical, of evangelization; the unification of faith and practice in evangelization; the unification of evangelization and evangelizer; the unification of evangelization and the evangelized; and the consequences of a unified evangelization.

THE CHURCH'S ESTABLISHMENT THROUGH EVANGELIZATION

Thesis 1: The Church draws its identity from its mission of evangelization. The deepest meaning of the foundation of the Church by Christ is that he makes the Church his historical body and continuer of his mission. All of the Church's structures— doctrinal, sacramental, and organizational—attain their fulfillment only when they are at the service of evangelization. The ultimate horizon of the Church's work of evangelization is the kingdom of God.

The Church's Fulfillment in Its Mission

According to *Evangelii nuntiandi* "the task of evangelization is to be regarded as the Church's specific grace and calling and the activity most fully expressive of [its] real nature. The Church exists in order to evangelize" (14). Moreover, what may be called the internal life of the Church—prayer, listening to the word, the practice of fraternal love, and the sharing of bread—"cannot attain its full meaning and vitality unless it issues in witness, stirs wonder and leads to conversion, and finds expression in the preaching and proclamation of the gospel" (15).

These statements, though formal and made prior to the study of the content and methods of evangelization, are important. They make two key points: the Church's identity is found in a mission it is to carry out and the internal life of the Church attains its fulfillment only when it serves this mission. Here the relationality that is constitutive of the Church is clearly expressed.

These statements follow logically from the teaching of the Vatican Council, but in conceptual clarity and radicalness they go beyond it. At the Council the need was to move beyond a hierarchical and mystical conception of the Church, to emphasize its historical nature and its existence as a people. This is why so much stress was put on the idea of the Church as the "people of God" (LG 9–17). But once the emphasis on hierarchization has been overcome in principle, once the historical character of the Church has been assured, again in principle, we must ask ourselves what the purpose or finality is that gives the Church its coherence and its reason for existence. The Council answers in a formal way by recalling that the Church is the body of Christ (LG 7). The Council means to emphasize the union of the Church with its head, while the mission that derives from this union is considered in terms of the internal life of the Church and the establishment of the community. *Evangelii nuntiandi* goes further and says, in speaking of the relation of the Church to Christ, that its "primary duty is to carry on his mission and work of evangelization" (15).

The Second Vatican Council's systematic use of "sign" and "sacrament" in describing the Church was also important. These two notions express a varied content. They can refer to communion with God or to the unity of the entire human race (LG 1) or to the visible and salvific nature of the Church, which offers itself to the Spirit as a body through which he works salvation (LG 8). The Council thus chooses a systematic concept that is extremely important. For a sign is a reality that is not autonomous but exists to signify something to someone. The emphasis is on what I have called the constitutive relationality of the Church, although in the Council this emphasis is expressed at a formal level that needs to be further determined and concretized.[2]

Origin of the Church

This assertion of the constitutive relationality of the Church does not represent a modern discovery but rather a rediscovery of the earliest truth about the Church, a truth present from the very beginning. As a help in penetrating more deeply into our subject let me offer some thoughts, necessarily brief, on the origin and foundation of the Church.[3]

There are two dinstinct models for understanding the establishment of the Church by Christ: the *juridical* model and the *historical* model. The first of these was the only accepted one until recently. Briefly summarized, it means that during his earthly life Jesus founded an institution called the "Church" and expressly endowed it with hierarchical, doctrinal, and sacramental structures.

Nowadays this model is challenged, and with good reason. It is challenged, first of all, by the exegetes who in their study of the historical Jesus do not come across sure evidence of the Church's being founded in this manner. Even more important for my purpose here is critical systematic thinking on the subject. According to the juridical model, the founding of the Church is connected with an arbitrary act of Christ; the importance of the act does not make it any less arbitrary. In other words, Jesus founded a Church when he could just as well not have founded it. According to this explanation the Church has certain doctrinal, hierarchical, and sacramental structures that are logically prior to its mission and therefore also logically independent of it. In principle, of course (as the history of the Church shows), this does not keep the Church from also having a mission; but this mission is as it were a second phase of the Church and not really its reason for existence.

The juridical model of the Church does not deny the relationship between Church and mission, but the relationship is not constitutive of the Church. I shall show that all this is contrary to the essence of the New Testament. The practical conclusion from the juridical model is that the Church as institution takes precedence over the Church as mission, even though the Church obviously does dedicate itself to this mission. It follows, too, that the Church as institution already knows who it is before any question arises of its evangelizing task, and therefore that it also knows in principle how it must evangelize, what it must say, and to whom it should address itself prior to reflection on the mission. In short, the juridical model supposes that the Church can be constituted in logical independence of mission.

These are, of course, logical deductions and have never been stated in their purity in the history of the Church. That same history does, however, give evidence of serious mistakes with regard to mission, of European and Roman centralization, of a lack of inculturation, of presenting a message already possessed without regard to the recipients and so on. The logical basis for these historical defects is the practice of regarding the institutional Church as already constituted prior to any consideration of mission, or, in other words, the failure to make the relation to mission constitutive of the Church as institution. This logical basis is made possible by taking the view that Christ founded a Church in the juridical sense, for this makes it possible to separate what the Church is in itself from what it must do for others.

Over against this juridical model of the founding of the Church I set the historical model.[4] This model holds that the life and resurrection of Christ as historical realities gave rise to the thing we call the Church and that the content of the life and resurrection of Christ, even apart from any formal statements by Christ, automatically became normative for the new thing we call the Church. I cannot here go into this complex problem in full detail; after all, it is coextensive with the entire history set down in the New Testament. But I do want to indicate some points here that will help shed light on the relationality that is constitutive of the Church.

In the first stage of his public life Jesus proclaimed the kingdom of God. Here we have the basis for the relationality proper to Jesus: he preached the kingdom of God, not himself. He did not preach the Church nor did he endeavor to found an institution with the characteristics spoken of in the New Testament as belonging to the "Church" after Jesus' resurrection. Nonetheless, from the very beginning Jesus did have people who shared in his mission. This way of putting the matter is deliberately vague, yet it is important in order to understand the reality of the subsequent Church. The synoptic gospels tell us that Jesus chose the Twelve (cf. Mk. 3:13-19).[5] The commentators agree that the number twelve is symbolic and meant to express the fullness of the kingdom that is being proclaimed. More important for our subject here is the fact that the "appointment" of the Twelve appears in a specific context: "He called to him the twelve, and began to send them out" (Mk. 6:7). In a summary a few verses later, Mark explains what the appointment of the Twelve implies: "So they went out and preached that men should repent. And they cast out many demons, and anointed with oil many that were sick and healed them" (Mk. 6:12-13).[6]

This passage certainly does not speak of a Church; in fact, it was not possible to speak of any kind of stable institution, since at this time Jesus believed that the coming of the kingdom was at hand. It is important, however, to note that the calling of the twelve gets its meaning primarily from a mission: they are sent to do and preach basically what Jesus himself does and preaches. The reason for the existence of the Twelve is clear and it is essentially relational: they are to preach the kingdom to others and be the signs that show this kingdom has come.

In the second stage of his public life Jesus passed through a crisis designated the "Galilean crisis" because the gospels place it in the environs of Capernaum. At this time Matthew places in the mouth of Jesus the words referring to the founding of the Church. Although it is not historically certain that Jesus spoke these words, it is important to see how the history of Jesus at this period of his life lays the foundations for the Church and its relationality. I shall focus attention on one detail, an important one for understanding the later relational character of the Church.

The crisis in question consisted in the gradual desertion of Jesus by the crowds, in the fact that his disciples, while continuing to follow him, did not understand or even completely misunderstood him (cf. Mk. 8:31–33), and in the intensification of persecution against him by the powerful. Jesus was for all practical purposes left in isolation with his disciples; he must have been tempted to withdraw from his mission. Mark points to such a temptation by a geographical shift, for Jesus now makes his way through the Transjordan outside of Israel. In other words, he spends this period of time far from Jerusalem, the center of his people.

This temptation to withdraw (expressed in geographical terms) and go ever further from Jerusalem expresses in turn another temptation that is even more fundamental for an understanding of the future Church. The most reasonable alternative offered to Jesus after the failure of his mission was to form a sect comparable to the sects of Qumran, which were quite numerous at this time. The temptation was to think of his mission as limited to a group in which the message of Jesus might perhaps be lived with great purity but at the cost of isolation from the world.

Jesus overcame this temptation and went to Jerusalem. This ascent to Jerusalem is extremely important for the Church, both by reason of the historical events that took place in connection with it and by reason of the subsequent theological interpretation of it by the synoptics. The historical fact is that Jesus resisted the temptation to form a sect consisting of himself and a small group of disciples, and instead he turned back to the people as a whole. The "going up to Jerusalem" was a clear expression of Jesus' fidelity to his mission, which consisted not in creating closed groups, even if the internal life of such groups might have been a good one, but in continuing to preach the kingdom of God and offer it to all, even if the form was quite different from that at the beginning of his public life. In their theological interpretation of the ascent to Jerusalem the synoptic writers draw their inspiration from the Servant of Yahweh as they show Jesus setting out on a road that means salvation for all; the universal scope of his mission will find clear expression at the Last Supper in the phrases "for you" and "for the many."

In this ascent to Jerusalem the foundations of the future Church and its relational character are clearly present. From a sociological point of view a sect is characterized as being "against" or "apart from" others; it will be characteristic of the Church to be "for" and "with" others. Even at the most critical moments the life of

Jesus does not have its meaning in and for itself but in relation to others, more specifically to that unlimited majority of "others" who are represented by "Jerusalem." Jesus counters the temptation to self-centeredness with a relationality that is the fundamental law governing his life. The concrete content of this relational existence is clearly expressed in the "for": it is an existence in behalf of others. Whatever the form taken by the Church, the visible institution that comes on the scene after the resurrection, these two traits will be essential to it. It is usually said, and with good reason, that the objective foundations of the Church were laid at the Last Supper. To interpret the Last Supper as laying the foundation of a new people grounded on the law of the "for the many" is to have the germ of a truly profound theology of the Church.

After the resurrection the Church was established in the proper sense of the term; this is true historically and logically. Historically, because such is the testimony of the New Testament documents, for example, the Acts of the Apostles and the Pauline letters.[7] Logically, because only after the resurrection was there truly faith in Christ, that is, an acknowledgement that in Jesus of Nazareth the Son of God had revealed himself. The important thing is that even after the resurrection the Church did not lose its relational character. It might seem that after the resurrection the Church was simply the group of Christians who gathered to confess their faith in Christ, a sect.

On the contrary, according to the New Testament the appearances that were the basis for a definitive faith in Christ led to mission. According to the New Testament those to whom Christ manifests himself are not simple spectators brought to faith through the experience; they are "witnesses," that is, persons whose realization of the resurrection is accompanied by a readiness to testify about it to others. "Spectators" of the resurrection might have turned into individual Christians but not into a Church. The Church came into existence when the spectators became witnesses, that is, when they accepted a mission. I can here only assert the fact without demonstrating it fully. The passage from faith in Christ to the existence of the Church was accomplished through mission. The distinction between "spectators" and/or "witnesses" is not simply a matter of words. Had there been only "spectators" the result might well have been a sect that had the worship of the risen

Jesus for its focus and that did not look outside itself; but that would not have been the Church according to the New Testament. That Church is constituted in the carrying out of a mission, in bearing witness to others. Even though a great deal changed for the disciples of Jesus after his resurrection there was a basic continuity: the historical Jesus demanded that his followers carry out a mission for which he himself served as the model; the risen Christ likewise inaugurated a mission.

Relationality of the Church

These scriptural considerations on the origin of the Church show that the juridical model of institution is not only historically inaccurate but also theologically impoverished. The Church has its foundation not in an arbitrary act of Christ's will but in his entire existence. Because the being of Jesus is relational, relationality belongs to the Church, which has come into being as the continuation of Jesus. During his historical life Jesus gathered disciples for the sake of a mission; after his resurrection he inaugurated the mission of bearing witness. We have not yet explained what this mission of the Church is, what it means to proclaim the kingdom or to preach Christ as risen. I shall discuss this point further on. One important conclusion can already be drawn: the Church's reality lies not in itself but in a mission it is to accomplish. This mission, taken as a whole, is "evangelization."

In asserting relationality as constitutive of the Church I am not forgetting the complex dialectic of theo-logy and history. From the theo-logical standpoint we must remember that God's action antecedes the mission of the Church. The fact that "he [God] first loved us" (1 Jn. 4:19) is the condition for the very possibility of the Church's existence. But this love does not mean God's love for the Church but rather his love for the entire human race. And the Church is constituted not simply by becoming conscious of this love on God's part but by communicating it effectively to human beings. From the historical point of view, the Church exists—at least at a descriptive level—before a specific mission exists; but it is the Church itself that sends us out on this mission.

My point in saying that the Church is constituted by its mission is to say that the Church is not something abstract but comes into possession of its own concrete nature through the exercise of mission; that the Church does not keep itself in existence through history by maintaining its structures but by constantly carrrying out its mission. "What we must learn is not that the church 'has' a mission, but the very reverse: that the mission of Christ creates its own church. Mission does not come from the Church; it is from mission and in the light of mission that the church has to be understood."[8] It is in this deeper sense that we must understand the words of *Evangelii nuntiandi*: "The task of evangelization is to be regarded as . . . the activity most fully expressive of her real nature" (14).

THE WAYS OF EVANGELIZING

Thesis 2: The ways of evangelizing are (1) the proclamation of the word of God as the expression both of the overall meaning of history and of gratuitousness; (2) the living witness of Christians who as "subjects" of faith can and must transmit the "objects" of faith; (3) action that changes the world and thus brings to pass what the word says, the implantation of the kingdom of God. Since the world in which the Church carries out its mission is a sinful world, evangelization includes not only proclamation but also (4) a prophetic denunciation of everything that radically hinders or denies the kingdom of God.

Fundamental Forms of Evangelization

"Ways of evangelizing" refers to the fundamental forms the Church must use to offer the good news and thus to continually constitute itself. I am not speaking of concrete methods but of fundamental forms. It is important to make these ways or forms explicit because until very recently evangelizing was practically synonymous with preaching, announcing, and proclaiming, as *Evangelii nuntiandi* acknowledges (22). The fundamental form taken by the work of evangelization was the activity of verbal proclamation of the good news.

The Church's mission throughout history has embraced much more than verbal preaching. The Church has engaged in various practices; these were normally thought of not as evangelization but as an accompaniment or an ethical requirement of the Christian faith. This conception of evangelization traditionally had a privileged place because revelation in Christ was thought of as primarily doctrinal. Revelation took the form of the words of Christ or of words about Christ as these were set down in the New Testament.

Vatican II moved beyond this conception of revelation when it said that "this economy of Revelation is realized by deeds and words, which are intrinsically bound up with each other" (DV 2).[9] *Evangelii nuntiandi* takes this new vision of the forms of revelation and draws conclusions from it for evangelization. It lays down a fundamental principle when it says that we are to derive the meaning of evangelization from observation of the evangelizing activity of Jesus, "the first and greatest herald of the Gospel" (7). The result is a new approach to evangelization. Before bringing Christ in as object of evangelization the Exhortation refers to Jesus as the subject or agent of evangelization. He evangelized by preaching (11) and by signs, that is, by historical practice (12). Here effective practice becomes part of evangelization. In a section that is of special importance for systematic thought on the subject the document says that "every aspect of the mystery of Christ—the Incarnation itself, the miracles, the teaching, the sending of the apostles, the cross and resurrection—is a part of his evangelizing activity" (6).

This approach puts an end to the unilateral understanding of evangelization as simply a verbal communication of the good news and, in the case of Christ, the first evangelizer, makes his entire historical existence part of the concept: his teaching and his activity, his historical situation, and his destiny. From this vision of Christ as evangelizer *Evangelii nuntiandi* draws conclusions for evangelization today: it names three fundamental and mutually complementary forms of evangelization.

According to this document evangelization is accomplished (1) through verbal proclamation of the good news; (2) through the witness of Christian life; and (3) through a transforming practice. Although *Evangelii nuntiandi* does not discuss the relationship among these three, it nonetheless performs an undeniable service in putting an end to a simplistic conception of evangelization, saying that "no . . . partial and imperfect definition can do justice to the rich, complex and dynamic reality we call evangelization. In fact, it risks impoverishing and even distorting it" (17).

According to the first and most traditional meaning of evangelization—which is therefore least challenged and least open to disagreement—to evangelize means to announce or proclaim a message. This is the verbal aspect of evangelization. "There is no authentic evangelization unless the name and teaching, the life and promises, the kingdom and mystery of Jesus the Nazarene, Son of God, are preached" (22; cf. 2-6, 8, 11, 12, 43-45, 47). Under the heading "preaching of the word" evangelization includes life-giving preaching (42), the liturgy of the word (43), catechesis (44), and the sacraments (47), while the use of the mass media for spreading the word is recommended (45).

This first meaning does not exhaust the concept of evangelization. The document wisely asserts that "this announcement—in kerygma, preaching, or catechesis—is so important a part of evangelization that it has often become a synonym for it. Yet, it is in fact but a part of the whole" (22). To this aspect two others must be added; they produce practical consequences for the Christian understanding of evangelization and for the activity of the Church both in relation to the outside world and to its own internal life.

The second form of evangelization is the testimony of a Christian life. "The Good News must be proclaimed first and foremost in the form of witness" (21). "It is . . . above all by her conduct and way of life that the Church can evangelize the world, that is, by the living witness which is a manifestation of her fidelity to the Lord Jesus, her poverty and detachment, her freedom in the face of all earthly powers and, in a word, her holiness" (41). Without this living witness preaching is ineffective (76), for preachers must in their own life be servants of the word they preach (78).

The third form of evangelization is transforming action. This is the most novel aspect of evangelization and the one most likely to cause conflict because of that novelty and its practical consequences. The document says that the gospel must "change" our contemporaries (4). It states indirectly that the eternal salvation it preaches must be a reality that begins in the present life (27). The document asserts that the new commandment of love cannot be properly preached without an accompanying effort to promote justice (31). It states in direct terms that the Church has the duty not only of announcing the liberation of millions of human beings but also of "helping the process of liberation to get underway, of testifying in its behalf and of working for its completion" (30). *Evange-*

lii nuntiandi is aware of the novelty of making liberating action a part of the concept of evangelization and therefore it adds, rather timidly but nonetheless pointedly, that "all this is by no means unrelated to evangelization" (30).[10]

The Christian Content of Evangelization

I will show how the three fundamental ways or forms named above pertain to evangelization precisely because it is Christian and that therefore they may not be regarded as dispensable. That Christian evangelization is a proclamation and announcement of good news is due not so much to its verbal character as to its symbolic character. "Symbolic" here refers to symbols that pull together the overall meaning of human existence and human history. When Jesus says, for example, that "the kingdom of God is at hand" or that "whoever would save his life will lose it" or that "greater love has no man than this, that a man lay down his life for his friends," he is not simply making statements to be registered and reflected on by the mind; he is summing up the ultimate meaning of life in limited statements. Insofar as evangelization proposes this same meaning to hearers, it must likewise make use of the same kind of statements, since they take life in its totality and assert its Christian meaning. Evangelization is therefore not primarily a presentation of doctrine that must cover certain points; it is primarily a proclamation of life's deepest meaning.

This kind of proclamation is not peculiar to Christian evangelization; it is a constant that has its basis in human nature. Any "missionary" movement, be it religious or political, must use key statements to express the meaning of its claims. The reality of what it is trying to accomplish must be formulated in words. Any reality that does not press for such formulation would be neither definitive nor a source of motivation.

What is Christian in proclamation as a form of evangelization comes from Christian content. I shall make two points in this regard: The Christian God is a God of history, and he has a specific will for human beings.

The Christian God is not an absolute that can be regarded simply as a "universal reason," in principle discoverable by the human mind. That God is love and not condemnation; that he sides with the oppressed; that he wants to re-create the entire human person and not merely reward one according to one's actions; that he is a crucified God and not simply all-inclusive power—these are not truths that human beings can discover in the inertia of their existence or by their own power to reason. In order, therefore, that the absolute mystery of God may be concretized in a way corresponding to its reality, words are needed that will shatter the ambiguity implied in the idea of God as an abstract absolute.

This explains the abiding importance of proclamation as part of evangelization. No matter how often the message may have been repeated, no matter how trivial it may seem to have become, it is absolutely necessary to go on preaching that God is love and not arbitrary power; that the kingdom of God is at hand and not infinitely distant; that to love other human beings is to fulfill the law. This is the deepest meaning of the New Testament statement that Christ is the Word. He is the Word not because he comes to offer us a developed doctrine about God, a theology for our reflection, but because when he comes to earth he incarnates the meaning of God's being and thus breaks out of the notion that God may choose either to save or to comdemn. Christ tells us that God does not maintain that kind of objectivity and balance, that the ultimate mystery is not uncommitted, so to speak, either to meaning or to absurdity, but rather that God and his mystery are fundamentally a God and a mystery of "salvation." This is the content that the Church must proclaim.

The proclamation of the good news is important for its relevance to the Christian grasp of meaning. If the content of this meaning is good news, the way of grasping it is gratuitousness. According to the New Testament the good news is not something invented or discovered by humankind, but something given; for this reason it must be spoken. The fact that the good news must be spoken does not mean that something which has always been known needs further clarification, but rather that something by no means evident in a world of sin and wretchedness needs to be proclaimed. It does not mean that what we grasp in hope needs further explanation, but rather that the present partial reality of what we hope for needs to be asserted.

Through this proclamation the hearers of the good news experience meaning, because they find their lives being drawn back again into the ambit of an Other who liberates them from their self-centeredness. The meaning of their lives derives from an Other, and in Christianity (which perhaps differs in this from other ideologies) the experience of this derivation is an integral part of the experience of meaning.

If evangelization is to be Christian, the element of proclamation may not be forgotten, for it gives expression to the concrete historical character of God's will for the world; it states the positive content of this will; and because of it human beings will be those whose existence gets its meaning through reference to an Other who is different from and greater than they. For all these reasons proclamation is not merely something said but something that has to be said.

Evangelization takes the form of living witness because of the efficacy of God's word and the intersubjective character of Christian faith. By "the efficacy of the word" I mean that it would be an open contradiction for one to proclaim the good news from God and not make this good news a reality in one's life. It would be absurd to talk of a liberating God if no liberation had taken place, of a merciful God if there were no exercise of mercy, or of a God who sides with the poor, if poverty were not voluntarily accepted and shared.

In a different but relevant context medieval theologians said that if no real faith existed in the Church no eucharistic consecration would be possible. They meant that if Christ were not really present in the lives of Christians neither would he be really present in the Eucharist. They were pointing to a basic principle: in Christianity symbols do not have a life of their own, but draw their life from the reality that makes them possible. This principle applies to evangelization: the good news cannot be proclaimed as God's word unless it has to some degree become a good reality, at least in those who proclaim it.

Individual preachers of the good news will differ in the extent to which they make this good news a reality in their lives. But in the Church as a body—universal Church, local Church, basic community—this embodiment of the good news in Christian living cannot be lacking. Such a failure would amount to saying that God has good news for the world but unfortunately it cannot become a reality. Then we would no longer be dealing with the effective word of God, which is what we want to transmit.

In regard to "the intersubjective character of Christian faith," the New Testament makes it clear that the personal appropriation of faith depends on the faith already lived by others. To say this is to suppose not only that the good news should be embodied in the lives of the evangelizers, but also that access to faith always involves overcoming a stumbling block and that therefore an evangelizer must offer to others a faith embodied in action, which has overcome this stumbling block. This is precisely what we are told in, for example, chapters 11 and 12 of the Letter to the Hebrews. These chapters set before us not only objects of faith but also subjects of faith, namely the "cloud of witnesses" (12:1) who have gotten over the stumbling block and attained to faith.

The witness of faith is therefore essential to evangelization. But "witness" is not a matter of communicating information about something or someone; it is a matter of making present the reality that is being proclaimed. Living witness is thus not simply a help to evangelization nor an ethical demand made of the evangelizer, but an essential ingredient of evangelization.

The third fundamental form taken by evangelization is action. This I define as everything that succeeds in really transforming human beings and structures in accordance with the plan of God. In this sense the two forms of evangelization already discussed are also actions; the specific character of action is that it is the practice that effectively leads to establishment of God's kingdom.

Any action—education, conscientization, organization, political work—that effectively leads to the creation of a world more in accord with the gospel ideal is evangelization. I thus reject a conception of Christian action as an ethical requirement of evangelization or a preparation for the acceptance of the gospel.

Here we have the unique contribution to the idea of evangelization and the contribution most likely to cause conflict, both because of its theoretical novelty and because of its practical repercussions. For, as we shall see, this kind of action requires Christian creativity; it can cause one to suffer the disagreeable consequences of all authentic evangelization: persecution from the sinful world in which one attempts to exercise a transforming activity.

Action is necessary because the word preached is an efficacious word. It has already proved its efficacy to some extent in the living witness of the evangelizer, but it must also prove it to the addressee.

If the general content of the proclamation is a God who is love, then the proclamation must be a matter of deeds as well as of words. To speak to human beings about God's love without a concrete exercise of this love toward them would be to fall into gnosticism. The gnosticism would be the more pronounced if the addressee were one of those who have been oppressed for centuries.

Evangelization takes three forms; evangelization includes action. These two points are extremely important.

Evangelii nuntiandi lists the three forms of evangelization without showing how they are united. It is satisfied to deny that any one of the three is either the only element or the most important one. It says, for example, that proclamation is only one part of evangelization (22); that living witness is inadequate if not accompanied by explicit proclamation (22); and that proclamation must be accompanied by work for justice and peace among all (30). For the moment it is enough to say that all three are integral parts of evangelization; the priority of any one of them will depend on the form the evangelization takes in a real situation.[11]

Evangelization in a World of Sin

In connection with these three forms of evangelization I must discuss something mentioned in *Evangelii nuntiandi* only in passing when it says that part of evangelization is "the preaching of the mystery of iniquity" (28) and presupposed when it speaks of the situation in the Third World (30–38).

To evangelize is to present good news but in a world of sin. The proclamation seeks to lead its hearers not from a neutral existence to an existence in hope but from a real world marked by affliction to a real world that is renewed. If anything is sure in Latin America it is the reality of sin and inevitable wretchedness.

Sin has a subjective side inasmuch as it is an internal human act; it also has an objective, visible, structural side. The result of sin is death in the literal sense of the word: the spiritual death of the sinner and the human death of the one sinned against. To sin is to cause the death of human beings, either violently or slowly through unjust structures.

Evangelization is certainly a proclamation of the good news, but it must also include a denunciation of all that hinders this good news and keeps it in chains. Evangelization must therefore—unfortunately—include the curses uttered by Jesus as well as the beatitudes.

Proclamation and denunciation alike are in the service of the same reality: the kingdom of God. Proclamation is more typically Christian; but denunciation is—even if indirectly—historically necessary as long as there exists a world of sin that is the negation of God's reign. Proclamation and denunciation are therefore not on an equal footing as if evangelization involved proclaiming positive and negative sides equally. No, in both cases the aim is positive, but in different ways.

Denunciation is required in evangelization in order that people living in a world of sin may grasp the point of proclamation by seeing its opposite. The positive content of proclamation is a utopia that can be validated only by hope, whereas the wretched conditions of the real world actually exist and can be readily identified. Denunciation's first purpose is thus to point by way of negation to the reality with which evangelization is concerned.

The two aspects of proclamation are directed to the good of all, both those to whom the good news is immediately announced and those who are the addressees of denunciation. The aim in both cases is humanization. For those who have been dehumanized by wretched poverty and oppression the good news begins as a word of hope: the power of God is greater than the wretchedness of his oppressed people. For those who have been dehumanized by their own wrongful use of oppressive power the good news begins as a call to conversion.

These two aspects of proclamation can be seen in the first words of Jesus with which he began his program: "The kingdom of God is at hand; repent" (Mk. 1:15). In a sense, all human beings are both oppressors and oppressed; all need both a hope and a summons to conversion. But in historical and concrete terms, some addressees of the good news are fundamentally oppressors while others are fundamentally oppressed. Depending on the case, therefore, the emphasis in evangelization must be either on offering hope or on calling to conversion. In both cases, the purpose is to humanize human beings and to bring them the good news in an effective, not an idealistic way. At every point in the process of evangelization we must bear in mind that the oppressed need conversion and that oppressors may be being deprived of the proclamation of the good news. At the historical level, however, the concrete approach will differ.

Evangelization requires not only proclamation but also prophetic denunciation. Today this general truth becomes utterly clear and calls for urgent application.[12] Evangelization also makes necessary an analysis of what sin is, how it is to be eliminated, and how sinners are to be converted so that they too may be told that the kingdom of God is at hand.

THE TRANSCENDENT AND HISTORICAL CONTENT OF EVANGELIZATION

Thesis 3: The content to be communicated in the three forms of evangelization is twofold (the two parts being closely connected): (1) the good news as a transcendent reality, that is, God's love for human beings as manifested in Christ and the hope of final fulfillment; (2) the good news as a historical reality, that is, the accomplishment of this love at various periods of history. In Latin America, love, without neglecting other forms, must take the form of justice as the indispensable means of creating unity among human beings and thus turning them into children of God.

Evangelii Nuntiandi *and Evangelization*

Evangelii nuntiandi gives a general description of evangelization: "to bear simple and direct witness to the God whom Jesus Christ revealed" (26). Here again, the document shows an awareness of complexity. We must note from the beginning that one of the most serious reasons for attending to this complexity is the situation of the churches now evangelizing the Third World. The chapter on the content of evangelization has two parts: one on the essential content of evangelization throughout the history of the good news (26–29), another on the meaning of the good news and the problems it raises in the countries of the Third World (30–38).

The first of these two sections begins by recalling the great truths Christian tradition has always seen as comprising the good news: that God loves the world in his Son; that he calls human beings to eternal life; that we are children of God and therefore brothers and sisters; that salvation begins in the present life even though it will attain its full form only in eternity. Accompanying this statement of traditional themes is a declaration of general principles regarding the historical concretization of these great truths:

> Evangelization cannot be complete, however, unless account is taken of the reciprocal links between the Gospel and the concrete personal and social life of man. For this reason evangelization requires a message which is explicit, adapted to varying situations and constantly related to the rights and obligations of each individual, to family life without which the development of the individual becomes extremely difficult, to common life in society, to international life and to peace, justice and development. Finally, it must be a message, especially strong and pointed today, of liberation (29).

In this context the document moves on to consider the special problems of evangelization in Third World countries. It begins by describing the situation in the Third World:

> These peoples, as we know, are striving with all their might to overcome the conditions which force them to live such a marginal life: hunger, chronic illnesses, illiteracy, penury, injustice at the international level and especially in commercial relations, and economic and cultural neocolonialism which is sometimes as cruel as political colonialism (30).

Given this situation, the document says that "the Church has the duty . . . of proclaiming the liberation of millions of human beings, many of whom are her children. She also has the duty of helping the process of liberation to get underway, of testifying in its behalf and of working for its completion. All this is by no means unrelated to evangelization" (30). The document bases the positive relationship between evangelization and human promotion on the several kinds of connections between the two: anthropological, since it is one and the same human being to whom the good news is preached and who experiences the problems mentioned; theological, since it is impossible to dissociate creation and redemption; and evangelical, since it is not possible to proclaim love without also promoting justice and the elimination of injustice (31).

The document asserts that given the situation in our countries the struggle against injustice and the restoration of peace is part of evangelization. "The Church certainly considers it highly important to establish structures which are more human, more just, more respectful of the rights of the person, less oppressive and coercive" (36).

Unity of the Transcendental and Historical Aspects of Evangelization

Although *Evangelii nuntiandi* does offer some thoughts on the transcendental and historical aspects of the content of evangelization (32), the document does not develop the unity of the two in a detailed way. Such a development is left to theological reflection and in fact is the most topical and the most revolutionary theme in contemporary theology.

Here I offer two brief considerations showing the unity and relationship of the transcendental and historical aspects of evangelization. This relationship can be understood in two ways: (1) the transcendent is what occurs after history is finished (it is what *Evangelii nuntiandi* refers to as the call of human beings to eternal life); and (2) the transcendent is that which gives ultimate meaning to the present.

Contemporary theology finds no difficulty in the historical aspect of the relationship because it is aware of the historical character of God's revelation in the Old Testament and especially in the incarnation of Christ. It is clear that "the history of salvation supposes salvation taking place in history."[13] Throughout the Old Testament the God who wants to liberate a people effects concrete liberations. These historical liberations, partial though they be, motivate faith in a savior God. To say that history already is or should be the locus of salvation is to say nothing more than that the word of God is efficacious and must be understood not in gnostic fashion as information about content but historically as the word that brings to pass what it says.

The unity of the two histories becomes even clearer with the incarnation of the Son. Provided this incarnation is, once again, not understood in gnostic fashion, then earthly history does not get its meaning from outside, from some possible teaching of Christ about history; its meaning comes from within, at least from the segment of history that is the life of Jesus and, in dependence on that life, from the subsequent history of his historical body, the Church. A denial of this unity of the two histories would be a modern version of the christological heresy known as monophysitism. If Jesus is indeed Emmanuel, "God with us" (Mt. 1:23), then it is absurd to say that his presence in history is not a manifestation of the reality of the saving God. Moreover, the concrete life of Jesus makes clear what this salvation in history is.

The two histories are also related in the understanding of the transcendent as the end of history. It is clear that history has not yet reached its fulfillment. This fulfillment is a utopia and as such cannot be adequately analyzed by human reason but can only be grasped through hope. At the same time, faith tells us that the present is not simply a time of trial in preparation for a future destiny as though there were no continuity between present and future. As a matter of fact, the present "trial" consists in making present under the conditions of history that which we await in hope as the ultimate fulfillment: the kingdom of God. The trial consists in making real the love, justice, and unity among human beings that are the symbols used to describe the fullness of the endtime. Therefore, even though this fullness is a free gift brought about by God, and in this sense is discontinuous with present history, a profound continuity does exist. Only those who build a new earth here will share in the new heaven. The content of transcendent salvation is not different in kind from present salvation, nor can present history be conceived of as a series of arbitrary demands made of human beings who will later on receive "heaven" as a recompense. The demands made of human beings in this world are simply the expression of a future fulfillment.

When the evangelists proclaim the transcendent in the twofold sense of absolute future and absolute meaning of the present, they cannot oppose the transcendent to the historical nor can they be satisfied with presenting them as parallel. Because we are dealing not with evangelization in some vague sense but with Christian evangelization, emphasis must be placed on the unity of the two histories, the two good news. They are phases of a single reality, the one good news being lived in the conditions of historical existence, the other being lived under the conditions of the eschaton and therefore able to be grasped only in hope.

Dangers

When *Evangelii nuntiandi* deals with the two dimensions—the historical and the transcendent—of evangelization, it points out two dangers. The more basic of the two, and one that is frequently met with, is to reduce evangelization to human liberation of an economic, political, social, or cultural kind (32–35); the other is to place the hope of liberation solely on a change of structures without any conversion of heart (36). Throughout this section of the document (30–38) we see a struggle between the positive assertion of liberation as an integral part of evangelization and the awareness of the dangers this task carries with it. Nonetheless the chapter draws to a close with this positive statement:

> Having said this, We must also say how happy We are that the Church is becoming ever more conscious of the true and wholly evangelical way in which she is to collaborate in the liberation of man. . . . The Church constantly strives to link the Christian struggle for liberation with the comprehensive plan of salvation which she proclaims (38).

In mentioning these dangers, the pope is thinking primarily of evangelizers in the Third World. This means that his words must be read in the context of the Third World. It is quite possible, of course, that some minds are really in danger of completely identifying human liberation and Christian liberation; it is also possible that they make completely absolute certain ideologies and concrete methods as the means of achieving this liberation. But, while this danger may indeed be real as far as the intentions of some evangelizers are concerned, we must take a different approach to it when we look at the objective situation of Latin America.

What is called the "eschatological proviso" (a theological concept developed in the First World), that is, the proviso or reservation that the coming eschaton sets against any and every human achievement, applies differently in different situations. Despite the economic and social achievements of affluent societies in which the basic problems of human subsistence have been resolved, these societies are still not the kingdom of God. This is so because in these societies the fullness of the endtime has not been reached, and, above all, because the affluence of these societies depends on the wretched poverty of the rest of the world.

In the Third World the eschatological proviso has a different meaning, since the problem among us is not that the kingdom of God has not yet come in its fullness, but that this kingdom is formally denied. We must therefore not be too quick to invoke the eschatological proviso against the present reality, even if it needs to be invoked against the intentions of some individuals.

The statements of Medellín are still valid. "Misery . . . besets large masses of human beings in all of our countries. . . . That misery, as a collective fact, expresses itself as injustice which cries to the heavens" (*Justice* 1). "The lack of solidarity . . . on the individual and social levels, leads to the committing of serious sins, evident in the unjust structures which characterize the Latin American situation" (*Justice* 2). We live "in an unjust situation which promotes tensions that conspire against peace" (*Peace* 1), in a situation of "institutionalized violence" (*Peace* 16).

In these circumstances, the primary aim of evangelization should not be to make relative the mediations of the kingdom but rather to do everything possible to promote a more just society (to which, of course, when achieved, the eschatological proviso will have to be applied). We have a long way to go before the problem of the eschatological proviso becomes relevant in Latin America as it is in the First World. Evangelizers would be indulging in sarcasm if they began by emphasizing the point that the kingdom of God has not yet come, when the very things that make the "not yet!" caution meaningful do not exist, and when reality makes it perfectly clear that the kingdom has not yet come.

Similarly individuals may be excessively preoccupied with the structural aspect of problems and solutions. Evangelization cannot and may not overlook the personal dimension of human beings, for the Christian faith makes clear the absolute value of the human person and the person's unavoidable obligation to make decisions that are inalienable. In Latin America, however, this value of the human person and the person's capacity for decision have for centuries been threatened and nullified by the structures in which people live. Consequently, although evangelizers must not equate the complete renewal of the person (the "new man") with a transformation of structures, they must nonetheless be utterly serious about the need for change in unjust structures. These structures are a formal negation of the kingdom of God in its communal aspect and a serious obstacle in the way of a people's efforts to regain and deepen their dignity as children of God.[14]

THE UNIFICATION OF FAITH AND PRACTICE
IN EVANGELIZATION

Thesis 4: Evangelization must combine faith and practice, without making either independent of the other. Faith provides the ultimate Christian meaning of action; action is the Christian practice of this ultimate meaning. Christian reality is the historical process of believing in the God of the kingdom by bringing this kingdom to pass.

Everything I have said about evangelization supposes a new basis, one that requires reflection. We need to reflect in depth on all this so that we will not be satisfied with simple declarations and we will be able to resolve the problems that arise from this new conception of evangelization. The problems may take theoretical form but they will have important repercussions on the practice of evangelization. One of the most basic problems in my view lies in the need of unifying various aspects of evangelization. These aspects may be reduced to three: (1) the unity of faith and practice; (2) the unity of evangelization and evangelizer; and (3) the unity of evangelization and the evangelized.

The Integration of Historical Practice

Evangelization takes the forms of proclamation and Christian action; its content includes transcendent meaning and historical realization of this meaning. Both pairs of concepts have to do with the general problem of the relation between faith and Christian practice in evangelization and in those who are the addressees of this evangelization.

This integration of historical practice into the concept of evangelization is something new; it is therefore important to establish what the unity is between practice and faith. In bringing practice and faith into a higher unity, I am recalling the specific originality of Christianity. In the course of history this originality has often been neglected in favor of a merely "religious" conception of Christianity.[15]

In the New Testament and throughout the history of the Church it has always been maintained at the theoretical level, and with greater or less success in practice, that both dimensions—faith and practice—are necessary for real Christianity. The theoretical problem, which has major practical implications, has been that of the relationship between the two aspects and of the priority that has in theory or in practice been given to one aspect over the other.[16]

The history of the Church and of theology also tells us that if we presuppose that one aspect can be known independently of the other, we find ourselves with an insoluble theoretical difficulty. If we start with two separate things—with a "faith" and a "practice" that are fully constituted autonomously and independently each of the other—then there is no theoretical solution to the problem, and we fall into a religiosity that is not necessarily Christian (this has happened with great frequency) or into a practice that may degenerate into mere activity without any element of gratuitousness or transcendence.

We must begin with some kind of unity within which "faith" and "practice" are dialectically related components that stand in essential need each of the other. In order to launch into a consideration of this unity, and without claiming to offer even a nominal definition, I may describe "faith" as the ultimate meaning of practice, and "practice" as the making real of this meaning. Giving a principally Christian content to these formal definitions, I may go further and describe "faith" as unconditional hope in the Father of Jesus, and "practice" as the making real of the content of this hope; I can describe "faith" as hope in the "God" of the kingdom, and "practice" as the building of the "kingdom" of God.

Jesus Unifies Faith and Practice

The justification for this thesis is christological, both in the sense that I methodically set aside any ideas on the question without first observing Jesus, and in the sense that he provides the criterion for the Christian unification of the two aspects.

Jesus did not preach himself; he did not make himself the center, either for himself or for others. The unity of his entire life and of his mission comes from what the synoptic gospels call "the kingdom of God." This statement is basic and has far-reaching consequences. It means that the ultimate frame of reference for Jesus is not simply "God" (indicating the priority and autonomy of "faith") nor simply the "kingdom" (indicating the priority and autonomy of a practice geared to the building of the kingdom). From the beginning of his life Jesus' ultimate point of reference is the one, unifying reality of the "kingdom of God." In formal terms this means that the "vertical" and "horizontal" dimensions of his preaching and activity are united from the outset.

The kingdom of God supplies the ultimate point of reference, the horizon for the mission of Jesus. This explains the unity of the various aspects of his mission, which are obviously separated in their temporal embodiments. The preaching or proclamation of Jesus, that which insofar as it consists of words expresses the meaning of life for Jesus and looks for a response of faith from his hearers, is also something that by its nature has to be done, put into practice. If what Jesus proclaims in his preaching, kerygma, and parables is the love of God, the reality of a God in whom human beings can trust and hope; if what Jesus denounces in his controversies and anathemas is the legalism of those who have turned God into a matter of oppressive legalism and not of love—then Jesus can credibly speak this message only if he also puts it into practice.

On the other hand, the activity of Jesus enables him to speak his message and indeed calls for him to do so. His cures, miracles, and exorcisms, his prophetic gestures in the temple, eating with the oppressed and leaping social barriers—all these make it possible to give verbal expression to the ultimate reality of God as liberating love. They call for the explicit reference of Jesus to the Father, whether this be expressed in a prayer of thanksgiving giving voice to the fullness of meaning (cf. Mt. 11:25–30) or in a prayer of search and acceptance as in the Garden (cf. Mk. 14:36).

Jesus' preaching of faith in God and his accompanying action are thus interconnected. Neither is autonomous, even if there are different moments for each to come into play. At the very source of his activity, at least as this is communicated to us by the synoptic writers, Jesus' personal vocation (explicit relationship with the Father) and his mission of spreading on earth the right to justice form a whole. I think, therefore, that the kingdom of God—with its two aspects of transcendence and history, proclamation and action, call for faith and call for practice—is the unity (one that unifies and is not itself only subsequently united) that explains the mission of Jesus.

The Theology of John

All the New Testament writings (after the resurrection, when the Church in the proper sense makes its appearance), show that both faith and practice are required for Christianity. But it is the theology of John that best helps us to understand not only the existence of these two dimensions but also their necessary mutual relationship.

In carefully composed statements John says that "God is love" (1 Jn. 4:8); that this love has manifested itself in history by sending the Son for the salvation of the world (1 Jn. 4:10; Jn. 3:16); and that this love is gratuitous and prior to any action on the part of human beings (1 Jn. 4:10). Here we see the element of faith, of coming to understand, on the basis of God's love, that life and history have a positive meaning. John goes on in a surprisingly radical statement: "If God so loved us, we also ought to love one another" (1 Jn. 4:11). What John is saying is that the proper way of responding to God's love is to love one another; that the proper way of responding in faith is to practice love; and that without this practice faith is empty and cannot become what it ought to be. John is, of course, speaking of Christian love for God as the expression of Christian faith, but what is unique to John is his statement that the right relation to God and the right relation to others are identical.

We are shown here the true Christian way of responding to the word of God. In general terms, to respond to the faith offered us is nothing less than to conform to the reality of God; therefore, if God loves us, a response of faith to this God will mean conformity to him in the practice of love. Here we have a unified vision of faith and practice that is grounded in the very reality of the Christian God.

The practice of love sustains faith: "We know that we have passed out of death into life, because we love the brethren" (1 Jn. 3:14). The rejection of this practice makes faith impossible: "This is the judgment, that the light has come into the world, and men loved darkness rather than light, because their deeds were evil"(Jn. 3:19).

We thus find an important dialectic in John. Faith is the gift of knowing oneself to be loved by God; the first result of this knowledge is love of our sisters and brothers. And those who love others and do good works pass from darkness to light and acknowledge the light. Faith and practice are closely united, not only in virtue of an anthropology that sees both meaning and action as dimensions of the human person, but also in virtue of the very concept of God.

Conclusion

From these brief reflections on the historical Jesus and the theology of John it follows that, as the communication of the Christian totality, evangelization must hold tight to both aspects, for these, though separated in time, are united in reality. Unless we love human beings we cannot communicate to them the truth that God loves them, nor can we love human beings unless we have passed from darkness to light. For a long time now a purely doctrinal conception of God, transcended at best by a significant but limited personalist approach to him, has tended to give the element of proclamation a privileged place in evangelization and to concentrate on the response of faith. But if God is in fact the God of the brethren, as John says, then we must communicate him as he really is.

THE UNIFICATION OF EVANGELIZATION
AND EVANGELIZER

Thesis 5: The action of evangelizing and the person of the evangelizer must be united. Evangelization supposes that its agents already know what they are going to proclaim and bring about. However, evangelizers are not fully constituted as such except in the act of evangelizing. Their initial faith becomes ever more real and concrete and grows in the course of their history, not apart from or prior to but through their evangelizing activity.

Reciprocity between Evangelizer and the Act of Evangelizing

After the unity of faith and practice, the next important and necessary form of unity is that of evangelization and evangelizer, whether the latter be considered as an individual or as a group, a Church. It is obvious that within the Church there must be a special preparation prior to the activity of evangelization of those who will expressly devote themselves to this work (priests, catechists, lay ministers of the word, and the equivalents of these). The way to become an evangelizer is precisely in and through the action of evangelizing, for Christian meaning and Christian practice alike are deepened and intensified in and through the work of evangelization and not simply through the acquisition of methods for evangelization or by simply intending to do this work. It is through evangelization that the evangelizer is constituted as such.[17]

This means, moreover, that evangelization necessarily involves a process of growth for the evangelizer (individual or group) and that this growth comes about through the activity of evangelizing.

Christological Justification

The justification for this thesis is christological. I showed earlier that in the mission of Jesus to others proclamation and practice form a unity. I wish now to show how this same mission to others led Jesus to a growth in faith and in his consciousness as an evangelizer.

For Jesus the kingdom of God serves as the ultimate horizon within which everything is located and seen. But the unification of everything in the consciousness of Jesus did not take place once and for all because Jesus was subject to the conditions and potentialities imposed by history and to the historical process. In short, even Jesus became an evangelizer through his evangelizing mission.

According to the synoptic writers Jesus began his evangelizing activity with a notion of God and God's kingdom that derived in substance from the best traditions of his people. The predominant element in his conception of God was the idea of God as good, provident, just, sovereign, and partial to the oppressed. For this reason Jesus could assert that the coming of the kingdom would be essentially grace and salvation. In his conception of God prophetic and apocalyptic traditions were at work: the kingdom of God supposes a transformation of a world of sin into a world of human unity, which Jesus expected would be definitive and transcendent but which he also sought to promote even during the present life on earth. "Kingdom of God" meant to Jesus a type of human unity in which all are brothers and sisters and therefore children of God.

This first understanding, this first "faith" of Jesus,[18] took historical shape in his mind as he lived out his life, that is, his evangelizing mission. The course of this life saw expressions of meaning and expressions of crisis, depending on the ongoing course of his work of evangelization. This life had an impact on the consciousness of Jesus, on his understanding of the meaning of his own life, of the kingdom of God, and of his evangelizing mission. Like every human being, Jesus experienced the ambiguity of existence with its times of fulfillment and its times of crisis. In and through this ambiguity, and not independently of it, Jesus in the course of his life grasped the meaning of his evangelizing activity. This activity in turn gave meaning to him as an evangelizer.

More concretely, the faith that Jesus proclaimed is not something one possesses once and for all inasmuch as it grows even in the person who proclaims it. Therefore even though Jesus maintained the same formal idea of God his Father from the beginning of his life to its end, the content of this idea became ever more concrete and profound. The trust in God that Jesus expressed at the beginning of his public life is quite different from the trust he expressed in his "Abba! Father!" when he prayed in the Garden. Jesus' faith in the Father, that is, his complete and unconditional surrender to him, was there throughout his life. But what made this faith a concrete and historical reality in his human existence was not merely the intention of Jesus to go on trusting in the Father, but his actual evangelizing practice. In this practice Jesus deepened his conviction that despite everything God is really a Father, an eminently positive reality that can justly be described as Love.

The same can be said of Jesus' growth in his practice of the kingdom of God. From the beginning of his life Jesus put his entire self and all he had at the service of this kingdom: his abilities, his mind, his power to perform miracles and exorcisms, his followers, his disputes with and denunciations of those who were hindering and destroying the kingdom. Through his historical development he came to realize that the building of the kingdom required not only all the positive abilities of an evangelizer but also a readiness to suffer, to deny himself, to give his very life. This discovery by Jesus was not the result of mere reflection on the need for self-surrender; it sprang from the realization of the historical power that sin wields against those who try to establish the kingdom of God. It sprang from the realization that the sin of the world must resist all the positive values brought by the evangelizer, and that the evangelizer in turn must be ready to carry the sin of the world, must try to overcome this sin, even from within, inasmuch as he or she is ready to let it conquer.

The Letter to the Hebrews sums up the entire life of Jesus when it says in the course of a description of his priesthood that he was "made perfect" (5:9). The Letter uses the vocabulary not of evangelization but of priesthood, but it is making the same formal point. It defines priesthood as activity "on behalf of men" (5:1); this priestly life on behalf of others elicits from Jesus "loud cries and tears" (5:7); it is a process in which "he learned obedience" (5:8). Through all this he reached "perfection," which is elsewhere defined as the perfection of the "faith" of Jesus (12:2). His priestly or, as we would say, evangelizing mission made him what he was.

The Evangelizer Grows in Faith

The model supplied by Christ can help us to a systematic grasp of the reciprocal relationship between evangelizer and evangelization. Evangelizers must be persons of faith, "witnesses" to the faith, if they are to begin any kind of evangelization. The very work of evangelization will continually reconstitute persons as witnesses to the faith and thus enable them to carry on with the work of evangelization. Evangelization is therefore not simply the activity of an already constituted evangelizer; it also makes the person an evangelizer.

We are now in a position to understand that the evangelizer should grow in faith through the work of evangelization. Johannine theology says something important about the nature of Christian faith when it speaks of faith as a "victory" (1 Jn. 5:4); faith is not something evangelizers possess once and for all, but something they must go on taking possession of. Evangelization is the concrete form in which faith wins its victory and proves itself something that is not simply possessed but attained ever anew.

The relationship between the faith of the evangelizer and the mission of evangelization is a dialectical one; it is important therefore to see the relation as processual. In analyzing the relationship we must also consider how the process advances, both insofar as it begins with the "initial" faith of the evangelizer and insofar as it begins with the "initial" practice of evangelization.

Viewed from the standpoint of faith, the process may be described as follows. Christian faith begins with the hearing of the word. This word is God's message regarding human beings, history, and God himself. Faith thus involves a "hearing," a freely offered reference to another, and thus an acquisition of meaning. But according to Christian faith the word that is heard must be put into practice, both in order that faith may yield its ethical fruit and in order that it may be constituted as truly faith. At this point the response of faith means conformity to God through an action like his. It means making God's will for the world an efficacious will— this is simply evangelization in the sense explained. Finally, faith thus put into practice becomes once more a word of meaning, thanksgiving, and response. This is the doxological side of faith.

From the standpoint of faith, at the moment when the word of God is first heard, the process involves a response of acceptance. But according to the pattern just described, between God's word to the human person and the human person's word to God there must intervene a Christian practice, that is, evangelization. If then faith as such is to be constituted a response to God, it requires a practice that is a conformity with the action of God.

From the standpoint of practice, the process can be described as follows. Initially there is some kind of communication of the good news to other persons; as we have seen, this must include some practice of love or humanization of others. This practice is always undertaken in the wretched conditions of the real world and in confrontation with the power of the world's sin, against which this practice of love is directed. The historical practice of love must thus come to grips both with the meaning of human life and with the crisis of meaning. History raises the question whether the practice of love is the ultimate source of meaning for human life; in other words, it raises the challenge to faith. If the challenge is met, the crisis surmounted, and the practice of love sustained, then the ultimate supremacy of love is proved at the level of practice and the human person proves that he or she effectively believes in the God of love. The proper expression of Christian faith is to sustain to the end the practice of love in a sinful world, for this perseverance asserts love as the ultimate reality and makes possible the specifically Christian way of asserting transcendence: the way not simply of "faith" but of "faith in the face of unbelief" or, in the language of the Bible, of "hope against hope."

Christian practice, therefore, determines either the failure of the evangelizer's faith or the attainment of its plenary form. Apart from this practice it is not possible for the evangelizer to attain to the fullness of Christian faith, since only through it and in confrontation with the sin of the world can faith establish itself as a victory and not simply as a possession of God.

THE UNIFICATION OF EVANGELIZATION AND THE EVANGELIZED

Thesis 6: In evangelization the action of evangelizing and the addressee of evangelization must form a unity. The addressee is not simply a passive subject of the action of evangelizing, but a condition enabling the content of evangelization to be constituted as such. The privileged place for effecting this constitution is the evangelization of the poor, since the poor make it possible to know and preach the Christian God.

Reciprocity of Evangelization and the Evangelized

In the traditional concept of evangelization (though this was never completely verified in the concrete practice of evangelization) the following scheme was presupposed:

Evangelizer → evangelization → the evangelized

In chronological terms, some such scheme is of course implied. The same is not true however when the matter is subjected to a logical analysis.

We saw in the previous section of this chapter that it is not easy to separate evangelizer and evangelization because the latter is constitutive of the evangelizer as evangelizer. I wish to make the same point now in regard to evangelization and the evangelized. Specifically, I wish to deny the view that the evangelized is simply the addressee of evangelization and to show that the evangelized constitute an element that makes Christian evangelization possible. This matter is of great importance, especially in the Third World. I shall therefore go into it in some detail.

The theological problem raised by a consideration of the addressee of evangelization springs from the fact that Scripture contains two parallel statements: evangelization must be directed to all human beings; and evangelization has certain privileged addresses, namely the poor. Both statements have their basis in the nature of the Christian faith and are simply descriptions of what actually happens. The universality and the partiality are both called for by the Christian faith. How do these two aspects fit together? What is the importance of the duality for evangelization?

Universality of Evangelization

Evangelization is to be direced to all human beings. Matthew's classical text expresses this: "Make disciples of all nations" (Mt. 28:19). Another text gives the presupposition for this universal mission: "God our Savior . . . desires all men to be saved and to come to the knowledge of the truth" (1 Tim. 2:3–4). This position, which seems so obvious, actually emerged from a lengthy historical process in Israel and in the new Christian communities. The process reached its completion in the decision to "turn to the Gentiles."

More important than the simple fact are its theological presuppositions and its consequences. In ways that differ according to different theologies, Scripture presents us with the idea of a single God who stands over against and in relation to the whole of reality. His lordship extends to history (Ps. 78), embracing both its beginning (Gen. 1–2) and its end (1 Cor. 15:28). Within this history there is no individual and nothing in any individual that does not stand in need of a saving word from God. In positive terms: the whole person and all persons need evangelization. This presupposes that all human beings are in some way sinners in need of conversion and that all are loved by God and therefore in possession of hope.

The universality of evangelization is fundamental to the Christian faith and cannot be abandoned without the very substance of that faith being destroyed. This universal mission is the source of the Church's duties and rights as evangelizer. Its first duty is to take seriously the need for concrete mediations by which evangelization can reach all and not simply a single social group or a single region of the world or a single cultural epoch. It is a duty of inculturation in the fullest and deepest sense of the term, that is, in the sense of a "cultivation of reality . . . an action that cultivates and transforms reality."[19] The universality of evangelization means, therefore, the "cultivation" of saving reality in all periods of history and in all places using the means that diversity requires.

The universality of the Church's evangelizing mission also gives the Church the right to evangelize the whole of reality. Its addressees are not only all human beings but the whole human being in his or her personal and social, historical and transcendent dimensions. The task in universal evangelization is therefore to proclaim the good news and make it a reality by addressing not only the religious dimension of the person but the economic, cultural, social, and political dimensions as well.

The universality of evangelization is thus of the very essence of evangelization and is not adequately explained by simply repeating that "all must be evangelized." It supposes a nonsectarian conception of the Church; it supposes the discovery that in God's sight there are "neither Greeks nor Jews"; it supposes that access is gained to God not only through that which is "religious" but through any and every human reality. It supposes, finally, the basis of everything else: that God cannot be fully apprehended through a particular dimension of human existence nor a particular social group. In positive terms, God is greater than any created thing and therefore all aspects of created reality are addressees for evangelization. It supposes, too, that God is really love and therefore wishes to re-create every area of creation.

Partiality of Evangelization

I now turn to the other dimension of evangelization: its partiality. This aspect is important first because it is clearly in Scripture. It is also important from a systematic viewpoint because consideration of this partially or partisanship will enable us to give a properly Christian meaning to the universality of evangelization and will make possible the specifically Christian content of evangelization. The subject is an urgent one for Third World peoples if we take seriously these statements of Medellín: "We wish the Latin American Church to be the evangelizer of the poor and one with them" (*Poverty* 8). The poor "place before the Latin American Church a challenge and a mission that [it] cannot sidestep" (7). Moreover, a new kind of atheism exists, "a rejection of the Lord himself," wherever unjust "social, political, economic and cultural inequalities" exist (*Peace* 14).

I shall begin my discussion of these problems with some terminological and conceptual observations regarding the "poor."[20] The Hebrew term *rash* is neutral in meaning and is the least used of the various Old Testament terms. Preference is given to other more concrete terms describing the kinds of poor individuals: *ebyon* is the person who wishes for something, the beggar, the person who lacks something and hopes to receive it from another; *das* is the weak, emaciated person; *ani* is the person who is stooped, carrying a burden, the person who does not enjoy full use of his or her abilities and strength, the person who has been humbled. The New Testament uses the Greek word *ptochos*: the person who does not have the necessities of life, the wretchedly poor person who is forced to beg. Scripture thus acknowledges the existence of the poor, those who are materially poor. It condemns such poverty as a scandal, something that should not be because it is contrary to God's will. It also interprets this poverty as having a social meaning because it is not inevitable but is due to the actions of other human beings. The poor are, at least in part, those who have been reduced to penury.

In addition to these terms referring to material poverty others speak of poverty in a theological sense. The *anawim* are those who humble themselves before God; the *ptochoi* of the beatitudes are those who are ready to do God's will (this is clearly the meaning in Matthew; it is also the meaning in Luke but here has more nuance). Unlike material poverty, which is a scandal, this new kind of poverty is a good thing and is praised. But some qualifications are called for if its true value is to be grasped. First, the poverty that is called theological or spiritual is not simply material poverty practiced at the intentional level or, in other words, an indifference toward possessions. It is a positive attitude of openness to the will of God and may include not only an affective indifference to things but an effective indifference as well.

Second, the words used to express this theological poverty are the same words that are used to express material poverty (*ptochos*, *anaw*). This suggests that if theological poverty is to be a historical reality it must be accompanied by some kind of material poverty or at least that the materially poor are structurally in a better position to attain to spiritual poverty, to openness and docility toward God, since in historical fact the possession of material goods is a hindrance to this openness. Finally, neither material nor theological poverty have anything to do with a "metaphysical" poverty that affects all human beings because of their limited nature; material and theological poverty are historical realities in the sense that individuals are poor because others have impoverished them or because they have made themselves poor, that is, open to the will of God.

Against this terminological background we can better understand the precise sense of the statement that the poor are the addressees of evangelization. The poor who are the addressees of evangelization are the materially poor. This is clear from the history of both the prophets and Jesus. We see Jesus addressing himself with great frequency to the impoverished and the social outcast. This is consistent with his version of the kingdom as involving the restoration of human unity. Material impoverishment dehumanizes relations among human beings, and the aim of Jesus' activity is to reestablish human relations as far as possible. In this sense, it is obvious that in Latin America the materially poor continue to be the privileged addressees of evangelization; since it is to them that the good news must first be proclaimed and for them that it must first be made real if the preached message of God's love is to be credible. It is also obvious that the materially poor are sinners and that therefore conversion must be preached to them. If we want to summon them to conversion to a loving God, we must effectively show them our own love for this God.

The poor, however, are not only the privileged addressees of evangelization; they are also the condition for the possibility of evangelization, inasmuch as the evangelization of the poor is constitutive of the very content of evangelization.

If by "poor" we mean the *anawim*, they of course are themselves witnesses to the faith, and their lived faith is a way of evangelizing the evangelizers who have come to them. Even when the poor to whom evangelizers address themselves are the materially poor, the outcast, the oppressed and impoverished, these poor are essential to the very content of evangelization. This is something uniquely Christian; it has often been repeated but we must go into it more fully. It has all too often been taken for granted that evangelizers preach a God whom others do not yet know but whom they (the evangelizers) already know. Such a pattern may make sense for a philosophical concept of God, but it does not hold for the Christian God. Evangelizers do, of course, already have some knowledge of God before they address themselves to the poor, but it is precisely through contact with the poor that they will acquire the specifically Christian knowledge of God they must then preach and put into practice.

This is because the Christian God is not just any God but the Father of Jesus. Formally, this God is a God who is ever greater and transcendent. This transcendence does not receive adequate Christian expression when God is described as the origin and absolute future of all things; it finds Christian expression only when God is a crucified God. The transcendence of God is here expressed as a "stumbling block" and "folly" (cf. 1 Cor. 1:23-24). The clearest historical mediation of this "annihilation" is the poor person, both because he or she expresses the fact of annihilation or humbling and because he or she shows that this annihilation is a consequence of the sin of the world and not a natural state. The great truth regarding the transcendence of the Christian God, namely, that he is crushed by human beings, is mediated for us in a privileged way by the situation of the poor.

At the noetic level this means that the poor are the ones who can cause the epistemological break that is needed to understand the Christian God and to proclaim him. The poor break through the inertia that affects natural understanding whenever it deals with the divinity; they are the hermeneutical instance that makes it possible to read the Scriptures with the necessary sense of surprise and without attributing to it a naturalistic concept of God.

From the viewpoint of content, the Christian God is love but, once again, love in a specific sense. This love contains a "Yes" and a "No" to the real world. Logical priority belongs to the definitive "Yes" that God says to the world. But this "Yes" requires that we first hear the "No" that God says to oppression. When God hears the cry of the oppressed he emerges from his own history (cf. Ex. 3:9; 6:5). The poor in their reality are the concrete mediation given to evangelizers in order that they may learn that God's love for us contains a clear "No" to the world of sin. The presence of the poor causes this "No" (which the natural human being and even the evangelizer tend to ignore, forget, or water down) to remain alive as the initial expression of God's love for the world.

In positive terms, the poor serve as a constant reminder to us of how love as understood by the God of Jesus is to be practiced. God wants to save the poor and to bring to fulfillment even now his desire for the reign of unity and justice. To go forth to the poor with the intention of liberating them is to understand God's vision for the world and to conform to the reality of God. In this historical way the evangelizer becomes ever more Christian and, in the deepest sense of the term, is divinized.

The poor, then, are not simply the privileged addressees of evangelization; they are also the required condition for evangelization to have a Christian content. Contact with the poor is an indispensable condition for the break needed at the noetic level in dealing with the reality of God; it makes possible Christian action in harmony with that of God.

In what, concretely, does "contact with the poor" consist? The question is complicated partly because of the background of the evangelizer and partly because of the means that must be used to effectively announce the good news to the poor and make it a reality for them. Some models for such contact are found in the life of Jesus. There is physical contact: Jesus draws near to the oppressed and lives among them. Then there is Jesus' experience of material poverty during certain periods of his life and certainly at his death. In a society divided into oppressors and oppressed, Jesus stands with the poor and defends them against those in power. Finally, Jesus suffers the consequences of his solidarity with the poor; the power of the oppressors is clearly brought to bear against him and puts him to death.

Let me repeat that the question of how the evangelizer draws close to the poor concretely is a complex question, but one or other of the ways just indicated must lead to something that is of fundamental importance: the acquisition by evangelizers of the outlook of the poor. In other words, as they evangelize the evangelizers must acquire partiality for the poor. Only the poor can give this to them. The evangelizers must want to break with a naturalistic, an insufficiently Christian conception of evangelization, and this is something that only a poor person can do.

This is the meaning I am trying to convey when I say that the poor are not only the addressees of evangelization but also its privileged addressees and the condition for a truly Christian evangelization. I want to bring out the inadequacy from the Christian standpoint of the model of evangelization that I sketched earlier. In schematic form the natural model of evangelization would be:

Evangelizer → evangelization → the evangelized

From the Christian point of view, however, the proper model should show a dialectical relationship among the three elements:

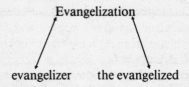

I have been considering in detail the role of the evangelized in the entire evangelization process. In the previous section I dealt with the role of evangelization. In the model I have proposed the important thing is to consider the entire process precisely as a process in which the three elements are interrelated so that the whole unfolds in a Christian way.

Partiality for the Poor and Totality of Evangelization

When I speak of the poor as addressees of evangelization, I am not trying to idealize them. They too are sinners; they too must have conversion preached to them. The gospels make it clear that Jesus died for all, for the sins of all, and that at the end of his life even the people abandoned him and desired his death. Whatever qualifications need to be made about these statements on historical grounds, they remain theologically valid. There is no question, therefore, of idealizing the poor or indulging in casuistry to the effect that if the poor are not poor in the sense described they cannot help establish the content of evangelization.

I have tried to state a principle regarding one of the fundamental dimensions of the Christian faith: its partiality. This is clearly indicated in the Scriptures and is an urgent matter in our present ecclesial situation. Many Church documents of our time bear witness to this Christian partiality, even when they issue clear warnings about the risks accompanying it and about the dangers of reductionism.

Statements must be nuanced and interpretations must be carefully thought out. We labor under the disadvantage of having inherited a God who is more Aristotelian than biblical. This notion of partiality must defend itself against difficulties, accusations of inconsistency, and criticisms. However, a straightforward reading of the gospels puts this partiality beyond doubt: "The Spirit of the Lord is upon me, because he has anointed me to preach good news to the poor. He has sent me to proclaim release to the captives and recovering of sight to the blind, to set at liberty those who are oppressed, to proclaim the acceptable year of the Lord" (Lk. 4:18–19; cf. Is. 61:1–2). Even if an attempt is made to spiritualize these passages (the classical and most frequent form of reductionism), the partiality is unaffected, as *Evangelii nuntiandi* declares: "But one sign stands out to which he himself attributes great importance: the 'little ones' or the poor have the Good News preached to them, become his disciples . . ." (12).

This partiality is not opposed to the universality of evangelization, which I spoke of earlier; it is in fact the concrete way of achieving this universality. Totality is not achieved directly and precisely as totality in any philosophy or religion or even in the Christian faith. In fact the most effective way to destroy totality is to try to grasp it and to act directly upon it. Such a grasp and such direct action are possible only if one deals with abstractions; then there can indeed be a totality, but one that is merely conceptual. Every approach to real totality must, consciously or unconsciously, have some concrete target.

The Christian faith holds that in order to achieve the totality that evangelization calls for we must start with the poor. This obviously does not mean that at the level of concrete methods of evangelization we are to take no account of the cultural, social, and historical characteristics of the various groups of people who are to be evangelized. *Evangelii nuntiandi* devotes several paragraphs (51–58) to this point. There is no question, therefore, of ignoring the relative autonomy of the various addressees of evangelization or of overlooking the fact that they too can and must contribute to establishing the content of evangelization. A Christian structuring of the various contexts to which evangelization is directed cannot ignore, but must integrate into the picture, the viewpoint of the poor. Then it is possible to grasp what it means to evangelize the intellectuals, the middle classes, and even those in power.

Once this standpoint of the poor is adopted it becomes possible to unify the evangelization of the various social groups (those in power, the middle classes, the poor), the various age groups (children, youth, adults), the various functional sectors of society (the intellectuals, the professionals, the workers). To all of these the good news must be proclaimed, but this will not happen if the "proclamation" is at the expense of the poor or if it forgets about them. This same standpoint must be adopted if we are to grasp the universality of the concrete means of evangelization: direct work with the oppressed; structural work in schools, universities, and publications; the work of conscientization and of the promotion and organization of peasants; the work of denouncing oppressors and oppressive structures. Everyone cannot do everything equally, but no one may forget the standpoint of the poor.

This kind of partiality may seem excessive and opportunistic. The real issue here, however, is the very essence of the Christian faith. The characteristic temptation of that faith is to brush under the rug the scandal that is necessary if the faith is to be grasped. At the doctrinal level the Church has for centuries repeated orthodox statements that are perfectly valid and greatly scandalous: that God became human; that the sin of the world has had more power in the course of history than the love of Jesus has had; that the wisdom of God is manifested in the cross of Jesus; that whoever wants to secure life must lose it; that the poor, the calumniated, and the persecuted are blessed. All these truths are paradoxes for natural reason and give the Christian faith its originality. We should not be surprised if a similar originality marks evangelization and its privileged addressees. If originality at this level still surprises us, it is because we have not made the uniqueness of Christianity part of us or because we have asserted it at the level of orthodox statement but have not allowed it to have any real repercussions on our lives.

This partiality in regard to the addressees of evangelization is another way of showing both the uniqueness and the scandal of the Christian faith. It coincides with the content of this faith; it shows the love of God for all, but especially for those to whom no love is shown; it gives hope to all, but especially to those who humanly have least reason to hope; it is concerned about all, but especially those about whom no one else is concerned.

The poor keep alive in history the question that human beings, even Christians, try to forget: What is God really like? What does "salvation" really mean? What must we do so that our human life may have meaning? What kind of action on our part justifies our hope for ultimate fulfillment, for resurrection?

CONSEQUENCES OF A UNIFIED EVANGELIZATION

Thesis 7: The consequences of this unified evangelization can be foreseen and are verifiable after the fact. They are: the conversion of one's own Church; the union of the various ecclesial groups around this mission of evangelization; and a consequent separation from those who do not accept this model of evangelization; the persecution of the Church not only or primarily as an institution but precisely as missionary; credibility in the eyes of the world and especially of the oppressed; an awareness on the part of the Church that it is the body of Christ in history.

Actualizations of the Theoretical Model

The theoretical model of evangelization that I have developed here is based on a deep understanding of the Christian reality (one that is not satisfied with just any kind of evangelization) and on the practice of the Churches in Latin America. To a degree, the truth of the model can be tested by its actualizations, even though these will never exhaust the full reality of the Christian model.

These actualizations give clear form to that which has always been the fact but which has not always been put into practice with a sense of urgency. The model's embodiment in practice helps us at the historical level to grasp this truth, which is one of the deepest elements in the Christian faith. These are among the more novel actualizations of the model proposed: the joining of prophetic denunciations and of action as a mode of evangelization (the word in which the message is proclaimed is joined to the testimony of the evangelizer's own life); the emphasis on the building of a world that resembles the kingdom of God (without prematurely appealing to the eschatological proviso although the latter continues to be true); the stress on action in behalf of justice as the privileged, though not the only, form of love; the acceptance of the conflict to which this model of evangelization leads; the emphasis on the element of partiality in the Christian faith, as the poor are made the privileged addressees of evangelization.

Consequences of the Model in Latin America

The implementation of this model of evangelization has had visible consequences in Latin America. Insofar as these consequences are really Christian they will in turn prove, really and not conceptually, the truth contained in the model. The most important consequences are the following.

The new manner of evangelization, and especially the effective adoption of the vision or outlook of the poor, requires a conversion, both at the level of the theoretical understanding of the Christian faith and at the level of real changes in lifestyle and ways of acting. Since the Medellín Conference (1968) many of the official documents of Latin American episcopates show a kind of thinking different from that of the past. New approaches to life and action can be seen throughout the continent.

The new model of evangelization has brought persecution, especially when it has been consistently employed and has included both prophetic denunciation and action for the building of the kingdom. This persecution has been directed not against the Church as an institution but against the mission of the Church, its agents of evangelization, and the addressees of evangelization.

The new model of evangelization has led to a notable intensification of Church unity. This unity cuts across all the estates within the

Church: hierarchy, priests, religious women and men, laity, peasants, intellectuals. The bond of unity lies in a common mission and a shared suffering. The new model has unfortunately also led to disunity. Independent of the subjectivities involved and of moral judgments on individuals and groups on one or other side, the important thing is that the power to unite or separate exists not in the Church as an abstract entity but in its mission. From this standpoint, achieving the unity desired for the Church (cf. Jn. 17:22) is a task to be carried out by concrete means and it cannot be achieved at the price of ignoring what is the heart of the Christian mission. In our time it is evident that the word of God cuts deeper than any two-edged sword (cf. Heb. 4:12).

This new model has brought a recovery of the Church's credibility. It is becoming increasingly clear that the Church lives in human history and exists for human beings; that it really does share the joys and hopes, the griefs and anguishes of the people. The Church's credibility comes into play not so much when the Church tries to explain a teaching that has been attacked or challenged as when it displays the signs of the reality that it proclaims. This is the criterion running through the New Testament. No one has greater love that those who give their lives for others. The Church is regaining credibility because of the readiness of its members to surrender everything in behalf of human beings.

This kind of evangelization, because it is based on the example of Jesus as "the first and greatest herald [evangelizer] of the Gospel" (EN 7), makes the Church realize that it has found the right road for our time in Latin America. The Church is completing in Christ's body what was lacking in the sufferings of Christ (cf. Col. 1:24) and is also seeing him as the firstborn to the risen life (cf. Col. 1:18). It feels itself inwardly united to Christ in his sufferings and in the hope of fulfillment, since both spring from a single mission conceived and practiced as the mission of Christ himself.

The Church in Latin America makes this model of evangelization a reality only to a degree of completeness. To that degree, it perceives itself to be what it is meant to be: the continuation of the person and mission of Jesus down through history.

10

Religious Life in the Third World

This chapter presents some general thoughts on religious life in Latin America. They may help us to understand the present situation of religious life there, the legitimacy and necessity of the change now going on in it, and the guidance needed to take this change in a Christian direction. When I speak here of religious life I am referring to the orders and congregations that exercise an apostolate, not to those devoted solely to the contemplative life.

I will limit myself to the fundamental traits of religious life as these emerge from its recent history and as they can be inferred from the Christian reality present in all religious life. I have no intention of analyzing in detail the countless and complex problems raised by each of the points I shall be treating. I am interested in a general model of religious life for the Third World.

In general, when I speak here of religious life I mean a way of becoming a Christian within an apostolic group following in a Christian way the charism of a founder and practicing the three vows in the following of Jesus—and this in the Third World. This is less a formal definition than a cumulative description of the various elements essential to religious life. To a certain extent it is also a polemical description inasmuch as it brings out what is positive in religious life by denying traditional ways of understanding religious life and inasmuch as the elements included in the definition— the historical context of religious life, for example—are not usually included in definitions of an essentialist kind.

I shall now explain the various elements of the definition from a theological and historical standpoint. I shall attempt to show how the Christian faith calls for a kind of religious life that cannot be deduced in isolation from other religious ideals and how the concrete embodiment of Christian faith in religious life depends on the historical context.

RELIGIOUS LIFE AS A WAY OF BECOMING CHRISTIAN

The affirmation that religions life is a way of becoming Christian is fundamental to a Christian understanding of religious life. The affirmation is positive, but it is set in a deliberately polemical context. In the past the structures of religious life have been thought of as enjoying a certain autonomy with respect to the ideal required of every human being: to become a Christian. I shall begin by stating what is essential to the Christian faith; I shall then explain in a dialectical way how religious life can neither exist nor be understood except within this Christian reality.

Christian Faith, the Foundation of Religious Life

The foundation of religious life is this: the ultimate identity of religious comes from their Christian faith. From the anthropological standpoint this means that religious, like all human beings, must make a basic choice in favor of certain values. They must choose either to make themselves and their congregation or community the center of their life or to see their life in terms of others and for the sake of others. They must choose to give their life—the ultimate gift—for the sake of others or else keep it for themselves and thus deny in practice the ultimate value that on the surface they profess.

From the theological standpoint Christian religious must choose love as the ultimate reality that gives meaning to everything and in light of which all else human is to be judged. They must therefore make certain beliefs their own: that God is love and not law or power or knowledge; that this God of love seeks unity in the present world; that as religious work for this unity the love they practice takes the form of justice (because the world is a world of sin in which human beings dehumanize one another either by using power in an oppressive way or by suffering under oppressive power and because the justice of God must re-create all human beings according to the state of dehumanization in which they exist); that this God is partial to the oppressed and reveals himself in them in an effective as well as in an ideal way. Religious must make their own the truths that God is always greater than the ideas we human beings can form of him; that his demands, because they affect historical reality, are more important than any created reality, including the structures of religious life; that we must continually try to build his kingdom without ever identifying the result with the definitive plenitude of that kingdom and without ever ceasing to build it despite the power of sin that hinders the building.

From the christological standpoint, Christian religious must choose the following of Jesus as the way in which they live their belief in God. This is how they must express the fundamental choice that governs their life. They must believe in Jesus as the risen lord and believe it precisely because Jesus lived on earth as the Son. They must look upon Jesus as the primordial model of a Christian because Jesus lived the life of faith to the full. He was the great pioneer, the forerunner (cf. Heb. 12:2). Even as religious invoke Jesus as the firstborn into the risen life (cf. Col. 1:18), they must follow him as the one who was the firstborn even during his earthly life, for Jesus was not ashamed to call us his brothers and sisters (cf. Heb. 2:11).

This following of Jesus brings together in harmony both the meaning implied in faith in God and the historical practice of building the kingdom. Out of this following comes the hope of a fulfillment that shall not pass away.

Religious Life as a Process

I have defined the purpose of religious life by describing it not simply as a way of *being* a Christian but as a way of *becoming* a Christian. To succeed in becoming a Christian is a person's greatest success. It is said of Jesus that he was the first of all believers; it is also said that he *was "made perfect"* (Heb. 5:9), that he *became "perfect through suffering"* (Heb. 2:10); and that he *"learned obedience"* (Heb. 5:8).

The following of Jesus, then, does not consist simply in being and doing what Jesus was and did; it consists in experiencing the same process that he experienced. It means learning through historical experience the reality of a God who is always greater and cannot be manipulated, the ways of God in creating his kingdom, the power and impotence of love, the necessity of suffering, the hope that does not die.

At work here is the Johannine concept of faith as a victory over the world (cf. 1 Jn. 5:4). To believe means to become a believer. This assertion is important because it points to the dimension of newness that is essential to faith. Faith remains to the extent that it renews itself and gives rise to a new history. This point is especially important for religious life. For if the idea is accepted, consciously or unconsciously, that faith is something done once and for all, any attempt at renewal and, much more, any attempt at a break with the past will face not only the difficulties attendant upon any conversion but also a fundamental theological difficulty: the unceasing and unresolved tension between a faith conceived as ec-static and the clear calls for change that are making themselves heard in the consciousness of present-day society and Church, between religious life understood as a permanent structure and religious life viewed as a structure requiring renewal.

Theories and Practices of Religious Life

Throughout history there have always been religious men and women who were convinced, often to a striking and heroic degree, that "Christian" is the identifying mark of religious life. And religious life has been a means of growth in true Christianity. I state this because I want to radicalize the presuppositions of which I have been speaking. Religious life tends to and is tempted to think of these presuppositions in a nonradical manner and to justify itself by an appeal to a theory of religious life. I shall try now to clarify in a positive way what I have been saying and to contrast it with theories and, above all, practices of religious life generally. The purpose of the contrast is to emphasize the *positive* content of religious life.

First, even though this is not an important theoretical problem at the present time, I must emphasize that religious life cannot be understood on the basis of its supposed superiority to other states of life. This is why I have described religious life as *one* way of becoming a Christian. The idea of "superiority" is a formal one expressing a relation to something else; to define religious life in terms of superiority, whether unwittingly or with deliberate cunning, would be to define it in relation to secular life, which religious life would then negate and transcend. This would be to introduce into the idea of religious life a rejection of a criterion that appeals to an absolute content and, specifically, to the criterion of "becoming a Christian." Over and above the fact that the supposed superiority of one state of life over another seems an anachronistic notion, we must not let our attention be drawn off on a false scent when we set ourselves to thinking about religious life. We must not allow the fact of the religious "not being" a layperson—even if the intention in making the point is to bring out a positive and perhaps even higher value—to make us forget the positive "being," which is the ground of religious life. The question at issue here is not solved by appealing to the supposed inherent excellence of the vows.

Second, we must do away with any sacral idea of the structures of religious life. On the positive side, the traditional structures of religious life (vows, life in community, spiritual practices) are structures that can be the basis for becoming a Christian. However, a fundamental truth must be kept in mind if these structures are in fact to be vehicles of christianization. God is a holy mystery that cannot be manipulated, and we must let him be God. This God, to whom Christian faith is conformed, accepts no limitation of himself by any created structure as though the latter were an absolute and would automatically ensure possession of him. Even "religious" structures can set limits to the reality of God. Religious have often thought and acted as if there were something sacred, inviolable, and eternal about specific channels of spirituality and religious life. They have really thought that one thing is certain about religious life: it is an almost automatic way of access to God (this represents a kind of application to religious life of the mechanistic *ex opere operato* principle).

The eschatological proviso extends even to the structures of religious life. In other words, a Christian faith that endeavors to respond to the ever greater God cannot find a definitive way in religious life or in a particular spirituality; rather, any "definitiveness" must be achieved over and over at the historical level by a process of seeking and finding ever new ways that effectively respect the initial presupposition, namely, the mystery of an ever greater God. This point, which I raise here in criticism of any sacralization of the structures of religious life, also poses a condition for the possibility of any meaningful discussion of, for example, the vows. Neither are other natural structures besides those of religious life—marriage, possession, and free disposition—absolute in God's eyes.

Third, religious life is a process of "christianization," a word I use in order to avoid bringing in too quickly the idea of "sanctification." The difference is not simply one of terminology; it is a problem of substance. It often happens, especially in religious life, that when persons have lived the Christian faith in a certain way for many years they think of themselves as "possessing the faith." A shift to a new form of Christian faith often produces insecurity with regard to what they have thought of as most characteristically Christian and religious. The result is the easily verifiable experience of anxiety at the appearance of new types of spirituality and religious life. The anxiety may be accompanied by an understandable fear of moving from a new formulation of faith in Jesus to a new practice, a conscious or unconscious fear that the new formulations of the faith may have very real consequences for the concrete life of the religious, the communities and the entire congregation.

This experience is undeniable and is common to laity and religious alike. The problem arises because of the traditional structure of religious life. Those within it may find a justification for not accepting the changes. Religious life is seen as a state of sanctification. The paradoxical situation may arise then in which laypersons require of themselves a really Christian change and religious reject this change on the grounds that they have already chosen the way of sanctification.

For this historical reason we must insist that religious life is first and foremost a process of christianization. The statement may seem polemical and scandalous, but it is not. I am not saying that entrance into a religious order and, even more, perseverance in it do not represent a beginning of growth in Christian life. My aim is to bring home the truth that the most important thing a Christian, lay or religious, can do is to become a Christian. Although religious life offers one way of being a Christian, it does not provide a recipe that eliminates the difficulties and temptations inherent in the process of becoming a Christian. Concretely: before assuming the peculiarities of religious life are the essentials and the source of any difficulty in the life (celibacy, for example, or obedience, or community life), we must inquire into the Christian reality that these peculiarities are to help bring into being. We must not overlook or shunt aside the specifically Christian problem by premature concentration on peculiarities.

If religious presuppose that just because they are religious they know what Christianity is, that they are living it, and are already in possession of the Christian faith, then they are in fact losing sight of the very heart of the faith. Any renewal of religious life based on such a supposition is clearly inadequate. The most important thing in the life of a religious is the ongoing experience of following Jesus and the progressive transformation of his or her reality in accordance with the ideal of the reign of God.

Conclusion

My aim has been to show that religious life cannot be independent of Christianity and, furthermore, that the theology of religious life cannot concentrate solely on religious life, as though the basic theological principles regarding Christianity were sufficiently clear and certain. A religious will be tempted to understand Christian theology from the standpoint of religious life. An exactly contrary approach must be taken, at least at the logical level; in practice of course, living religious life will condition one's theological vision.

I have spent time on this first point because, although it is obvious at the logical level, it is not so clear at the historical level. If I have made the point in a somewhat polemical manner, I have done so in order to explain the basic thesis with greater cogency. The deepest truths of the Christian faith provide a constant criticism of concrete religious life and help to bring to light the temptations that would turn religious life into something unchristian. At the same time religious life offers a means of living the Christian life in Latin America; its characteristic structures make possible today an authentic Christian life.

RELIGIOUS LIFE WITHIN AN APOSTOLIC GROUP

The Group Aspect

Unlike religious life in ages past, religious life today is lived in groups. I have deliberately chosen the term *group* because it is broad enough to allow for a variety of characteristics and does not from the outset determine the meaning of "living in a group."

This first statement is obvious but no less important. Whatever religious life may be, whatever the process of christianization a religious undergoes in religious life, the process is carried on not by the individual in isolation but by the group. In this sense religious life makes clear something fundamental to Christianity, namely, that the Christian faith is lived not by the isolated individual but by the group. This fundamental assertion is implicit in the reality we call "Church" and in the various theological formulations of the nature of the Church that we find in the New Testament: "body" of Christ, "people" of God, "temple" of the Spirit. Even though it is individuals who have faith, they cannot have it except within the group called the Church. From the outset (and this is not specific to the Christian Church but is a sociological characteristic of many institutions), the conversion or renewal of the individual takes place in a group. Baptism not only brings the forgiveness of sins and the renewal of the individual but also inducts her or him into a group that promises salvation.

The group aspect of religious life has an importance that goes beyond the advantages demonstrable by psychology and sociology. Faith and the substance of the Christian faith are lived in a group.

For religious, then, religious life is the place where they strengthen others in the faith and allow others to strengthen them. It is the place for mutual support and mutual consolation in the faith; it can also be the place of temptation against faith.

If this is taken seriously and not dismissed as mere pious chatter, it means that the group dimension will play a key role in the manner of conceiving the various structures of religious life: vows, rules, and so on. This first Christian determination that the faith is lived within a group is also a first principle for determining what is to be

Christian about the structures of the group. It is a first principle for judging the Christian truth of a particular community, a particular regional division of a congregation, or a particular congregation—for judging, that is, whether it is a place, environment, or group in which faith does in fact grow. The judgment is not a matter of seeing whether or not the concrete means of achieving faith exist and what kind they are (forms and practices of spirituality, for example); it is a matter of seeing what the overall result is. To the extent that religious life is a place of growth in faith for the religious, it is immediately justified; to the extent that it is not, its value becomes dubious, no matter how excellent its constitutions, structures, and spiritual practices may be.

The Two Dimensions of the Group

I use the term *group* with regard to the living of religious life because it is applicable both to life within the group and to the relation of the group to those outside it; in other words, the group is both "community" and "apostolic body." I am not trying to solve problems by setting up definitions; I am interested simply in calling attention to the two fundamental dimensions of religious life and in transcending from the outset the traditional notion that religious life automatically has a salvific meaning when considered internally but not, or not so clearly at least, when considered in relation to the outside world.

This amounts to saying that the religious "group" should influence individuals at various levels. In terms of its internal life, it must offer individuals a place where witnesses to the faith already exist; it must require of individuals a disposition to build a Christian community, which will be the place whence they derive their identity. This building of a Christian community (as distinct from mere integration into existing social structures) in accordance with ultimate Christian values that are specified by a way of life made possible by the vows is one of the two Christian tasks a religious has. In terms of its relations with the outside world, the group must offer to religious and require of them a task that is to be carried out as a group task. In other words, religious life exists in order to build a broader community extending into the outside world.

It is not enough to show the two dimensions of religious life. It is also necessary and more important to see how they are related to each other. Each dimension involves a distinct area of life and a distinct set of problems that must be resolved by using appropriate means. Thus, the proper functioning of the religious group in either its internal life or its external life will not automatically solve the problems of the other area.

In principle, religious life, like any form of Christian life, derives its ultimate identity and justification from its mission. From the theological standpoint, therefore, the "community" does not exist for its own sake nor does it offer the criteria by which the truth of religious life is ultimately to be judged. The community exists rather for the sake of its mission. The "apostolic body" is what turns a religious "community" into a Christian community. Only by going out of oneself (in either an individual or a communal sense) and to others does one gain a properly Christian identity. Even though the building of a community has a Christian value and raises specific problems that must be dealt with, it is nonetheless mission that makes the community. The "edification" (literally, the building of the house) of the community only has meaning (unless religious life is to be turned into a sect) and is only possible by building a larger home in the world, namely, the kingdom of God.

This is another way in which the necessary desacralization of the structures of religious life is carried out, religious life being considered here in its historical origins. In the genesis of the various orders and congregations an apostolic ideal lived in an inchoative way came first: only later did an order or congregation come to be established. Religious life is therefore not an "enclosure for holiness" within which religious then begin to inquire about what they ought to be doing. The real movement is just the opposite. When there is something to be done, some mission to be accomplished, then it makes sense to ask whether a "religious enclosure" should not be established with specific structures to facilitate the carrying out of the mission at a particular point in history.

Theological Meaning

The fact, then, that religious life is lived in a group and not by isolated individuals has profound theological meaning. Religious life is a way of overcoming the egocentric self, and thus becomes one of the mediations through which human beings acknowledge and accept a God who is greater than their own subjectivity. It is an expression of the basic Christian law of "carrying and being carried." The fact that the group is "apostolic" points to the law of eccentrism that characterizes the Christian faith: only outside of oneself can one find one's own center; only by building a house for the world can one build one's own house.

RELIGIOUS LIFE AND THE CHARISM OF THE FOUNDER IN CHRISTIAN TERMS

I have stated some principles that are fundamental for religious life but that are true of all Christian life and are not specific to religious life. I turn now to points that are peculiar to religious life.

Relevance of the Charism of the Founder

Anyone today entering a religious order or congregation chooses a way of life that, in principle and in practice, can be traced back to the founder and that founder's charism. The very existence of a religious depends, among other things, on the persistence of this charism. If it were to disappear, the particular order would no longer have any justification for existing.

In calling the charism of the founder an essential element of a religious order I am supposing that the charism gives concrete embodiment to something truly Christian and evangelical. At the same time, it is not possible to pass over the theoretical and practical problems attendant upon the meaning of the founder's charism and on the concrete use made of it.

The theoretical problem is to relate the charism of the founder, on the one hand, to the following of Jesus, and, on the other, to the historical situation in which the effort is being made to maintain the charism. The need is to discover in the charisms of the various founders (charisms that may be authentic, but are partial) some kind of totality that corresponds to the totality of the gospel.

The practical problem has to do with the use made of the charism, with the appeal to the charism of the founder as a way of resolving problems that arise in the course of history. It can happen that in the history of an order the charism loses its potency or is replaced: although the charism of the founder is nominally maintained it has in fact disappeared. It can happen that the charism of the founder is turned into an absolute: even though the gospel is nominally accepted as the ultimate norm for religious life, the founder in fact becomes the ultimate criterion of understanding and activity. It can also happen—and does happen quite frequently —that in the name of the charism or, more accurately, in the name of a particular conception of the charism, other types of spirituality and apostolate are rejected, which, though not explicitly envisaged by the founder, are required by the reality of the situation. It can happen, too, that the concrete historical embodiment of a particular charism becomes a way of ignoring the totality of the Christian faith or the core reality that gives meaning to the whole.

The claim has not infrequently been made that since it is impossible to imitate everything about Christ, it is good for each religious order to "specialize" and reproduce certain of his traits: his teaching ministry, his works of mercy, his sufferings, his liturgical prayer and praise. The problem here is different. Even though it is impossible to imitate everything about Christ and even though there are Christians and religious who concentrate especially on one or other activity, none of them may ignore what is central to the following of Jesus: his building of the kingdom of God, his partiality toward the poor, his struggle for justice, his unconditional trust in the Father. Moreover, the presence of this center or core justifies the existence of varied historical mediations as expressed in various charisms and makes possible the exercise of a "partial" charism to be Christian.

In appealing to the charism of the founder one must be conscious of one's real intentions. A formal appeal does not automatically solve the problem of religious life at a given moment. We may not forget that a founder is a Christian who at a particular time in history tries to follow Jesus. The basic question here is whether or not the charism which he or she embodied at a particular point in history is still able today to launch a Christian history.

Analysis of a Charism

I shall now analyze in a Christian manner what the charism of a founder must mean if the appeal to it is to be legitimate and necessary. I shall try to clarify the issue by using the example that is best known to me. It could be replaced by the charisms of other founders. The example I choose is the charism of Saint Ignatius Loyola, founder of the Society of Jesus. My analysis is not exhaustive; I do not even claim that all the details I adduce are exact, since complete exactness would require a more complete historical study. My interest here is to show how to analyze the structure of the charism of a founder so that an appeal to it may be possible and even required.

In order to make the analysis manageable and useful, I shall distinguish three levels in Ignatius's charism as founder and first General of the Society. The first level is that of expressions that are external and clearly conditioned by the age in which he lived. Examples are external forms of the manner of life, the kind of dress, the concrete forms of prayer, the time spent in prayer, certain kinds of apostolate (such as work in hospitals), certain apostolates rejected (such as work in parishes), the philosophical presuppositions manifested in the Spiritual Exercises. That these points belong to this level does not mean that they are unimportant; they are, after all, the expressions at a particular time of something that is important. Because they are concrete expressions, however, they do not belong to the central core of the charism.

At the second level, deeper things appear; but these still do not represent the deepest reality although they are indeed connected with what I call the third level. At the second level are the points traditionally associated with the Jesuits: unqualified obedience, suppression of the communal recitation of the divine Office, and, in a different order of things, a broad and solid academic formation. These things are obviously important, so much so that if they were to disappear, the historical form of the Society's life and activity would be transformed. However, they are not the deepest reality of the Society, even though they may seem to be most characteristic at a descriptive level. That which differentiates is not necessarily what is deepest although it may also be this.

The third level is the most profound: conformity, at a stage in history, with the gospel of Jesus. Without aiming at completeness, I mention the following points as belonging at this level.

1. *The experienced reality of an ever "greater" God.* This is translated at the operative level into an attitude of seeking God's will and not presupposing one already possesses it; into a correla-

tive need for discernment in order to find this will; into an attitude of always trying to do what is for the "greater" glory of God.

2. *The following of the poor and humiliated Jesus who is committed to human service.* This following embraces both the mission of building the kingdom of God (cf. the meditations of the eternal and temporal king in the *Spiritual Exercises*) and the manner of building it (cf. the meditations on the two standards and the third mode of humility).

3. *The superiority attributed to apostolic practice over the theoretical formulation of it,* to "works of love" over words of love, as is clear from the contemplation for obtaining love.

4. *"Contemplation in action"* (as distinct from other classical models of contemplation, such as "communicating to others the fruits of one's contemplation" [*contemplata aliis tradere*]). Here the important thing is to carry the contemplation into not just any kind of action but into action that makes possible and calls for contemplation, namely, the following of Jesus.

5. *An openness to and disposition for the whole,* in the form of a readiness to accomplish a greater good, wherever the greatest need exists (in this sense the fourth vow is fundamental).

6. *The essentially apostolic concept of the Society,* according to which Jesuits are "friends in the Lord" (a community) insofar as they form the body of the Society. This is what Ignatius calls a *communitas ad dispersionem,* a community meant to be scattered.

7. *The supremacy, in principle, of "the interior law of charity and love which the Holy Spirit writes and imprints in hearts"* (as we read at the beginning of the Jesuit Constitutions) over any "external law." External law, however, is also necessary.

8. *"Thinking with the Church."* This does not mean an infantile or servile acceptance of rules and orders (the life of Ignatius gives the lie to such an interpretation) but a profound solidarity with the Church as depository of the tradition of Jesus.

In terms of the above outline, the heart of a founder's charism is at the third level. The first level is conditioned by a given age and therefore requires translation for other ages. The second level is important for the character of a particular order; its ultimate meaning, however, lies not in itself but in its relation to the third level.

I have analyzed this problem in detail because it is of real importance. The temptation most typical of Christianity has always been the temptation to "sacralize" things. It has been assumed, without valid reason, that sacralization is the characteristic Christian way of declaring something or someone to be supremely important. But, in addition to being an attack on the transcendence of God, the process of sacralization often leads to a watering down of what is authentically Christian. Sad to say, sacralization has often occurred in direct proportion to dechristianization. It is for this reason that I have tried to offer a *Christian* but not a *sacral* conception of the charism of a founder. In practice a sacral conception of this charism serves as an ideologized justification for not carrying out the renewal of religious life called for by the Second Vatican Council, by many religious, and by the reality in which we live.

Two points must be made about founders: (1) they are not Christ; and (2) if they as founders launched a manner of Christian life then they were related to Christ at a very deep level. If these statements are accepted in a real, operative way, religious life can and should be renewed in accordance with the charism of the founder. To put the same point abstractly: the charism of the founder must be accepted as a *norma normata* and not a *norma normans*. The *norma normans* is Christ alone; the charism of the founder can and should continue to be a norm as long as it is subordinate to Christ and to the history to which Christ continually gives rise.

If, for some historical reason, a charism can no longer give rise to a history that is in accordance with Jesus, then its *kairos* has passed. From the theological standpoint, another basic principle must be kept in mind: a religious order is not the Church. The Church, as depository of the tradition about Jesus, has been guaranteed indefectibility throughout history. Religious orders have no such guarantee. Consequently, a readiness to disappear must be part of a religious order's Christian self-understanding—uncertain and frightening though this may seem.

This readiness, which at first can sound negatively like resignation to or passive acceptance of historic destiny, is the condition for the possibility of something very positive: the disposition to a renewal that does not have as its end the *defense* or *maintenance* of a specific religious order, but rather the *adaptation* of the order to the word of God and to the needs of the present situation. Religious orders tend toward a typical "concupiscence" to make themselves absolute according to a model that only theologically corresponds to the totality of the Church. Only by overcoming this "concupiscence" can religious life renew itself.

The history of the embodiments of religious life shows religious life to be an authentic form of Christian life. In the following sections of this chapter I shall show the logical possibility and excellence of such a way. I want to insist again that the charism of the founder will be maintained in a Christian way and may legitimately be appealed to as long as, at the third level of the charism, a truly Christian nucleus exists and makes possible necessary innovations at the first level and can find at the second level historical mediations that justify the existence of a special religious order.

If the charism of the founder does not have this power today, then from the Christian standpoint it is dead. If it does have this power—the test being history—then there should be no hesitation about appealing to it, since it is truly a source of Christian life within religious life.

THE VOWS AND THE FOLLOWING OF JESUS IN THE THIRD WORLD

Various Conceptions of the Vows

Religious life is one way of becoming Christian by living in accordance with basic Christian values. But the religious, unlike the layperson, does this through the mediation of the three traditional vows of poverty, chastity, and obedience.

These vows are concerned with bringing into focus three areas important in the life of every person: sexuality, affectivity and parenthood; the free disposal of oneself; and the use and possession of things. These three areas are not specific to religious life but are part of every human life. For this reason, all who want to become Christians must consciously organize these three areas in accordance with the values of Christ. In this sense, every Christian has an obligation to "take vows" in regard to the three areas, although not in the juridically appointed way proper to religious life. Moreover, all Christians must grow in faith and become Christian in these three important areas of life. Religious life with its three vows provides one possible way of organizing life in a Christian manner.

The vows in themselves are no more than possible channels of Christian life. Whether in fact they serve as such depends on the concrete way in which they are lived. Paradoxically, a person can grow in faith or decrease in faith through the three vows. The actual outcome cannot be determined a priori but can be observed only after the fact. It is typical of the theology of religious life to try to show in an a priori way the excellence of that life. I shall survey briefly the various theories of the vows and point out the a priori conception that makes of the vows an authentic possibility for Christian life. The criticisms of the various theories are derived from observation of the practice to which the theories lead.

Ascetical theory. According to the ascetical theory, the vows relate the religious to the three important areas of life by a rejection of their use. Religious reject the natural exercise of sexuality, of free will, and of the free disposition of material things. This rejection supposes a sacrifice of natural human tendencies, including those willed by God. This sacrifice has an inherent religious value; it is an act of religion. It must be said in criticism, however, that the correct religious relation to the God of Jesus does not consist first and foremost in the offering of sacrifices even though sacrifices are necessary in the following of Jesus.

Imitational theory. According to the imitational theory, the value of the vows is that in them the person makes her own or his own certain virtues and attitudes of Jesus. The point here is certainly valid and Christian, but its presuppositions are not entirely correct. First, while Jesus seems to have been a celibate, the obedience and poverty he practiced cannot without qualification be identified with those reflected in the vows. Jesus was indeed poor and obedient, but the ways in which he was were not the ways of religious life. Jesus had no superior and no juridical regulations on his possession of things. Second, Jesus called not for imitation but for following. Following implies that one also act like Jesus, that is, imitate him, but following and imitation cannot be equated. According to the imitational theory, one might vow to travel about, to preach in parables, to clash with the powerful, and so on. Without denying the good intention of this conception, I must emphasize that the vows should be a channel or way of following Jesus, not of imitating him. This distinction is all the more necessary since in the history of religious orders, after the first enthusiasm has vanished, imitation through the vows is used as a reason not to "imitate" other fundamental aspects of the life of Jesus.

Personalist theory. The personalist theory was in part a reaction to the ascetical theory. According to the personalist theory, the vows are apt means of bringing the religious to fulfillment as a person. They provide a way to mature development of one's sexuality and affectivity, one's freedom, and one's proper use of material goods. This conception has the historical advantage of putting an end to a type of infantilism in the practice of the vows and of proclaiming that nothing that is ideal in itself need be simply sacrificed by a human being and a Christian. Everything involving sacrifice and negation is in the service of something positive, which in this case is the religious himself or herself. Nonetheless, this conception, though correct in what it rejects, stops at a liberal kind of Christianity and religious life. For, important though it is (especially in view of the infantilization of religious life) to keep in mind the value of the human person and the need for the religious to find fulfillment as a person, we must also keep in mind that personal fulfillment is not the ultimate ideal of the Christian or, to put the matter more precisely, that personal fulfillment is paradoxically never attained directly but by the detour of "losing one's life." The crisis in religious life has not been overcome when communities have passed from infantilism to personalism, but only when they have taken a further step, which I shall discuss later.

Communitarian theory. Whereas the ascetical theory relates the religious to things and the personalist relates the religions to himself or herself, the communitarian theory connects the vows with other persons, usually the other people in one's own order and community. According to this view the vows are ways of building the community: chastity is the condition that makes possible mutual friendship and love; poverty makes it possible to share things in common; obedience emphasizes the communal hearing of the word of God (though there is a superior who makes the decisions). This conception obviously embodies a series of Christian values. The danger is the tendency of the community to a self-centeredness ending in the building of a home for the religious rather than a home for the world.

Eschatological theory. The eschatological conception of the vows takes two forms: (1) religious life by reason of the structure of the vows is an anticipation of the definitive future; and (2) religious life is a way of living the substance of the Christian faith in the manner proper to the eschaton, but doing so in the here and now. The first form emphasizes the fact that by reason of the vows religious *are not* (descriptively) like other Christians and that this *are not* brings into view the difference between the state of nonmaterial plenitude and the present historical state. The vows are a way of anticipating the eschaton and its specific structures of nonmateriality: love not mediated through the body, material things no longer being needed, and so on. This conception is naïve, not because it sees in religious life an anticipation of the eschaton but because it sees in it an anticipation of the structures of the eschaton.

The second form of the eschatological conception is legitimate, since according to it what is anticipated is not so much the structures as the content of the eschaton, namely, unconditional love. Religious life makes it possible to live, in a manner proper to the eschaton but under the conditions of historical existence, that which we are told will characterize the fulfillment proper to the eschaton. However, not only religious life but any Christian life that is truly a following of Jesus is eschatological in this sense.

Apostolic theory. The apostolic conception of the vows puts those areas of life that are shaped by the vows into the service of the reign of God. The vows are historical structures that exist for the sake of the following of Jesus. That the vows exist for the sake of God's reign implies that God's reign is the ultimate justification for what is "abnormal" in the vows, and above all, that the building of the kingdom will make it known whether or not the vows are effective channels for Christian life.

These, I think, are the most important theories employed in order to show the a priori possibility of living a Christian life under vows and to demonstrate the excellence or superiority of religious life to other ways of Christian life. Before proceeding further, there are a couple of points I wish to emphasize. First, even though the various theories appeal to different justifications, they are not inherently exclusive. The ascetical conception recalls every human being's need of self-control in the important areas of life; the personalist reminds us of the danger of turning religious life into something infantile. Although the various theories are not mutually exclusive, it is important to determine which of them gives logical coherence to all the others and explains the possibility of religious life at the present time.

I choose the apostolic conception because I think it has roots in the gospel that the others do not have and because it sets forth in a satisfactory manner both the ideal and the real possibility of religious life: religious life is a life for the reign of God. This implies that religious life is basically a following of Jesus. Insofar as it is a following of *Jesus,* it must embody the ultimate values of Jesus; insofar as it is a *following* of Jesus, it must unequivocally take into account its own historical and geographical location, which in my case is the Third World. I am thus introducing historical location into the very essence of religious life and not treating it simply as a desideratum.

Second, even in the apostolic theory or conception, the vows are not sacral in themselves. The Christian justification of the vows lies in the living of them and in whether or not they give rise to a life spent in the following of Jesus. The traditional conception of the vows strains the relationship between vows and attaining to faith. In the apostolic conception of the vows the pattern is different: exercise of the vows leads to the kingdom of God and the attainment of faith.

Channels for the Following of Jesus

The reality or the content to be brought into being through the three vows is nothing else than the following of Jesus. This following is the absolute norm for every Christian as it is for religious. It also confirms the Christian value of the vows, without any overhasty, ideological sacralization of them. I wish now to offer some brief thoughts on the following of Jesus (these are developed at greater length in my *Christology at the Crossroads* [Maryknoll, N.Y.: Orbis Books, 1978]) and to reflect on some of the typical structural aspects of this following. By reason of these aspects the vows seem to be an adequate structural channel.

The following of Jesus unites two basic dimensions of Christian existence: faith and practice. To follow Jesus simply means to prolong his reality. This following is, therefore, a practice, a historical activity, and its truth is to be judged by what is objectively done. It is also the way of attaining to faith in Jesus as the Christ.

The following of Jesus is the condition for the possibility of a christological epistemology. Christian recognition of the truth of Christ is possible only within a life like that of Jesus. In the measure that we make ourselves sons and daughters of God by following Jesus we are able to confess him as the Son; in the measure that we travel the way of Jesus in a real and objective manner we come to know the truth of Jesus. This truth resides in the relationship that is constitutive of Christ as a way to the Father; consequently we recognize the truth of Christ in our own life insofar as it is a way to the Father.

The way of Jesus can be described with a certain objectivity, despite the fact that different situations require different concrete mediations. It is a way to the Father who is love and who has shown his partiality for the poor and oppressed; the Father who is, moreover, effective love, that is, who wants to establish his reign on this earth. And since the world is ruled by sin, which reduces the lowly and the poor to a state of subjection, this love finds its privileged form in justice. God not only wants to love human beings; he also wants to re-create them when they have been dehumanized by oppressive power or by the results of the exercise of this power.

This is the real purview of the way of Jesus that must be followed. But this way calls for its own mode or manner of traveling: it adopts the attitudes practiced and taught by Jesus. These attitudes are found in the spirit of the beatitudes, in the radicality of the demands made, in fidelity to the end, and in the posing of problems in the form of clear alternatives, since there is no complementarity or dialectical relationship between "God and mammon," "putting one's hand to the plough and turning back," "gaining one's life and losing it."

Such is the ultimate *norm* for living that is offered to and imposed on every Christian who wants to become precisely that, a Christian; it integrates orthopraxis and orthodoxy. This norm is imposed on religious, too, as the ultimate norm for living. Precisely by reason of the vows, however, the following of Jesus in religious life has an element of *abnormality*. I turn to this element now. The basic content of the following of Christ has already been stated. What do the vows, considered as a structural channel, contribute to this following?

Religious life is not normal but abnormal by reason of the structure given it by the vows. Yet this very abnormality brings out what is characteristic of the following of Christ. Christian existence has its origin in Christ's call and in our response; in other words, it is structurally a calling or vocation. This is true for every Christian. That is what Paul is telling us when he says that God has chosen us from all eternity. It follows from this that the vocation of those who are not religious (those who are married, single, in a chosen profession) follows the same pattern as the vocation of religious. But the religious vocation, because it involves vows that are not normal, brings out more clearly the origin of the following, namely, God's call to follow Jesus. This call has no justification beyond itself; to hear this call and respond to it is the first step to Christian faith.

Further, the vows by their very structure allow and demand that the radicality of the call be extended into areas beyond those that are normal. Using a geographical image, I might say that the vows allow and require the religious to live in the desert, on the periphery, and on the frontier. By "living in the desert" I mean that the religious goes where no one else is; thus throughout history religious have worked in hospitals and schools and, nowadays, in neglected parishes. By "living on the periphery" I mean that the religious is not at the center of power but in the place characterized by powerlessness. By "living on the frontier" I mean that the religious exists where there is greater scope for Christian imagination and creativity to experiment; where the risks may be greater; where there is need of prophetic activity in order to shake off the inertia that is continually immobilizing the Church as a whole or in order to denounce sin more energetically.

Finally, the abnormality of religious life expresses the hope of final fulfillment—hope against hope. By reason of the structural indifference to the here and now, which the vows embody, the religious can effectively represent the hope of fulfillment.

The vows are thus meant to be a channel for the following of Jesus, and they entail structural abnormalities that highlight certain aspects of the following of Jesus. This does not mean that religious are the only ones to live in the abnormal way described nor even that historically they have done so better than others. The important thing is that religious life contains the possibility for this abnormal following.

Here we find the gravest reasons for the crisis of religious life as a structure (independently of the personal reasons leading individuals to continue in or to abandon religious life). If religious life by its very structure involves a certain abnormality, then that life will experience crisis when it seeks to become normal and when it is no longer lived in the desert or on the periphery or on the frontier. The religious then feels that he or she is caught up in an abnormal personal structure (that of the vows) and yet is trying to do what is normal, what everyone else is doing. Religious then ask whether they should not follow the lead of everyone else and make their own the normal structure, marriage and the free disposition of themselves.

This difficulty is structural, and consequently it cannot be resolved by appealing simply to purity of intention and to the supposed value that the vows have in themselves. If religious life is to continue to be meaningful it must be based on the following of Jesus and must focus its attention on something beyond the merely normal. If this does not happen, good people will go on doing good and useful things, but we must ask whether they are really religious.

When I say that religious life by its structure means taking the following of Jesus as the norm amid a certain abnormality, I am simply recalling the historical origin of almost all the orders and congregations. They came into existence at moments when some desert or periphery or frontier existed for them. The danger that confronts religious orders today is that, because of a poorly understood charism, they may turn these places into comfortable and established centers.

The result will be a profound lack of coherence between the abnormal structure of the vows, on the one hand, and, on the other, the normality of work, of lifestyle, of inflexible criteria. If the apostolate and lifestyle have even a spark of madness about them, the vows will be an expression of the Christian folly of the cross. If, however, the apostolate and lifestyle are characterized by tidiness, adaptation, and acceptance of the comfortable center, then the vows will not represent a sharing in the Christian folly of the cross but will be seen, at least by the more perceptive, as responsible for a deep division in the Christian and psychological consciousness of the religious. Under these circumstances, young people will turn to other institutions, which, supposedly or really, offer them a challenge in their following of Jesus.

By way of conclusion and in order to prevent any misunder-standing, let me add that the structural abnormality characteristic of a life according to the vows has nothing to do with eccentricities or excesses. The abnormality of this way has a clear norm: the following of Jesus. The purpose of this way or channel of the following of Jesus is to show forth clearly the values and attitudes of Jesus, which I have already described. If this norm is not taken into account, some religious may, as has happened in the past, seek to justify their life by "follies" that are not necessarily those proper to the following of Jesus.

Following Jesus in the Third World

The following of Jesus that I have described must be lived in the Third World. In emphasizing this point I reject an atemporal, ahis-torical, and autonomous conception of religious life. The vows must be lived in a concrete situation and this situation is part of their historical essence. Both the following of Jesus as the norm and what I have called the structural abnormality of the vows must be given concrete shape in a particular situation. Here I am simply restating the embodiment or incarnation that is required if the following is really to be a continuation of Jesus and not a mere imitation of him.

Religious life in the Third World calls for one incarnation of a generic kind and for another that is more specifically Christian. In generic terms, religious live within a particular set of historical and geographical coordinates. The history of the last third of the twen-tieth century has been marked in Latin America by widespread wretchedness, a consciousness that this wretchedness is due to op-pression by powerful groups at home and abroad, and a conscious longing for liberation. In geographical terms, the obvious fact is that our religious life must be lived in Latin America and not in some other part of the world. This observation is important for those religious men and women who, because of their place of birth or because of their tradition (the European or North American ori-gin of their religious order or congregation), may tend to suppose that forms of religious life or apostolate valid in other places will automatically be valid here as well.

Geographical location also determines a basic sociological situa-tion. Only on the surface is Latin America a single unit. In fact it consists of various social groups: First World enclaves, peasants, natives, the marginalized, and so on. Religious life cannot, deliberately or indeliberately, remain aloof; it must choose an embodiment.

This initial, generic definition of the Third World is not a kind of postscript to religious life. It exercises a positive influence on the understanding and living of the vows. Being poor, chaste, and obedient is not or should not be the same in Latin America as in Rome or New York. A historical consciousness of oppression, a longing for liberation, and a deliberately chosen location among and for the sake of specific social groups are all necessary conditions if the life of the vows is to be meaningful and a real Christian possibility in our day.

Over and above this generic definition of the Third World a Christian definition of its reality shows its convergence with the vows of religious life. I can here allude only briefly to matters I have analyzed in greater detail elsewhere. The Third World is by and large a world made up of the poor and the impoverished. Whether the poverty is due to natural causes (the poor) or due to historical causes (the impoverished), the situation is scandalous in the eyes of God. Poverty is the objectification of sin and the product of the sins of human beings. To this world God says an unconditional "No" because unjust poverty brings death to the children of God. In this first sense the Third World is sinful. This statement, however much it needs to be analyzed, discussed, and nuanced, is a basic truth. To ignore this would be to turn any Christian and religious life into a hoax.

God, who "hears the cry of the oppressed," wants to save this sinful world. To the ought-not-to-be that describes the Third World, God opposes an ought-to-be, a being of a different kind, a liberation. Paradoxically, this Third World, which suffers and needs to be set free, also offers the possibility of salvation to the entire world and to the other "worlds." The pattern God adopts in saving is a pattern of redemption: if sin is to be done away with, its burden must be shouldered. Life for others comes through the giving of one's own life; it is by continuing to hope in the midst of wretchedness that one gives true hope to others.

To put the whole matter in a nutshell: the Third World is the contemporary historical version of the Servant of Yahweh, though in making such a statement we must avoid oversimple parallels. In this perspective, religious life is incarnated in the Third World when it incarnates the basic values of the Servant of Yahweh. This means entering the world of the poor, making one's own the cause of the poor, bringing justice to the poor, and suffering the destiny of the poor.

Vows taken for the sake of God's kingdom provide an excellent opportunity to enter the world of the Servant of Yahweh. By their structure the vows suppose a redemptionist theology; that is, they suppose that the attainment of faith involves a negation, a detachment from something positive, and not simply a building upon it.

There is here a structural convergence with the Servant of Yahweh who in order to reach salvation had to travel the way of negation. The vows provide the structural possibility for at least a relative distancing from a society that is the source of sin as well as a structural disposition to make one's own the cause of the poor. However distorted the vow of poverty may have been, the name at least has not disappeared; a religious is or should be "poor" and have a certain affinity for the world of the poor. The vows provide a structural possibility for keeping alive the attitude typical of the Servant of Yahweh: hope against hope. Religious should be privileged exemplars, witnesses to faith, not by reason of any theological professionalism but by reason of their very lives; that is, because amid their own insecurity they find security in God, because amid their own loneliness they are united to God, because they look beyond their own judgment and seek God.

This structural convergence between the life of the vows and the Third World may of course remain at the level of mere ideas. The intention inherent in the vows is not enough to make us part of the Third World; that will happen only if we really act like the Servant of Yahweh. Then the vows will bring home a truth that requires no further clarification through theological reflection; they will have become transparent in themselves. The embodiment of the vows in the Third World, after the manner of the Servant, will concretize them in a Christian manner.

In order to see whether or not there has been such an embodiment or incarnation we need only ask whether religious are experiencing and sharing the lot of the Servant. If they are establishing justice among the peoples, if they are suffering persecution, if they are keeping hope alive, then there has clearly been an authentic incarnation.

Up to this point I have tried to show that the vows must be a channel of Christian life. In a summary that is both positive and polemical I may say that what needs to be brought into being through the channel of the vows is the following of Jesus with *his* basic values, even though these values will be lived out in a different way. We must therefore not presuppose, perhaps erroneously, perhaps overhastily, that the vows are already a following of Jesus. By their structure the vows suppose a form and state of life that, even in descriptive terms, is not normal; it is this abnormality that enables them to bring out certain aspects of the following of Jesus. This means that lifestyle and apostolic work are not to be established in a comfortable center, even though good things might be done there. To do so would be to create a tension between state of life on the one hand and lifestyle and work on the other.

The vows are then a structure that makes it possible to live in the Third World after the manner of the Servant of Yahweh. Whatever types of incarnation are necessary in other parts of the world, this is the kind of incarnation that is needed in Latin America. If it is not implemented, then religious life here will become inflexible and useless; any value the vows may have will be entirely a matter of intention; and the ultimate criterion of truth, which is the actual following of Jesus after the fashion of Jesus, will have no place. The deep crisis of religious life arises when religious desire to follow Jesus but cannot find an objective channel for doing so. This incongruence also accounts for the lack of credibility among those outside the order or congregation and for the distressful need to maintain in intention what is not there in objective reality. However, if religious live after the fashion of the Servant, an objective congruence will exist between the intention of living the vows and the service rendered to the Third World.

CELIBACY, POVERTY, AND OBEDIENCE
AS A FOLLOWING OF JESUS IN THE THIRD WORLD

Before analyzing each of the vows in detail I have some introductory observations to make. I pass over here the question of whether the three vows are present in the gospel and whether there may not be other "evangelical counsels" for the following of Jesus besides those to which the vows are related. The three classical vows highlight three important areas of life within which the other attitudes or "counsels" of Jesus can find their place. We must also note that religious life does not consist in the exercise of "three" vows, but rather that the reciprocal interaction of the three constitutes religious life.

If what is said here of each vow is to be meaningful, each must be viewed in its relation to the others. I shall show briefly what properly belongs to each vow by its structure, even though the actual living of the vow depends on the living of the other vows as well. Finally, I shall say something about the special problems of each vow. In covering so much ground I have no choice but to be brief; I will therefore be unable to offer the reasons for many of the positions I take.

Christian Celibacy

Celibacy has to do with an important area of human life: sexuality, affectivity, parenthood, and sociability. Celibacy chosen for the sake of God's reign is a way of bringing this area into conformity with the kingdom. Celibacy is not the same as continence, although it presupposes continence; celibacy in religious life, then, does not simply mean persevering in continence.

In the course of history a great many reasons have been put forward to show the excellence of celibacy: the sacrificial value of continence, the purity continence bestows, the imitation of the angels, the preservation of an undivided heart, a special affective relationship with Christ. Although there is something of value in each of these, they do not capture what is most specific to Christian celibacy. Here, then, in my estimation are the positive reasons for Christian celibacy.

Celibacy is an exercise of faith in a *God who is greater*. In the Old Testament, marriage was seen as a blessing of the created order and willed by God; according to rabbinical teaching in the time of Jesus, marriage was obligatory. Jesus dealt in a matter-of-fact way with women (behavior that in his day was regarded as scandalous) and he gave them a new social standing. Nonetheless, he was a celibate. In his historical context this choice embodied a great truth and even a religious revolution. The truth is this: for the God of Jesus, no created structure, not even the "good" structures of the created order, can set limits to his will. The fact of the celibacy of Jesus is a proclamation that his God is utterly beyond human power to manipulate.

Herein lies the first value of Christian celibacy: it is a confession, incarnated in a way of living, of the transcendent God. Celibacy, moreover, represents a special modality of this faith in transcendence. By reason of its structure, celibacy puts the religious in a condition of psychological solitude that is not normal in comparison with the rest of humankind. This solitude serves to express an important aspect of faith in God, namely, the poverty of the human person who comes before God without any support or protection. The solitude proper to celibacy is one of the important historical mediations of something essential to faith: perseverance in faith even when there is no basis to support it.

Celibacy as an exercise of faith has repercussions in the Christian community. All the great believers, of the Old Testament and of the New, have allowed God to be God without attempting to manipulate him, and they have always passed through a period of solitude or isolation. In the Old Testament the classical example is Abraham, who was required to hope against hope; in the New Testament the classical and definitive example is Jesus, who was required to trust in God at the moment of his own greatest isolation on the cross. Because he persevered in faith Jesus became the one who "lived the life of faith to the full and as the pioneer." From this kind of faith the faith of others draws support. If we are to succeed in begetting faith in others we must live our own faith in the transcendence of God to the bitter end. Here, in my opinion, is to be found the first Christian value of celibacy: those who have the courage to stand before God in detachment from things (a detachment mediated in an effective historical way by detachment from marriage) themselves grow in faith and beget faith in others.

Celibacy is an exercise of faith in a *God who is love*. Although to be "greater" formally defines the God of Jesus, the substance of this God is love. Celibates cannot and may not renounce love. But as celibates they exercise a love that has two special traits. At the level of interhuman love, celibates are by their very condition geared to building a community that (though using the normal means of building applied in every human community) will empha-size the constructive aspect of love rather than the aspect of mutual gratification. In their relationships as religious with those outside celibates must not only seek to love others in effective ways but must also seek to channel the unused residue of feeling in such a way that their apostolic work will become a passion. In this special way celibates will clearly show forth their faith in a God who is love.

Celibacy is an exercise of the *following of Jesus*. According to the New Testament, celibacy is, in the words of Jesus, "for the sake of the kingdom of God." According to Saint Paul, celibacy allows the person to be "anxious about the affairs of the Lord," the word *affairs* having a historical not a spiritualist meaning. According to Jesus this connection between celibacy and the kingdom of God is something "ultimate" or "eschatological," something for which one must be ready in principle to sacrifice "everything." For a celibate, the concrete—though not the sole or exclusive—media-tion of this requirement is the renunciation of that to which the human psyche normally tends: marriage as a form of mutual self-giving and complementarity, a form that is in principle a source of gratification. Celibacy is a historical expression of the ultimateness of the reign of God and makes possible one kind of following of Jesus for the sake of the kingdom. It makes possible a kind of structural freedom for service to the kingdom because it fosters a detachment from society; the affective vacuum created allows the celibate to embrace a large number of people. Celibacy enables the person to live, as I put it earlier, in the desert, on the periphery, on the frontier.

Whether celibates in fact do all this and whether they alone do it, are questions of historical fact. My concern here is to show that the celibacy proper to religious life is much more than the preservation of continence. In the concrete, religious celibacy is authentic if it engenders faith in a God who is allowed to be what he is—beyond manipulation and always greater; if it engenders faith in a God who is real, historical love and not simply a "pure" spirit. It is authentic if it engenders a following of Jesus that is marked by detachment, a position on the frontiers of the Church, and a readiness to accept danger and persecution. Celibacy is authentic if it renders the celi-bate capable of building a community.

Obedience

Obedience has to do with a second important area of human life: the person's free decision about what she or he is to do. In this summary description the emphasis can be put either on the "free" or on the "do."

In Christian terms, obedience cannot have as its object the denial of one's own will. Neither can it consist in delegating to another person the final responsibility for oneself when this responsibility is for important and ultimate matters. It cannot consist in a formal imitation of the obedient Christ, for Christ obeyed God his Father and in so doing made relative, even as he accepted it, obedience to human authorities.

The ultimate meaning of the vow of obedience is to be found by connecting it with the "do" in the summary definition above. This vow too is an exercise of faith in God. The Christian God is not an eternal God in the atemporal sense of the word *eternal,* nor can his will be deduced from the created natural world. He is the God of the word, through which he makes known his concrete will for history and the concrete way in which that will is to be carried out. Obedience, then, is to be understood in the light of its etymology: *ob-audire,* "to go forth *(ob)* to meet or hear *(audire)* the word." Thus understood, obedience is first an exercise of faith since it presupposes that a limited human person cannot automatically know what he or she must do by attending to the declarations of the Church or the documents of the religious congregation. It is once again an exercise of faith in the God of the word.

Given this meaning, there exists what I call a first and a second obedience. The first obedience is exercised by the religious order as a whole or by its concrete embodiments in regions or individual communities. From this point of view there is no juridical distinction between superiors and subjects. There is no room for asking what the will of the superior is but only for asking what God's will is. This point may seem obvious but it needs emphasizing. Many crises of obedience and many difficulties that are created by any superior-subject or authority-obedience relationship among human beings come about because the second kind of obedience is too quickly invoked without having taken seriously the first and fundamental level of obedience.

What I call the first obedience is not strictly speaking the object of the vow; it is, however, the reality that will give meaning to the vow. The object of the vow is the second obedience, that is, the relationship set up within religious life between subjects and superior whose will they promise to obey. This will must be understood in the light of all the qualifications, nuances, and reservations set down in the constitutions of the various orders and congregations. The vow, or second obedience, is simply one of the possible ways of giving concrete historical form to the first obedience. The vow thus derives its Christian meaning from its connection with the first obedience, and is not to be understood as something purely mechanical, the repetition of which would be good and salvific in itself.

The vow of obedience supposes a reality that is historical, traditional, and now in force. If this particular way is to be a vehicle of the first obedience, then its exercise must be accompanied by the use of the other means of finding God's will, such as prayer and personal and communal discernment, attention to the signs of the times, an effort to gain an objective knowledge of reality around us, and this both from the theological standpoint and from that of the social sciences.

Taking a vow of obedience is a clear way of showing that one is absolutely serious about seeking the will of God. The purpose of the vow, then, is not to delegate to another human being one's personal responsibility for this search, but rather to assure that in the search one's own judgment will not be swayed by self-interest. The second obedience thus makes no sense without the first, and the first makes no sense unless it seeks some concrete historical means that will make it easier to hear the word of God effectively. For this reason, the vow of obedience, taken in conjunction with other means of seeking God's will, is an exercise of faith in the God of the word.

This understanding of obedience is apostolic. It has to do with God's will for the building of the kingdom. The aim is not simply to know God's will but to put it into practice; the second obedience is a practical way of reaching a decision to act. The passage from an inward looking community to an apostolic body is always mediated by some discipline of obedience.

In this brief explanation of the meaning of the vow of obedience I do not go into the complicated casuistry that has always existed to which is added today the tension felt by some between the lack of obedience to the word of God and the demand for the second obedience. This is perhaps the most serious Christian difficulty in the way of obedience today, although of course, characteristic difficulties still persist and are felt by the religious as an individual who, like every human being, will be tempted to self-assertion, especially as rather inhuman forms of the exercise of authority are still to be found. I want to stress, however, that the vow of obedience is basically an exercise of faith in the God of the word. The exercise of the vow involves both discerning the will of God and carrying it out. In order that this openness to the God of the word not remain at the ideal or sentimental level, concrete means must be adopted that make it possible to hear the word of God at a particular point in history. The vow of obedience sets a seal on one of these means, but the vow must be exercised along with the other means that faith, psychology, and sociology regard as apt for discovering God's will.

This is what I mean by saying that obedience is apostolic and exists for the sake of God's kingdom. This is why the mere fact of obeying another human being has no intrinsic value and why obedience in the concrete is a means whereby the kingdom may really come into existence.

One final clarification is applicable to the Third World: there is a "boom," so to speak, in what I have called the first obedience, an abundance of documents and declarations from religious congregations on what their existence means in the Third World and what their mission there is. At this level the various congregations are exercising the first obedience, which consists in listening to the word of God. The usual difficulty has to do with the coherence, or lack of it, between the word heard in the first obedience and the word demanded in the second. The word that has been heard may pass through so many filters, including the tradition of a given religious order, that it dies the death of a thousand qualifications. Consequently, when there is talk of a crisis in obedience, we must determine at which of the two levels the crisis is felt, and what form the fundamental crisis takes.

Poverty

The vow of poverty has to do with another important area of human life: the possession and use of material goods. A human being is not a pure spirit but a spirit enfleshed. We become human beings through the mediation of the material, and the material mediates our relations with other human beings. The relationship of the person to material things causes that person to develop in a particular way as a spiritual person; the relationship causes human beings to give particular form to their social relationships.

The area covered by the vow of poverty thus includes much more than the juridical determination of how, in accordance with the constitutions of the congregation, the individual may use material things. Expressions of this "more than" are to be found in contemporary thinking about poverty. In virtue of poverty religious are required, for example, to live lives of austerity; to live by their work; to share with the community and with other communities whatever goods they possess.

All these aspects of poverty are important because they fit in with the demands of the human makeup of the religious and with Christian ideals. These aspects, however, do not capture what is most profound in poverty. Its most profound aspect is to be found in the idea of poverty as an exercise of faith in God. Poverty signifies a partiality or partisanship that is not to be taken for granted but that is nonetheless characteristically Christian. Poverty points to God's revelation in behalf of the poor, the revelation of God who "hears the cry of the oppressed," the revelation of God in the poor, "in the captive, the sick, the hungry," the revelation of God to the poor to whom "the Good News is to be preached." However often we may hear these last words nowadays, we must not take them as obvious, for they introduce into the being of God a partiality that, today as in the past, is "a stumbling block to Jews and folly to Gentiles."

In its concrete reality the vow of poverty must first of all relate the religious to the poor. This relationship takes various forms: a real entrance into the world of the poor, effective efforts to change the lot of the poor, a stripping of self in behalf of the poor, a defense of the cause of the poor, a sharing of the lot and destiny of the poor. This relationship to the poor will continually shape the person and life of the religious by demanding and leading to characteristic traits of poverty, such as a lowering of economic and social level and the development of an apostolate that mediately or immediately, but in any case verifiably, works for the poor.

The most important thing religious state in making a vow of poverty today is that they want to make their own the outlook, the cause, and the death of the poor. Precisely in this we find what is called "poverty of spirit." This phrase does not mean simply a detachment of spirit from things we possess, but rather a complete openness to God and availability to him. Once again the God in question is the God of Jesus and not just any divinity whatsoever. Therefore a clear mediation exists for this openness, namely, the poor. This is so because Christian openness to God is not an openness attainable on the basis of inertial human existence. It is an openness that rejects the naturalistic conception of God as power, law, or knowledge. *This* kind of openness is made possible solely by the poor, from the poor Jesus to the oppressed poor of our day. To be open to God (that is, to be poor in spirit) is to have succeeded in opening oneself to God; it is to be converted. According to Christianity, though perhaps not according to other philosophies, the poor alone are the created reality that has power to convert us. The condition for the possibility of religious being poor in spirit and open to God in the midst of material goods, knowledge, and power (things that they will have to a greater or lesser extent and that they never can or should avoid completely) is for them to acquire the outlook of the materially poor and to make their own the cause and destiny of the poor.

All this is very important for religious life in the Third World. Whatever the particular meaning of the vow of poverty in a given congregation (austerity, use of things with permission, disposition of possessions only for purposes of the apostolate) the most important thing religious do when they publicly vow poverty is to declare themselves in solidarity with the cause of the poor. When this element is lacking, poverty becomes a form of infantilism, a matter of juridical fictions, or worse, a bit of sad irony.

Conclusion

In this short analysis of the vows I have tried to view them in broad terms, to not reduce them to a single known function (already known at the juridical and canonical level), to relate them to key areas in the life of every Christian and therefore of every religious. This approach makes it possible to concretize in a given historical situation what is most important in each of the vows. I have thus tried to explain the meaning that the three symbols, poverty, chastity, and obedience, ought to have in our day.

By not reducing the vows to a specific and predetermined function, I am also saying that they enjoy no autonomy in themselves. The taking of the three vows is simply an expression of a readiness to give these three areas of life a Christian form. The vows correspond to structural areas of a Christian's life and provide structural channels through which the person can grow (or decrease) in Christianity; they are structural ways of becoming Christian. I have tried to point out the way in which the vows are channels and how they make possible growth in Christianity.

The three vows display a theological character that goes beyond that which has been attributed to sacrifice. Because God is love and always greater, because he is partisan and has a specific will that is made known through his word, the vows provide structural ways of growth in faith.

The three vows are ways of following Jesus. They make it possible for us to do what Jesus did as he did it by providing us with the freedom and detachment to live the beatitudes at our moment in history, to live the prophetic role of Jesus, and to act as he did for justice and the building of the kingdom.

Because of their theological character and because they are a historical following of Jesus, the vows have what has traditionally been called eschatological and apostolic dimensions. This duality is characteristic of any Christian life and manifests itself also in the vows. Here, however, the form it takes is not parallel to that in other modes of Christian life. The historical practice of the following of Jesus makes possible a growth in the theological dimension and thus in eschatological existence.

The vows are ways of relating the religious not to "things" (one's own body, material goods, one's own will) but to other persons. I am not denying that religious attain to perfection as individuals; I am saying rather that they do so to the extent that through the vows they help others to perfection or, to put it differently, they help build the kingdom of God. Applied to our world, the vows are structural channels that lead the religious to the Servant of Yahweh. If the religious grows in painful self-giving to others, in work for justice, and in the hope of liberation, then the vows have proved themselves really able to turn human beings into Christians, and religious life will continue to be a possibility and a great aid to the entire Church.

Notes

1. THEOLOGICAL UNDERSTANDING IN EUROPEAN AND LATIN AMERICAN THEOLOGY

This essay is a revision of a paper read at the Encuentro Latinoamericano de Teología (Mexico City, August 11–15, 1975). It was published in the acts of the meeting (*Liberación y cautiverio: Debates en torno al método de la teología en América Latina,* ed. E. Ruiz Maldonado [Mexico City: Organizing Committee, 1976], pp. 177–207). The contrast drawn here between two ways of doing theology may seem overly sharp. I omit the conversation that ensued with some European theologians who are closer in their views to Latin American theology than to the progressivist theology of Central Europe. I do not analyze the limitations of Latin American theology; this was done in another paper at the same meeting.

If I include this essay in a book on the basic problems of the Church in Latin America, it is not chiefly because I consider theology to be one of these problems. Rather, I hope that the essay will help the reader to evaluate correctly both the concern that moves us to tackle these problems and the way in which they are approached. This essay includes indirectly the points that I regard as fundamental to the christology that guides my thinking on the Church.

1. "What Is Enlightenment?" in *The Philosophy of Kant: Immanuel Kant's Moral and Political Writings,* ed. Carl J. Friedrich (New York: Modern Library, 1949), p. 132.

2. Ibid.

3. Cf. Rudolf Bultmann, et al., *Kerygma and Myth: A Theological Debate,* ed. Hans Werner Bartsch, rev. and trans. Reginald H. Fuller (New York: Harper & Row, 1961), p. 49.

4. A discussion of contemporary Protestant thinking from the perspective of the theology of liberation is provided by Rubem Alves in *Cristianismo: ¿Opio o liberación?* (Salamanca: Sígueme, 1973); Eng. original: *A Theology of Human Hope* (Washington, D.C.: Corpus Books, 1969).

5. Wolfhart Pannenberg, *Grundfragen systematischer Theologie*, 2 vols. (Göttingen: G. Mohn, 1967), 2:291. English translation by G. H. Kehm, *Basic Questions in Theology* 2 (Philadelphia: Fortress Press, 1971.)

6. Pannenberg, "Wie wahr ist das Reden von Gott?" *EvKomm* 4 (1971): 631.

7. Pannenberg, "Zur Theologie des Rechtes," *ZEE* 7 (1963): 8–9.

8. Pannenberg, "The Revelation of God in Jesus of Nazareth," in *Theology as History,* ed. J. M. Robinson (New York: Harper & Row, 1967), p. 133.

9. Pannenberg, *Basic Questions in Theology,* 1:50.

10. Ibid., 1:53.

11. Pannenberg, *Theology and the Philosophy of Science,* trans. Francis McDonagh (Philadelphia: Westminster Press, 1976), p. 157.

12. Ibid., p. 409, n. 769.

13. There is a good description of the historical and theological genesis of the concern that motivates the theology of liberation in Gustavo Gutiérrez, "Evangelio y praxis de la liberación," in *Fe cristiana y cambio social en América Latina* (Salamanca: Sígueme, 1973), pp. 231–45. See also "Liberation Praxis and Christian Faith," Chapter 3 in *The Power of the Poor in History,* trans. Robert R. Barr (Maryknoll, N.Y.: Orbis Books, 1983).

14. Claude Geffré, "A Prophetic Theology," in *The Mystical and Political Dimension of the Christian Faith,* ed. C. Geffré and G. Gutiérrez, Concilium 96 (New York: Seabury, 1974), p. 9.

15. Ibid.

16. Cf. Juan Luis Segundo, "Teología y ciencias sociales," in *Fe cristiana y cambio social,* pp. 285–95; Ignacio Ellacuría, "Tesis sobre la posibilidad, necesidad y sentido de una teología latinoamericana," in *Teología y mundo contemporáneo,* Homage to Karl Rahner (Madrid: Cristiandad, 1975), pp. 336–50.

17. Cf., J. L. Segundo, *The Liberation of Theology,* trans. John Drury (Maryknoll, N.Y.: Orbis Books, 1976); Hugo Assmann, *Teología desde la praxis de la liberación* (Salamanca: Sígueme, 1973), pp. 171–245. [This section is not included in the English translation, *Theology for a Nomad Church,* trans. P. Burns (Maryknoll, N.Y.: Orbis Books, 1975)—Trans.]

18. Cf. Gustavo Gutiérrez, *A Theology of Liberation,* trans. Sr. Caridad Inda and John Eagleson (Maryknoll, N.Y.: Orbis Books, 1973), pp. 155–220.

19. Cf. Juan Carlos Scannone, "The Theology of Liberation: Evangelic or Ideological?" in *Jesus Christ and Human Liberation,* ed. E. Schillebeeckx and B. Van Iersel, Concilium 93 (New York: Seabury, 1974), pp. 147–56.

20. Cf. Ignacio Ellacuría, "Hacia una fundamentación filosófica del método teológico latinoamericana," in *Liberación y cautiverio.*

21. In Europe Bonhoeffer had written of the following of Jesus in his *The Cost of Discipleship* (1937), 2nd ed., trans. R. H. Fuller and I. Booth (New York: Macmillan, 1963). Cf. also Hans Urs von Balthasar, "Who Is the Church?" in *Church and World,* trans. A. V. Littledale and A. Dru (New York: Herder and Herder, 1967), pp. 112–65, and Jürgen Moltmann, *The Crucified God: The Cross of Christ as the Foundation and Criticism of Theology,* trans. R. Z. Wilson and J. Bowden (New York: Harper & Row, 1974), pp. 53–65. The theme of the following of Jesus as the practice of christological understanding has been absent from many of the great systematic christologies such as Paul Tillich's *Systematic Theology,* vol. 2, *Existence and the Christ* (Chicago: University of Chicago Press, 1951), or Wolfhart Pannenberg, *Jesus, God and Man,* 2nd ed., trans. L. L. Wilkens and D. A. Priebe (Philadelphia: Fortress Press, 1977). In the two large volumes of *Mysterium Salutis* III (Einsiedeln: Benziger, 1969), which are devoted to christology, there are few references to the following of Jesus and none to this following as a mode of theological understanding.

22. Cf. D. Wiederkehr, *Mysterium Salutis* III/2, pp. 560–61; Pannenberg, *Jesus, God and Man,* pp. 115ff.

23. European theology has of course developed a practical conception of faith. Cf. J. B. Metz, *Theology of the World,* trans. W. Glen-Doepfel (New York: Seabury, 1969); Edward Schillebeeckx, *The Understanding of Faith: Interpretation and Criticism,* trans. N. D. Smith (New York: Seabury, 1974); and various writings of Moltmann: "The Cross and Political Religion," in J. Moltmann et al., *Religion and Political Society* (New York: Harper & Row, 1974), pp. 9–47; "Evangelio" in his *Esperanza y planificación del futuro* (Salamanca: Sígueme, 1971), pp. 215–44, Eng. trans., *Hope and Planning,* trans. M. Clarkson (New York: Harper & Row, and London: SCM, 1971); *The Crucified God,* pp. 317–40.

The fundamental criticism voiced by the theology of liberation is that the European theology of practice continues to be too abstract; that is, it remains a matter of thinking rather than of doing. For criticism of Moltmann, cf. Assmann, *Theology for a Nomad Church,* p. 94; Gutiérrez, *A Theology of Liberation,* pp. 182, n. 41, and 216–18; Enrique Dussel, "Domination-Liberation: A New Approach," in Concilium 96, pp. 52–53, and especially Alves, *Cristianismo.* On the other hand, a positive influence of the theology of liberation is discernible in Moltmann's latest book, *The Crucified God.*

24. Cf. Barth's radical position in *The Epistle to the Romans,* trans. E. C. Hoskyns (London: Oxford University Press, 1933), and *Nein! Ein*

Antwort an Emil Brunner, Theologische Existenz heute 14 (Munich, 1934), and his more nuanced position in *Church Dogmatics,* vol. 1, *The Doctrine of God,* trans. T. H. L. Parker et al. (Edinburgh: T. and T. Clark, 1957).

25. Rudolf Bultmann, *Glauben und Verstehen,* vol. 2, 5th ed. (Tübingen: Mohn, 1968), pp. 117-32; Eng. trans. *Faith and Understanding,* ed. Robert R. Funk, trans. Louise Smith (New York: Harper & Row, 1969).

26. Dietrich Bonhoeffer, *Letters and Papers from Prison,* rev. and enlarged ed., trans. R. H. Fuller (New York: Macmillan, 1967).

27. Moltmann, *Hope and Planning,* pp. 3-30; and *Man: Christian Anthropology in the Conflicts of the Present,* trans. J. Sturdy (Philadelphia: Fortress Press, 1974), pp. 105-17.

28. Pannenberg, *Basic Questions in Theology,* 2:65-119; *What Is Man? Contemporary Anthropology in Theological Perspective,* trans. D. A. Priebe (Philadelphia: Fortress Press, 1970), pp. 1-40.

29. Cf. José P. Miranda, *Marx and the Bible: A Critique of the Philosophy of Oppression,* trans. John Eagleson (Maryknoll, N.Y.: Orbis Books, 1974), pp. 44-67.

30. Cf. Dussel, "Domination-Liberation," pp. 40-42.

31. Cf. J. L. Segundo, "Capitalism-Socialism: The Theological Crux," in Concilium 96, pp. 105-23.

32. Leonardo Boff, "Salvation in Jesus Christ and the Process of Liberation," in Concilium 96, p. 90.

33. Hugo Assmann, "Conciencia cristiana y situaciones extremas en el cambio social," in *Fe cristiana y cambio social,* pp. 335-43; C. Padín, "La transformación humana del tercer mundo, exigencia de conversión," in *Fe cristiana,* pp. 265-81.

34. Cf. Dussel, "Domination-Liberation," pp. 48-49.

2. THE PROMOTION OF JUSTICE AS AN ESSENTIAL REQUIREMENT OF THE GOSPEL MESSAGE: SYSTEMATIC REFLECTIONS

This paper was read at the Society of Jesus' Eighth International Congress of Ecumenism (Barcelona, August 25-31, 1979). The paper was first published in *ECA* 33 (1979): 779-92. Although the general theme of the Congress was strictly ecclesial, that is, it dealt with ecumenism in the Churches, the article concentrates on a basic problem of Christian life and practice. It refers indirectly to ecclesial life and practice insofar as these are Christian, and thus offers help in correctly orienting ecumenism on the basis of its own fundamental presuppositions.

1. Jon Sobrino, "Una visión latinoamericana del ecumenismo," *ECA* 31 (1977): 830–31.

2. In this paper I shall concentrate on the positive and unifying potential of the promotion of justice. This very promotion divides the Church internally and divides the various Churches among themselves. On this point, see my article "La unidad y el conflicto dentro de la Iglesia," *ECA* 32 (1978): 787–804 [translated as Chapter 7 of this book].

3. Karl Rahner, too, though from a different viewpoint, calls attention to the dangers of this reduction; cf. his *Foundations of Christian Faith: An Introduction to the Idea of Christianity,* trans. W. V. Dych (New York: Crossroad, 1978), p. 13.

4. Cf. Edward Schillebeeckx, *Jesus: An Experiment in Christology,* trans. H. Hoskins (New York: Crossroad, 1979), p. 103.

5. The "kingdom of God," formally defined, is "the reign of God in action"; materially defined, it is "the ideal of the king of righteousness." For these definitions, see Joachim Jeremias, *New Testament Theology: The Proclamation of Jesus,* trans. J. Bowden (New York: Scribner's, 1971), vol. 1, p. 98.

6. Cf. Oscar Cullmann, *Jesus and the Revolutionaries,* trans. G. Putnam (New York: Harper & Row, 1970), pp. 24ff.

7. Cf. Ignacio Ellacuría, "Fe y justicia," *Christus* 42 (Mexico) (1977): 23–24; Jon Sobrino, *Christology at the Crossroads: A Latin-American Approach,* trans. John Drury (Maryknoll, N.Y.: Orbis Books, 1978), pp. 170–74.

8. Cf. José I. González Faus, *Acceso a Jesús: Ensayo de teología narrativa* (Salamanca: Sígueme, 1978), pp. 172–80.

9. Cf. Carlos Escudero Freire, *Devolver el evangelio a los pobres* (Salamanca: Sígueme, 1978).

10. Cf. P. Benoit, M.-E. Boismard, and J. L. Malillos, *Sinopsis de los cuatro evangelios* 2 (Bilbao: Desclée de Brouwer, 1977), pp. 96–110, 215–17, 333–37. Original French, *Synopse des quatre évangiles* (Paris: Cerf, 1972).

11. Cf. Hugo Assmann, "Tecnología y poder en la perspectiva de la teología de la liberación," in *Tecnología y necesidades básicas* (San José: DEI, 1979), pp. 29–44, and "Technology and Power in Liberation Theology," *Theology Digest* 28 (1980): 239–243.

12. Gustavo Gutiérrez, *Teología desde el reverso de la historia* (Lima: CEP, 1979), pp. 23–59; Eng., "Theology from the Underside of History," in *The Power of the Poor in History,* trans. Robert R. Barr (Maryknoll, N.Y.: Orbis Books, 1983), pp. 169–221.

13. I have not given examples for the various points I have made. I make an exception here and note that persecution and martyrdom are wide-

spread in the Churches of Latin America as a response to the promotion of justice. The Puebla Document recognizes this fact, although it does so with a certain timidity; cf. 92, 265, 668, 1138.

14. Even the practice of justice is, of course, historically open to disordered desire and is subject to the risks inherent in any historical way of responding to the gospel. There can be no denying this, any more than it can be denied, for example, that the way of the contemplative life has, along with its positive values, its disordered affectivity and dangers. My effort has been to describe the positive values to which the way of justice can give rise.

15. Cf. Ignacio Ellacuría, "Fe y justicia," *Christus* 42 (Mexico), August 1977, pp. 26-33, and October 1977, pp. 19-34; Miranda, *Marx and the Bible;* idem, *Being and the Messiah: The Message of St. John,* trans. John Eagleson (Maryknoll, N.Y.: Orbis Books, 1977); José Alonso Díaz, "Términos bíblicos de justicia social y traducción de 'equivalencia dinámica,' " *Estudios Eclesiasticos* 51 (1976): 95-128; José Míguez Bonino, *La fe en busca de eficacia: Una interpretatión de la reflexion latinoamericana de la liberación* (Salamanca: Sígueme, 1977); Gutiérrez, *A Theology of Liberation,* especially pp. 194-285; Jon Sobrino, "La vida religiosa a partir de la Congregación General XXXII de la Compañia de Jesús," *Diakonia,* Supplement 1 (May 1978): 49-70 [partially translated as Chapter 3 of this book]; W. Kerber, K. Rahner, and H. Zwiefelhofer, *Glaube und Gerechtigkeit* (Munich, 1976); J. C. Haughey, ed., *The Faith That Does Justice* (New York: Paulist Press, 1977).

16. Cf. Leonardo Boff, *La experiencia de Dios* (Bogotá: Indo-American Press Service, 1975), pp. 35-44.

17. Rahner, *Foundations of Christian Faith,* p. 297.

18. Moltmann, *Hope and Planning,* pp. 45-46.

19. J. B. Metz, "Unbelief as a Theological Problem," in *The Church and the World,* Concilium 6 (New York: Seabury, 1965).

20. M. Horkheimer, *Die Dehnsucht nach dem ganz Anderen: Ein Interview mit Komentar von H. Gumnior* (Hamburg, 1970), p. 62.

21. Decree on Ecumenism, in *Vatican Council II: The Conciliar and Postconciliar Documents,* ed. A. Flannery (Collegeville, Minn.: Liturgical Press, 1974), p. 462, n. 11.

22. Declaration "Jesuits Today," no. 8 in *Documents of the Thirty-first and Thirty-second General Congregations of the Society of Jesus,* ed. and trans. J. W. Padberg (Saint Louis: Institute of Jesuit Studies, 1977), p. 403.

3. THE SERVICE OF FAITH AND THE PROMOTION OF JUSTICE

This essay is part of the lengthier study, "La vida religiosa a partir de la Congregación General XXXII de la Compañia de Jesús" (Supplement to *Diakonia,* May 1978, pp. 49–70). It elucidates the theoretical and practical difficulties attending the new definition of the mission of the Society of Jesus as "the service of faith and the promotion of justice"; to show that this bipartite formulation expresses what is most characteristic of Christian existence; and to emphasize the importance of such a mission for the renewal of religious life in the Society. Although these reflections are addressed directly to the Jesuits working in the special circumstances of Central America, I think they are valid for religious life in general and for every form of Christian life.

1. Cf. *Documents of the Thirty-first and Thirty-second General Congregations of the Society of Jesus.* The decrees are cited in this chapter by number and paragraph; e.g. 2:11 means second decree, para. 11. The second decree is entitled "Jesuits Today"; the fourth, "Our Mission Today: The Service of Faith and the Promotion of Justice."

4. THE CHURCH OF THE POOR: RESURRECTION OF THE TRUE CHURCH

This essay is a revision of one published earlier in *Cruz y resurrección: Presencia y anuncio de una Iglesia nueva* (Mexico City: CRT, 1978), pp. 82–159. Its title was "Resurrección de una Iglesia popular." It may be helpful to recall the context in which the essay was originally written. In connection with Puebla many writings were published by theologians and basic ecclesial communities which called for "a Church of the people," "a Church born of the people," or "a Church of the poor." CELAM and its official theologians carried on a campaign of disparagement against everything that could be called a "Church of the people." The book in which my essay appeared was intended to be a theological analysis of the "Church of the people" idea and was an effort to move beyond a purely sociological approach to the subject. It was this sociological approach on which the campaign against the notion was focused and which was the object of its attack.

In that context my essay aims to show that the Church of the poor is a "true" Church because it manifests the root of ecclesiality or, in other words, the substance of Churchness according to the faith. But the purpose of the essay is also to show theologically that this new way of being Church is "truer" than others. For this reason, the rise of the Church of the poor is seen as a resurrection of the Church. As a concrete way of going about my task I have chosen to justify the Church of the poor on the basis of the traditional four marks of the true Church. But in approaching the four marks of the true Church from the vantage point of the poor, we find that they cease to be abstract and really serve to identify the true Church.

1. Gutiérrez, "Theology from the Underside of History," in *Power of the Poor,* p. 211.

2. Karl Rahner, in *Christologie, systematisch und exegetisch,* Karl Rahner and Wilhelm Thüsing (Freiburg: Herder, 1972), p. 38.

3. Jürgen Moltmann, *The Church in the Power of the Spirit: A Contribution to Messianic Eschatology,* trans. M. Kohl (New York: Harper & Row, 1977), p. 98.

4. Cf. B. Klappert, *Diskussion um Kreuz und Auferstehung* (Wuppertal: Aussaat, 1967), pp. 40-52, where he shows the various aspects of Christ's resurrection that have a bearing on Christian existence.

5. Julio de Santa Ana, *Good News to the Poor: The Challenge of the Poor in the History of the Church,* trans. H. Whittle (Maryknoll, N.Y.: Orbis Books, 1979).

6. Ibid., p. 39.

7. I have attempted this kind of historical study in remarks on the passage at the beginning of the Church's history from a Christian existence based on the following of Jesus to a different kind of Christian existence based more one-sidedly on the risen Christ; cf. my *Christology at the Crossroads,* pp. 273-310.

8. Cf. Chapter 2 of the Dogmatic Decree on the Church *(Lumen gentium),* especially no. 12.

9. Cf. Yves Congar, "The Church: The People of God," in *The Church and Mankind*, ed. E. Schillebeeckx, Concilium 1 (New York: Seabury, 1965), pp. 11-38; Hans Küng, *The Church,* trans. R. and R. Ockenden (New York: Sheed and Ward, 1967), pp. 107-50; M.-D. Chenu, "Vatican II and the Church of the Poor," in *The Poor and the Church,* ed. N. Greinacher and A. Muller, Concilium 104 (New York: Seabury, 1977), pp. 56-61.

10. Jürgen Moltmann, *La Iglesia, fuerza del Espíritu* (Salamanca: Sígueme, 1978), p. 413. [I have translated from the Spanish edition here because it differs significantly from the English, which adds a second "not": "The Church is not yet sanctified by poverty if it does not become 'the church for the poor' and especially honors alms given for the poor": *The Church in the Power of the Spirit,* p. 356—Trans.]

11. Ignacio Ellacuría, "La Iglesia de los pobres, sacramento histórico de liberación," *ECA* 31 (1977): 717.

12. Ibid.

13. I cannot stop here to analyze the theological meaning of "poor." For this cf. Gutiérrez, *A Theology of Liberation,* pp. 287-306; the whole of *The Poor and the Church,* Concilium 104; *ECA* 31 (1977) on the Church in Latin America.

14. Ellacuría, "La Iglesia de los pobres," p. 717.

15. Cf. Sobrino, *Christology at the Crossroads,* pp. 226-72.

16. DS 150.

17. DS 3013: "To the Catholic Church alone belong all the many and wonderful qualities arranged by God to make perfectly clear the credibility of the Christian faith. The Church by its very nature—that is, by reason of its marvelous spread, its outstanding holiness and inexhaustible fruitfulness in every kind of good, its catholic unity and unshakeable stability—is a great and permanent motive of credibility and an unassailable testimony to its divine mission."

In its *Dogmatic Constitution on the Church of Christ,* Vatican I argues in a different way. An internal structure of the Church, namely, "the sacred apostolic primacy on which the strength and stability of the entire Church is based," is expressly mentioned "in order that [the Catholic Church] may be believed and maintained by all the faithful" (DS 3052). [I have translated DS 3052 here according to the author's interpretation of it in his Spanish version. The words "in order that . . . faithful" seem to represent the Latin (*doctrinam*) *cunctis fidelibus credendam et tenendam*—Trans.]

18. Küng, *The Church,* p. 269.

19. I shall briefly present the way the marks are treated by H. Küng and J. Moltmann in the works cited. The main point of summarizing their analyses is to restore history to its rightful place as a source of proof of the Church and to reestablish the historical form which the marks of the Church must take if the Church is to be true.

20. Moltmann, *The Church in the Power of the Spirit,* p. 126.

21. It is no accident that the Church of the poor has given rise to basic communities and that these understand themselves differently than is customary in the First World. The key point about the basic communities is that they form the real—sociological and material—base of the Church and the people. They are basic not because they are "different" but because they are of the people. For this reason they show, from the base of the pyramid, how all are to become part of the Church of the poor.

22. Unification is not a matter simply of convoking and assembling Christians. Only the Word, which evokes and challenges, effects true

unity; cf. Leonardo Boff, *Los sacramentos de la vida,* 3rd ed. (Salamanca: Sígueme, 1980), pp. 14ff.

23. Ellacuría makes this acute observation: "A bishop apart from his local Church is a bishop cut off from the body of the local Church; consequently he is not a bishop of this Church however much he may have received episcopal consecration and a jurisdictional mandate which he does not carry out": "Entre Medellín y Puebla," *ECA* 32 (1978): 121. With the example of Archbishop Romero before me, I recently sketched a portrait of a bishop of the Church of the poor: "Mons. Romero, mártir de la liberación: Análisis teológico de su figura y su obra," *ECA* 35 (1980): 253–76. More specifically, I developed the idea of the bishop as the real symbol of a diocese and therefore as unifier and expression of unity (pp. 264–65).

24. Cf. J. Sobrino, "La unidad y el conflicto dentro de la Iglesia," *ECA* 32 (Oct.-Nov. 1977): 771–86 (translated as Chapter 7 of this book).

25. Küng, *The Church,* pp. 320ff.

26. Moltmann, *The Crucified God,* pp. 343ff.

27. Still valid are Karl Rahner's reflections on the intrinsic necessity of the Church being holy, in his *The Church and the Sacraments,* trans. W. J. O'Hara, Quaestiones Disputatae 9 (New York: Seabury, 1963), pp. 11–19. So are his thoughts on the sinfulness of the Church as such and not simply of the Church as having members who are sinners: "The Church of Sinners," in *Theological Investigations* 6, trans. K.-H. and B. Kruger (Baltimore: Helicon, 1969), pp. 253–69.

28. Cf. E. Dussel, *America Latina en la historia de la salvación* (Barcelona: Nova Terra, 1972), and the CEHILA project of writing the history of the Church in terms of the poor. Such an approach is in strong contrast to most histories of the Church in Latin America and elsewhere, which are written basically in terms of the exercise of ecclesial or political power.

29. Cf. Gutiérrez, "Theology from the Underside of History," pp. 200–201; Roberto Oliveros Maqueo, *Liberación y teología: Genesis y crecimiento de una reflexión, 1966–1976* (Mexico City: CRT, 1977), pp. 101ff.

30. Gutiérrez, "Theology from the Underside of History," p. 199.

31. Neither does it attempt to deny the truths and general directives proposed by the universal magisterium; rather it aims at making these real by concretizing them. Therefore, and rightly, the Preparatory Document for Puebla was subjected to a good deal of harsh criticism precisely because it tried to impose an ecclesial universalism that was not concretized in the local Latin American Church. Cf. E. Dussel, "Sobre el 'Documento de Consulta' para Puebla," *Christus* 43 (Mexico) (1978): 55f.; I. Ellacuría, "Entre Medellín y Puebla," pp. 123f.; Roberto Rivero Mendizábal, "Re-

flexión cristiana. De Medellín a Puebla," *Diálogo* 8 (Guatemala) (1978):16ff.

32. *Lumen gentium,* in *The Documents of Vatican II,* ed. W. M. Abbott (New York: Guild Press, 1966), p. 15, no. 1 (italics added).

33. In response to the memorandum of a hundred German theologians in favor of the theology of liberation, a Latin American priest wrote to Karl Rahner and in doing so brought out the new meaning of catholicity: "When you in Germany support this theology you are bringing life and hope to the lowly who courageously suffer, hope, and struggle and who are members of the same body to which you belong. We thank you from our hearts, Father Rahner, for this moral support. I tell you from experience that when a person feels weak and threatened, he becomes more sensitive to brotherly affection," *Diálogo* 8 (Guatemala) (1978): 36.

34. Cf. Sobrino, "Una visión latinoamericana del ecumenismo," *ECA* 31 (1977): 30f.

35. An example of Church unity based on general truths and not created from below can be seen in Alfonso López Trujillo, *Teología liberadora en América Latina* (Bogotá: Paulinas, 1974), pp. 73ff.

36. Trans. in *The Pope Speaks* 21 (1976): 10–11.

37. Gutiérrez, "Theology from the Underside of History," p. 200.

38. Ibid., pp. 200–201.

39. I have developed these thoughts in "Evangelización e Iglesia en America Latina," *ECA,* 31 (1977):723–48 (translated as Chapter 9 of this book); "Iglesia y evangelización en el Tercer Mundo," *Búsqueda* 5 (San Salvador) (1977): 7–31.

40. Gutiérrez, "Theology from the Underside of History," p. 207.

41. Jeremias, *New Testament Theology,* vol. 1, p. 116.

42. Carlos Escudero Freire, *Devolver el Evangelio a los pobres,* p. 270.

43. Ibid., p. 273.

44. Cf. Gutiérrez, "Theology from the Underside of History," p. 208: "Hunger and justice are not just economic and social questions; they are global questions, and they challenge our way of living the faith in its very roots." An inestimable contribution of the poor in the Church has been to show that a misnamed "secular" practice can be combined with the practice of the faith. Cf. J. I. González Faus, "La declaración de la Comisión Teológica Internacional sobre la teología de la liberación," *Christus* 43 (Mexico) (1978): 8–22.

45. Gutiérrez, "Theology from the Underside of History," p. 208.

46. This concretization supposes a break and a qualitative leap. Given the many efforts at renewing the Church after Vatican II, we must apply to the renewal of the Church what Gutiérrez says about the renewal of theology: "Any attempt to make progress in theology apart from the hope

of the poor—a hope from within their world and in their own terms—could gain a little here and a little there, perhaps, but would not give us the quantum leap we are looking for," ibid., p. 201.

47. The correct "hierarchization" of the marks of the Church is an academic problem, but it is also a practical one. The ecclesiology emanating from CELAM stresses Church unity, communion, and participation, and makes apostolicity in the form of mission a secondary matter. The Church of the poor, however, gives first place to the apostolate of the Church, that is, to its mission. From this vantage point it determines in what concretely the holiness of the Church should consist, and brings about the unity of the Church in this and not in any other way. Because this mission is utterly concrete it also prescribes the correct form to be taken by the tension, involved in catholicity, between "local" Church and "universal" Church.

48. Cf. the classical treatment by I. Salaverri, *Sacrae theologiae summa* 1 (Madrid, 1958), pp. 891–950, which ignores the historical form that basic ecclesiality must take if the Church is to be true.

49. This raises a basic problem which I cannot go into here. The question is whether an ecclesiology can be purely a priori in form or whether it must not include as an essential part a "story" about the Church. To put it another way, the question is whether there be an ecclesiology that does not necessarily bring in the history of the Church. To the extent, of course, that this history is one of sinfulness it will not be normative for the construction of an ecclesiology. But insofar as it is a history of grace, it presents us with something new that cannot be thought out a priori in its concreteness. The ultimate criterion for the truth of the Church is whether the story of its history sounds like the story of the history of Jesus. Ecclesiology will, moreover, be constantly forced to lay hold anew of the truth of what is narrated in order to make this historical criterion of truth, until a new action on the part of the Spirit of Jesus causes the history of the Church to be told in a different way and gives the criterion of truth a new concrete form.

50. Ellacuría, "Entre Medellín y Puebla," p. 126. A sociological description to go along with the theological description of the two forms of Churchness may be found in R. Muñoz, "The Function of the Poor in the Church," in *The Poor and the Church,* Concilium 104, p. 82: "On the one side, there is the model of the 'great institutional' Church, with its sociological and cultural center outside the world of the poor, in the rich sectors of the country and the rich nations of the world; a Church that values discipline more and seeks greater functional cohesion; that practices organized aid to the poor; a Church with the power to negotiate with political and military authorities and exercise some pressure on them in order to obtain an amelioration of the social conditions brought about by the re-

gime; a Church that teaches doctrine with authority and can make itself heard through the mass media of communication.

"The other model is that of the 'communications-network' Church, with its sociological and cultural center in the world of the poor, among the poor who make up the bulk of the population of this country and of the poor countries of the world; a Church that values fraternity more and looks for a greater sharing of responsibility; that lives and preaches solidarity in the midst of the people, fulfilling its role of prophetic denunciation of injustice, discreetly maybe, but still accepting the concomitant risks, so as to awaken a consciousness of their dignity in the poor together with hope for a better world; a Church that, in and from the world of the poor, seeks to bear witness to the Gospel, generally without disposing of any means of communication beyond person-to-person contact."

51. In this chapter I have offered a theological analysis of the historical marks of the Church. There is still need of showing how this historical channel of the Church of the poor also makes it possible to live the transcendental aspect of the Christian faith as faith in God. This I shall do in the next chapter.

5. THE EXPERIENCE OF GOD IN THE CHURCH OF THE POOR

This chapter was a paper read at a theological symposium held at Marquette University (Milwaukee, March 29–31, 1979) in honor of the seventy-fifth birthday of Karl Rahner. This explains why the essay makes references to the theology of Karl Rahner and to what I consider a basic point in his thinking: the relation of humankind to the mystery of God. My purpose in discussing this theme from the vantage point of the Church of the poor is a positive one, inasmuch as no Church can avoid explicitly confronting this important theme. But my purpose is also polemical: The Church of the poor has been accused of a reductive horizontalism, and I want to show that the best Christian possibility of experiencing God is to be found in a Church of the poor.

1. Karl Rahner, "Questions of Fundamental Theology and Theological Method," in *Theological Investigations* 5, trans. K.-H. Kruger (Baltimore: Helicon, 1966), p. 6.

2. Karl Rahner, "The Need for a Short Formula of Christian Faith," in *Theological Investigations* 9, trans. Graham Harrison (New York: Seabury, 1972), p. 122.

3. Rahner, *Foundations of Christian Faith,* p. 13.

4. Ibid., pp. 51–52.

5. It is true that liberation theology has not given as much attention to the theme of God as to other themes. It is also true that when it has done so, it has tended to concentrate on reflections concerning the knowledge of God and the practice of justice. See, for example, Miranda, *Marx and the Bible.* Nevertheless, from its very beginnings liberation theology has preserved the dimension of the mystery of God as mystery, even if it has done so in the context of an examination of the spirituality of liberation rather than in the context of a systematic study of God. See, for example, Gutiérrez, *A Theology of Liberation,* pp. 189–208; Boff, *La experiencia de Dios.*

6. Rahner, *Foundations of Christian Faith,* p. 12. For the different pastoral perspective, in a profound sense, of European and Latin American theology, see J. Sobrino, "El conocimiento teológico en la teología europea y latinoamericana," *ECA* 29 (1975):427–34.

7. This was the fundamental goal of my previous work, *Christology at the Crossroads,* especially pp. 41–235.

8. Leonardo Boff, *Jesus Christ Liberator,* trans. Patrick Hughes (Maryknoll, N.Y.: Orbis Books), p. 113.

9. Rahner (*Foundations of Christian Faith,* p. 343) also presents this truth generically: "By the very nature of man and by the very nature of God, and by the very nature of the relationship between man and God when God is understood correctly, the social dimension cannot be excluded from the essence of religion. It belongs to it because man in all of his dimensions is related to the one God who saves the whole person. Otherwise religion would become merely a private affair of man and would cease to be religion." He comes even closer to the intention of my own reflections when he states (ibid., p. 389): "No one develops and unfolds from out of the purely formal and antecedent structure of his essence. Rather, he receives the concreteness of his life from a community of persons, from intercommunication, from an objective spirit, from a history, from a people and from a family, and he develops it only within this community, and this includes what is most personal and most proper to himself. This is also true for salvation and for the Christian religion, and for the Christianity of the individual."

10. I do not mean to belittle in any way the contribution of Vatican II to an understanding of the Church as the people of God. One may even find in the Vatican II documents references to the poor as the privileged within the Church and to the persecution that characterizes the status of the Church as a pilgrim (e.g., *Lumen gentium,* 8). However, the Council did not attempt to restructure the Church around these truths. In his excellent and now classic study of the Church as the people of God, Yves Congar ("The Church: The People of God," pp. 11–37) shows the uses and the limitations of this concept in the Second Vatican Council. Thus, for exam-

ple, God is said to have saved his people from Egypt, but the oppressed whose cries reached God are not mentioned (ibid., pp. 20–21). Likewise, the inequality that exists within the people of God is said to be organic and functional, so that in effect certain benefits accrue to the entire people of God. However, social inequality is not mentioned, so that the partiality of God with respect to his people does not appear (ibid., pp. 21–22).

11. On the Church of the poor, see Francisco Soto, ed., *Cruz y resurrección: Presencia y anuncio de una Iglesia nueva* (Mexico: CRT, 1978); Gutiérrez, "Theology from the Underside of History"; *Iglesia de los pobres y organizaciones populares* (San Salvador: UCA Editores, 1979); *ECA* 31 (1977), issues devoted to the state of the Church in Latin America; Gutiérrez, "The Poor in the Church" and R. Muñoz, "The Function of the Poor in the Church," in *The Poor and the Church,* Concilium 104, pp. 11–16, 80–87. On declarations of Latin American episcopates that reflect this type of theology, see *Los obispos latinoamericanos entre Medellín y Puebla* (San Salvador: UCA Editores, 1978).

12. For a theological analysis of what is meant by "the poor" in Latin America, see Gutiérrez, *A Theology of Liberation*, pp. 287–302; Ignacio Ellacuría, "Las bienaventuranzas como carta fundacional de la Iglesia de los pobres," in *Iglesia de los pobres y organizaciones populares*, pp. 105–18.

13. John Eagleson and Philip Scharper, eds., *Puebla and Beyond: Documentation and Commentary*, trans. John Drury (Maryknoll, N.Y.: Orbis Books, 1979), The Final Document, 32–39.

14. Ibid., 1142.

15. The document cited above in n. 14 attempts to do this in 1141–44, 1148–52.

16. According to Joachim Jeremias (*New Testament Theology*, vol. 1, p. 116) the good news was directed "to the poor alone."

17. Gutiérrez, "Theology from the Underside of History," pp. 201 ff.

18. Ellacuría, "Las bienaventuranzas," p. 177.

19. Ellacuría, "La Iglesia de los pobres, sacramento histórico de la liberación," *ECA* 33 (1977): 707–22.

20. Rahner, *Foundations of Christian Faith*, pp. 295–98. See also Rahner, *Ich glaube an Jesus Christus* (Einsiedeln: Benziger, 1968).

21. Rahner, " The Experience of God Today," in *Theological Investigations* 11, trans. David Bourke (New York: Seabury, 1974), p. 150.

22. Rahner, *Foundations of Christian Faith*, p. 12.

23. Jeremias, *New Testament Theology*, vol. 1, p. 104.

24. See Dussel, "Domination-Liberation: A New Approach," pp. 34–56.

25. Rahner, *Foundations of Christian Faith*, p. 91.

26. I have examined this choice between the God of Life and the gods of death in greater detail in another work: *La aparación del Dios de vida en Jesús de Nazaret*, Eng. trans., "The Epiphany of the God of Life in the Life of Jesus," in *The Idols of Death and the God of Life: A Theology*, trans. Barbara E. Campbell and Bonnie Shepard (Maryknoll, N.Y.: Orbis Books, 1983), pp. 66–102.

27. Karl Rahner, in *The Jesuits: The Year Book of the Society of Jesus*, 1974–75 (Rome: Curia Generalizia, S.J., 1975), p. 32.

28. Karl Rahner, *The Dynamic Element in the Church*, trans. W. J. O'Hara, Questiones Disputatae 12 (New York: Herder and Herder, 1964), p. 91.

29. Liberation theology was well aware of this dialectic from the very beginning, e.g., Gutiérrez, *A Theology of Liberation*, pp. 299–302; Ellacuría, "Las bienaventuranzas," pp. 117–18.

30. Miranda, *Marx and the Bible*, p. 57.

31. Rahner, "On the Theology of the Incarnation," in *Theological Investigations* 4, trans. Kevin Smith (Baltimore: Helicon, 1966), pp. 107–11.

32. This is an experience which J. Moltmann, following D. Bonhoeffer, has described in his work, *The Crucified God*, and which takes place daily in the Church of the poor in the presence of the crucified majorities.

33. Ellacuría, "La Iglesia de los pobres," p. 717.

34. Sobrino, "Historical Understanding in European and Latin American Theology," Chapter 1 in this book. Revised from original form in *Liberación y cautiverio*.

6. THE WITNESS OF THE CHURCH IN LATIN AMERICA: BETWEEN LIFE AND DEATH

This chapter is a revision of a paper read at the Fourth International Ecumenical Congress of Theology (São Paulo, Brazil, February 20–March 2, 1980). It was first published in *ECA* 35 (1980, pp. 427–44); in English see "The Witness of the Church in Latin America" in *The Challenge of Basic Christian Communities: Papers from the International Ecumenical Congress of Theology, February 20–March 2, 1980, São Paulo, Brazil* (Maryknoll, N.Y.: Orbis, 1981). The aim of the essay is to determine the objective and subjective nucleus of the Church's witness in the boundary situation in which it exists in various countries, as well as to show how this boundary or limit character of the situation has influenced the reformulation of witness as defense of the just life, and the reformulation of the readiness for martyrdom as both persecution and liberation.

1. The thoughts that follow have been inspired by the activity of ecclesial groups in El Salvador, Nicaragua, and Guatemala. Since the essay is theoretical and not descriptive I sketch the basic character of the activity of these Christians to the extent needed to present theological reflections; I do not however analyze their concrete activity, which is obviously much more complex.

2. The apostles are to bear witness to the resurrection of Jesus (cf. Luke 24:48; Acts 2:32; 3:15; 4:33; 5:32; 13:31; 22:15) but also to the whole of his public life (cf. Luke 1:2; John 15:27; Acts 1:22; 10:39ff.).

3. Cf. G. Gutiérrez, *The Power of the Poor in History*.

4. Cf. ibid., p. 195.

5. Cf. the collective volume, *The Idols of Death and the God of Life*.

6. Among the episcopal statements dealing with these new problems see the Episcopal Commission for Social Action of the Bishops of Peru, *La justicia en el mundo* (1971), the Bishops and Religious Superiors of Northern Brazil, *He oído los clamores de mi pueblo*; and the excellent commentary on both documents by J. Hernández Pico, "El episcopado católico latinoamericano, ¿Esperanza de los oprimidos?" *ECA* 32 (1977): 749-70. See also the *Mensaje al Pueblo Nicaragüense* (June 2, 1979), and *Compromiso cristiano para una Nicaragua nueva* (November 17, 1979), both by the Episcopal Conference; the Sunday homilies of Archbishop Oscar Romero of San Salvador beginning with that of January 20, 1980.

7. Cf. Sobrino, "The Epiphany of the God of Life in the Life of Jesus," *The Idols of Death and the God of Life,* pp. 66-102, Theses 1 to 1.5.

8. Cf. Sobrino, "Espiritualidad de Jesús y espiritualidad de liberación: Reflexiones sistemáticas," *Dialogo* 9 (Guatemala) (1979): 24-31.

9. Among the various collections of documents see, e.g., *Persecución de la Iglesia en San Salvador* (San Salvador, 1977): *Signos de lucha y esperanza: Testimonio de la Iglesia en America Latina, 1973-1979* (Lima: CEP, 1978); *El Salvador:Un pueblo perseguido* (Lima: CEP, 1980).

10. Cf. Sobrino, "The Epiphany of God," p. 96-97.

11. In these analyses my point of reference is the Church and Christians, but something similar must be said of those who are not explicitly Christian but work really, though anonymously, for the kingdom and who make it present or fail to make it present in their lives.

12. On the new concept of the church's holiness as one of its distinctive notes cf. Leonardo Boff, *Eclesiogénesis* (Santander: Sal Terrae, 1979); Jon Sobrino, "Resurrección de una Iglesia popular," in *Cruz y resurrección*, pp. 110-16. See also Chapter 4 of this book. Moltmann moves in the same direction in his *The Church in the Power of the Spirit*, pp. 352-57.

13. This is how Rahner formulates the usual concept of martyrdom as treated in dogmatic and fundamental theology; see "Martyrium, II. Theologisch," *LTK* 7:136.

14. Working document of Puebla, note on martyrdom, n. 223.

15. For a theological discussion of violence see Ignacio Ellacuría, *Teología política* (Buenos Aires: Latin America Books, 1975); in English see *Freedom Made Flesh: The Mission of Christ and His Church* (Maryknoll, N.Y.: Orbis, 1976).

16. *Summa theologiae* II–II, q. 124, a. 2, ad 2.

17. I must remind the reader here, with even greater reason, of what I said in n. 11.

18. Cf. I. Ellacuría, "Las buenaventuranzas," pp. 105–18.

19. *Summa theologiae* II–II, q. 124, a. 5, ad 3.

20. Cf. I. Ellacuría, "El pueblo crucificado: Ensayo de soteriología histórica," in *Cruz y resurrección*, pp. 49–82.

21. Paul VI, Address at Mass on Development Day in Bogotá, August 23, 1968, quoted in the Medellín document *Peace*, n. 19.

22. I have developed these ideas with reference to the situation of the Church in El Salvador in my essay "La Iglesia en el actual proceso del país," *ECA* 34 (1979): 918–20.

7. UNITY AND CONFLICT IN THE CHURCH

The first version of this chapter appeared in *Christus* 41 (Mexico City, 1976): 19–29, under the title "La conflictividad dentro de la Iglesia"; in its present form it appeared in *ECA* 32 (1977): 787–804. Its purpose is to show the root causes of ecclesial conflicts as these are to be seen in El Salvador and in the Latin American Churches generally. Despite recent events in the Church (the Puebla meeting, for example), conflict in the Church does not seem to have disappeared; for this reason, the reflections offered here may still be of value.

1. The element of structural conflict in theological pluralism as this developed in connection with Vatican II has been formulated as follows by Karl Rahner: "Granting all this [the role of the magisterium in the new pluralistic situation], we must still say that the way in which the church exercises this right and this duty will have to take on a wholly new cast in the light of the new pluralism. . . . If the church does take conscious note of this new pluralism, and if she realizes that it cannot be overcome in an instant, how can she reshape her way of preserving the oneness of her profession?" ("Pluralism in Theology and the Oneness of the Church's

Profession of Faith," in *The Development of Fundamental Theology*, ed. J. B. Metz, Concilium 46 [New York: Crossroad, 1969] p. 113).

2. At both the Escorial meeting of 1972 and the Mexico City meeting of 1975, it could be seen that the theology of liberation is not a monolithic entity but serves rather as the focus for a whole family of options. I am therefore simplifying things when I speak of "two" options or currents. In general, however, especially by reason of their reciprocal opposition, we may speak of a liberationist current and "another," which is not well defined but forms a current precisely insofar as it is against the theology of liberation.

3. Gutiérrez, *A Theology of Liberation*, p. 273.

4. J. L. Segundo, "Las 'élites' latinoamericanas: Problemática humana y cristiana ante el camino social," in *Fe cristiana,* p. 209.

5. Gutiérrez, *A Theology of Liberation*, p. 277.

6. López Trujillo, *Teología liberadora*, p. 78.

7. Ibid., pp. 73–74.

8. Ibid., p. 73. López Trujillo's whole discussion of unity and division in the Church is quite revealing. He distinguishes three possible levels of unity: unity in faith, unity in brotherhood, and political unity. He admits that faith is mediated by brotherhood, but he does not make it clear what place the political order plays in the exercise of faith. From the concrete examples given it seems he is against allowing it any role. I see two major defects in this position: 1. The analysis of the unity of the church is derived chiefly from Paul, who speaks of unity built up from within. But, as I have noted, such considerations as these are insufficient. In order to pose the problem of unity among Christians we must go on to the carrying out of the Church's mission *ad extra*, because the Church is not an end in itself but is in the service of something else. 2. The ecclesiology of López Trujillo is conceived in intraecclesial terms. There is no serious analysis of the relation of the Church to Jesus of Nazareth or to the God of Jesus. This narrowness of vision makes possible unqualified assertions about the Church and its characteristic traits. It is possible, moreover, to draw from a particular conception of the Church (in this case the Pauline conception) general conclusions that pay no attention to the historical forms the Church has taken in the name of Jesus. When an ecclesiology is absolutized, certain marks of the Church (unity, for example) are also automatically absolutized. But the real problem is to determine in what Christian unity consists, and this cannot be done on the basis of an analysis of the Church but only on an analysis of that which gives the Church its meaning: the kingdom of God, which Jesus proclaims and makes a reality.

9. Karl Rahner, "Heresy, II. History of Heresies," *Sacramentum Mundi*, 3:20.

10. Hugo Assmann, "El pasado y el presente de la praxis liberadora en América Latina," in *Liberación y cautiverio*, p. 296.

11. Ernst Bloch, *Atheism in Christianity: The Religion of the Exodus and the Kingdom*, trans. J. T. Swann (New York: Seabury, 1972), pp. 9, 266. [I have translated the second brief passage from Sobrino's Spanish version of the German original. The English translation reads: "Where there is hope there is religion, but where there is religion there is not always hope, not the hope built up from beneath, undisturbed by ideology"— Trans.]

12. Ignacio Ellacuría, "Entorno de la 'cuestión fundamental' de la pastoral latinoamericana." *Sal Terrae* 64 (1976): 567.

13. Ibid.

14. The dispute between Peter and Paul can serve as an example. "When Cephas came to Antioch I opposed him to his face. . . . For before certain men came from James, he ate with the Gentiles; but when they came he drew back and separated himself, fearing the circumcision party" (Gal. 2:11–12). What Peter is casting doubt on is not the theoretical truth of the gospel but its concrete practice and visible consequences. When this attitude of Peter becomes public, Paul not only does not think it unseemly to rebuke him publicly but even considers himself obliged to do so. "Paul opposed such a practical and objective denial of the truth of the gospel. The result was a public dispute, an open indictment of Peter by Paul. A public scandal in the church must be publicly criticized and publicly removed" (H. Schlier, *Der Brief an die Galater*, 4th ed. [Göttingen, 1965], p. 50).

15. J. L. Segundo, *The Liberation of Theology*, p. 9.

16. Ibid., p. 8.

17. Declaration "Jesuits Today," no. 8, in *Documents of the Thirty-first and Thirty-second General Congregations of the Society of Jesus*, p. 403.

8. THEOLOGICAL SIGNIFICANCE OF "PERSECUTION OF THE CHURCH" APROPOS OF THE ARCHDIOCESE OF SAN SALVADOR

This chapter appeared first in *Persecución de la Iglesia en El Salvador* (San Salvador: Secretarido Social Interdisocesanos, 1977, pp. 30–75). In the first five months of 1977 persecution of the Church began and repression of the people intensified. The situation called for reflection on those two facts and their connection and for a minimal description of the Church's reaction to persecution. The situation in El Salvador and other Latin American countries in the years since then has not rendered these initial, inchoative reflections invalid but demands rather that they be carried further.

1. LG 8 and AG 42. The translations of the documents of Vatican II are from *Vatican II: The Conciliar and Postconciliar Documents*, ed. A. Flannery (Collegeville, Minn.: Liturgical Press, 1975).

2. The translation of the Medellín documents is from *The Church in the Present-Day Transformation of Latin America in the Light of the Council*, vol. 2, *Conclusions*, ed. L. M. Colonnese (Bogotá and USCC, Washington, D.C., 1970).

3. [That is, in *Persecución de la Iglesia en El Salvador*, in which this essay of Fr. Sobrino first appeared. See the introductory note to this chapter—Trans.]

9. EVANGELIZATION AS MISSION OF THE CHURCH

This chapter appeared as "Evangelización y Iglesia en América latina," in *ECA* 31 (1977): 723-48. It had previously been presented in a shorter form to a gathering of clergy at which the theme was "Evangelización según la *Evangelii nuntiandi*." This explains why the essay contains so many references to that papal document. In its present form the essay is a brief and systematic presentation of the various aspects of evangelization as the mission of the Church; I have developed the material as a set of theses. The basis I have chosen for this systematization (it was also the basis called for by the occasion) is *Evangelii nuntiandi* as reread in the Latin American context. I had already undertaken such a rereading—not of evangelization as such but of *Evangelii nuntiandi*—in "Iglesia y evangelización en el Tercer Mundo," *Búsqueda* 5 (San Salvador) (1977): 7-31; that essay is not reprinted in this book.

The translation of *Evangelii nuntiandi* is from *The Pope Speaks* 21 (1976): 4-51. The translation of the documents of Vatican II is from *Vatican II: The Conciliar and Postconciliar Documents*. The translation of the Medellín documents is from *The Church in the Present-Day Transformation of Latin America in the Light of the Council*.

1. It is already clear in the Apostolic Letter *Octogesima adveniens* of Pope Paul VI to Cardinal Maurice Roy on the 80th Anniversary of the Encyclical *Rerum novarum* (May 14, 1971) that the local Churches are to read the various documents of the universal Church in a creative, not a passive way. "In the face of such widely varying situations, it is certainly difficult for Us to enunciate one way of thinking which will provide a suitable solution for all parts of the world. . . . It is the obligation of Christian communities to scrutinize the true situation in their own region, to clarify it

in the light of the Gospel's unchanging words, and to derive principles of reflection, norms of judgment, and guidelines for action" (4 [translation of the document in *The Pope Speaks* 16 (1971–72), 137–64]).

Evangelii nuntiandi, too, invites "all God's people in the Church to reflect on these matters" (5). It makes clear the service to be rendered by the universal Church to the local Churches and vice versa: "Any local Church which deliberately cuts itself off from the universal Church loses its place in God's plan and much of its ecclesial character. On the other hand, the Church spread throughout the world would become an abstraction if [it] did not derive embodiment and life from the local Churches. Only if we keep these two aspects of the Church always before us will we be able to comprehend the rich relationship which exists between the universal Church and the local Churches" (62).

2. The ecclesiology based on sign must be completed by what is said in the *Decree on the Missionary Activity of the Church* (2): "The Church on earth is by its very nature missionary." This solemn statement is very important in our present context.

3. I cannot here supply the evidence for all that follows. The subject of the Church's relation to the historical Jesus has been extensively studied. I refer the reader to Leonardo Boff, "El Jesús histórico y la Iglesia. ¿Quiso el Jesús pre-pascual una iglesia?" *Servir* 12 (1976): 263–84. In this article the exegetical and systematic views commonly accepted by scholars today are summarized. Cf. L. Boff, *Eclesiogénesis*.

4. The "historical conception," as I call it, holds that the New Testament must be read as a history within and through which the teaching contained in the New Testament is to be understood. The recognition of this fact is important for our present problem. Even though exegetes have difficulty in accepting the classical text in Matthew 16:6–20 as the unaltered historical words of Jesus and in specifying the precise place and time at which he supposedly said them, this does not mean that they are ignoring the basic fact that Christ founded the Church; rather they look to the history of Jesus for that which really gave rise to the Church.   .

5. "He appointed twelve, to be with him, and to be sent out . . . " (Mark 3:14). According to P. Benoit and M.-E. Boismard: "In the theology of Mark 'being with Jesus' does not mean a passive concentration on the person of Jesus; it means a connection with his mission in its entirety. The 'disciple' is one who is at the side of Jesus and accompanies him wherever he goes" (*Synopse des quatre évangiles* [Paris: Cerf, 1972], vol. 2, p. 124). "Being with Jesus" does not therefore have the one-sidedly personalist sense of focusing on the person of Jesus. The contrast in v. 14 between "being with Jesus" and "being sent to preach" is a contrast be-

tween accompanying Jesus on his mission and being sent as missionaries
without Jesus.

6. In the theology of Mark this text marks the climax of a noncontinu-
ous series of texts on mission: "The appointment of the twelve for a mission (Mark 3:14–15), instructions on mission (Mark 6:8–11), and finally
the departure for the mission (Mark 6:12–13)" (Benoit and Boismard, *Synopse* 2: 216).

7. The reader will be familiar with the thesis put forward by E. Peter-
son in 1929 and then adopted and nuanced by R. Guardini, H. Schlier, and
J. Ratzinger, among others. According to this thesis the historical condition for the possibility of the Church coming into existence after the resurrection included these elements: (1) the Jews, who were the chosen people,
did not accept Jesus; (2) the return of Christ did not occur immediately and
was no longer imminently expected; and (3) the apostles decided to go out
to the Gentiles.

8. Moltmann, *The Church in the Power of the Spirit*, p. 10.

9. It was not easy for Vatican II to move beyond an intellectual conception of revelation because the Church's official theology supposed that
revelation was basically a communication of truths. In adding "deeds" to
"words" as part of revelation the Council was asserting a more inclusive
concept of revelation. The same problem crops up again with evangelization. However novel it may seem to introduce action into the concept of
evangelization, it is in fact simply a conclusion to be drawn from the primal
instance of evangelization, namely, the self-revelation of God.

10. The need of action is very clearly stated in *Octogesima adveniens*.
The context of the Letter differs in two important ways from that of
Evangelii nuntiandi: (1) *Octogesima adveniens* is formally speaking not of
evangelization but of the Church's position on social problems; and (2) a
distinction is made between the role of the hierarchy, whose function is
basically to provide the light needed for activity, and that of the laity, who
are called upon to engage directly in action. But, these reservations made, it
is enlightening that the Letter insists: "It is not enough to recall general
precepts to [people's] minds, to state intentions, to condemn grave injustices, and to pronounce judgments in a prophetic tone." Rather, it goes on,
"the laity have the duty of using their own initiative and taking action in
this area—without waiting passively for directives and precepts from
others. They must try to infuse a Christian spirit into people's mental out-
looks and daily behavior, into the laws and structures of the civil community" (48).

11. When I use the term *integral* I am not taking a position in the traditional disagreement over *substantial*, *essential*, and *integral* parts. I wish

only to say that for the reasons given, if any one of the three is lacking there will be no evangelization in the Christian sense of the term.

12. We must not fail to estimate properly the pastoral and theological value of the many denunciations issued by the Latin American bishops ever since Medellín. These have been collected in J. Hernández Pico, "El episcopado latinoamericano: ¿Esperanza de los oprimidos?" *ECA* 32 (1977): 749–70. This is historical proof that the good news can be proclaimed on our continent only if it is accompanied by denunciation.

13. Ellacuría, *Teología política* (San Salvador: UCA, 1973), pp. 1–10.

14. *Octogesima adveniens* notes the influence of structures on personal life and even speaks of them as playing a determining role (cf. 50).

15. The distinction between Christianity as faith and Christianity as religion is developed in my *Christology at the Crossroads*, pp. 273–310.

16. There is a thorough treatment of this problem in Ellacuría, "Fe y justicia," and a more summary discussion in my article, "La oración de Jesús y del cristiano," *Christus* 42 (Mexico City) (1977): 40–44.

17. In speaking of evangelization I shall not consider the various kinds of evangelizers and their different functions as is done, for example, in *Evangelii nuntiandi* (59–73). This diversification of persons and functions is required by the structure of the Church. My thesis here is concerned with a stage prior to this differentiation of evangelizers. The thesis that the evangelizer is constituted as such in and through the activity of evangelization holds for each of these various agents.

18. I am speaking here of Jesus in his human reality as this is made known to us in the Gospels. I have gone into the problem more fully in *Christology at the Crossroads*, pp. 79–108.

19. Ellacuría, "Diez años después: ¿Es posible una universidad distinta?" *ECA* 29 (1975): 609.

20. Cf. Gutiérrez, *A Theology of Liberation*, pp. 287–306; also *The Poor and the Church*, Concilium 104.

10. RELIGIOUS LIFE IN THE THIRD WORLD

This chapter is an expanded version of a paper read at the General Assembly of the Conference of Religious Men and Women of El Salvador (October 1, 1977). It was first published in *Diakonia* 4 (Panama) (1977): 2–30. Its purpose was to offer a reinterpretation of religious life in view of the situation of conflict in El Salvador and in view of the new and urgent demands being made of religious men and women by the poor majorities and by the pastoral program of the Church under Bishop Romero. Against this background I try to take up all the important aspects of religious life, although it is not possible to do more than suggest directions in which solutions may be sought in each area.

Index

Compiled by James Sullivan